Presidents and
Prime Ministers

Presidents and Prime Ministers

Edited by Richard Rose and Ezra N. Suleiman

Foreword by Richard E. Neustadt

American Enterprise Institute for Public Policy Research
Washington, D.C.

Library of Congress Cataloging in Publication Data

Main entry under title:

Presidents and prime ministers.

(AEI studies ; 281)
1. Comparative government. I. Rose, Richard,
1933–   II. Suleiman, Ezra N., 1941–
III. Series: American Enterprise Institute. AEI
studies ; 281.
JF51.P68   351.003'13   80-17898
ISBN 0-8447-3386-5

AEI Studies 281

Printed in the United States of America

CONTRIBUTORS

CARLOS R. ALBA is associate professor of political science at the Autonomous University of Madrid. He received a Ph.D. in law from the University of Granada in Spain and an M.A. and M. Phil. in political science from Yale University. He has been a visiting research fellow at Princeton University and has held awards from the March Foundation, the Western European Council, and the Spanish-American Committee for Cultural Affairs. He is the author of various articles on political socialization and political elites in contemporary Spain and on the Marxist and neo-Marxist concepts of the state. He is now completing a research project on bureaucracy and politics in Spain.

COLIN CAMPBELL, S.J., is associate professor of political science at York University and also serves as academic director of the Ontario Legislature Internship Program and president of the Canadian Study of Parliament Group. In 1979, he was a guest scholar at the Brookings Institution in Washington, D.C. He is the author of *The Canadian Senate: A Lobby From Within* and is co-author of *The Superbureaucrats: Structure and Behaviour in Central Agencies; The Contemporary Canadian Legislative System;* and *Parliament, Policy and Representation.* He is presently co-authoring a book that compares central agencies in the United States, the United Kingdom, Switzerland, and Canada.

SABINO CASSESE is professor of administrative law at the Scuola Superiore della Pubblica Amministrazione and a member of its Steering Committee. He also serves on both the Superior Council of Public Administration and the Steering Committee of the European Group of Public Administration. He is president of the governmental commission for the transfer of public corporations to the regions. He has written on public enterprises, on the history of administrative culture and Italian public administration, and on the formation of the administrative state in Italy.

RENATE MAYNTZ, professor of sociology at the University of Cologne, received a B.A. from Wellesley College, a doctorate in sociology at the Free University in Berlin, and honorary doctorates from the universities of Uppsala and Paris. She has held chairs at the Free University in Berlin and the Hochschule für Verwaltungswissenschaften in Speyer. She has taught at Columbia University and the New School for Social Research in New York, at the University of Edinburgh, and at FLACSO (Facultad Latino-americana de Ciencias Sociales) in Santiago de Chile.

JOHAN P. OLSEN is professor of public administration and organization theory at the University of Bergen. He has been a visiting professor and fellow at Stanford University and at the University of California, Irvine. He is co-author of *Ambiguity and Choice in Organizations* and has written several books in Norwegian on political macro-organization, public bureaucracies, corporatism, and direct actions and movements. He is currently conducting a study of power in Norway.

RICHARD ROSE is director of the Centre for the Study of Public Policy at the University of Strathclyde, Glasgow. He is also secretary of the Committee on Political Sociology of the International Political Science and International Sociological Associations. He has been a visiting scholar at the American Enterprise Institute, the Brookings Institution, and the Woodrow Wilson International Center in Washington, D.C., and a visiting professor at the European University Institute, Florence, Italy. He is the author or editor of, among others, *Politics in England; Governing without Consensus: an Irish Perspective; Electoral Behavior: a Comparative Handbook; Managing Presidential Objectives; Can Government Go Bankrupt?;* and *Do Parties Make a Difference?*

EZRA N. SULEIMAN is professor of politics at Princeton University, where he is also chairman of the Council on International and Regional Studies and of the Committee for European Studies. He has held awards from the Guggenheim Foundation, the Ford Foundation, the American Council of Learned Societies, and the German Marshall Fund. He is the author of *Politics, Power, and Bureaucracy in France* and *Elites in French Society: The Politics of Survival.*

CONTENTS

FOREWORD

Comparing governmental institutions from one country to another can be fun, especially if the comparisons confront the actualities of practice as the essays here assembled try to do. But beyond fun are rewards of insight. Few of us can ever hope to understand another governmental system as well as—if we work at it—we have a chance to understand our own. The nuances of language, culture, and history raise barriers too high for that. But looking at another system helps illuminate our own, which is precisely what these essays do.

"By contrast with Washington," writes Richard Rose of leadership in London, "a Prime Minister does not depend upon personally loyal but bureaucratically amateur advisers. By contrast with Paris, a Prime Minister does not turn civil servants into his political agents, looking to the President for their future career." That last is an allusion to Ezra Suleiman's essay on the Elysée. Of all the differences between our Presidential system and the "Presidentialist" regime under the Fifth Republic up to now, none is more striking than the network of relationships nurtured by the present French President with former colleagues from the bureaucratic elite. In Washington, who are their counterparts? Who could be his?

This book is addressed mainly to Americans. It looks at the contemporary roles of political leaders in Britain, Canada, France, Italy, Norway, Spain, and West Germany. Each chapter frequently reminds us of the White House. In his concluding essay Rose makes the contrast explicit, playing off the others against ours, posing likenesses among them against differences with us, highlighting what our Presidency lacks:

> The distinctive feature of Cabinet government is that all
> of the participants . . . are bound politically to collective deci-

sions. The strongest phrase is not the expression of the volition of an individual politician, but rather a collective statement: The Cabinet has decided. . . . *In the Cabinet system, there is a government as well as sub-governments. . . .*

The strongest phrase in Washington—the President wants this—is usually voiced as an aspiration. The people whom the President can immediately command in the White House do not have their hands on the operating agencies of government. Even those whom the President appoints to direct the major departments of government are only overseers of the bureaus that collectively constitute the principal operating agencies of the executive branch. The President can fire an appointee, but this is itself an admission of failure to gain satisfaction from the person appointed. It is not an augur that he can do any better with a successor. Moreover, most of the money that the government spends is effectively uncontrollable. . . . In domestic policy, the federal government gives almost as much money to state and local governments to administer as it manages itself. In national security affairs, the President's position is relatively stronger as commander-in-chief, but it would be a bad thing if he spent all his time thinking of war.

It may be that a German or a Spaniard reading here of London or of Paris will find no less light shed on his own regime than an American can gain from reading all. Still, as Rose points out, the fascinating differences among the Europeans pale by comparison with trans-Atlantic differences:

Nonetheless, there remains an ocean of difference between the collective authority of a Cabinet and the American political system. The primary contrast is a matter of balance —or the absence of balance. The Cabinet provides collective authority sufficiently strong to reconcile differences among sub-governments. The force of a Cabinet is not that of a dictator; instead, it is the force of government based upon elected politicians with common loyalties and a common need to secure reelection. Conflicting interests can and do state their case in Cabinet. But after that is done, there is a government there, that is, a Cabinet with the political and institutional strength to reconcile differences.

The American system, by contrast, is best described as lopsided, because the power of sub-governments is so great in relation to collective authority. The Supreme Court can make binding decisions upon other branches of government,

but its authority is strong only when other branches act
unconstitutionally. . . .

Interestingly, European governments most nearly resemble
Washington when they meet in the institutions of the European Community. The explanation is simple: the nine member nations of the European Community meet as sovereign
states—even more sovereign than the committees of Congress or well-entrenched Washington bureau chiefs.

Refreshingly, Rose does not deplore sub-governments. Rather, he
finds them useful:

The American system of politics is especially good at dealing
with a large number of small-scale decisions. . . . To decry
the institutional atomization of contemporary American
politics is to miss an important point. An atomized political system should be good at making small-scale decisions.

For us the difficulties lie, rather, in dealing with a small number of
big decisions, on problems that are themselves big in their scale,
their complexity, and the externalities and jurisdictional entangle-
ments they involve. Stagflation dramatically poses such a problem
today, and so does energy. Rose urges us to concentrate on institutional adjustments that might help us deal with such as these, never
mind everything else.

Rose offers good advice, specific, focused, interesting, arguable,
and always within range of discretionary acts or legislation. He does
not traffic in the unattainables of constitutional reform. He argues
that the access of colleagueship in our government requires short steps,
where and as we can, to rebuild party ties and organizations. He
argues also that increased reliance on career officials offers dividends
of expertise well worth the sacrifice of questionable loyalty from
assorted "In-and-Outers." Following the leads that comparison affords,
Rose plunges deep into contemporary issues of performance and
direction for the American Presidency. Without necessarily accepting
every twist and turn, one cannot but applaud his vivid demonstration
of the insights to be drawn from a comparative approach.

And insights are accompanied by warnings. A number of the
essays in this book recall that the assessment of intentions or performance even by close allies, even by "similar" governments, are
fraught with hazards, hidden traps. This is an old refrain of mine.
The subtlety of differences beneath the similarities, the shades of
cultural conditioning, the shifts of language even (or especially)
among American, Canadian, and British English—all these spring

to mind afresh. Reading these essays is at once to be informed and to be put on guard. We learn so much, yet there is so much more to *grasp*. Caution is called for. Happily these authors seem to know that.

RICHARD E. NEUSTADT

Harvard University
Cambridge, Massachusetts

PREFACE

While the American Presidency is a unique institution, its primary tasks are not unique. The need to give direction to government is universal and persisting. Every country, from the Egypt of the Pharoahs to contemporary democracies and dictatorships, faces the challenge of organizing political institutions so that leaders can make authoritative decisions about collective problems of society. The commitment to representative as well as effective government increases political complexity in order to increase popular consent.

Today, there is no presupposition that any one country has discovered the formula for good government; signs of difficulties are everywhere, in the Second and Third World as well as in Western nations. Differences in historical traditions and in contemporary circumstances inevitably lead to differences in institutions and in processes of government. Yet it would be an unusually arrogant citizen who proclaimed that his country had nothing to learn from the experience of other nations in governing itself—if only to learn from their mistakes. The less confidence Americans have in national institutions, the more reason there is to look elsewhere in a spirit of open inquiry.

Comparisons of national systems of government reveal both constants and variations. For example, each of the national studies in this book emphasizes the extent to which heads of government are and must be *political* animals. A suave European will be as concerned with mundane calculations of political support as any brash Washington politician. National contexts greatly influence the practical significance of political universals. One cannot begin to understand, for example, how European politicians act without understanding the nature of party loyalties in Europe. The fact that similar labels are used does not mean that European parties are like American parties, that Cabinets in a parliamentary system are like the American President's Cabinet, or that the President of the United States is like the President of Italy, let alone the President of France. The essays in this book show what accounts for the variations among these institutions, how governmental processes differ, and what the consequences are for political systems.

The greater the observed differences between national systems of government, the more desirable it is to consider the consequences of these differences, since their causes can most readily be explained by history. While institutional differences cannot compensate for deficiencies in a nation's economy or, for that matter, in a nation's electorate, institutions do affect the processes of government. The American Constitution two centuries ago was, in its time, a revolutionary innovation in political processes. Today, as in the past, there can be strong disagreements among citizens concerning specific government policies. But unless citizens agree about the process for reconciling differences of opinion, their political system is in real trouble.

Becoming aware of differences among nations is an important step toward understanding better both the strengths and weaknesses of one's own national system of government. In cases where the comparison shows very different countries to have similar political difficulties, one can conclude that the problem is a general one and requires a response that is applicable to many countries. In such a case, it is apparent that merely changing the individuals in charge of a nation's government will not remove difficulties that are more deeply rooted. Conversely, in cases where comparison emphasizes the distinctiveness of a nation's problems, the solution should be sought first in nation-specific circumstances.

Comparison starts from the premise that there are sufficient similarities to justify the exercise. It would be of little avail to compare the American system of government with that of Third World countries, or with a system like that prevailing in Iran past or present. The justification for the countries chosen in the present volume is simple and clear: Britain, France, Germany, and Italy are the four largest nations in Europe, and each is sufficiently distinctive in itself to merit special attention. Norway stands as a representative of the successful Scandinavian variant of smaller European democracies. The example of Canada shows what happens when British-type parliamentary institutions operate in a country whose federal structure, geographic expanse, and party politics are closer to that of the United

States. To test the extent to which the difficulties of directing government are not restricted to democracies, a chapter is included on Franco Spain, one among many nations along the Mediterranean littoral that have had, for a time at least, political power fall into the hands of a general. The authors of all the chapters combine both a scholarly approach to the study of politics and a practical knowledge of governmental and bureaucratic processes.

The final chapter addresses the question: What are the most significant differences between the American and European systems of governing today? It finds that the common reliance on collective authority in Europe constitutes an important contrast with government in the United States. The essay stresses the implications of these differences for the political process in Washington today, especially in facing such challenging issues as inflation, energy, and national security. The chapter concludes by showing why American government must gain greater collective authority if it is to respond effectively to the collective political challenges facing it in the 1980s.

The initial stimulus for this book came from a meeting on political administration organized under the auspices of the Committee on Political Sociology of the International Political Science Association at its World Congress in Edinburgh in August 1976.

The preparation and publication of this book was made possible by a grant from the American Enterprise Institute in its dual role as an imaginative sponsor of public policy research and as a publisher of studies on matters of current public importance. The editors would like to thank the president of AEI, William J. Baroody, Jr., and the codirectors of AEI's program of Studies in Political and Social Processes, Austin Ranney and Howard R. Penniman. Carol Rosen and Cynthia Barry in the AEI publications department have our very special thanks for having coped cheerfully and expeditiously with manuscripts submitted by authors who among them have six different native languages. Bringing the book promptly to publication was facilitated by Richard Rose's being a visiting scholar at AEI for three months in early 1980, where he enjoyed the very congenial atmosphere of a "think tank" set in an environment more conducive to reflection on weekends than week days, namely, downtown Washington.

An acknowledgment is also due to the University of Strathclyde, whose Centre for the Study of Public Policy provided a European base for the preliminary stages of the work, and whose Loch Lomond conference center, Ross Priory, was an ideal setting for the authors to meet to discuss first drafts of their manuscripts in July 1979. The Rt. Hon. Lord Trend and Richard E. Neustadt were very constructive and well-informed general discussants from both academic and practical vantage points. The Ross Priory staff dispensed hospitality in the best fashion of the Scottish Highlands.

Individual authors have given their personal acknowledgments in each chapter.

Presidents and Prime Ministers

1

British Government: The Job at the Top

Richard Rose

The imperative must always have priority.

—Old Treasury maxim

Viewed from the top, British government looks more like a mountain range than a single pyramid of power. The Prime Minister is preeminent among these peaks, but the political significance of this preeminence is ambiguous. The person on top can be remote from what is happening on the ground.[1] Those who observe government from the dizzy heights of Downing Street are subject to what Lord Rosebery described as "hallucinations" about the allegedly "universal power" of the person at the top. The claim that contemporary eminence makes a British Prime Minister similar to an American President is to ignore the many studies of the American President that emphasize the weakness of that office.[2] Perhaps the person on top is better described as the "least weak" member of government instead of the most powerful.

NOTE: I am particularly indebted to Richard Parry for intelligently compiling the tabular material required, to George W. Jones of the London School of Economics, and to a variety of necessarily anonymous politicians and civil servants for comments and insight over the years.

[1] Major studies that endorse the apex theory include John P. Mackintosh, *The British Cabinet* (London: Stevens and Sons, 1963), and R. H. S. Crossman, "Introduction" to Walter Bagehot, *The British Constitution* (London: Fontana, 1963), pp. 1-56. For a critique of these views, see especially George W. Jones, "The Prime Minister's Power," *Parliamentary Affairs*, vol. 18, no. 2 (Spring 1965), pp. 167-85; and A. H. Brown, "Prime Ministerial Power," *Public Law* (Spring and Summer 1968), pp. 28-51 and 96-118.

[2] Lord Rosebery (Prime Minister, 1892–1895), in his *Life of Sir Robert Peel*, quoted by Harold Wilson in the epigraph of Wilson's *The Governance of Britain* (London: Sphere Books, 1977), p. 5. For my view on the Presidency, see Richard Rose, *Managing Presidential Objectives* (New York: Free Press, 1976), especially chap. 10, and see also chap. 9 of this book.

A Prime Minister cannot participate in the government of Britain without becoming enmeshed in established institutions of governance. Formally, these institutions are described as Her Majesty's Government. But this phrase begs the question: Who exercises the powers of the Crown? To describe British government by the name of the Prime Minister of the day, as the Thatcher government, is to emphasize what is personal and transitory about durable and impersonal institutions. The Victorian custom of emphasizing the administration of Mr. Gladstone or Mr. Disraeli better conveys the permanence of the structure that party politicians head. Constitutional lawyers use impersonal terms, typically referring to parliamentary government or Cabinet government. This usage is preferable, for these are the institutions that shape the office of the Prime Minister, defining what must be done—and what cannot be done—whatever the personality of the individual incumbent.

To understand the role of the Prime Minister of Great Britain, one must see it from the base of the pyramid as well as from the top. The object of this paper is to analyze what the Prime Minister does and does not contribute to the ongoing process of British government. Identifying what a Prime Minister *must* do is important for understanding the economy of influence; a Prime Minister has limited political resources to invest in the job. Identifying what a Prime Minister does *not* do is important in mapping the geography of influence. Testing generalizations about the office against the experience of eight Prime Ministers since 1945 ensures that generalizations do not reflect the experiences of a single individual in that office.[3]

The first section of this paper sets out systematically the tasks that every Prime Minister must undertake, and shows what is and is not involved in discharging imperative responsibilities. The second section reviews the staff organization—both ad hoc and civil service—that the Prime Minister has at hand to meet these responsibilities. Because political influence affects particular policies, the third section examines the role of the Prime Minister in three different policy arenas: foreign affairs, the economy, and education. The concluding section views the job of Prime Minister across time and space.

---

[3] Mrs. Thatcher's tenure of Downing Street had recently begun when this paper was written. The argument here is that her behavior in office will be more determined by the ex officio characteristics outlined herein than by her political ideology or personal characteristics.

For assessments of Mrs. Thatcher's first year in office, in which her style was to seek to dominate the Cabinet, see, for example, the articles in *The Sunday Times Magazine* (London), "Her First Year," April 27, 1980, and Adam Raphael, "Our Gutsy Iron Lady is a Warrior, not a Healer," *The Observer*, April 27, 1980.

The Imperatives of Office

Respect for organizational imperatives is the first rule of political survival for the incumbent of 10 Downing Street. With limited time and political capital to invest, a Prime Minister cannot be involved personally in every action of government. Twenty or so active and ambitious Cabinet colleagues undertake the bulk of the political work of government. The job of a Prime Minister is to do those things that only he or she can do, and to do them well enough to continue in office.

Doing the Possible and the Essential. Upon moving into 10 Downing Street a Prime Minister does not need to ask "What am I to do?" Pressures to act come with the job and they come from many directions: from Whitehall departments and their ministers, from members of Parliament (MPs), from the party, from the media, from news on the ticker tape, and, not least, from abroad. Responding—or fending off—pressures to act takes up most of the Prime Minister's week. Richard Neustadt's description of the President—as "the prisoner of first-things-first. And almost always, something else comes first"—is also applicable in Westminster.[4]

To speak of political imperatives in government is to emphasize that governing is an active process; it is about acting in response to what must be done. Action-forcing routines set tasks for the occupant of 10 Downing Street on a daily, weekly, or quinquennial basis. Some of these imperatives are relatively unimportant, such as submitting a weekly report of government business to the Queen. But most are important, whether affecting the personal standing of the Prime Minister or conditions in the country as a whole. What Richard Neustadt says of the President is also true of a Prime Minister:

> Priorities are set not by the relative importance of a task, but by the relative necessity for *him* to do it. He deals first with the things that are required of him next. . . . The net result may be a far cry from the order of priorities that would appeal to scholars or to columnists—or to the President himself.[5]

---

[4] Richard E. Neustadt, *Presidential Power* (New York: John Wiley and Sons, 1960), p. 155. For first-hand accounts of time pressures on a Prime Minister, see Wilson, *Governance of Britain*, pp. 108ff: and for pressures on Cabinet ministers and senior civil servants, see Ernest Marples, "A Dog's Life in the Ministry," and Lord Strang, "Permanent Under-Secretary," in Richard Rose, ed., *Policy-Making in Britain* (London: Macmillan, 1969), pp. 128-31 and 132-48.

[5] Neustadt, *Presidential Power*, p. 155.

Party Management. A Prime Minister may be self-interested, but he or she is not self-employed. To become Prime Minister, a politician must spend years in the service of the party in Parliament. Since 1945 the length of the average parliamentary apprenticeship of a newly installed incumbent has been twenty-eight years. A Prime Minister gains office in competition against colleagues by building up expectations about how well he or she can do the job. A Prime Minister holds office only as long as he or she retains the confidence of a broad spectrum of opinion in the governing party.[6]

A Prime Minister manages a party as one manages a horse: by giving sufficient rein to avoid a straight test of will between horse and rider in which the latter might be overthrown. The office is often conferred upon a politician because he[7] is seen as a person who will let the party have its head. Clement Attlee, Harold Wilson, and James Callaghan achieved leadership as mediators between different wings of the Labour party. Harold Macmillan and Sir Alec Douglas-Home became Prime Ministers because each was broadly acceptable in the Conservative party, unlike their chief competitor, R. A. Butler. Edward Heath lost the Conservative leadership to a relatively unknown Margaret Thatcher in 1975 because his autocratic style cost him the confidence of Conservative MPs.

Patronage is the most immediate and tangible resource that a Prime Minister can use to ensure loyalty within the governing party. The first priority of a newly installed Prime Minister is to give office to many of the party's supporters in the House of Commons. The Constitution vests this power solely in the hands of the Prime Minister. From the exercise of patronage—or the anticipation among backbenchers of receiving favor—flows much of the Prime Minister's influence upon colleagues, both senior and junior. The only MPs immune to the lure of patronage are those relatively few who, for personal or other reasons, have foresworn any desire for the office or honors that a Prime Minister can bestow.[8]

Every recipient of a ministerial appointment, whether in Cabinet or at sub-Cabinet level, becomes bound by the doctrine of collective responsibility. This doctrine precludes a minister from publicly disagreeing with government policy or attacking the actions of the Prime

---

[6] See Richard Rose, *The Problem of Party Government* (London: Macmillan, 1974), chap. 14.

[7] Strictly speaking, the term "his" is appropriate when referring to the Prime Minister here, for this study generalizes about the office from 1945 to 1979, when all the incumbents were male.

[8] See R. K. Alderman, "The Prime Minister and the Appointment of Ministers: An Exercise in Political Bargaining," *Parliamentary Affairs*, vol. 29, no. 2 (Spring 1976), pp. 101-134.

Minister. Any minister who wishes to do so must resign and risk indefinite (or permanent) exclusion from office. Behind the veil of collective responsibility, ministers may pursue personal ambitions, interdepartmental battles, and even, on occasion, intrigues against the Prime Minister, but not to the point of the "free enterprise" politics that characterizes official Washington.

The patronage in the hands of a contemporary Prime Minister immediately assures him of the formal loyalty of more than half the votes needed to command the governing party in the House of Commons. A governing party normally has at least 318 of the 635 members of the House of Commons. A Prime Minister will appoint about twenty MPs to posts in the Cabinet and about sixty more to ministerial posts of sub-Cabinet rank. Furthermore, upward of three dozen MPs are appointed to the unpaid (and technically nonministerial) post of parliamentary private secretary. These MPs, too, are expected to be loyal to government policy and thereby swell the number in receipt of patronage to about two-thirds of the total needed for a majority in a parliamentary party.

The cumulative extent of Prime Ministerial patronage is large and has been growing since 1945 (see table 1–1). In more than six years of office, Clement Attlee appointed only 109 different MPs to paid ministerial offices, a ratio of 1 job for every 3.6 Labour MPs initially elected in 1945. By contrast, in six years of office Harold Wilson appointed 136 MPs to a paid office, equivalent to 1 job for every 2.7 MPs. Conservative governments, too, have distributed more patronage to MPs through the years. In 1951 Sir Winston Churchill initially gave paid posts to 61 MPs. In 1979 Margaret Thatcher initially gave jobs to 77 MPs. Whereas only 17 percent of MPs retiring from 1918 to 1944 had held a ministerial post, the proportion had risen to 33 percent for the 1945–1974 period.[9]

In making appointments, a Prime Minister can use any of four criteria: personal loyalty (rewarding friends); personal disloyalty (bribing enemies); representativeness (naming a woman or a Scot, for example); and departmental competence.[10] Of these four criteria, three are meant to maintain the solidarity of the governing party in support of the Prime Minister; only one relates to skills instrumental in running the government. Every Prime Minister wishes to appoint MPs who are administratively competent *and* contribute to his personal support. But a Prime Minister cannot afford to err on the side of

---

[9] Michael Rush, "The Members of Parliament," in S. A. Walkland, ed., *The House of Commons in the Twentieth Century* (Oxford: Clarendon Press, 1979), p. 92.

[10] Rose, *Party Government*, pp. 363ff.

TABLE 1–1

The Cumulative Extent of Prime Ministerial Patronage

Prime Minister	Number Initially Appointed[a]	Total Appointees[a]	MPs in Governing Party[b]	Appointees as Percentage of Governing Party
Attlee, 1945–51	66	109	393	28
Churchill, 1951–55	61	83	321	26
Eden, 1955–57	67	84	345	24
Macmillan, 1957–63	65	118	365	32
Douglas-Home, 1963–64	67	70	365	19
Wilson, 1964–70	86	136	364	37
Heath, 1970–74	64	85	330	26
Wilson, 1974–76	82	95	319	30
Callaghan, 1976–79	92	114	319	36
Thatcher, 1979–	77	N.A.	339	(23)
Average	73	99	344	28

N.A. = not available.

[a] All figures are paid appointments given members of the House of Commons. They exclude members of the government in the House of Lords and unpaid parliamentary private secretaries.

[b] Highest level of party strength at the general election during the Prime Minister's period of office.

Sources: D. E. Butler and Anne Sloman, *British Political Facts, 1900–1975* (London: Macmillan, 1975), chap. 1; and House of Commons, *Parliamentary Debates* (London: Her Majesty's Stationery Office), sessional indexes.

having too little support in the Cabinet, for fear that the resulting government, no matter how competent, may no longer be his.

Because the disposition of patronage immediately affects the Prime Minister's management of the party in Parliament, it is not a task that can be delegated. A President may delegate congressional relations to a subordinate and remain President even if things go wrong. A Prime Minister who comes unstuck in relations with the parliamentary party runs the risk of being forced from office by disaffection among the legislators. Moreover, a Prime Minister must always eye senior colleagues warily for fear of a crown prince anxious to replace him. Harold Wilson was particularly conscious of playing off rivals in the Cabinet. At one crucial point, Wilson claimed to have no less than six would-be heirs so positioned that their mutual suspicion would assure his retention of office, if only for lack of trust in any other candidate.[11]

---

[11] Wilson, *Governance of Britain*, pp. 51ff.

A Prime Minister is continuously reviewing the disposition of ministers, in order to reshuffle posts to weed out the obviously incompetent, promote the ambitious, reward the loyal, and cloak with collective responsibility the potentially disloyal. In the course of a Parliament, a Prime Minister is likely to make at least one major reshuffle and several other significant postings of ministers. Ministers already in office will tread warily at such times, hoping for promotion or fearing being dropped. MPs aspiring to office will be biddable at such times, hoping that their show of loyalty will be rewarded by an appointment.

Party politics in Britain is first of all parliamentary politics. A Conservative or Labour Prime Minister does not have to worry about fighting for renomination in party primaries. Effectively, the parliamentary party makes a running judgment on his performance as a potential winner of elections. Moreover, a Conservative Prime Minister can control the party organization by virtue of appointing the chairman of the Conservative central office. The annual conference of the Conservative party has neither the formal status nor the political predisposition to challenge policy laid down by a Conservative government. By contrast, a Labour Prime Minister has no sure authority in the Labour party's extraparliamentary headquarters or annual conference, both dominated by trade union votes. A Labour Prime Minister can choose among three strategies vis-à-vis the party organization: He can try to control it by collaborating with trade union leaders; he can appeal directly to party rank and file through the media and public meetings; or, at worst, he can treat relations with the Labour party as "a necessary exercise in damage limitation."[12] Attlee, Wilson, and Callaghan each tried all of these strategies.

Timing and Winning a General Election. The solidarity of the governing party is most evident in a common partisan concern with winning the next general election. Only if this is done can MPs retain or aspire to office and party supporters identify their leader as successful. To gain the Prime Ministership, a British MP need not lead his party to a general election victory; five of the nine postwar Prime Ministers first entered Downing Street in the middle of a Parliament. But to retain the leadership of the nation, a Prime Minister does need to win the next general election.

---

[12] See "How Jim Won the Battle of the Manifesto," *The Observer*, April 8, 1979; and generally, Lewis Minkin, *The Labour Party Conference* (London: Allen Lane, 1978).

The British Constitution gives to the Prime Minister alone the power to choose the date of a general election. A Prime Minister may consult formally or informally with colleagues about an election date, but he or she retains the right of deciding when to risk an appeal to the people. A Prime Minister may enter office on the crest of electoral victory, but no Prime Minister can expect to stay at the peak for a five-year period. The Prime Minister's task is to time the next general election so that it occurs when the party has risen from a trough to the crest of another wave of popularity. Unpopular actions (such as economic deflation) should be taken at a point in the electoral calendar when the government can afford to face criticism. Good news (such as a rising standard of consumption) should be timed as the prelude to a general election.[13]

Within the lifetime of a Parliament, the Prime Minister's party standing waxes and wanes with the party members' evaluation of their leader as an electoral asset. By-election results emphasize the electoral vulnerability of the governing party. Because by-elections immediately affect membership in the House of Commons, they are peculiarly salient to MPs. In every Parliament except one since 1945, there has been a swing against the governing party in by-elections (table 1–2). Usually, the average swing is big enough to unseat the government if repeated in a general election, and the average number of by-election defeats suffered by government has been increasing. By-election results remind MPs in the governing party of their electoral mortality.

Opinion polls provide an additional reading of the electoral fortunes of the party in office. In nearly every Parliament since 1945, the opposition party has usually been ahead of the governing party in the monthly Gallup Poll. In the extreme case of the 1970–1974 Conservative government, the Labour opposition was ahead in thirty-seven of the forty-two monthly Gallup inquests (table 1–2). Overall, the opposition party has led the governing party in the Gallup Poll in eight months in every twelve. At some point in a typical Parliament, MPs who saw their Prime Minister as the party's electoral champion might conclude from this record that the Prime Minister was leading the party to defeat.

A Prime Minister can usually extract personal popularity from the ex officio status of incumbency. Because a general election is not a straight contest between party leaders, the Gallup Poll normally

---

[13] See W. L. Miller and M. Mackie, "The Electoral Cycle and the Asymmetry of Government and Opposition Popularity," *Political Studies*, vol. 21, no. 3 (September 1973), pp. 263-79.

TABLE 1–2
GOVERNMENT STANDING IN BY-ELECTIONS AND MONTHLY OPINION POLLS

	By-Elections		Number of Months Leading Gallup Poll			% of Total Months Government Ahead in Gallup Poll
Parliament	Number of seats contested	Swing to govern-ment (per-centage)	Govt.	Oppos.	Tie	
1945–50	38	−4.9	5	23	3	17
1950–51	14	−4.4	8	9	0	47
1951–55	42	+0.1	9	25	1	26
1955–59	41	−4.7	14	32	0	30
1959–64	39	−5.5	21	35	2	37
1964–66	11	−1.5	10	5	0	67
1966–70	25	−12.0	8	39	1	17
1970–74	17	−5.4	5	37	0	12
1974	1	−1.4	6	0	0	100
1974–79	22	−10.5	13	38	2	25

NOTE: Minus sign shows swing from government.
SOURCES: *By-Elections:* Chris Cook and John Ramsden, *By-Elections in British Politics* (London: Macmillan, 1973), p. 389; for 1974–1979, data supplied by F. W. S. Craig, Parliamentary Reference Service. Also, *Gallup Poll: The Gallup Election Handbook* (London, June 1970) and the Gallup Poll monthly *Political Index* thereafter. Calculations exclude polls taken during the election month and the month preceding.

asks whether voters separately approve of each party's leader; it would be electorally meaningless to ask: Which leader would you vote for as Prime Minister? The replies show that the Prime Minister is normally given a higher rating than the leader of the opposition (table 1–3). But it also shows that Harold Wilson was always more popular than any of his four Conservative opponents, whether Wilson was in government or opposition. In the period for which public opinion data are available, the "Wilson effect" appears as important as the incumbency effect.[14]

The Prime Minister is almost always better known and registers more popular approval than his party in the Gallup Poll. This was

---

[14] This is a major limitation on generalizing from data reported in David Butler and Donald Stokes, *Political Change in Britain*, 2d ed. (London: Macmillan, 1974), chap. 17. Monthly Gallup Polls from June to December 1979 again showed Prime Minister Margaret Thatcher less popular than the leader of the opposition, James Callaghan.

TABLE 1–3

POPULAR APPROVAL OF THE PRIME MINISTER COMPARED WITH
THAT OF THE OPPOSITION LEADER IN MONTHLY GALLUP POLLS

Competitors	Prime Minister			Average Lead (%)
	Ahead	Behind	Equal	
Eden vs. Gaitskell, 1956	3	3	0	9.0
Macmillan vs. Gaitskell, 1957–59	13	0	0	12.0
Macmillan vs. Gaitskell, 1959–63	15	10	2	11.0
Macmillan vs. Wilson, 1963	0	10	0	−16.0
Douglas-Home vs. Wilson, 1964–64	0	9	0	−20.0
Wilson vs. Douglas-Home, 1964–65	9	0	0	21.0
Wilson vs. Heath, 1965–70	46	9	1	9.0
Heath vs. Wilson, 1970–74	4	36	2	−12.0
Wilson vs. Heath, 1974–75	9	0	0	15.0
Wilson vs. Thatcher, 1975–76	6	5	2	1.0
Callaghan vs. Thatcher, 1976–79	26	7	2	6.0

SOURCES: George H. Gallup, ed., *The Gallup International Public Opinion Polls: Great Britain, 1937–1972* (New York: Random House, 1976); and the Gallup Poll monthly *Political Index* (London).

always the case from 1945 through 1964, and only once did Harold Wilson run behind Labour in monthly Gallup surveys taken from 1964 to 1970. Notwithstanding the relative unpopularity of Edward Heath against Harold Wilson, from 1970 to 1974 Heath ran ahead of his party in twenty-seven months and behind in only three. Paradoxically, the interpretation of this evidence may be that the Prime Minister can offer little or no "coattail" help to his party's candidates. Voters can distinguish between their views of an individual and a vote for a party. This was shown spectacularly in 1945, when the electorate refused to endorse Winston Churchill leading a Conservative government in peacetime.

The Prime Minister's responsibility for timing and fighting a general election is a double-edged sword. As the incumbent, the Prime Minister has most to lose, and in six of the eleven general elections since 1945 the Prime Minister of the day has led his party to defeat. Of the defeated Prime Ministers, only Winston Churchill and Harold Wilson were retained long enough as leader in opposition to win a subsequent general election victory. In advance of a general election, a Prime Minister may use his relative popularity—vis-à-vis that of the opposition leader or the party's own national support—

to claim to be a potential winner or at least the party's best leader in bad circumstances. But the more portents of electoral defeat confront the governing party, the more the Prime Minister's authority is eroded. Defeat for a Prime Minister not only threatens to terminate his or her career but also offers a crack at the top job to an ambitious colleague.

The Presentation of Self in Parliament. A Prime Minister does not need to attract publicity; attention is always focused on the incumbent of Downing Street. What a Prime Minister needs to do is to turn this attention to his or her political advantage. The image of self that the Prime Minister presents is important within as well as outside government. The more favorable the reputation, the greater the Prime Minister's ability to influence others. This is true even though Whitehall is "a stock exchange for the brokerage of information without the discipline of a market price."[15]

Parliament is the chief constitutional forum for the presentation of self to politicians, and the mass media is the chief electoral forum. The two are intimately connected, for political journalists look to Parliament for cues. The Westminster view is well expressed by Marcia Williams (now Lady Falkender), Harold Wilson's long-time aide:

> The Prime Minister, if he is to maintain his authority in his own party, has to demonstrate his authority over the Opposition. If he does it well, it impresses first his Cabinet colleagues and also his back-bench supporters. Then it has its repercussions on television and in the newspapers. There is nothing like a good press on the following morning [after Prime Minister's question time] for heartening a party leader. Afterwards, it is possible to sense the reaction in the country as the effect of newspaper stories and the reports of MPs to their constituencies have their effect throughout the rest of Britain.[16]

So great is the role of Parliament that until World War II the Prime Minister (or his deputy in coalition) was also leader of the House of Commons, a strategic position for taking the temper of MPs of all parties. The sacrifice by the Prime Minister of this role because of exigencies of time has not reduced concern with parliamentary business.

---

[15] J. M. Lee, "Central Capability and Established Practice," in B. Chapman and A. Potter, eds., W.J.M.M.: Political Questions (Manchester: University Press, 1974), p. 167.

[16] Marcia Williams, Inside Number Ten (London: Weidenfeld and Nicolson, 1972), p. 78.

Personal contact is a necessary condition of maintaining personal confidence. A Prime Minister cannot delegate to political surrogates the task of maintaining confidence in himself. Only by attending personally to relations with Cabinet colleagues, junior ministers, and backbench MPs can a Prime Minister hope for understanding and loyalty in moments of difficulty. Fortunately, the ethos and architecture of the palace of Westminster require a Prime Minister to be accessible to all members of the governing party. No appointments secretary stands like a grand vizier between the Prime Minister and the MPs and journalists who hold his reputation in their hands.

Parliamentary Question Time. The Prime Minister is required to appear twice a week in the House of Commons to answer parliamentary questions. These appearances are among the highlights of the political week in Westminster. They offer an opportunity for the Prime Minister to demonstrate his or her skills, and an opportunity for opposition MPs to test themselves in parliamentary combat with the country's chief politician. Both MPs and Prime Ministers welcome this very public and political trial of wits, aptly described as "a twice-weekly confrontation about the competence of the governors."[17]

Prime Ministers have frequently paid tribute to the intimidating character of question time. It exposes the country's leading political figure to verbal assault by unanticipated supplementary questions, and to the risk of coming off second best in a verbal duel with the lowliest of backbench MPs. In such circumstances, a Prime Minister has more to lose than any individual MP seeking to make a name. The skillful fielding of questions strengthens a Prime Minister's reputation, especially when the unsuccessful assailant is the leader of the opposition.

Question time consumes a significant portion of the Prime Minister's time whenever Parliament is sitting, which is most of the year. One Downing Street private secretary is assigned to prepare answers in consultation with the relevant departments. Even though the Prime Minister will have to defend what a minister is doing, privately a rebuke or a prod may be given the minister if the question has a valid point. Because the questions are often opaque—the sting being in the supplementary question—preparation involves elaborate efforts to spot nonobvious implications in a query. On two nights a week, the Prime Minister receives up to three boxes of files in prep-

---

17 George W. Jones, "The Prime Minister and Parliamentary Questions," *Parliamentary Affairs*, vol. 26, no. 3 (Summer 1973), p. 263; Wilson, *Governance of Britain*, pp. 164, 171n; and D. N. Chester and Nona Bowring, *Questions in Parliament* (Oxford: Clarendon Press, 1962), pp. 162ff.

aration for the next day's ordeal, reading these ahead of Cabinet papers or Foreign Office telegrams. The Prime Minister and the private office and political staff then meet for a final rundown of topics for forty-five minutes in advance of each appearance. In anticipation of question time, Harold Macmillan reported that he nearly became physically ill.

MPs consciously regard question time as an occasion for personally testing the Prime Minister, when he or she is unprotected by a speechwriter's script. The overwhelming proportion of parliamentary questions are for oral, not written answer. For example, in 1971–1972 the Prime Minister answered 515 questions orally as against 104 questions for written answer. By contrast, the secretary of state for the environment received one-tenth that many questions for personal answer in the House and twenty times more for written answer. As a Prime Minister gains confidence in his or her role, he or she is readier to answer questions on any and all topics, in order to demonstrate the breadth of Prime Ministerial concern and knowledge; fewer questions are transferred to ministers actually responsible for the subject of the question. MPs are increasingly anxious to put questions to the Prime Minister. The number has risen with each Prime Minister and increased nearly three times from 1961 to 1977 (see table 1–4).

Prime Ministerial questions concentrate on a few themes, often outside the responsibility of particular departments. About one-fifth of all questions analyzed for sample years in table 1–4 address general concerns of government and are properly directed to the Prime Minister as the government's chief nondepartmental official. A quarter or more of the questions concern international affairs for which the Prime Minister is a unique spokesman. Increasingly, questions concern economic affairs, 27 percent of the total in the 1976–1977 session. These questions are addressed to (and accepted by) the Prime Minister because of their pervasive political significance, even though they could be referred to established departments. An innovation of the 1970s has been questions asking the Prime Minister whether he has plans to visit a given constituency or a scene of international concern. On December 11, 1975, for example, the places included Costa Rica, Cyprus, Shoreham, and Sweden. The point of proposing a visit is to allow the MP to follow it with a pointed supplementary, which may or may not obviously relate to the place in question.

Prime Minister's question time is also revealing for the range of government concerns that are ignored. Half the questions concern

TABLE 1-4

THE SUBJECT OF PARLIAMENTARY QUESTIONS TO THE PRIME MINISTER, SELECTED YEARS

Subject	1961–62 N	1961–62 %	1963–64 N	1963–64 %	1968–69 N	1968–69 %	1972–73 N	1972–73 %	1974–75 N	1974–75 %	1976–77 N	1976–77 %
General government[a]	65	17	130	28	203	29	120	16	204	21	216	21
International[b]	202	54	171	37	254	37	243	32	249	26	239	23
Economy[c]	41	11	78	17	120	17	147	19	300	31	281	27
Home office[d]	19	5	14	3	15	2	38	5	12	1	16	2
Welfare[e]	25	7	21	5	31	4	40	5	28	3	31	3
Environment[f]	7	2	15	3	20	3	65	9	23	2	34	3
Agriculture	2	—	9	2	5	1	16	2	—	—	3	—
Scotland, Wales, and Northern Ireland	15	4	30	6	45	6	37	5	49	5	47	5
Visits	—	—	—	—	—	—	49	6	103	11	161	16
Total	376	100	468	101	693	99	755	99	968	100	1,028	100

NOTE: Percentages may not add to 100 because of rounding. Compiling data for consecutive years requires tedious clerical effort, and many years may be atypical, for example, interrupted by a general election or the choosing of a new party leader; data are therefore given only for sample years representative of the Parliament in question. Before 1961–1962 parliamentary questions to the Prime Minister were organized on a different basis; earlier years are therefore excluded from the table.

a Includes parliamentary matters, ministerial responsibilities, speeches by the Prime Minister, the civil service, the press, and other questions not classifiable by department.

b Includes the Foreign Office, defense, EEC, nuclear issues, visits abroad.

c Includes Treasury and Department of Economic Affairs, nationalized industries, and energy.

d Includes broadcasting.

e Includes health, social security, and education.

f Includes transport.

SOURCE: House of Commons, Parliamentary Debates, index for appropriate years, including both oral and written answers.

foreign affairs or the economy and another quarter government generally. Established major departments such as the Home Office receive very little attention from the Prime Minister at question time. The major spending departments—Health and Social Security, and Education—receive equally short shrift. The departmental policies of two-thirds to three-quarters of the Cabinet are rarely the subject of Prime Ministerial questions.

Accounts or broadcasts of the repartee of Prime Ministerial question time demonstrate two characteristics. The first is the imaginative dexterity of both interrogator and respondent in finding unlikely connections between topics. The second is the superficiality of the exchanges. The lack of substantive discussion of policy is not accidental. In the opinion of a former civil servant, "The perfect reply to an embarrassing question in the House of Commons is one that is brief, appears to answer the question completely, if challenged can be proved to be accurate in every word, gives no opening for awkward supplementaries, and discloses really nothing."[18] A statement that provokes a laugh can be more effective than a statement full of facts or analysis. The essence of question time is that MPs seek to score debating points and catch headlines rather than to analyze a problem of British government.

Debating Policy. The bulk of the time of the House of Commons is spent on legislation or debate on policy, but the Prime Minister rarely participates in the principal business of the House. Unlike an American President, who is personally identified with legislative proposals in his State of the Union message, the Queen's Speech is a collective Cabinet document. Individual legislative proposals are the responsibility of particular Whitehall departments. In a debate concerning an issue within the scope of a department's responsibilities, the minister in charge is meant to state government policy.

The Prime Minister speaks far less in debates on substantive policy issues than do other major politicians in the Commons, whether those on the government frontbench or the leader of the opposition (table 1–5). In the course of a year, a Prime Minister will on average participate in only six debates. These are normally on only three issues: international affairs, the economy, and the business of government. The Prime Minister will also make about half a dozen statements to the House of Commons on important events in these fields. Within the government, the Prime Minister takes a back seat to the

---

[18] H. E. Dale, *The Higher Civil Service of Great Britain* (London: Oxford University Press, 1941), p. 105.

TABLE 1–5
Participation in Debates by Leading MPs

Session	Prime Minister No.	Subject	Chancellor of the Exchequer	Home Secretary	Leader of the Opposition No.	Subject
1947–48	7	Foreign 4, govt. business 3	13	12	8	Foreign 4, govt. business 4
1952–53	6	Foreign 4, govt. business 1, environment 1	11	14	9	Foreign 6, govt. business 2, economy 1
1955–56	13	Foreign 9, govt. business 2, economy 1, Home 1	8	9	13	Foreign 7, govt. business 1, economy 4, Home 1
1961–62	4	Foreign 2, govt. business 2	3	6	12	Foreign 2, govt. business 3, economy 2, Home 2, education 1, EEC 1, Scotland 1
1963–64	5	Foreign 2, govt. business 3	7	16	9	Foreign 1, govt. business 3, defense 2, economy 2, education 1
1968–69	4	Govt. business 3, employment 1	6	15	7	Foreign 1, govt. business 3, economy 2, employment 1
1972–73	6	Govt. business 2, economy 3, N. Ireland 1	8	7	9	Foreign 2, govt. business 1, economy 5, N. Ireland 1
1974–75	4	Govt. business 1, economy 2, EEC 1	8	5	5	Govt. business 1, economy 3, EEC 2
1976–77	6	Govt. business 4, economy 1, Scotland/Wales 1	7	7	6	Govt. business 3, economy 2, Scotland/Wales 1
Average	6		8	10	9	

Note: A speech is defined as three continuous columns of *Hansard*; government business includes debate on the Queen's Speech; committee stages of legislation are excluded.

Source: Derived from *Hansard* index for sessions.

Chancellor of the Exchequer and the home secretary in initiating or concluding debates about substantive policies. The Chancellor is on average involved in eight major debates a year, and the home secretary in ten. These ministers are in charge of operating departments, with immediate and clearly defined executive responsibilities for the national economy, for prisons and police, and for a host of other major activities of government.

The leader of the opposition speaks more often and on a wider range of policy issues than does the Prime Minister. This reflects the political weakness of an opposition party, with fewer senior front-benchers able to participate effectively in debates.[19] It also reflects the need of the leader of the opposition to establish himself or herself in Parliament. The leader of the opposition is relatively eminent because of a lack of important colleagues, whereas the Prime Minister is often overshadowed by departmental ministers when the House debates major policy questions.

The Prime Minister's presentation of self to Parliament reflects personal priorities and constraints, not the work of government. The Prime Minister appears twice weekly in question time to test his or her political superiority by fielding questions about general political concerns much more than specific departmental responsibilities. Once this is done, the Prime Minister leaves the House to Cabinet colleagues, who expound and defend the work of government, as determined by the responsibilities of their departments.

Press Publicity. For a century the press has been the principal means by which Prime Ministers have presented their personalities and ideas to a mass electorate. The British press (and television shares many of its characteristics) is divided into small-circulation, elite newspapers, read by about one-tenth of the electorate, and popular entertainment dailies containing little political information. Since 1945 social change and the advent of commercial television have led to the abandonment of the sacerdotal approach to public affairs, in which a Prime Minister was a remote and grand object of deference.[20] Instead, the persona of the Prime Minister receives greater emphasis.

The Prime Minister and the media have a symbiotic relationship; each feeds off the other. The Prime Minister is interested in being

---

[19] An opposition newly turned out of office will for a time have a substantial number of experienced frontbench spokesmen, but they may or may not be assiduous in attending to parliamentary duties.

[20] See Jay G. Blumler, "Producers' Attitudes towards Television Coverage of an Election Campaign," in Richard Rose, ed., *Studies in British Politics*, 3d ed. (London: Macmillan, 1976), pp. 266-91.

reported, and reporters live by the doctrine that names make news. As the biggest personality in politics, the Prime Minister is ex officio the most newsworthy. The institutions and arrangements of Westminster give parliamentary journalists easy access to a Prime Minister, and vice versa. Prime Ministers are concerned not only with managing their fellow MPs but also with using the press to their ends. Harold Wilson, the longest serving postwar Prime Minister, was also the most assiduous cultivator of the press. Churchill and Macmillan, too, were inveterate consumers of daily newspapers, typically reading the first editions of morning newspapers before going to bed.[21]

Parliamentary journalists are professional skeptics. Since they are not assigned to follow the Prime Minister exclusively, they are not dependent on a single source of news as are their U.S. counterparts who cover the White House. They are concerned with personalities—but personalities in conflict make better stories than personalities in the abstract. Hence, British journalists are always seeking evidence of disagreement within the Cabinet. In the words of one journalist, "We are war reporters wanting to know who is winning a battle in Cabinet." After reflection, he added, "We are not so much concerned with what the war is about."

An indication of the relative publicity given the Prime Minister can be obtained from the *Index to The Times*. While *The Times* is not a typical English newspaper, it is the one most read by the political class with whom the Prime Minister comes in contact. Other serious daily and weekly papers are likely to share *The Times*'s news emphasis, if not its evaluation of individual politicians. If anything, the popular press is likely to exaggerate the patterns revealed in *The Times*, since the popular press deals only with the highlights of political news and personalities.

For the past quarter century the Prime Minister has received more press attention than three leading ministers combined—the foreign secretary, the Chancellor of the Exchequer, and the leader of the House of Commons (table 1–6). Only in the exceptional circumstances of Clement Attlee's tenure of office have Cabinet colleagues (Sir Stafford Cripps and Ernest Bevin) garnered as much press attention as this unnaturally shy incumbent of Downing Street. Since

---

21 See Sir David Hunt, *On the Spot* (London: Peter Davies, 1975), pp. 58ff; and James Margach, *The Abuse of Power: The War Between Downing Street and the Media* (London: W. H. Allen and Co., 1978). More generally, see Jeremy Tunstall, *The Westminster Lobby Correspondents* (London: Routledge and Kegan Paul, 1970), and Colin Seymour-Ure, *The Press, Politics and the Public* (London: Methuen, 1968).

TABLE 1–6

NUMBER OF REFERENCES TO SENIOR POLITICIANS IN THE TIMES (LONDON)

Year[a]	Prime Minister (1)	Leader of Opposition (2)	(1) as % of (2)	Chancellor of Exchequer (3)	Foreign Secretary (4)	Leader of House of Commons (5)	(1) as % of Total of (3–5)
1949	Attlee 94	Churchill 62	152	Cripps 110	Bevin 96	Morrison 56	36
1952	Churchill 302	Attlee 64	472	Butler 136	Eden 197	Crookshank 38	81
1956	Eden 193	Gaitskell 70	276	Macmillan 93	Lloyd 111	Butler 50	76
1960	Macmillan 303	Gaitskell 88	344	Amory 44	Lloyd 76	Butler 109	132
1964	Douglas-Home 278	Wilson 169	164	Maudling 47	Butler 106	Lloyd 23	158
1968	Wilson 147	Heath 50	294	Jenkins 46[b]	Brown 45	Crossman 14	140
1972	Heath 141	Wilson 82	172	Barber 18	Douglas-Home 74	Whitelaw 24	122
1977	Callaghan 170	Thatcher 78	218	Healey 37	Crosland/Owen 39[c]	Foot 59	126

[a] The January-March quarter.
[b] Stories concerning the March budget.
[c] Stories on the death of Crosland and the appointment of Owen are omitted.
SOURCE: The quarterly Index to The Times (London).

1960 the three leading Cabinet colleagues together have received less than four-fifths of the Prime Minister's press mentions in *The Times*.

The Prime Minister has consistently had more publicity than the leader of the opposition. The importance of office in securing press notice is demonstrated by the fact that when Clement Attlee was Prime Minister and Winston Churchill leader of the opposition, Attlee's press coverage was 1.5 times greater than Churchill's. When their roles were reversed, Churchill received much greater publicity. Similarly, when Harold Wilson was Prime Minister and Edward Heath leader of the opposition, Wilson enjoyed 2.9 times as much attention as Heath; when the roles were reversed, Heath had the advantage of 1.7 times the attention of Wilson.

During general election campaigns, the Prime Minister also dominates the television presentation of the governing party. The Prime Minister is likely to receive more than half of all attention given by the broadcasters to the party's personalities; the remainder tends to be fragmented among many politicians, with only one or two colleagues mentioned as much as one-tenth of the time (see table 1–7). A similar pattern prevails in the opposition party. The requirements of fairness imposed upon the broadcasting authorities give the leader of the opposition almost as much publicity as the Prime Minister—

TABLE 1–7

REFERENCES TO PARTY LEADERS IN ELECTION CAMPAIGN TELEVISION
(percentage)

Year or Month	Prime Minister		Leader of Opposition	
	All mentions[a]	Lead over closest colleague	All mentions[a]	Lead over closest colleague
1964	36	23	47	32
1966	45	23	59	51
1970	53	44	50	34
Feb. 1974	59	46	66	58
Oct. 1974	55	47	50	38

[a] Figures combine mentions on both British Broadcasting Corporation and Independent Television News.

SOURCES: Martin Harrison, in D. E. Butler and others, *The British General Election of 1964* (London: Macmillan), p. 170; *1966*, p. 130; *1970*, p. 208; *February 1974*, p. 341; *October 1974*, p. 143. Data for 1979 are omitted because they are not fully comparable.

and leave his or her colleagues even more in the shadow. The concentration of television on party leaders strengthens the leaders (and especially the election victor) in relation to their own frontbench colleagues.

Whether the Prime Minister is in the ascendant or under attack, presentations of self in Parliament and in the media reinforce each other. The media do not create the Prime Minister's image; they amplify it. Journalists of both the popular and elite media mingle on intimate terms with politicians in Westminster. Media people turn to Parliament for cues about what is news, and the mood of the House provides their basis for evaluating how well politicians are doing, especially the Prime Minister. A Prime Minister who is successful in securing the good opinion of the House at question time can expect to be successful in the mass media as well.

The Prime Minister gives the appearance of having a finger in many pies. He or she is challenged about anything that government does or has failed to do. The media—especially the popular media—intensify the personalization of government, viewing Prime Ministerial activities in short catchy phrases. Parliamentary question time demands that a Prime Minister appear a jack-of-all-trades. The analysis of major debates and legislation in the Commons emphasizes that the Prime Minister is also a master of none.

Chairing the Cabinet. The task of chairing the Cabinet automatically brings the Prime Minister face to face with the ongoing problems of government, as distinct from problems of party management, electioneering, and personal public relations. Moreover, it is the weekly or bi-weekly occasion when the Prime Minister sits down with leading party colleagues to discuss political issues about which they must present a united front.

The chief function of the Cabinet is to maintain the political solidarity of the government.[22] As Lord Melbourne is supposed to have said about a Cabinet decision in the days before minutes were taken: "It is not much matter which we say, but mind, *we must all say the same.*" Most decisions of government will be made outside the Cabinet room—in departments, in Cabinet committees, or in informal colloquies among a few senior ministers including the Prime Minister.

---

[22] For views of the same Cabinet by different members, see accounts of the 1964-1970 Labour Cabinet by Patrick Gordon Walker, *The Cabinet* (London: Jonathan Cape, 1970); R. H. S. Crossman, *Inside View* (London: Jonathan Cape, 1972), and his *Diaries;* Sir Richard Marsh, *Off the Rails* (London: Jonathan Cape, and Nicolson, 1978); George Brown, *In My Way* (London: Victor Gollancz, 1971); and Wilson, *Governance of Britain.*

But all decisions are collective, in the sense that any minister must be sure that his colleagues agree with what he is doing and will give public support (or at least not voice public criticism) for his particular actions. The rule of collective responsibility binds the Prime Minister as well as departmental ministers. Since the Prime Minister lacks a major department of state as a base for taking specific policy initiatives, he or she is particularly dependent on collective agreement. Although the Cabinet meets only a few hours a week, its authority is continuous.

As chairman of the Cabinet, the Prime Minister is its authorized spokesman and in an emergency can considerably prejudge its room for maneuver. In the course of a week, a considerable amount of Prime Ministerial time is devoted to organizing and occasionally filtering out issues for collective discussion in the Cabinet. In doing this, the Prime Minister consults almost daily with the leader of the House of Commons, the chief whip, and the secretary of the Cabinet. The first two advise about issues that Parliament and the governing party wish Cabinet to pronounce upon. The secretary of the Cabinet informs the Prime Minister of matters that have progressed sufficiently through the deliberations of Whitehall to come forward for Cabinet discussion, endorsement, or dispute.

In the course of a political year, the chairmanship of Cabinet should bring at least one concern from every department of government across the Prime Minister's desk. Problems heading for the Cabinet are likely to involve the Prime Minister in informal discussion with the responsible minister well before a document finally and formally goes forward to the Cabinet. The Prime Minister will wish to make sure that the minister in charge is handling the issue satisfactorily and is aware of all its extradepartmental implications, especially those affecting the Prime Minister as party manager and election campaigner. The responsible minister will want to solicit Prime Ministerial support for his line of policy and sympathy for departmental difficulties. Contact is most frequent with the foreign secretary and the Chancellor of the Exchequer. But any minister can lobby (or be lobbied) by the Prime Minister at almost any time.

Increasingly, the Cabinet formally and collectively endorses decisions already resolved in Cabinet committees. The growth of governmental activities has disproportionately increased potential points of friction between departments, and the scope of Cabinet committees has expanded greatly. Among the matters usually decided without full discussion in the Cabinet are changes in public expenditure, whether increases or cuts, and arrangements for future legislation. In neither case does the Prime Minister chair the relevant Cabinet committee.[23]

Every Cabinet agenda includes regular topics, such as the following week's parliamentary business, presented by the leader of the House, and a review of international issues, presented by the foreign secretary. The Chancellor is likely to make a statement to colleagues about economic problems. If not, he will certainly have things to say about the financial implications of measures promoted by other departments. For a time, a "hot" item, such as negotiations on entry to the European Community or the troubles in Northern Ireland, may automatically appear on the Cabinet agenda. Some topics arise periodically, such as the annual White Paper on defense.[24]

In addition to recurring topics, Cabinet meetings deal with political issues that are deemed urgent because of their substantive scale. For example, local government reorganization affects the delivery and coordination of many central government services, and also the interests of local councillors who see MPs (including ministers) in their constituencies. Topics such as capital punishment may be discussed at Cabinet level because they generate much controversy. The Prime Minister must seek full Cabinet discussion to evolve a party line before a controversial issue blows up in Parliament.

As chairman of the Cabinet, the Prime Minister's first task is to ensure that the views of its members are fully elucidated. Normally, the discussion of an item on the Cabinet agenda is opened by the departmental minister responsible. Comments—positive and negative —flow from this oral presentation and from such disagreements as ministers have with written briefs. The course of the discussion is meant to show everyone, including the Prime Minister, the extent and intensity of agreement and disagreement in the Cabinet. Harold Wilson was prepared to have a Cabinet go through a White Paper or Green Paper paragraph by paragraph prior to its release so that no minister could afterward claim that he had not been consulted.[25] The Prime Minister can use a chairman's prerogative to raise important topics that might otherwise be overlooked and to stop discussion from becoming irrelevant. If a Prime Minister senses that disagreement will be intense, then he or she may first direct potentially rancorous debates to a Cabinet committee to maintain political harmony.

[23] On Cabinet committees, nominally a state secret, see, for example, Walker, *The Cabinet*, chap. 3.
[24] "Edward Heath and Lord Trend on the Art of Cabinet Government," *The Listener*, April 22, 1976; and, more generally, Walker, *The Cabinet*, chap. 7.
[25] Wilson, *Governance of Britain*, p. 72. More generally, see Brown, "Prime Ministerial Power," pp. 49-51.

Because the Cabinet does not make decisions by voting on resolutions, as does the Commons, it is up to the Prime Minister to announce the sense of the meeting. This summing up of the discussion is formally recorded in Cabinet minutes as a government decision. In summing up, a Prime Minister may influence the expression of that decision, but he or she is limited by what Cabinet colleagues have actually said. The minutes of a Cabinet meeting cannot depart greatly from the sense of the meeting itself without generating acrimonious disputes and distrust—procedural as well as substantive—at the next Cabinet meeting.

Constitutionally, a Cabinet decision takes precedence over the wishes of an individual minister, including the Prime Minister. No minister wishes to be bound to a decision that goes against the interests of his department or his personal political position. One card to play in a Cabinet battle is the threat of resignation. This would put the minister out of a job—but also leave him free to attack the Cabinet publicly. A Prime Minister does not want to be open to attack from within the party. Hence, whatever his personal views on the matter at hand, he will go to considerable lengths to avoid making a decision when the Cabinet threatens to split.

> The Prime Minister, curiously enough, was never keen on making decisions on matters that did not demand immediate action. Unless one had to be made, he liked to discuss the pros and cons at length and would then adjourn the meeting for further thought, particularly if the decision was likely to be one which went against the grain.[26]

The above is not a description of one of nature's temporizers, such as Harold Wilson, but of a man who outside the Cabinet room had the reputation of being a man of action, Winston Churchill.

The simplest means for a Prime Minister to be in the right is to suspend judgment until the Cabinet has discussed an issue fully, and then to side with the majority there. Often this stratagem is unnecessary because the Prime Minister will learn, in the course of informal discussions about any emerging problems, where the balance of opinion lies within the Cabinet, and formulate his or her views in the light of a lengthy process of give-and-take. Unlike an American President, a Prime Minister cannot make decisions by himself. A Prime Minister is bound to the Cabinet just as much as any other member. To take a position in advance of agreement in the Cabinet and then to find oneself in a minority is to risk loss of office. When Harold

---

[26] Sir Ian Jacobs, in Sir John Wheeler-Bennett, ed., *Action this Day: Working with Churchill* (London: Macmillan, 1968), p. 191.

Wilson did just this, in a Labour government dispute on industrial relations legislation in 1969, he had to abandon his policy rather than risk ejection from Downing Street. Peter Jenkins stated the moral: "The power of the Prime Minister was thus sufficient for him to remain in office, but insufficient for him to remain in office *and* have his way."[27]

Form Follows Function: Staffing the Prime Minister

The most important political tasks of a Prime Minister are those that he or she must do personally. Only the Prime Minister can determine how best to dispense patronage to party colleagues and potential rivals. Only the Prime Minister can advise the monarch about the date of a general election. When question time comes in the House of Commons, the Prime Minister is literally "on his own" against the combined forces of the opposition. Sophisticated journalists will judge the Prime Minister by impressions made in personal contact and not by handouts from press secretaries. The job of the Prime Minister is first and foremost to look after his or her personal interests; it is a one-person job.

Number 10 Downing Street is not a great London townhouse, let alone a royal palace. It is a not particularly large eighteenth-century terrace house that happens to be used by Prime Ministers. Douglas Hurd, a former political secretary to Edward Heath, aptly characterized it:

> Number Ten Downing Street is a house, not an office, and that is its most important characteristic. In the summer, tourists throng the little streets outside. Probably most of them go away a little disappointed, convinced that the right adjective for Britain is quaint. Number Ten ranks with Anne Hathaway's cottage and the Bluebell railway line. The Kremlin, the Elysée and the White House, by contrast, look like real seats of Government. It is hard to imagine anyone governing anything substantial from Number Ten.[28]

The staff of the Prime Minister must be fitted into a single residence, now enlarged with annexes. The back-up services are not located in the Prime Minister's office but in the Whitehall departments directed by Cabinet colleagues or in the Cabinet Office itself. Only three

---

[27] Peter Jenkins, *The Battle of Downing Street* (London: Charles Knight, 1970), p. 163.

[28] Douglas Hurd, *An End to Promises* (London: Collins, 1979), p. 32.

groups of péople work exclusively for the Prime Minister: the private secretaries, press secretary, and political advisers.[29]

Private Secretaries. The point of contact between the Prime Minister and government departments, collecting information from departments and communicating messages to them, are the six private secretaries of the private office. All are mid-career civil servants, specially picked by the Civil Service Department because of outstanding qualities and future promise as leaders of the civil service. The principal private secretary, the head of the private office, is not a chief of staff because he has no army—only another five civil servants —underneath him.[30] The group works as a team in two rooms, listening in on each other's conversations and dipping into each other's mail. In this way, the private office coordinates the flow of information in and out of 10 Downing Street. While the individuals in the team are not without ambition, each can best serve this ambition by showing skill in working as a team under a politician, an essential attribute for promotion in the civil service.

The civil servants in Downing Street are meant to be nonpartisan, but in no sense are they meant to be nonpolitical. As Richard Crossman once remarked, "There is nothing like a civil servant for being a politician and denying that he is one."[31] Private office staff are selected for their political sensitivity, the ability to see the difficulties in an issue, and to assess the mind of the Prime Minister and sense the purport of messages flashed from the departments. As the primary link between Downing Street and the operating departments of the Cabinet, they must be good at picking up messages on the "jungle telegraph" of Whitehall and alerting the Prime Minister to danger signals.

The Press Secretary. The link between the Prime Minister and the media is the press secretary, who sees the press twice daily to engage in the give-and-take of political journalism. This means giving information about the Prime Minister's activities and taking cues from

---

[29] For an up-to-date (as of the Callaghan government) and succinct description see George W. Jones, "The Prime Minister's Men," *New Society*, January 19, 1978. For a historical description, see George W. Jones, "The Prime Ministers' Secretaries: Politicians or Administrators?" in *From Policy to Administration: Essays in Honour of William A. Robson* (London: Allen and Unwin, 1976), pp. 13-38.

[30] Peter Hennessy, "Why the Best Job in the Civil Service Means Carrying the Prime Minister's Bag," *The Times*, November 10, 1976.

[31] Crossman, *Inside View*, p. 78.

journalists about topics that may blossom into major stories, whether favorable or unfavorable to the Prime Minister. In this way, the press secretary can brief the Prime Minister about things to keep an eye on, as well as try to put his employer's point of view to skeptical journalists. The post is usually filled by a civil servant, backed up by a few government information officers.

The press secretary is more than a public relations adviser to the Prime Minister. He is also expected to assist the coordination of the activities of departmental information officers and to present positively the main themes of government policy at home and abroad. In this, a press secretary is not making policy, nor is he acting for the Prime Minister. Instead, he is seeking to promote collectively agreed-upon policies on behalf of the whole Cabinet.

Political Advisers. Political advisers are partisan and personal appointees, given an office in 10 Downing Street for the duration of their patron's pleasure. There is no standard job description for a political adviser, since the post is a relatively recent innovation. Until the late 1950s a Prime Minister might have only civil servants to work for him in Downing Street.[32] As Harold Wilson once remarked, "In less hectic days, ministers were their own political advisers."[33] In the 1970s advisers have included an alleged eminence grise (Marcia Williams, now Lady Falkender, for Harold Wilson), a junior political secretary (Douglas Hurd, for Edward Heath), a party adviser concerned with extra-Whitehall affairs (Tom McNally, for James Callaghan), and a policy adviser concerned specially with Whitehall affairs (Dr. Bernard Donoughue, for Harold Wilson and James Callaghan). On occasion, a policy adviser may have a staff of up to six persons—but most advisers are appointed as individual *confidants*; being a trusted crony is a one-person job.

Political advisers are meant to complement the work of Downing Street's civil servants by keeping the Prime Minister in contact with the views of the governing party in Parliament, the party organization, and, not least, the electorate. From time to time, cronies are given sinecure appointments in Downing Street to serve as the Prime Minister's confidential companion. Civil servants would neither seek

---

[32] For accounts of life in Downing Street as a personal adviser, see Lord Egremont (formerly John Wyndham), *Wyndham and Children First* (London: Macmillan, 1968), chap. 6; Williams (Lady Falkender), *Inside Number Ten*; Hurd, *An End to Promises*; and, more generally, George W. Jones, "The Prime Ministers' Advisers," *Political Studies*, vol. 21, no. 3 (September 1973), pp. 363-75; and Sir Charles Petrie, *The Powers behind the Prime Ministers* (London: MacGibbon and Kee, 1958).

[33] *Governance of Britain*, p. 245.

nor be qualified to do this work. An individual political adviser is not difficult to assimilate into 10 Downing Street, as long as the individual stays close to his patron and does not become involved in work normally undertaken by departments or civil servants. Normally political advisers concentrate on aiding the Prime Minister in the presentation of self.

Advisers concerned with matters that are the responsibility of Whitehall departments must also understand the civil service and cultivate good personal relations with those who command the flow of information about emerging policies and problems. A Downing Street policy adviser cannot prepare or implement a given policy, for this is not the responsibility of his patron. Doing this is a departmental responsibility of individual Cabinet ministers. As the name declares, a policy adviser can suggest that a Prime Minister adopt a certain view—but he cannot tell ministers what they must do when the Prime Minister himself lacks that authority.[34]

Because the Prime Minister's staff is small—numbering less than a hundred inclusive of typists, with less than a dozen concerned with politics and policy—a Prime Minister does not have the problem of staff "going into business for themselves." Since most of the staff are civil servants whose ambition makes them emollient, there are not the personal frictions that a houseful of political appointees would generate. The chief source of potential friction is between the short-term political appointees who have no job security, an ill-defined role, and only nominal responsibilities, and civil servants who reckon to know exactly what the Prime Minister is expected to do.[35]

As chairman of the Cabinet, the Prime Minister is also involved with a second group of persons, who serve the Cabinet collectively. This status effectively constrains the personal use the Prime Minister can make of the Cabinet Office, the Civil Service Department, and the Central Policy Review Staff. They tend to be extroverted, looking outward from the Cabinet table, and do not merely concentrate their gaze on the Prime Minister. Because nearly all are civil servants, they wish to maintain a reputation for acting impersonally in order to serve the successors of the Prime Minister of the moment.

The Cabinet Office. In his role as chairman of the Cabinet, the Prime Minister is closest to the Cabinet Office, the principal task of which

---

[34] On the overall role of political and policy advisers, see Rudolf Klein and Janet Lewis, "Advice and Dissent in British Government: The Case of the Special Advisers," *Policy and Politics*, vol. 6, no. 1 (September 1977), pp. 1-25.

[35] For accounts of frictions, see Williams, *Inside Number Ten*, and Joe Haines, *The Politics of Power* (London: Jonathan Cape, 1977).

is to organize and draft reports for the myriad interdepartmental committees of the Cabinet that deal with contentious issues affecting more than one departmental minister. Much of the groundwork for negotiating agreement between affected departments is undertaken by committees of civil servants. Ministers then deal with the unresolved issues. By staffing these committees, the Cabinet Office becomes a vast repository of intelligence about agreements and disagreements within Whitehall. This information is conveyed to the Prime Minister, whose views as chairman of the Cabinet are solicited about how disagreements might best be resolved. With the growth of government, the Cabinet Office has grown—but it still measures its core administrative staff in dozens rather than hundreds.[36]

The secretary of the Cabinet stands in an unusual position as a seeker of agreement among politicians and civil servants collectively. As one of the three leading members of the civil service, specially charged with securing interdepartmental agreement, the secretary of the Cabinet must try to exert influence on departmental officials. His influence is enhanced insofar as he can correctly claim that the views enunciated are endorsed by the Cabinet, or that it is the opinion of the Prime Minister that they are suitable for Cabinet endorsement. But those subject to such influence will be able to resist any recommendation that has not, in fact, been formally written in the minutes of the Cabinet. The Cabinet Office seeks consensus; it does not have clout of its own. Its strength lies in its freedom from departmental interests. If it were perceived as a partisan for the Prime Minister alone, this could create opposition. As one of its staff has commented, "We always have to carry the rest of Whitehall with us. If the departments ganged up on us, we would always be defeated."[37]

The Civil Service Department. Nominally, the Prime Minister is the chief minister of the Civil Service Department (CSD), but to a large extent it is self-regulating in the management of the civil service. The effective head of the CSD is a civil servant, and one of the permanent secretary's chief responsibilities is to preserve the civil service from partisan influence by the Prime Minister or Cabinet ministers, individually or collectively.

---

[36] See Lee, "Central Capability and Established Practice," p. 184; and also George W. Jones, "Development of the Cabinet," in William Thornhill, ed., The Modernization of British Government (London: Pitman, 1975), pp. 31-62; and, historically, S. S. Wilson, The Cabinet Office to 1945, Public Record Office no. 17 (London: Her Majesty's Stationery Office, 1971).

[37] Quoted in Peter Hennessy, "The Cabinet Office: A Magnificent Piece of Powerful Bureaucratic Machinery," The Times, March 8, 1976.

The Central Policy Review Staff. The origins of the Central Policy Review Staff (CPRS), a would-be Cabinet gadfly, are perhaps more instructive than its present operations. In opposition in the late 1960s, Edward Heath conceived the need for what one of his associates, David Howell, described as *A New Style of Government*, with a "central capability unit" to provide the necessary intelligence and direction for a radical program of cutting back government in accord with Conservative political principles. The unit was assumed to require "the highest political authority with the direct backing of the Prime Minister."[38] While never stated explicitly and publicly, the Heath approach envisioned the creation of a Prime Minister's department to give direction to what the then Conservative leader saw as "his" Cabinet.

After the Conservative victory in 1970, the collective weight of jealous departments, led by a politically powerful Iain Macleod as Chancellor of the Exchequer, and civil servants at the highest level squashed plans for anything resembling a Prime Minister's department in Whitehall. The CPRS was established in 1970 to serve the Cabinet collectively. Its chief function is to put forward briefs from a nondepartmental (that is, bureaucratically disinterested) point of view.[39] As the chief nondepartmental minister, the Prime Minister has the most to gain from briefs' being submitted to Cabinet free from normal departmental biases. But as the "licensed" critic of departmental interests, the CPRS is guaranteed to have opponents, and it has no political patron. The Prime Minister cannot take a case to the Cabinet on the basis of a CPRS brief without abandoning his role as chairman of a controversial discussion and risking his authority on the strength of the CPRS's judgment.

The fewness of the Prime Minister's responsibilities is further underlined by the lack of staff. A Prime Minister does *not* have staff units comparable to those in the Executive Office of the President in Washington,[40] even though they may be found elsewhere in Whitehall.

1. The Prime Minister has no budget staff similar to that of the U.S. Office of Management and Budget: The power to review the

---

[38] David Howell, *A New Style of Government* (London: Conservative Political Centre, 1970), p. 17. For background on the period, see Hugh Heclo and Aaron Wildavsky, *The Private Government of Public Money* (London: Macmillan, 1974), chaps. 6-7.

[39] See Lord Rothschild, *Meditations of a Broomstick* (London: Collins, 1977), especially pp. 111ff.

[40] See Richard Rose, "The President: A Chief but Not an Executive," *Presidential Studies Quarterly*, vol. 7, no. 2 (Winter 1977), pp. 5-26.

annual budget rests with the Treasury. It is exercised by a Cabinet member, the chief secretary of the treasury, acting under the overall authority of the Chancellor of the Exchequer.

2. There is no Council of Economic Advisers, as in the U.S. President's Executive Office: The Treasury is the sole source of economic advice for the Prime Minister and the Cabinet collectively, as well as for the Chancellor of the Exchequer. From time to time an individual economic adviser has been attached to 10 Downing Street or to the Cabinet Office, but such individuals have never been successful in challenging the economic assumptions on which the Treasury bases its major (and sometimes politically unwelcome) policies.

3. There is no National Security Council as in the White House: Although the Prime Minister invariably concentrates much time and attention on foreign affairs and defense, the briefings are supplied by the Foreign and Commonwealth Office, or the Ministry of Defense.

4. No staff prepares the Queen's Speech for annual legislation, whereas a special White House staff is available to compile the State of the Union message. In Great Britain legislative proposals are developed within departments under the supervision of a particular minister. The chairmanship of the Future Legislation Committee of the Cabinet is normally in the hands of the leader of the House of Commons, not the Prime Minister. The final judgment on legislation is made by the Cabinet, not by the Prime Minister.

A Prime Minister is not the chief executive of government; the responsibility for doing anything in particular is vested by Parliament in particular departmental ministers. As long as the Prime Minister is a nonexecutive minister, he or she does not require a large department, nor could it be justified in conventional terms: "The major political difficulty which stands in the way of giving an executive department to the Prime Minister is constitutional, not technical."[41]

The Prime Minister and the Policy Process

Governing Britain cannot be a one-person job. By any criterion, the direction of 7 million public sector employees spending more than £60 billion each year is far more than any one person could supervise, let alone direct. Nor is there any constitutional reason for the

---

[41] Lee, "Central Capability and Established Practice," p. 171.

myth of Prime Ministerial government. Organizationally, British government is made up of departments, each headed by a Cabinet minister.[42] Collectively, Cabinet ministers have far more time to devote to specific policies than does the incumbent of 10 Downing Street, and ministers, too, find it difficult to keep up with their departmental responsibilities.[43] Constitutionally, government is the responsibility of the Cabinet, which brings together the ministers in charge of operating programs to make or to legitimate the policies of Her Majesty's Government.

The Prime Minister, as a nondepartmental minister, is detached from the day-to-day work of government. Others are charged with responsibility for foreign affairs, the economy, pensions, education, housing, health, and so on. A former private secretary to three Prime Ministers, Sir Philip de Zulueta, describes the position thus:

> Once a government is formed, the Prime Minister will find to his surprise that in one sense he has nothing to do. He has no large administrative machine for whose day-to-day running he is responsible. This sensation of idleness—the still in the centre of the whirlpool—is an illusion. But as Prime Ministers are normally men of active habit, they face a considerable test in adjusting themselves to the situation at No. 10. For while not directly responsible for very much, they are indirectly responsible for everything, and can meddle in anything they choose.[44]

Instead of having a large department, with many policies immediately under his direction, a Prime Minister can influence policies only indirectly, through responsible ministers. No wonder that Harold Macmillan's Downing Street adviser, John Wyndham, described it as only natural for an activist Prime Minister to "ache to collar a department for himself."[45]

The first questions to ask about the Prime Minister are whether he or she is involved with a given policy and which policies are most

---

[42] Since the delivery of services for much of the work of government is in the hands of local government, nationalized industries, or other "extra-Whitehall bodies," the structure is far more complex—and far less amenable to central direction—than can be described here. See Richard Rose, *Politics in England*, 3d ed. (Boston: Little Brown and Co., 1980), chap. 10.

[43] See Bruce Headey, *British Cabinet Ministers: The Roles of Politicians in Executive Office* (London: Allen and Unwin, 1974).

[44] "The Power of the Prime Minister," *The Swinton Journal*, vol. 12, no. 2 (Autumn 1966), p. 39.

[45] Egremont, *Wyndham and Children First*, p. 167.

frequently treated at Downing Street. In a formal sense, the Prime Minister is always involved, sharing collective responsibility for everything done in the government's name. But in a practical sense, a Prime Minister can be only selectively involved in government policies. There is not world enough and time to be informed about all that is done in the name of the government, let alone to influence everything. A Prime Minister who boasts of digesting 500 policy briefs in a weekend[46] can give equal attention to each only if they are skimmed very quickly as background information.

In general, the Prime Minister is involved in any "hot" issue, that is, any that is the subject of major discussion in Parliament, the party, and the press. The action-forcing processes described above will direct questions and comments to 10 Downing Street, whether the responsibility for the problem at hand rests with a particular departmental minister or a foreign government, or is an act of God. Foreign affairs, economic issues, and often the two in relation to each other are most frequently thrust forward for Prime Ministerial attention.

The next question to ask is how the Prime Minister relates to policy issues. At a minimum, the Prime Minister, as the government's chief spokesman, is forced to answer questions about an issue in the House of Commons, in party conclaves, and in discussions with journalists. A Prime Minister is also forced to take up issues that are the subject of international discussion among the heads of foreign governments. Summit meetings are held as the apex of intensive discussions and briefings by major departments, especially the Foreign Office.

As an experienced politician, the Prime Minister does not want to spend all of his or her time simply speaking from briefs supplied by affected departments. By virtue of having more free time to scan the horizon, looking for opportunities and difficulties and seeing the interconnections among policies, a Prime Minister can make a distinctive contribution to the formulation of many policies, especially when more than narrow departmental interests are at stake. Yet the absence of departmental staff limits what a Prime Minister can contribute. At best, the incumbent of 10 Downing Street can steer policies toward certain broad political objectives, and away from recognizable difficulties.

The advice and opinions that a Prime Minister offers are often general, even to the point of vagueness. One reason for this is the absence of detailed information "in house." A second reason is that

---

[46] See Harold Wilson's farewell speech as Prime Minister, reported in *The Times*, March 17, 1976.

another minister (or ministers) are already dealing with the issue. A third reason is that if every alternative course presents difficulties, a Prime Minister may not wish to promote a move that is open to criticism. Only by avoiding commitment to a specific action can a Prime Minister leave himself in a position to chair Cabinet discussions as an impartial judge, making decisions in the light of the recommendations and arguments of affected ministers.

In chairing the Cabinet, the Prime Minister's primary responsibility is to secure consensus, rather than particular policy outcomes. This is no easy task, for as Barbara Castle has put it, a Cabinet is not a "political caucus" of like-minded politicians trying to determine priorities; it is an arena in which "departmental enemies" contest for power.[47] By virtue of being a nondepartmental minister, the Prime Minister stands above the clash of departmental interests. If a Prime Minister gets the reputation of being partial to a few departments or a few ministers, those who feel discriminated against may mobilize their political forces against him. No Prime Minister wishes to encourage a Cabinet split; the unity of the Cabinet normally comes first. In deciding which policy the Cabinet is to unite on, the Prime Minister has more leeway than an American congressional leader, for Cabinet decisions are not voted, but after opinions are voiced a decision is articulated that will maintain rather than threaten Cabinet cohesion.

Generalizations about policy making vary from one problem area to another. This point is brought out clearly by examining two areas of unquestionable significance—foreign affairs and the economy—and a third area, education, in which careful documentation shows the Prime Minister's role to be distinctive by its absence.

Foreign Affairs. The priority the Prime Ministers give to international affairs is even more evident in their memoirs than it is in *Hansard*, the written report of parliamentary debates. The historic international involvement of Britain and specific circumstances at the end of World War II explain why foreign affairs was immediately critical to the 1945–1951 Labour government. But Prime Ministerial interest has continued since, notwithstanding the decline in England's international standing. The concern is continuous, despite the major role of the Foreign and Commonwealth Office and the Ministry of Defense. Involvement is high whether a Prime Minister has previously been much concerned with foreign affairs or, like Harold Wilson, avoided such debates before becoming Prime Minister. The question must therefore be asked: Why do contemporary British

---

[47] Barbara Castle, "Mandarin Power," *Sunday Times*, June 10, 1973.

Prime Ministers devote so much of their scarcest political resource, time, to foreign affairs?

The first reason is that international diplomatic protocol requires heads of government to deal with each other. A British Prime Minister cannot delegate attendance at an international summit without appearing to insult other national leaders deliberating there. A second reason is that foreign governments wish a single statement of a unified national policy from Britain. Prime Ministerial authority is required to remove potential differences between the Foreign Office, Defense, and the Treasury. Third, international issues are often intrinsically important.

International meetings make preemptive and substantial claims upon the time of the Prime Minister. Harold Wilson reckoned that in a two-year period from 1974 he attended fifteen multilateral meetings of heads of state and six meetings with the American President; took thirteen trips abroad for bilateral meetings with heads of government; and hosted fifty-nine meetings with heads of government in London, most of which were "full-dress official or state visits, involving two days of discussion and hosted and reverse entertainment." Wilson adds that these tabulations

> exclude formal or informal visits by foreign ministers (including Dr. Kissinger, Mr. Gromyko and M. Sauvagnargues), deputy prime ministers, finance ministers, trade and other ministers, parliamentary delegations, Commonwealth Parliamentary Association or International Parliamentary Union visits with one full IPU annual conference, speakers and presiding officers of overseas parliaments, the ambassadors and high commissioners stationed in London, Her Majesty's ambassadors and high commissioners to major countries whenever they are in London (including those accredited to countries to be visited as well as our representative to EEC, and the British members of the Commission, and NATO), the London-based Secretary-General of the Commonwealth, and the secretaries-general of OECD and CENTO, personal emissaries from overseas heads of state or government and leaders of the Opposition in different countries, particularly from the Commonwealth. If these are included the total would be at least three to four hundred—an average of some three or four a week.[48]

The show of international diplomacy must go on, even if there is a domestic crisis that threatens the government's future.[49]

---

[48] Wilson, *Governance of Britain*, pp. 150-51.
[49] See, for example, Hurd, *An End to Promises*, p. 121.

Conventions of international diplomacy authorize the Prime Minister to speak for the British government in international meetings and even to make commitments for the government. Whitehall departments with operational responsibility for international issues accept the Prime Minister's primacy and therefore brief him or her intensively prior to and during meetings, in order to ensure that their case is well understood and well presented by the government's chief spokesman. Given the widely ranging nature of many meetings of heads of state, face-to-face briefings often involve the Treasury, Energy, and Trade as well as the Foreign and Commonwealth Office, Defense, and ambassadors. Although briefings cannot determine the outcome of diplomatic negotiations, they establish the objectives, the arguments, and the tolerance of government departments for possible outcomes of bilateral or multilateral negotiations. Failure to consult properly with Cabinet colleagues before going abroad to negotiate can leave a minister, even a Prime Minister, vulnerable to repudiation by the Cabinet.

In order to handle the incessant flow of issues all over the world, the Prime Minister must continuously monitor international affairs. Foreign Office confidential reports and minutes are sent daily to Downing Street. By following closely events around the world, the Prime Minister reduces time spent in briefing; but this also reduces the time available to follow domestic matters.

Because of the exigencies of international diplomacy, the Prime Minister and foreign secretary are substantially interdependent. The Prime Minister is dependent on the Foreign and Commonwealth Office for staff and departmental briefs and lacks an adviser to question such briefs or to prepare alternatives. A Prime Minister has a free hand in determining this relationship, by deciding who is (or is not) appointed to the sensitive post of foreign secretary. The range of possibilities is great, from a person as weighty politically as the Prime Minister (Ernest Bevin to Attlee, 1945–1951) to a political junior (Selwyn Lloyd, 1955–1960, or David Owen, 1976–1979) to a potential or frustrated candidate for the Premiership (Anthony Eden, Harold Macmillan, James Callaghan, R. A. Butler, and George Brown).

Involvement in international affairs enhances the Prime Minister's presentation of self. This is first and foremost true of the incumbent's own ego. It is ego-boosting to be in the same room with the leaders of half a dozen of the world's largest and most important nations. In the course of a discussion, heads of state find they have many things in common and can sympathize with the domestic difficulties of a discussion partner who does not pose a threat to them.

The Prime Minister can exploit international gatherings, both in the presentation of self in Parliament ("As I told President _____ last week") and in the mass media, for foreign travels are news events in themselves. Few diplomatic or lobby correspondents attack their Prime Minister for what is done abroad.

Only one hard-boiled question remains: What power does the Prime Minister exert through involvement in foreign affairs? The answer is: Not much. An obituary notice for Anthony Eden pointedly noted, "He was the last Prime Minister to believe Britain was a great power and the first to confront a crisis that proved she was not."[50] Whereas the British government's power has grown in domestic affairs in the past half century, simultaneously it has declined in international affairs. Harold Wilson unintentionally illustrates this national (and personal) weakness: "In the sixties I was much involved personally in the Rhodesian problem, South Africa, Vietnam, Anglo-American and Anglo-Soviet relations and later the Nigerian civil war, as well as in broader issues of Commonwealth affairs"[51]—a catalog of activities without any notable British diplomatic success. Douglas Hurd more accurately sums up the typical outcome of a foreign affairs crisis, in this case arms sales to South Africa in the Heath administration:

> It consumed a vast amount of time and energy of ministers which could have been better employed. It bore little re-lation to the central purposes of Mr. Heath's Government. . . . The whole issue turned out an irrelevance. Like so many bitter arguments in politics, it just dissolved with the passage of time.[52]

Nor does involvement in foreign affairs now influence electoral opinion. A Prime Minister can exploit foreign affairs domestically only if an issue is considered important. But public opinion polls report that foreign affairs are usually considered important by less than 2 percent of the national electorate.[53]

The Economy. Management of the economy is now the preeminent concern of British government, for economic problems tend to have a pervasive influence on government policy, both abroad and at home. Moreover, because of the links between parties and interest groups and economic conditions and electoral outcomes, economic policy is immediately important for party management and the timing and

---

[50] Lord Blake, quoted in Margach, *Abuse of Power*, p. 100.
[51] Wilson, *Governance of Britain*, p. 149.
[52] Hurd, *An End to Promises*, pp. 52, 55.
[53] Richard Rose, "The American Shield: How Others See Us," *Public Opinion*, vol. 2, no. 2 (March-May 1979), pp. 13-15.

winning of elections. No modern British Prime Minister can be indifferent to economic affairs, even though many have been unprepared for the complexities.

Immediate responsibility for the management of the economy is in the hands of the Treasury. The Chancellor of the Exchequer is personally accountable to the House of Commons and to the Cabinet for what happens to the economy. The Treasury is the focal point of pressures arising in the world economy, in the British economy, and within government itself. The Chancellor's greatest political strength is the Treasury's monopoly control of macroeconomic policy and its production of expert briefs upon which the Cabinet bases its discussions of economic policy.[54]

But the Treasury is not alone in being concerned with the state of the economy. Every Whitehall department is concerned with anything that affects the amount of money that it spends, and every politician in the Cabinet is concerned with the extent to which the government can maintain its electoral popularity by raising the nation's standard of living and averting the worst effects of economic difficulties. Within the Cabinet, the Departments of Trade, Industry, Employment, Energy, and Agriculture are directly involved in carrying out economic measures. The Scottish, Welsh, and Northern Ireland offices voice distinctive territorial concerns about the economy, and the Foreign Office speaks for international implications. Most major economic issues are interdepartmental and affect a substantial portion of the Cabinet.

In addition, many organizations outside Whitehall are much concerned with government economic policy. Pressure groups representing finance, industry, commerce, and trade unions all articulate demands and participate in determining economic results in a mixed economy. The heads of major nationalized industries are extra-Cabinet officials whose actions rebound to the credit or embarrassment of the government of the day. Local government, too, is an important pressure group in Whitehall, and if elected councillors become disaffected, this sours many in the party whom the Prime Minister is meant to manage.

As the minister most concerned with the broad aims of government policy, the Prime Minister is uniquely placed to see the interconnection between economic policy and other political objectives. In chairing the Cabinet, the Prime Minister receives different views on the wisdom of reflation or deflation from ministers whose departments institutionalize disagreement. But the Prime Minister's interests

[54] See Samuel Brittan, *Steering the Economy* (London: Secker and Warburg, 1969).

extend well beyond the clash of departmental briefs. He or she can take account of the exigencies of electoral timing and evaluate the effect of economic policies on the electorate or, more immediately, the unity of a Cabinet divided by left-right tensions.

In the politics of economic policy making, the relation between the Prime Minister and the Chancellor is crucial. From 1945 to 1957 the Chancellor dominated economic policy because a series of leading political figures served with Prime Ministers—Clement Attlee, Anthony Eden, and Winston Churchill—who had little interest in economic affairs. Since then, the political status of the two has fluctuated. The Chancellor of the day must always strive to convince the Prime Minister that the economic policy being recommended to the Cabinet is desirable or, rhetorically even more effective, "the only possible" policy. With the full weight of the Treasury's expertise behind him, the Chancellor can produce formidable briefs in support of any case argued. In turn, a Prime Minister can influence a Chancellor by remaining unconvinced, or asking that policies deemed politically unsuitable be examined again by the Treasury. But the Chancellor and, even more, a horde of sophisticated Treasury officials require convincing, too, before a Prime Minister's idea can be put into effect by the Treasury.[55]

The determination of the government's broad economic strategy is a matter for summit diplomacy among major figures in the Cabinet. On the one hand, the Prime Minister must be satisfied with the policy to be announced and, lacking a departmental responsibility, may be especially concerned with its purely political implications. On the one hand, the Prime Minister must be satisfied with the divides the Cabinet or causes the resignation of an important minister. Given internal divisions on economic principles in both the Conservative and the Labour parties, this political balancing act is never easy.

Unfortunately, many Prime Ministers find that, like the conduct of foreign affairs, the pursuit of economic objectives faces opposition from sovereign forces outside the control of Whitehall. These forces may be the trade unions, financial interests in the City of London, or the manufacturing industry within Britain, or the directors of competitive economies abroad. Even worse, impersonal secular trends may be so strong that successive Conservative and Labour governments make little difference in the performance of the British economy.[56]

---

[55] See Brown, "Prime Ministerial Power," p. 109.
[56] See Richard Rose, *Do Parties Make a Difference?* (London: Macmillan, 1980), chap. 7.

Education. Logically and empirically, many policies of government can be carried out with little or no personal intervention by the Prime Minister. Neglect of many policies is the price the Prime Minister pays for concentrating on international affairs and the economy. Education is a well-documented example.[57] The principal institutions for policy making are three: the Department of Education and Science, which lays down and monitors broad policy guidelines; local education authorities, which manage and deliver education services; and interest groups, which represent those immediately providing or receiving education. The multiple forces making for changes in education policy include demographic trends in the expansion of education in the 1960s; the demands of pressure groups for such things as raising the school-leaving age to sixteen in 1972; and shifting patterns of party policy, which led to the abandonment of selective secondary education from 1965.

The conduct of education policy is formally the responsibility of the secretary of state for education, who devotes all of his or her time and political energy to this office. It is a middle-ranking Cabinet post that can be a steppingstone to higher office or, if mishandled, a last post before being dropped from the Cabinet in a reshuffle. The relative importance of education issues to the secretary of state for education and the Prime Minister can be shown by the number of parliamentary questions on this subject. Each year a secretary of state for education receives upwards of 500 parliamentary questions; by comparison, a Prime Minister will deal with half a dozen or a dozen on this topic, less than 1 percent of those directed at the responsible minister. What is true of parliamentary questions is equally true of parliamentary debate. Both the Prime Minister and the education minister agree that it is the latter's job to answer for the subject in the Commons.[58] Only one postwar Prime Minister—Margaret Thatcher—has served a prior term as an education minister.

Two secretaries of state for education have given public testimony to the limits of Prime Ministerial involvement in education policy.

---

[57] See, for example, Maurice Kogan, *Educational Policy-Making: A Study of Interest Groups and Parliament* (London: Allen and Unwin, 1975); Edward Boyle and Anthony Crosland, with Maurice Kogan, *The Politics of Education* (Harmondsworth: Penguin, 1971); Ronald A. Manzer, *Teachers and Politics* (Manchester: University Press, 1970); and Paul E. Peterson, "British Interest Group Theory Re-examined: The Politics of Comprehensive Education in Three British Cities," *Comparative Politics*, vol. 3, no. 3 (April 1971), pp. 381-402.

[58] Kogan, *Educational Policy-Making*, chap. 1. The only reference to education that Macmillan makes in his memoir of the period, *The End of the Day, 1961-63* (London: Macmillan, 1973), is to the appointment of Boyle to the department.

Sir Edward Boyle, education secretary under Harold Macmillan has commented:

> The starting point for educational questions was the education world itself. Not the Prime Minister to any great extent, who after all had never been Minister of Education. . . .
>
> While I always had a sympathetic treatment from Mr. Macmillan about education, it was obvious that he'd lived with Housing in a way that he'd never lived with the education service.[59]

Anthony Crosland commented thus about his relationship with Harold Wilson: "When he moved me to the Board of Trade, he [Harold Wilson] remarked on the fact that he hadn't once had a conversation with me about education."[60]

Education policy is not just the property of education pressure groups and civil servants in departmental offices. It is also a matter of government policy, and on occasion, such as the abolition of selective secondary schools, it is cause for contention within Parliament. The Prime Minister has the power to decide, on the ground of patronage or policy, who should be appointed to head the department. As chairman of the Cabinet, the Prime Minister can review disputes arising between the Treasury and Education about spending on education, or even question substantive education measures. The occupant of 10 Downing Street shares collective responsibility for what is done in the field of education, but no Prime Minister in generations has claimed to be an education policy maker.

What is true of Education is similarly true in most departments of state: Health and Social Security, Environment (housing, local government, and transport), Agriculture, the Home Office, and Scotland and Wales. Collectively they account for the bulk of public expenditure and new legislation each year. Each of these departments has its own special network of policy-making institutions. Each also has an infinity of people and issues demanding attention. No Prime Minister has the time or the inclination to monitor all departments closely, let alone to deal with all their problems together. Even secretaries of state find that they cannot effectively determine all the matters regarded as important within their departmental purview.

The Prime Minister keeps in touch with their activities through the Cabinet and all that flows into and out of the Cabinet and the

---

[59] Boyle and Crosland, *The Politics of Education*, p. 90.
[60] Ibid., p. 35.

House of Commons. But "touch" is the word: These concerns are tangential to the imperative concerns of the Prime Minister. The limited contact between 10 Downing Street and the substance of problems is summed up by the departmental civil servant whose first reaction on being transferred to 10 Downing Street was: "It's like skating over an enormous globe of thin ice."

The strength of the Prime Minister's unique position within the Cabinet is that he or she is best able to see government as a whole. The job is not to substitute for departmental ministers, but to supplement them, by noticing what would otherwise be left out of consideration. As Sir Philip de Zulueta notes, "No one except the Prime Minister is in a position to give coherence to government policy as a whole."[61] If the Prime Minister is not doing the job properly, the work of government will continue, Cabinet agendas will be full, and legislation promptly enacted. But what will be lacking is any sense of a central theme or purpose in the government of the day.

The Office in Perspective

The office exists before the individual. Biographies and autobiographical memoirs inevitably overstate the personal element in the Prime Ministership; the style of the man sets the style of a biography. By contrast, historians—including such past Prime Ministers as Harold Macmillan and Harold Wilson—tend to emphasize the continuity of the office; actions by different Prime Ministers at very different times are cited as binding precedents, without regard to changes in the office. Any set of generalizations should therefore be tested for significant variations depending on the personality of the incumbent, changes through time, and international comparisons.

The Individual Term in the Equation. In the most trivial sense there *is* a difference in personality and style between Prime Ministers. Clement Attlee was not Winston Churchill, nor was Edward Heath the same sort of politician as Harold Wilson. Differences occur within parties as much as between parties. Yet as soon as one reviews a gallery of Prime Ministers, similarities also emerge: Harold Wilson was prepared to speak well of Stanley Baldwin, and Harold Macmillan was an admirer of Winston Churchill, whom he had served. In the 1979 election campaign, Margaret Thatcher spoke favorably of Clement Attlee.

---

[61] de Zulueta, "The Power of the Prime Minister," p. 40.

The conventional social science way in which to analyze similarities and differences in an office is to create an abstract typology of personal attributes or political roles, to which individual leaders are then assigned. While it is tempting to do so, it is difficult to find clear and meaningful criteria for discriminating between individual politicians. For example, though it is possible to differentiate Prime Ministers by their social origins, it is not practicable to generalize about their behavior in office from such evidence.[62] Moreover, there are certain roles that all Prime Ministers *must* undertake. While individual Prime Ministers may respond differently to the demands of office, the imperatives tend to remain constant.

The very high degree of institutionalization in British government—encompassing informal Whitehall norms even more than formal organizations—is the most powerful determinant of what a Prime Minister can and cannot do. Personal style influences how a Prime Minister carries out the demands of office, but it does not determine what is to be done. The first priority of a Prime Minister is to do what is expected of him or her. How a Prime Minister meets these role expectations reflects not only his or her basic personality, whatever that may be, but even more what the incumbent has learned in a quarter century of socialization in Westminster and Whitehall. Unlike a newly elected American President, who usually has little prior experience in the federal executive branch, a newly installed Prime Minister is already "institutionalized" by Whitehall. Three postwar British Prime Ministers—Harold Wilson, Edward Heath, and James Callaghan—initially worked in the civil service, and Clement Attlee would have done so too, if he had succeeded in an examination for a legal post in the Church or Charity Commission.

Political circumstances are more important than personality; in different situations, the same Prime Minister will behave differently. This is most evident in the contrasts between the wartime government headed by Churchill (1940–1945) and that of peacetime (1951–1955). Clement Attlee was not the same kind of Prime Minister in 1951 as in 1945, nor did Harold Wilson in 1974–1976 act the same as in 1964–1970. There are contrasts between a government with and without a parliamentary majority. Equally, a Prime Minister will act differently if, like Attlee, he has a Cabinet full of politicians with high standing in the party or, like Heath, one filled with political lightweights.

---

[62] For a careful consideration of the difficulties of drawing inferences about government behavior from social origins, see Dennis A. Kavanagh, "Changes in Political Leadership: From Gentleman to Players," in William B. Gwyn and Richard Rose, eds., *Britain: Progress and Decline* (London: Macmillan, 1980).

The scope for action by Margaret Thatcher is inevitably limited by the character of the job at 10 Downing Street. Initially, Mrs. Thatcher has been an active participant in many debates on major policies; she is a player, rather than an umpire, in the game of policy making. But like any player, she cannot win them all. Within her first six months in office, the Conservative government confirmed policies on measures, such as MPs' pay, the treatment of Vietnamese boat people, and Rhodesia, that differed from those Mrs. Thatcher had initially indicated. Robust discussions between the Prime Minister and Cabinet ministers have instructed her in the difference between a "gut" reaction to an issue and a considered policy acceptable to affected parties outside as well as inside Whitehall. Mrs. Thatcher's activist style has risks: "If and when things go badly wrong, there will be nobody else to blame."[63] One certainty is that the limits of time and space will confine her influence. As one colleague remarked, "I don't say she wouldn't like to run the economy, but she's away so much that she can't run it, however much she might want to."[64]

Long-term Trends. The most significant, though as yet relatively small, institutional change in the political direction of government in Britain since 1945 has been the introduction of political advisers into Whitehall offices, including 10 Downing Street. The change has been gradual, and there are ample historical precedents. Political advisers have little chance to make a real impact on the civil service because of their inexperience in Whitehall, temporary status, and fewness. Their greatest influence is likely to be in aiding the Prime Minister in personal political roles, such as party management and the presentation of self. It is noteworthy that the largest and best documented group of political advisers, the staff of Harold Wilson, have made their memoirs a litany of failure to influence the ongoing processes of government.[65]

The second major change has been in media coverage of the Prime Minister. The press is no longer respectful, even deferential— although newspaper publishers retain a liking for private and unpublishable briefings at Downing Street, a weakness that the Prime

---

[63] Peter Jenkins, "Matriarch with a Sense of Mission," *The Guardian*, August 1, 1979.

[64] Quoted in Graham Turner, "How the Tory Cabinet Works," *Sunday Telegraph*, July 8, 1979.

[65] See sources cited in footnotes 28-41 above, especially Williams, *Inside Number Ten*, and Haines, *Politics of Power*.

Minister of the day is usually ready to exploit. Members of the working press are today much readier to write stories of controversy within the Cabinet or to fasten on more or less trivial aspects of the personality of the Prime Minister of the day. Television accentuates the significance of personality and is peculiarly incompetent to deal with stories of government disagreements leaked anonymously on a "not for attribution" basis. From the evidence of public opinion (tables 1–2 and 1–3) it would be difficult to argue that changes in the media have made a Prime Minister more or less successful in the presentation of self. New media techniques are best seen as neutral. In the absence of direct election of a Prime Minister, they are not crucial to the incumbent's fate, which is immediately decided in Westminster, not in television studios.

Many major changes in British government have occurred since 1945. It has grown not only in size and scope but also in the extent of institutional fragmentation. Many of the most obvious changes are of little operational consequence in 10 Downing Street. The great changes occurred in the nineteenth century, when the affairs of state grew beyond the capacity of any one individual to supervise them, as Palmerston and Peel had once done.[66] The creation of the "new model" civil service following the Northcote-Trevelyan Report of 1854 meant the bureaucratization of Whitehall, laid a foundation for continuity in government by depersonalizing office, and placed many constraints on the behavior of ministers. The creation of the Cabinet Office in 1916 was probably the last major institutional reform greatly affecting the work of the Prime Minister today. It was, incidentally, a reform that strengthened the collective authority of the Cabinet. Without a Cabinet Office, a Prime Minister could, like a President, try to substitute personal inclinations and staff directives for an agreed written minute of a Cabinet decision.

If Prime Ministers were being assessed in terms of their power over a range of issues it might be argued that the power of the Prime Minister has declined with the expansion of British government. In the first half of the nineteenth century, the Prime Minister could and did give personal direction to the few activities of government. But as government does more and more, any individual is less and less involved in the majority of things done in its name. A Prime Minister can share in the credit or blame for the actions of a mammoth impersonal bureaucracy, but can influence it only very selectively. After a careful review of the historical record, A. H. Brown concludes:

---

[66] See Henry Parris, *Constitutional Bureaucracy* (London: Allen and Unwin, 1969), pp. 107 ff.

If a graph could be constructed to illustrate Prime Ministerial power from the time of the Second or even of the First Reform Act to the present day, it would show nothing as consistent as a steadily (far less a rapidly) rising curve. It would be a picture of ups and downs, in which it would be possible to imagine a Prime Minister in the early 1840s appearing at a higher point than one in the mid-1930s and one in the early 1920s above one in the mid-1960s. Unfortunately, however, the question of Prime Ministerial power cannot be tackled in this way. By a selective use of evidence, *as plausible a case could be made for the general proposition that the Prime Minister's power has declined as for the view that it has increased.* . . .

No Prime Minister in the twentieth century has exercised greater personal power than Lloyd George or Chamberlain. None has been more willing to interfere with, or completely by-pass their Cabinet colleagues. Nor is it entirely coincidence that both came to a sticky end.[67]

A Comparative Perspective. Politicians in very different political systems can be alike in one thing: a concern with status and power is at least as old as Machiavelli. But politicians must pursue these common goals in different ways, according to differences in national forms of government and national political values.[68] A person ambitious to become Prime Minister of Britain will behave differently from a Presidential aspirant in America or France.

One distinctive feature of a Prime Minister's job in Britain is the importance of party management. The party in Parliament elects the Prime Minister; by comparison, an American or French President is popularly elected, securing nomination by demonstrating vote-getting abilities with the general public. Because a Prime Minister can be dismissed by the electoral college that has chosen him or her, a Prime Minister is much more bound to the party and must be much more loyal to it than is an American or French equivalent. As long as the Prime Minister can dominate the party in fact as well as name, then his or her position is secure. Doing this is a continuing and imperative task.

Because of the dominance of the executive over Parliament, a Prime Minister need have little concern about losing votes on legis-

---

[67] A. H. Brown, "Prime Ministerial Power," pp. 33, 44; italics added.

[68] The office of Prime Minister cannot be reduced to a set of cultural norms, especially if the institutions are then cited as evidence of these norms. The argument of this chapter emphasizes institutions; values and role expectations are what the institutions themselves institutionalize.

lation in the House of Commons. Unlike votes in the U.S. House of Representatives, votes in the Commons can usually be taken for granted. Managing Parliament is not so much a matter of legislation as it is a party task. It means maintaining good relations with back-benchers whose confidence is important for the Prime Minister's successful presentation of self. Individual Cabinet ministers are left to get on with the task of drafting and securing the adoption of particular acts of Parliament.

The centralization of authority in British government greatly concentrates and simplifies the direction of government. A Prime Minister does not have to worry about managing a multiparty coalition government, as is always the case in Italy, in the Benelux countries, and often in Scandinavia. Nor is a Prime Minister faced with competition from provincial premiers, land presidents, or governors as is the case in Canada, Germany, or America. The absence of a politically independent legislature such as the U.S. Congress further reduces competitors for influence. A Prime Minister must "only" stay on top of the world of Westminster.

The collegial nature of British government does not make it consensual. Conventions of the Constitution require that all Cabinet ministers formally agree on major policies of government. But the policies of government institutionalize disagreement. The Treasury and spending departments disagree about how much money can be afforded for education, health, pensions, and other benefits of the contemporary welfare state. The Foreign Office is likely to remind ministers of awkward international implications of domestic policies, and of awkward domestic implications of troubles abroad. And the Scottish and Welsh secretaries of state press for territorial advantage.

The institutionalized divisions within government are common to many lands. It is important to point them out, however, lest the *appearance* of collective responsibility be taken to signify an apolitical amount of agreement within British government. The Prime Minister's unique role is to maintain the appearance of agreement, by seeing that the decisions to which ministers are collectively bound are decisions they can accept politically. The management of politicians is the first necessity of remaining in the job at the top. An agreed policy is, by definition, a good policy. Any initiative that the Prime Minister wishes to take must also be agreed on by responsible ministers before it can become government policy.

In the political management of government, a British Prime Minister is distinctive in the trust given civil servants. Civil servants not only provide the cadres formulating and implementing departmental policies but also most of the staff within 10 Downing Street. The private secretary and his handful of assistants are the source of most daily political intelligence and the chief means by which views and requests from the Prime Minister are directed to departments. The secretary to the Cabinet is a very senior civil servant in charge of Cabinet business and all the committee work that flows from this and is often an ad hoc adviser to the Prime Minister. The result is a considerable degree of security for those who serve the Prime Minister; as long as they play the game according to civil service rules, their permanent claim on a good government job is secure. In return, the Prime Minister is privy to great expertise about government. The insecure staff in 10 Downing Street are personal and political appointees. Their insecurity stems less from struggles between individuals to influence policy, as in Washington; it is more a collective insecurity arising from doubts about their status and scope for exerting any influence within Whitehall.

A Prime Minister, unlike the U.S. President, does not depend on personally loyal but bureaucratically amateur advisers. Nor does a Prime Minister turn civil servants into his political agents, such as those in France who look to the President for their future career. Instead, between civil servants and leading politicians there is what Richard Neustadt has described as "a reasonable treaty, a good trade," in which civil servants loyally serve ministers politically, and politicians protect the status and perquisites that mean most to civil servants.[69]

The view from the top of British government, like that from any other government, is remote. A Prime Minister presides over much that is done by others. In public policy, a Prime Minister is doubly constrained. Positive requirements to emphasize party management and the presentation of self limit the time that can be devoted to policy. The primary responsibilities of departmental ministers also constrain the involvement of Downing Street in policy making. Where the Prime Minister is most involved, British government is now inevitably weak; this is true of the management of the economy as well as of foreign affairs. As captain of the ship of state, the Prime Minister has a lofty eminence, but it is in the engine rooms below that the bulk of the work of government is done.

---

[69] Richard Neustadt talks to Henry Brandon, "10 Downing Street: Is It Out of Date?" *Sunday Times*, November 8, 1964.

2

Political Leadership in Canada: Pierre Elliott Trudeau and the Ottawa Model

Colin Campbell, S.J.

In recent years there has been a plethora of literature in Canada maintaining that Pierre Elliott Trudeau has transformed the Prime Ministership into a Presidential institution.[1] The concept of presidentialization reflects the tendency among Canadians to label substantial shifts in structures and conventions as "Americanization" and to invoke presumed principles of parliamentary government as absolute standards for evaluating all innovation in the political system. Such reactions to change are misguided. Those who appeal to the principles of parliamentary government sadly misunderstand two things: it is questionable whether the golden era in which the British Parliament is thought to have made law ever existed as a nineteenth-century phenomenon;[2] and the Cabinet-dominated government in

NOTE: I owe a debt to my colleague in the Central Agency Project, George Szablowski of York University, Toronto, for many insights contained here. Frank Howard's column, "The Bureaucrats," in the *Ottawa Citizen* has kept me abreast of recent developments in Ottawa. The Brookings Institution in Washington, D.C., graciously provided me with an excellent environment in which to write while on leave from York. The Social Sciences and Humanities Research Council has supported this project. Finally, I am immensely grateful to Lord Trend for his helpful comments on this paper given during the Loch Lomondside Conference.

[1] Thomas A. Hockin, ed., *Apex of Power: The Prime Minister and Political Leadership in Canada* (Toronto: Prentice-Hall, 1971, 1977); Robert J. Jackson and Michael M. Atkinson, *The Canadian Legislative System: Politicians and Policy-Making* (Toronto: Macmillan, 1974); and W. A. Matheson, *The Prime Minister and the Cabinet* (Toronto: Methuen, 1976).

[2] See Gerhard Loewenberg, "The Role of Parliaments in Modern Political Systems," in Gerhard Loewenberg, ed., *Modern Parliaments: Change or Decline?* (Chicago: Aldine-Atherton, 1971), pp. 5-7, 15-16. For a Canadian perspective, see a critique of Parliament from the nineteenth-century viewpoint in Roman R. March, *The Myth of Parliament* (Scarborough, Ontario: Prentice-Hall, 1974); and a statement of the inappropriateness of the golden-era model in Colin Campbell and Harold D. Clarke, "Some Thoughts on Parliamentary Reform," in

Britain today differs greatly from that in Canada, especially since the British Prime Minister is subject to more political constraints than the Canadian counterpart. Those who view change as Americanization often fail to realize that innovations within the political system address pressures for modernization which are felt every bit as intensely in Britain and America as in Canada.[3] In so far as the concept of presidentialization simply addresses the organizational and operational problems faced by all chief executives, the label, especially in Canada, loads the case against many reforms which might otherwise be adopted. Canadians delude themselves by looking at political leadership in Ottawa through White House, Westminster, or even bifocal lenses. A far more productive approach views Canadian political leadership from the standpoint of the "Ottawa model" and focuses on statutes, conventions, and operational vagaries that are peculiar to Canada's system of government.

Pierre Elliott Trudeau initially left himself open to accusations of presidentialization by conducting a vigorous media-oriented campaign in 1968 so effective that the public response was dubbed Trudeaumania. Trudeau projected a refreshingly different image from that of his predecessor, Lester B. Pearson. Throughout his tenure, Pearson had received criticism for running lackluster campaigns (he lost two elections and in two others failed to lead his party to a majority), and for not exercising fully his Prime Ministerial prerogatives.[4] During Trudeau's first three governments (1968–1972, 1972–1974, and 1974–1979), he reinforced talk of presidentialization by often manifesting contempt for his colleagues in Parliament, the media, and various segments of the public.[5] By 1976 Trudeau's arrogance had even harmed morale in the Communications Division of the Prime Minister's Office, which faced the difficulty of overcoming the public's increasing irritation with Mr. Trudeau's flamboyance.[6]

Harold D. Clarke, Colin Campbell, Arthur Goddard, and F. Q. Quo, eds., *Parliament, Policy and Representation* (Toronto: Methuen, 1980), pp. 307-19.

[3] This perspective finds support in Joseph Wearing, "President or Prime Minister," pp. 326-43; Richard E. Neustadt, "White House and Whitehall," pp. 344-55; and Thomas A. Hockin, "Some Canadian Notes on 'White House and Whitehall,'" pp. 356-59, all in Hockin, *Apex of Power*.

[4] Peter C. Newman, *Renegade in Power: The Diefenbaker Years* (Toronto: McClelland and Stewart, 1963), and *The Distemper of Our Times* (Toronto: McClelland and Stewart, 1968); and Matheson, *Prime Minister and the Cabinet*, pp. 164-69.

[5] Walter Stewart, *Shrug: Trudeau in Power* (Toronto: New Press, 1972), and *Divide and Con: Canadian Politics at Work* (Toronto: New Press, 1973); and George Radwanski, *Trudeau* (Toronto: Macmillan, 1978).

[6] Colin Campbell and George J. Szablowski, *The Superbureaucrats: Structure and Behaviour in Central Agencies* (Toronto: Macmillan, 1979), p. 68.

Trudeau also fed talk of presidentialization by relying heavily on organizational structures designed to serve the Prime Minister and the Cabinet. These structures appeared to give Trudeau immensely greater capacity to modulate his image, monitor operational departments, leave his mark on substantive policy decisions throughout the government, and win strategic battles with the bureaucracy, Cabinet, and Parliament. Critics, however, attributed too much importance to structural changes in describing the rise of the Prime Minister's profile. In fact Trudeau was simply implementing fully innovations made by Pearson to enhance the operation of the Cabinet as well as to improve the Prime Minister's position in the policy arena.[7] Trudeau accelerated the process, especially by permitting extremely rapid growth and sharp differentiation in central agencies. The fact remains, however, that Trudeau's commitment to executive leadership, which eventually became associated with his arrogance, fleshed out the skeletal legacy left by Pearson and breathed life into dormant or latent operations of both the central agencies and the Cabinet.

It is a disservice to Trudeau to say that he transformed the structures of the executive branch to fit a mold at variance with Canadian constitutional principles. On balance, his first three governments operated much more within structural and conventional bounds than the ill-fated 1979 Progressive Conservative government under Joe Clark. The nine months of Clark's government produced the longest dissolution of Parliament since Confederation (1867), U-turns on several key campaign promises, and a restructuring of Cabinet committees and central agencies that left both officials and interest groups reeling in a sea of cross-cutting responsibilities and brand new acronyms and buzz words.[8] Trudeau might have thought he was Moses leading his people across the Red Sea. By December 13, when the Progressive Conservative government fell, many Canadians had concluded that Joe Clark had turned into a Pharaoh who had led them into the path of an economic tidal wave.

Along with the distinctive development under Trudeau of the Ottawa model, there were changes in the volume and variety of action-forcing matters that confront any Canadian Prime Minister and

---

[7] Thomas A. Hockin, "The Prime Minister and Political Leadership: An Introduction to Some Restraints and Imperatives," in Hockin, *Apex of Power*, pp. 2-21; Fred Schindler, "The Prime Minister and the Cabinet: History and Development," in Hockin, *Apex of Power*, pp. 22-53; Matheson, *Prime Minister and the Cabinet*, pp. 164-69, 170-76; and R. M. Punnett, *The Prime Minister in Canadian Government and Politics* (Toronto: Macmillan, 1977), pp. 79-80.

[8] For that matter, there are clearly limits to Presidential leadership in the United States. See Richard P. Nathan, *The Plot That Failed: Nixon and the Administrative Presidency* (New York: Wiley, 1975).

Cabinet. The size and complexity of modern political administration have brought unprecedented pressure to bear on chief executives. When Prime Ministers assume office, they must select, from the myriad themes and promises of the campaign, those on which a viable government can be based and, ultimately, reelected. Even if they map out a reasonably coherent strategy for their mandate, they must constantly juggle programs, applying priorities consistently through substantive positions taken by the government and changing the strategy when events undermine them. Besides mapping out the mandate strategy, adjusting it along the way, and making day-to-day policy decisions, Prime Ministers are greatly pressured to become personally involved in at least four other executive functions. They are called upon to make key decisions and judgments concerning integrated economic and fiscal policies, the allocation and management of government resources, the development and selection of senior personnel, and relations with the provinces of the Canadian federal system. The greater the pressure on Prime Ministers to give personal attention to any one area, the more likely they are to establish institutions that will help them with the workload, by adding staff or distributing some of the weight to other ministers or Cabinet committees. The cumulative intensification of action-forcing pressures on the Prime Minister and the corresponding institutionalization of his response lead directly to the first question addressed below: Why is it that executive functions tend to focus on the Prime Minister?

This chapter will stress the fact that change depends greatly on who is at the helm and what mood he is in. In other words, Prime Ministers' styles and organizational preferences vary greatly both within and between administrations. This chapter focuses somewhat narrowly on the first Trudeau governments. Yet, a close examination of changes in Trudeau's attitudes toward his job and organizational priorities also goes much further toward an understanding of executive leadership during his three governments than a study focused on the premise that he adopted and maintained a Presidential style.

Legal-Formal Authority versus Conventional Authority

Camouflaging Authority. Canada's "unwritten" constitution, the British North American (BNA) Act of 1967, mentions neither the Prime Minister nor the Cabinet.[9] Rather, it states that as the Queen's

---

[9] The assertion that Canada lacks a written constitution is found, for example, in R. I. Cheffins and R. N. Tucker, *The Constitutional Process in Canada*, 2d ed. (Toronto: McGraw-Hill Ryerson, 1976), pp. 1-15. This assertion notwithstanding, constitutional lawyers in Canada would be hard pressed to ply their trade without reference to the BNA Act.

representative in Canada, the Governor General exercises various powers connected to the executive authority of the monarch. Pursuant to the Letters Patent of 1947, these powers include virtually all prerogatives of the monarch. In a strictly legal-formal sense, therefore, the Governor General serves as Canada's chief executive.[10]

This tidy legal-formal picture bears no resemblance to reality. In fact, the Prime Minister advises the Queen on the appointment of a Governor General, and the current monarch has never been able to exercise even a modicum of choice in the matter. Further, the Prime Minister possesses de facto all the Governor General's executive authority by virtue of the simple fact that the Governor General issues all regulations, appointments, and assents requested by the Prime Minister. The last-known independent executive actions on the part of the Governor General took place in 1926 when Lord Byng refused to grant dissolution of Parliament to Prime Minister Mackenzie King.[11]

How did an officer without so much as a mention in a country's basic constitutional document attain the prominence enjoyed by the Canadian Prime Minister? For an answer, one should note first that the BNA Act stipulates that "there shall be a Council to aid and advise the Government of Canada . . . chosen and summoned by the Governor General."[12] This seemingly vague passage combines with one in the preamble, "a Constitution similar in Principle to that of the United Kingdom," to vest, by convention rather than statute, the Prime Minister with all authority for effective government.[13] According to British practice, the council is the Privy Council of Canada. The Cabinet, that is, a committee of the Privy Council, effectively operates in its place. Either the Prime Minister or a minister delegated by him, on the basis of the principle of first among equals, must affix his signature to Cabinet initiatives before they become government bills or orders-in-council.[14] Thus, it can be said that one person's legal-

---

[10] As Campbell and Szablowski note (*Superbureaucrats*, p. 17), Prime Minister Louis St. Laurent described the effect of this legislation as follows: ". . . when the letters patent come into force, it will be legally possible for the Governor General, on the advice of the Canadian ministers, to exercise any of these powers and authorities without the necessity of a submission being made to His Majesty" (*House of Commons Debates*, 1948, p. 1126).

[11] A recent discussion of the role of the Governor General occurs in Matheson, *Prime Minister and the Cabinet*, pp. 8-11.

[12] *British North America Act*, 1867, 30-31 Victoria, C.3 (U.K.), sec. 11.

[13] Colin Campbell, S.J., and Harold D. Clarke, "Editors' Introduction," *The Contemporary Canadian Legislative System*, Campbell and Clarke, eds., a special issue of *Legislative Studies Quarterly*, vol. 3 (November, 1978), p. 530.

[14] See Matheson, *Prime Minister and the Cabinet*, pp. 80-81, for discussion of orders-in-council.

formal authority is another person's conventional authority. By convention, the Prime Minister serves fully as the chief decision maker of the land.

The fact that the Governor General still performs many ceremonial functions tends to obscure the status of the Prime Minister in the system. Several introductory textbooks steadfastly continue to speak of the Crown, as represented by the Governor General, rather than the Prime Minister and the Cabinet, as the trustee of executive authority in Canada.[15] Further, the office of Prime Minister appears to have only a very small "halo" effect on people. In a 1969 survey, only 14 percent of the respondents mentioned Pierre Elliott Trudeau as one of the Canadians they admire.[16]

Canadians, in fact, expressly choose myth over reality when it comes to recognizing the actual trustee of executive authority. This came across strikingly in 1978. As part of a constitutional reform bill written in response to the Quebec crisis, the government sought to include the provision that the Governor General "continue his role in Parliament in his own rather than in the Queen's name."[17] In other words, the Governor General would supplant the Queen as the formal source of federal executive authority in Canada. The same bill would specify actual practice by lodging the exercise of executive authority in the Cabinet as chaired by the Prime Minister:

> There shall be a council to be styled the Council of State of Canada [formerly Privy Council], in whose name aid and advice in the government of Canada shall be given . . . [including] the person holding the recognized office of Prime Minister of Canada and each other person who on the advice of the Prime Minister is to be chosen and summoned by the Governor General of Canada to be appointed. . . . The Cabinet [a committee of the Council of State] has the management and direction of the government of Canada and is responsible to the House of Commons.[18]

---

[15] See, for example, R. MacGregor Dawson, *The Government of Canada* (Toronto: University of Toronto Press, 1963), revised by Norman Ward, chap. 8; Rais A. Khan, James D. McNiven, and Stuart A. MacKown, *An Introduction to Political Science*, rev. ed. (Georgetown, Ont.: Irwin-Dorsey, 1977), pp. 182-85; J. R. Mallory, *The Structure of Canadian Government* (Toronto: Macmillan, 1971), pp. 32-41; W. L. White, R. H. Wagenberg, and R. C. Nelson, *Introduction to Canadian Politics and Government*, 2d ed. (Toronto: Holt, Rinehart and Winston, 1977), p. 123.

[16] The Canadian Institute of Public Opinion (The Gallup Poll), February 26, 1969.

[17] Government of Canada, "Explanatory Notes," *The Constitutional Amendment Bill*, June 1, 1978, pp. 42-48.

[18] "Text," *The Constitutional Amendment Bill*, secs. 48(3)-53(1).

These provisions of the constitutional reform bill faced a barrage of criticism from Anglophone Canadians who saw them as a repudiation of the monarchy. An October 1978 survey asked voters: "At the present time, Queen Elizabeth is the Canadian head of state. Would you prefer to see her continue in this capacity, or would you prefer to have the Governor General as head of state, except when the Queen visits Canada?"[19] A total of 59 percent of respondents preferred the status quo, with 71, 30, and 56 percent of those whose mother tongue was English, French, and "other," respectively, registering a preference for the Queen over the Governor General.

The P.M.: None Dare Call Him "Chief Executive." Even if Canadians are loath to recognize the fact in a revised constitution, no authority in the country performs such an imposing constellation of functions as the Prime Minister does (see figure 1). First, he exercises extensive conventional authority over appointments both to political office and to the senior civil service. Political appointees include governor generals (through the Queen), their provincial lieutenants, all provincial and federal judges, members of the upper house of Parliament (that is, senators), and representatives of the public in numerous government agencies, commissions, and task forces. The one systematic study of political appointments, those to the Senate, suggests that Pierre Elliott Trudeau regularly ignored demographic considerations in order to optimize the political payoff of such patronage.[20] When faced with a choice of rewarding party or business notables for services rendered or upgrading the representation of minorities or regions of the country, he usually opted for the notables. The unit in the Prime Minister's Office under the nominations secretary takes the lead in political appointments.

The Prime Minister's conventional authority over the selection of public servants for top positions extends both to senior personnel policy and actual appointments.[21] Regarding the former, he shares this authority with the Treasury Board, a committee of the Cabinet. The more important the policy issue, however, and the higher the grade of the officials to which it applies, the more likely it is that the Prime Minister will be in the lead. With respect to actual appointments, Trudeau personally reviewed proposed selections at the level of deputy and assistant deputy minister. On occasion, he would personally review appointments farther down the hierarchy.

---

19 The Canadian Institute of Public Opinion (The Gallup Poll), October 14, 1979.
20 Colin Campbell, *The Canadian Senate: A Lobby from Within* (Toronto: Macmillan, 1978), pp. 40-43.
21 Campbell and Szablowski, *Superbureaucrats*, pp. 46-49.

FIGURE 1

EXECUTIVE LEADERSHIP IN CANADA UNDER PIERRE ELLIOTT TRUDEAU, 1979

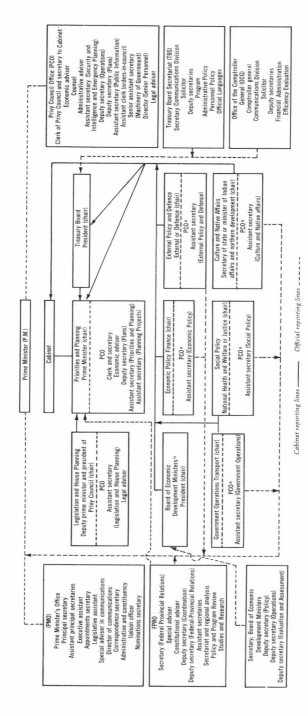

Cabinet reporting lines ——— *Official reporting lines* – – – – –

a Reporting to deputy secretary (Operations), PCO.

b Shadowed by a committee of senior officials, including the deputy ministers of member departments plus the clerk of the Privy Council, the secretary to the Cabinet, and the assistant secretary of the Economic Policy Committee, and chaired by the secretary of the Board of Economic Development Ministers.

c Member departments generate proposals; those with expenditure implications are reviewed by the Treasury Board; only major policy initiatives are reviewed by Priorities and Planning before going to the Cabinet.

Although most senior officials in Ottawa are permanent bureaucrats, Trudeau, like all Prime Ministers, could exercise discretion by advancing career officials who had caught his eye or even by recruiting individuals from outside government. In 1977, for example, Trudeau selected a New Brunswick bureaucrat to serve as deputy secretary to the Cabinet for federal-provincial relations, a Xerox executive to fill the newly created position of comptroller general at the highest deputy minister level (DM-3), and a former Cabinet minister who had failed to win a Commons seat in a by-election to work on national unity questions in his capacity as under secretary of state. British mandarins, of course, would look askance at such obvious departures from the career principle. Two units, one under the director of senior personnel in the Privy Council Office and the other under the deputy secretary for personnel policy in the Treasury Board Secretariat, shared the responsibility in this sector, with the former advising the Prime Minister directly on the more important issues and appointments.

A second function of the Prime Minister is that he shoulders considerable responsibility as the chief manager of his party. Since this role relates to his position as parliamentary leader of the party, it is based more on partisan than on constitutional conventions. Ultimately, it is the Prime Minister who, both in and out of season, must assure that party morale is high. He must see that senior Cabinet ministers assume responsibility for organizing and husbanding the party activities through large regions of the country and that junior ministers take adequate care of the constituencies that cluster within smaller regional divisions. Nationally, the Prime Minister must keep an eye on the Ottawa party office so that an organization exists to steer periodic policy conferences and advise on the timing of key political initiatives. The infrastructure the Prime Minister maintains might be hard to find in party directories. For instance, many lofty titles in the Prime Minister's Office roster conceal party influentials, and many senators fill key party jobs without being on the party payroll.[22] The point is that Canadian Prime Ministers must keep a hand on their party's organization if they want it to be responsive.

Third, the Prime Minister must act as salesman both for his government and for Canada. Both tasks are rooted in constitutional convention. Trudeau was perhaps unique in that he, not to mention his estranged wife, attracted the kind of attention usually reserved for "beautiful people" such as members of the Kennedy family. His international fame thus added to the domestic credibility of his constitu-

---

[22] Campbell, *Canadian Senate*, pp. 9-10.

tional role. The foreign eye, however, is a lot less discerning than the native one, and after the original bout of infatuation Canadians proved to be quite fickle about Trudeau. Thus, image builders gravitated to his inner circle. These included Senator Keith Davey, his campaign manager in 1974 and 1979, who actually controlled the release of all government announcements during both elections, and Dick O'Hagan, who gave up his communications post with the Canadian Embassy in Washington, D.C., in 1975 to join the Prime Minister's Office and lead the effort to sell the antiinflation program.

Fourth, the Prime Minister leads the parliamentary caucus of his party. Privately and by virtue of partisan convention, this means that he meets weekly with the members of his caucus in the House of Commons and the Senate to justify government legislative proposals, to hear sundry complaints about the overall performance of the government, to map out strategy for debates and committee work, and generally, to take the pulse of legislators and encourage them in their capacity as the party faithful in Ottawa with the strongest ties to the folks back home. Publicly and by virtue of constitutional convention, the Prime Minister as parliamentary leader of the government party must stand up to the loyal opposition in the House of Commons. In the tradition of adversary politics,[23] and certainly with the advent of televised debates,[24] this role leaves the Prime Minister vulnerable to attack but with an opportunity to impress on the public his competence as chief executive. Trudeau was more masterful than Pearson in his handling of this paradox. Although he stirred many a passionate protest by his domination of parliamentary debate and by the programs he introduced, few have denied that he was master in the House.

Fifth, as head of the government party, the Prime Minister chairs the Cabinet. The Canadian Cabinet, unlike the U.S. counterpart, meets at least weekly and deliberates on important issues facing the government, including contentious orders-in-council, appointments, legislative proposals, and policy initiatives.[25] The Canadian Cabinet, however, rarely votes. Thus, the Prime Minister finds considerable latitude in discerning the consensus.

An elaborate committee system (figure 1) enables the entire Cabinet to focus its attention only on those issues which cannot be

[23] Thomas A. Hockin, "Adversary Politics and Some Functions of the Canadian House of Commons," in Richard Schultz, Orest M. Kruhlak, and John C. Terry, eds., *The Canadian Political Process*, 3d ed. (Toronto: Holt, Rinehart and Winston, 1979), pp. 314-29.

[24] Anthony Westell, "The Press: Adversary or Channel of Communication?" in Clarke et al., eds., *Parliament, Policy and Representation*, pp. 25-34.

[25] Matheson, *Prime Minister and the Cabinet*, pp. 79-91.

resolved between departments at a lower level or those which concern certain strategic plans of the government. Within the committee system, the Prime Minister again assumes a key role. Trudeau chaired the Priorities and Planning Committee (P and P), which served both as an executive committee of the Cabinet and a standing committee on federal-provincial relations. The executive committee responsibilities of P and P included: (1) articulation of broad policy objectives and priorities for the long term and initiation of major policy reviews consistent with these priorities; (2) formulation of priorities for the annual budgetary expenditures and policy guidelines consistent with the fiscal (that is, spending) framework; (3) determination of macro-economic policy; and (4) overseeing personnel policy with respect to key executive appointments and promotions. Members of the committee included the chairmen of the other coordinating committees—the Treasury Board, the Legislation and House Planning Committee, the chairmen of various subject-matter committees, the minister of state for federal-provincial relations, and any other ministers who happened to have the Prime Minister's favor at a given time.[26] Trudeau ran P and P as a quasi-academic seminar through which he kept abreast of his colleagues' assessments of progress in various sectors of the policy process, got them to sort out the overall objectives of the government, and, on occasion, used them as a core group for resolving crises.

Sixth, the Prime Minister, again by constitutional convention, sits as first among equals in federal-provincial conferences of premiers which occur at least annually. Such meetings serve as the apex of Canada's surrogate Bundesrat, a complex array of hundreds of meetings between federal and provincial ministers and senior officials.[27] Such meetings attempt to resolve the vast number of policy and administrative issues that fall between federal and provincial jurisdictions. Provincial governments, thanks to favorable judicial decisions early in Confederation, exercise legislative and administrative authority over education, practically all of what is called health and welfare, the development of natural resources within their boundaries, municipal institutions, property and civil rights, administrative authority over justice, and concurrent authority with the federal government over agriculture and immigration. The federal government, however, retains much greater authority to raise revenues than the provinces

---

[26] Campbell and Szablowski, *Superbureaucrats*, pp. 152-53, 155, 160.

[27] Richard Simeon, *Federal-Provincial Diplomacy: The Making of Recent Policy in Canada* (Toronto: University of Toronto Press, 1972); and Donald V. Smiley, *Canada in Question: Federalism in the Seventies*, 2d ed. (Toronto: McGraw-Hill Ryerson, 1976), chap. 3.

do. The situation calls for considerable federal-provincial bargaining whereby the provinces permit the federal government to establish guidelines for provincial policies and administration in exchange for grants or greater "tax room." The Prime Minister plays the lead role in federal-provincial diplomacy.[28]

In sum, although Canadians are hesitant to admit the fact, a Prime Minister is the chief decision maker on the basis of several roles which fall to him either through partisan or conventional authority. The levers of power are probably as numerous and potent as any within the grasp of the principals in other political systems.

The Cabinet: Some Are More Equal Than Others. Although the Prime Minister enjoys full status as chief decision maker, the government of the day has other ministers as well. Before the May 22, 1979, election, Canada had thirty-two ministers. Unlike their British counterparts, all Canadian ministers belong to the Cabinet. Yet, representational and structural factors impinge on an individual's ability to participate in Cabinet-level decision making.

With respect to representation, the main base of a minister's power is his following among regional, economic, ethnic, or religious segments of Canadian society.[29] Each minister is responsible for party organization either in a part of a province, an entire province, or a region of the country. Although these roles are unofficial, voters in specific regions will often judge ministers on the basis of how well they have represented their area. Ministers, thus, can add to their influence on Cabinet decisions by a high standing as a regional representative. Economic, ethnic, and religious representational responsibilities often overlap with regional ones, thereby, intensifying a minister's standing in the policy arena.

Structural factors influence ministers' roles in several ways. Bruce Doern has noted that departments vary considerably in function and status.[30] In addition to central agencies, Doern includes the

[28] Smiley, *Canada in Question*, pp. 4-5, 62-64.

[29] This mode of representation has been termed consociational democracy. For descriptions of this mode as it is found in Canada, see Arend Lijphart, *Democracy in Plural Societies: A Comparative Exploration* (New Haven: Yale University Press, 1977), pp. 119-28; S. J. R. Noel, "Political Parties and Elite Accommodation: Interpretations of Canadian Federalism," in J. Peter Meekison, ed., *Canadian Federalism: Myth or Reality*, 2d ed. (Toronto: Methuen, 1971), pp. 121-40; Robert Presthus, *Elite Accommodation in Canadian Politics* (Toronto: Macmillan, 1973), pp. 3-19; and Matheson, *Prime Minister and the Cabinet*, pp. 22-46.

[30] G. Bruce Doern, "Horizontal and Vertical Portfolios in Government," in G. Bruce Doern and Seymour Wilson, eds., *Issues in Canadian Public Policy* (Toronto: Macmillan, 1974), pp. 310-36.

Department of External Affairs and the Department of Justice among "traditional horizontal coordination portfolios" whose functions cross-cut many other governmental departments. Two other types of horizontal coordination portfolios, "new" and "administrative," find much less leverage and influence in the policy process. The new include the Ministry of State for Science and Technology and the recently disbanded Ministry of State for Urban Affairs. Since a 1971 act of Parliament (Ministries and Ministries of State), the Prime Minister has been able to create up to five portfolios without seeking Parliament's approval. The Ministries of State have attempted to develop new and comprehensive policies in sectors of governmental activity which require special attention. Their tenuous status, how-ever, has militated against their assumption of operational respon-sibilities important enough to convince Parliament of the need for a permanent department. The administrative horizontal coordination portfolios, such as Revenue Canada, the Department of Public Works, and the Department of Supply and Services, simply perform services for other departments and therefore do not contribute greatly to a minister's power base. Finally, vertical constituency portfolios, such as the Department of Industry, Trade, and Commerce and the Depart-ment of Labour, actually administer the bulk of governmental pro-grams and usually develop strong clientele relations with the interest groups most affected. The status of a department's client groups can greatly affect its influence in the Cabinet. For instance, the two departments cited above have traditionally parlayed their relations with the business community and organized labor into significant influences on Cabinet decisions.

Ministers' committee positions reinforce advantages they receive by virtue of the functions and status of their departments. In fact, committee assignments can serve as surrogates for department-based standing. Under Trudeau, the Cabinet had three coordinating com-mittees: Priorities and Planning; Legislation and House Planning, which scrutinizes drafts of legislation and maps strategies for getting the government's legislative program passed; and the Treasury Board, which reviews all departments' expenditure forecasts, annual expendi-ture budgets, management and personnel policies, and program accounting. Just this array of committees endowed three ministers with high standing. Two had no departments: the deputy prime minister and president of the Privy Council, usually a gray eminence of the government party with a strong parliamentary orientation, chaired Legislation and House Planning; and the minister of state for federal-provincial relations took the lead on some federal-provincial matters before Priorities and Planning and the Cabinet. The president of the Treasury Board headed two powerful central agencies, the Treasury Board Secretariat and the Office of the Comptroller General, both of which contain deputy ministers of the highest rank.

In addition to the coordinating committees, standing committees review legislative proposals according to their subject matter. Under Trudeau these were Economic Policy, the Board of Economic Development Ministers (BEDM), Social Policy, External Policy and Defence, Culture and Native Affairs, and Government Operations. A pecking order existed here as well. Economic Policy, the Board of Economic Development Ministers, and External Policy and Defence provided forums where ministers of the major economic and international departments could express themselves on issues of concern to their sectors. In addition, somewhat less formal arrangements strengthened the hand of some key ministers. The president of the Treasury Board or delegated members could participate fully in any committee. The president of the BEDM was supported by his own secretariat, headed by one of Ottawa's top mandarins, Gordon Osbaldeston. The minister of finance and the minister of transport took the lead on Economic Policy and Government Operations respectively; the minister of national health and welfare or the minister of justice, the secretary of state for external affairs or the minister of defence, and the secretary of state or the minister of Indian affairs and northern development took the lead on Social Policy, External Policy and Defence, and Culture and Native Affairs, respectively. Finally, the lead position on a coordinating or a subject-matter committee was a key determinant of membership on Priorities and Planning.

The representational and structural factors behind a minister's standing in Cabinet point up the degree to which the principle "first among equals" can apply to individual ministers in Cabinet-level panels as well as to the Prime Minister. Yet, in every case, a minister is limited for two reasons. First, his representation of segments of the public and his committee or department obligations constantly draw his attention from Cabinet-level decisions to crises of the Liberal party in his region or to difficulties in a Cabinet committee or his department. Second, no matter how blessed by representational credibility or structural responsibilities, the minister must win and retain the favor of the Prime Minister to achieve full effectiveness in the Cabinet.

Behind the Scenes: Central Agencies and Departments

Servicing the Prime Minister. As a result of the many functions the Prime Minister performs, he receives countless letters, documents, requests for appointments, phone calls, and invitations which add to the pressures on his time. He needs a large staff to assist in "squeezing forty-eight hours out of the P.M.'s average day"[31] and to assure that he is adequately briefed at all times. For this he calls primarily on the Prime Minister's Office (PMO), the Privy Council Office (PCO), and the Federal-Provincial Relations Office (FPRO).

PMO under Trudeau housed a staff of close to a hundred, only thirty of whom were professionals. Most of the members, and certainly all the professionals, were exempt staff—that is, political appointees who do not belong to the permanent public service. The principal secretary headed PMO and reported exclusively to the Prime Minister. Although he was always a trusted partisan figure, his role adjusted to Trudeau's priorities. During his first government (1968–1972), Trudeau entrusted the position to a chancellor par excellence, Marc Lalonde. At the time, Trudeau had been in Ottawa only since 1965. In his efforts to get control of the bureaucracy he relied very heavily on Lalonde. As one PMO official put it, "Trudeau had to learn how to run a country from scratch. Lalonde helped him out and he was necessary at the time."[32]

The exercise of getting control of the ship of state did not endear the Prime Minister to the political faithful and the voting public. Trudeau came away from the 1972 election with a minority government. Martin O'Connell, an old political pro from the Toronto area and a defeated minister, succeeded Lalonde as principal secretary and set out to upgrade the Prime Minister's public image and relations with the party. He was not entirely successful in accomplishing these goals and virtually lost the PMO a role in policy advice. Yet, fate smiled on Trudeau in the election of 1974. A masterful campaign against the Progressive Conservative leader, Robert Stanfield, who advocated mandatory wage and price controls, resulted in a solid Liberal majority government. Trudeau saw a golden opportunity to leave his mark on the decade. To head PMO he chose Jack Austin, a deputy minister who had recently entered the permanent public service from the private sector and had Liberal party ties. Austin received a strong mandate to regain from PMO some of its former role in the policy process. He formed a unit in PMO which focused most of its efforts on prodding the Cabinet and permanent officials in what became known as the "priorities exercise." The exercise became too grandiose, however, given the slim resources of PMO, and foundered. Robert Stanfield had his vindication too. By the fall of 1975, the

---

[31] Campbell and Szablowski, *Superbureaucrats*, p. 60.
[32] Ibid., p. 62.

simultaneous inflation and unemployment became so acute that Trudeau had to eat both his hat and humble pie by installing mandatory wage and price controls and giving up hopes of introducing new social programs. It was time for Jack Austin to retire to the Senate and for the policy unit to retreat from the arena.

Jim Coutts, one of the two key architects of the 1974 election victory, took over as principal secretary and declared the PMO's job was to serve as "a switchboard" for the political operations of the Prime Minister. From early 1978, Coutts devoted most of his time to preparing the party for its fourth campaign under Trudeau as an election was expected in the spring or early summer. A subordinate picked up the slack in Coutts's more traditional responsibilities. A precipitous dip in the party's showing in public opinion polls and Trudeau's health[33] and marital problems coalesced at the time to counsel delay of the election. During the 1979 campaign, Coutts shed all but the title of principal secretary. He accompanied the Prime Minister on the campaign trail, working entirely as a political operative.

PMO, at the best of times, is a loosely differentiated cluster of functions rather than a hierarchical organization. Under Trudeau the agency housed policy advisers other than the principal secretary, and they, too, reported directly to the Prime Minister. Among these, Ivan Head, who served as international relations adviser from 1970 to 1978, is the only official who gained prominence in the Ottawa policy arena over a long period. During his tenure Head usually exerted more influence on Canadian foreign policy than the incumbent secretary of state for external affairs.

On the domestic side, the policy unit set up by Jack Austin was headed by Mike Kirby, a former political aide to a premier of Nova Scotia. The unit attempted to give organized and comprehensive advice to the Prime Minister, based on what the government sought to achieve at various stages of the mandate, on all major issues. The job description proved too vast for the small staff of four professionals with relatively little experience with the Ottawa scene. The unit disbanded in 1976 to be replaced by four assistant principal secretaries technically responsible for policy advice. In fact, the four officials focused on "desk work," that is, prodding ministers' work on behalf

---

[33] A Cabinet minister informed me that since fall 1977 the Prime Minister's health had been an important factor in delaying an election call. At the time, the Prime Minister informed his Cabinet colleagues that he did not have the physical stamina for a campaign even though at the time he was well ahead in the polls and under strong party pressure to go to the country.

of the party in various regions, monitoring the general political situation in these areas, and handling interest group consultations.

Officials in PMO also managed Trudeau's schedule. The executive assistant controlled commitments of the P.M.'s time, including those made to the PMO staff; his assistant, the appointments secretary, processed all requests for public appearances of the Prime Minister. A large nominations division handled the hundreds of recommendations for political appointments which each year come to the Prime Minister. It also advised on the political implications of appointments to the higher echelons of the career public service. A special adviser on communications, assisted by a press secretary, a director of communications, and several more professionals, attempted to manage the P.M.'s media image. Finally, a correspondence secretary directed the largest unit in PMO, the one assigned the task of answering the voluminous mail addressed to the Prime Minister.

Trudeau, in fact, received most of his policy advice from career public servants in the Privy Council Office (PCO) and the Federal-Provincial Relations Office (FPRO). These two offices were headed, respectively, by men who might be called the St. John the Evangelist and the St. Peter of Canadian officialdom. Those familiar with John's gospel will remember that he styled himself as the disciple most trusted by Jesus even though Peter was much older and eventually named vicar. Playing a role similar to that of St. John, Michael Pitfield claimed connections with Trudeau's cadre of Francophone intellectuals before Trudeau entered federal politics in 1965. He became an assistant secretary to the Cabinet at the precocious age of twenty-nine in 1966, and having established himself as the Prime Minister's most trusted official, he was chosen for the most vital advisory post in the public service, clerk of the Privy Council and secretary to the Cabinet, in 1975. Joe Clark, in fact, requested and obtained Pitfield's resignation when the Progressive Conservative government was sworn in after the May 1979 election, even though career officials are not normally removed with a change of government. Gordon Robertson, who had held Pitfield's post for almost twelve years, served as Trudeau's St. Peter. Although his headship of FPRO was virtually nominal, as the dean of the Ottawa mandarins, Robertson literally held the keys to the kingdom—that is, he advised the Prime Minister on all senior career service appointments. Robertson's gatekeeper role served as an essential counterweight to Pitfield's relative youth in Trudeau's credibility among career officials. Robertson's role continued until his retirement in September 1979, presumably safeguarding the merit principle through the transition period.

Strictly speaking, both PCO and FPRO are Cabinet secretariats. In addition, they house the only substantial advisory units with special responsibiltiies for briefing the Prime Minister. These units technically report to the clerk of the Privy Council and secretary to the Cabinet, but actually their briefing material is either channeled in written form through the clerk/secretary to the Prime Minister or presented personally. The advisory units are of three types. The first is fashioned as part of the clerk/secretary's advisory staff and include the clerk/secretary's economic adviser, his counsel, his administrative adviser, and the assistant secretary to the Cabinet for security and intelligence and emergency planning. Of these positions, the first and the last are the most important. The economic adviser provides an in-house counterfoil to economic advice being proffered elsewhere in government, especially that originating in the Department of Finance. The Security and Intelligence and Emergency Planning unit services various ad hoc Cabinet committees when, out of the potpourri of intelligence-related matters, some issue comes to the fore. As part of its daily routine, the secretariat, which by PCO standards is extremely well manned (nine professionals), processes and analyzes centrally reports from all other government intelligence units. Recently, the suspicion has developed that the unit served as a Canadian counterpart, albeit in-house, to Richard M. Nixon's Committee to Reelect the President of Watergate fame. Testimony before the McDonald Commission, the Royal Commission on the Royal Canadian Mounted Police (RCMP), has implicated the secretariat as a conduit for illegally gathered intelligence from the RCMP to the Cabinet. It has even suggested that a 1970 tip from the secretariat served as provocation for a 1973 RCMP break-in of the Parti Québécois offices in Montreal.

A second type of PCO secretariat reports bureaucratically to the deputy secretary of the Cabinet (Operations). Under Trudeau the assistant secretaries in this division headed units, each with four other professionals, which serviced subject-matter Cabinet committees. Each assistant secretary had two sets of staff responsibilities: those related to the operations of his committee, and those involving briefing the deputy secretary, the clerk/secretary, and the Prime Minister on committee issues. The latter responsibility hinges on an important procedural fact: the deputy secretary (Operations) serves as the clerk/secretary's principal lieutenant, providing policy advice to the Prime Minister on issues currently before the Cabinet and determining which items, among those that must be settled by the entire Cabinet, will get on the agenda for a given week. Under both Trudeau and Clark the deputy secretary has become so integral to the day-to-day management of government affairs that he joins the secretary/clerk and top PMO staff each morning at 9:30 to brief personally the Prime Minister on matters requiring immediate attention and on the Cabinet agenda. By virtue of the deputy secretary's role in the inner circle, assistant secretaries frequently gain access to the Prime Minister for further background briefing. Sufficient exposure of this type can lead to an assistant secretary's gaining direct access to the Prime Minister. Ian Stewart, while an assistant secretary (Economic Policy) obtained this enviable intimacy with Trudeau during the development of the 1975 antiinflation program. Stewart's status became official in 1976 when Pitfield tailored the title of economic adviser for him.

A third type of PCO secretariat reports bureaucratically to the deputy secretary of the Cabinet (Plans). Seven units fall within this category. Two service the Prime Minister in his capacity as chairman of the Priorities and Planning Committee (called the Inner Cabinet under Clark), three service the deputy prime minister in his capacity as chairman of the Legislation and House Planning Committee, and three service the Prime Minister as the chief executive authority for Machinery of Government, Senior Personnel, and Public Information. The Priorities and Planning unit and the Planning Projects unit, both headed by assistant secretaries and staffed by five other professionals, work through the deputy secretary (Plans) to the Prime Minister. The units played instrumental roles in the priorities exercise of 1974–1975, which attempted to map out a detailed strategy for maximizing the Parliamentary advantage obtained when Liberals regained majority control of the House of Commons in 1974. The strategy explicitly included the optimal timing of policies and program to assure re-election of the government before the end of its mandate in 1979.[34] The exercise was abandoned in 1975 in part because operational departments, remaining relatively immune to the zeal of the Cabinet, inundated committees with responses which were simply cosmetic reworkings of what they intended anyway for the next five years. In addition, the economic crisis of 1975 followed by the 1976 Parti Québécois election victory in Quebec drew the government's attention away from maximizing their mandate and toward political survival. The secretariats of Priorities and Planning and of Planning Projects turned their attention to issues that had to be settled within the relatively short term for the government to regain credibility. The fact that the Planning Projects unit under Trudeau commissioned an exhaustive study of trends in public opinion about a host of policy issues reflects both the survival orientation of the last three years

---

[34] Confidential memos provided by a member of the PMO.

of the government and a much greater politicization of a career public service unit than even the most attentive watchers of PCO would have suspected.

The three units working through the deputy secretary (Plans) to the deputy prime minister—that is, Legislation and House Planning, Orders-in-Council, and the Office of the Legal Adviser—advise on comparatively routine matters. These include guiding government bills through Parliament, processing orders-in-council, and assuring that government bills are consistent both with the original policy intentions of the Cabinet and with existing statutes. The first of these units is the only one likely to merit the direct involvement of the Prime Minister.

The three advisory units titled, respectively, Machinery of Government, Senior Personnel, and Public Information work almost exclusively for the Prime Minister. Their creation reflected the importance Trudeau ascribed to major reorganizational and jurisdictional issues in the public service, the development and selection of senior career officials, and the need to monitor the release of government documents. The senior assistant secretary for machinery of government and the assistant secretary for public information report directly to the clerk/secretary in his capacity as the principal adviser of the Prime Minister on these matters. Under Trudeau the director for senior personnel reported both to the clerk/secretary concerning general policy issues and to Gordon Robertson, the secretary to the Cabinet for federal-provincial affairs, regarding specific appointments.

The Federal-Provincial Relations Office (FPRO) evolved in 1975 from a secretariat of PCO. Bureaucratic politics dictated that Gordon Robertson yield the clerk/secretary position to Michael Pitfield. The creation of the title secretary of the Cabinet for federal-provincial relations, complete with an independent secretariat, provided Robertson a face-saving lateral transfer. Robertson maintained control of senior personnel appointments and, therefore, his deanship of the mandarins.

After the November 15, 1976, separatist victory in Quebec, the Cabinet committee originally serviced by FPRO, Federal-Provincial Relations, merged with the Priorities and Planning Committee, thereby adding to the seemingly contrived distinction between PCO and FPRO. Whether or not this distinction was contrived, the organizational differentiation of PCO and FPRO provided a framework for the further proliferation of units headed by officials at the assistant deputy minister level or higher with personal briefing responsibilities to the Prime Minister. Two of these officials, the constitutional adviser and the deputy secretary to the Cabinet (Coordination), command direct access to the Prime Minister without even the technical requirement that they work through the secretary. The constitutional adviser to the Prime Minister concentrates on developments in his constitutional reform initiatives; the deputy secretary advises the Prime Minister on strategy vis-à-vis Quebec separatism. The third official, deputy secretary for federal-provincial relations, although technically working through the secretary, is left pretty much a free hand. He advises the Prime Minister, in his capacity as chairman of Priorities and Planning, on day-to-day substantive issues concerning federal-provincial relations as well as on long-term strategy. He is assisted by three assistant secretaries. One heads a unit that serves as the secretariat processing federal-provincial matters through Priorities and Planning and the Cabinet and conducting analyses of regional issues; one heads a unit that reviews all departmental policy and program proposals from the standpoint of federal-provincial relations; one heads a unit that studies long-term strategic goals and proposes policy initiatives. The latter unit, for example, drafted a great deal of the 1978 Constitutional Amendment Bill.

This bird's-eye view of the staff at the disposal of the Prime Minister perhaps drives home one point. Although Trudeau lacked a sufficient number of partisan policy advisers, he had policy advice from a highly differentiated and well-staffed constellation of secretariats in his capacity as chief executive in charge of the Cabinet or as chairman of the Priorities and Planning Committee.

The Organizations behind Ministers. To use Doern's typology, whether a department is a central agency, a "traditional," "new," or "administrative" coordinating portfolio, or a vertical constituency portfolio with more or less prestigious clients contributes more than any factor to the organizational resources of individual ministers. But other factors are at play. First among these is the ability and prestige of a minister's deputy.

Deputy ministers serve as the principal policy advisers of ministers. Deputies who are well connected with others in the career public service and experienced in interdepartmental politics can greatly lighten their ministers' workloads. Ministers can rely on such persons to see that the departmental will is brought to bear, at the early stages of the policy process, in interdepartmental committees. Astute deputy ministers assure that they and other top departmental officials gain access to all vital panels of officials in town. They also see that their ministers adequately cover Cabinet committee meetings at which matters of major importance are at stake. Three conventions assist deputy ministers in this respect. First, a department can send a delegate to subject-matter committees to which it does not belong. Second, officials almost always accompany ministers to Cabinet committees and contribute to deliberations both by backing up ministers with expertise and by becoming full discussants. Third, officials often represent their department at Cabinet committee meetings which the minister is unable to attend. Campbell and Szablowski provide many insiders' views on the importance of deputy ministers and other officials to such a process. None, however, is more startling than this account:

> A cabinet-committee meeting was once rescheduled on short notice from its usual afternoon hour to the morning of the next day. All regular members and participants—with the exception of one deputy minister who was out of town and could not be reached—were advised by telephone of the change. The deputy minister had planned to return to Ottawa and attend the meeting in the afternoon originally scheduled. The meeting took place in the morning and an ADM substituted for the absent deputy minister. When the deputy minister returned he discovered that one item on the agenda had been resolved in a manner with which he strongly disagreed. He wasted no time and dispatched a terse and unequivocal memo to the minister who chaired the meeting. It read: "During my absence and without my knowledge a cabinet-committee meeting was held and a decision taken against which I had no opportunity to speak. This must not happen again." [35]

Deputy ministers use two means to ensure that their political masters have sufficiently developed advice and that their departments perform adequately in policy development. First, deputy ministers attempt to achieve optimal coordination of decision making in the department. All departments have management committees consisting of assistant deputy ministers and, sometimes, directors general, which attempt to resolve internal conflicts and decide the department's overall strategy as well as positions on substantive issues. All departments have a secretariat for managing communication within the department and with the Cabinet and its committees, other departments, Parliament, and the general public. In addition, several departments have large groups for coordination and evaluation which provide the management committee with analytic resources for determining plans and priorities.

---

[35] Campbell and Szablowski, *Superbureaucrats*, pp. 153-55.

Second, deputy ministers will take positive steps to upgrade the resources of their department in relation to those of other departments in various fields of expertise. Mickey Cohen's brief term as deputy minister of energy, mines, and resources (EMR) serves as an excellent example. Cohen served as an assistant deputy minister in the Department of Finance during the 1973–1974 energy crisis and the development and implementation of the 1975 antiinflation program. During this period, he had gathered a great deal of capital both with the Prime Minister and, although he is a lawyer, with the economists in town. Moving to EMR in the spring of 1978 after a sabbatical studying economics at Harvard, he chose to maintain prominence in the economics policy sector by upgrading EMR's advisory staff in this field. He eliminated several economist positions in operational branches of the department and centralized economic policy and analysis in a new branch. He was able as well to bring key personnel from the Department of Finance to assume the three most senior posts in the new branch. When Cohen moved on early in 1979 to become the deputy minister of industry, trade, and commerce, he left EMR the beneficiary of economic expertise from the biggest raid on Finance in years.

Although ministers rely for the most part on deputy ministers and other departmental career officials to support their policy roles, their resources for exempt staff (partisan appointees) have increased greatly in recent years. Currently, the typical minister employs one executive assistant, four special assistants, a private secretary, and between nine and fourteen support staff. Although the total bill for exempt staff cannot exceed $200,000, ministers may get around the limit by taking on consultants or seconding career officials to their personal staff. To date, ministers' staffs have not usually wielded much influence in the development of departmental policy or even in legislative liaison. They simply lack the time and expertise. But their performance of other crucial ministerial functions releases their bosses from many activities that otherwise would distract them from their departmental and legislative work. Such functions include organizing the minister's time and office, doing liaison work with organizations inside and outside of government, conducting public relations, and compiling available data and information for the ministers' speeches and press releases.[36]

Supporting Cabinet. Two types of secretariats work in support of the Cabinet and its committees: those in the Privy Council Office and

---

[36] Blair Williams, "The Parapolitical Bureaucracy," in Clarke et al., eds., *Parliament, Policy and Representation*, pp. 215-29.

the Federal-Provincial Relations Office, and those established as separate central agencies serving Cabinet committees. With respect to PCO and FPRO, the secretariats essentially center on briefing the Prime Minister, usually through the office hierarchy but often personally, on the timing and development of major issues before Cabinet and its committees. Officials within these secretariats also serve Cabinet committees in general and the chairmen in particular.

The key secretariats of this type are those under the deputy secretary (Operations) in PCO. The assistant secretaries for the five subject-matter committees staffed by PCO shoulder special responsibilities for briefing the chairman and for organizing the business of the committee. As a result, they play numerous bargaining and advocacy roles within the bureaucratic politics behind each major initiative. These include:

- Advising officials from operational departments on the best way to proceed on issues and, if the matter calls for an interdepartmental panel, which departments should be invited to join
- Monitoring development of the new policy in the department or the interdepartmental panel
- Deciding when the proposal is ready for initial discussion in the Cabinet committee
- Ensuring that any difficulties which emerged in the committee, especially those with the Department of Finance and the Treasury Board Secretariat, are ironed out before final consideration by the Cabinet committee
- Transmitting committee recommendations to the Prime Minister and the Cabinet
- Communicating Cabinet decisions to all concerned parties
- Ensuring that the decisions are actually implemented.[37]

This list of functions is quite a tall order for any assistant secretary. Throughout the formation of policy he must be sure to channel his energies in productive areas. Much of his work will be routine, but he will have to come to the rescue if a department is floundering on an issue especially important to the Prime Minister or to the committee. Under such circumstances departments which have played ball procedurally will likely get more sympathy and forbearance than those which have stepped on the toes of other departments or of PCO. During the implementation of policy the assistant secretary has to watch out for foot dragging in departments less than enthusiastic

---

[37] Campbell and Szablowski, *Superbureaucrats*, pp. 69-83.

about a decision. Here the official might ultimately call for artillery: "If a minister and his officials are dragging their feet on something that is dear to the P.M.'s heart, we might try to get a letter out of him to the minister saying in effect, 'get off your ass.' "[38]

In the final months of the Trudeau government, three secretariats serviced Cabinet boards and their presidents. Two of these, the Treasury Board Secretariat (TBS) and the Office of the Comptroller General (OCG), report directly to the president of the Treasury Board; one, the secretariat for the Board of Economic Development Ministers, established in December 1978, reported to the president of that board. Joe Clark changed the name of the board to the Economic Development Committee. Since this body was chaired by the minister of industry, trade, and commerce, the secretariat reported to him rather than to a full-time president. Clark was in the process of setting up a fourth secretariat, for a committee styled "Social Development," when his government fell in December 1979.

TBS and OCG, which together house several hundred professionals, advise the Treasury Board in the exercise of statutory authority given it by section 5 of the Financial Administration Act:

- The review of annual and longer-term expenditure plans and programs of the departments of government and the determination of budgetary priorities
- General administrative policy in the public service
- The organization of the public service
- Personnel management in the public service, including the terms and conditions of employment
- Financial management, including estimates, expenditures, financial commitments, accounts, fees or charges for the provision of services or the use of facilities, rentals, licenses, leases, revenues from the disposition of property, and procedures by which departments manage, record, and account for revenues received or receivable from any service.[39]

Three Treasury Board Secretariat branches (Program, Administrative Policy, and Personnel Policy) perform functions related respectively to the allocation of budgets and organization of the public service, administrative policy and the financial management of materials and services provided to all government offices, and personnel management. A fourth branch, Official Languages, monitors imple-

---

[38] Ibid., p. 81.
[39] Revised Statutes of Canada (RSC), 1970, chap. F-10.

mentation throughout the public service of the 1969 Official Languages Act and a 1973 resolution of Parliament, both of which mandate the expanded use of French in the federal government.

Within these various sectors TBS must share its authority with other central agencies. The Program Branch takes the lead in all budgetary review, but within the priority guidelines provided by the Privy Council Office and the fiscal framework set by the Department of Finance. Clark assigned budgetary review functions to the new Economic and Social Development secretariats as well, but it is too early to speculate on the consequences of these reforms for TBS even if they are maintained by the Liberal government. The fact that Treasury Board ministers or delegated officials attend all sectoral Cabinet committees and have the right to request copies of all departmental "Cabdocs" greatly contributes to the greatest resource of the Program Branch, a comprehensive grasp of expenditure proposals in the mill. The organization division of the Program Branch works on the general machinery of government, but the PCO unit, headed by a much more senior official, has greatly eclipsed TBS's role here. The Administrative Policy Branch serves as the government's in-house guardian of probity and prudence in the use of material and services. The more vital administrative issues, namely bureaucratic accountability, accounting, and evaluation of efficiency and effectiveness, are now under the aegis of the Office of the Comptroller General. The Personnel Policy Branch maintains a strong role in this field, with the exception of policy for and selection of senior personnel, an area dominated by PCO. The Public Service Commission, rather than TBS, actually administers most personnel policy below the senior levels. The functions subsumed under the Official Languages Branch moved from the Department of the Secretary of State when it was found that, without the direct backing of the Treasury Board, officials responsible for the implementation of related policies lacked clout.

The Office of the Comptroller General (OCG) evolved from two branches of TBS as a result of a chain of events that raised serious questions about the adequacy of financial administration in government. OCG focuses on one aspect of financial administration, program-oriented accounting. In addition to assuring that resources are actually expended in the program for which they were allocated, OCG assesses whether they were used efficiently and whether the program they supported was effective. The Financial Administration Branch of OCG upgrades department accounting systems while the Efficiency Evaluation Branch assures that departments routinely measure performance and conduct periodic in-depth studies of programs.

The various branches in the Treasury Board Secretariat and the Office of the Comptroller General have quite different working relations with the Treasury Board. Program Branch officials, especially the deputy secretary and the two assistant secretaries, attend most of the ninety meetings of the board each year. In these formal sessions, the officials brief the ministers, join in the cross-examination of departmental ministers and officials, and enter freely in board deliberations once departmental representatives have had their say. The remaining branches of TBS and all of OCG enjoy much less direct exposure to the Treasury Board. OCG suffers less from this lack of exposure to the ministers because its functions have been strongly supported by both the Trudeau and Clark governments, which have stressed financial administration. In addition, a strong affinity has developed over the years between officials, originally in TBS and now in OCG, responsible for evaluation and the various secretariats of PCO which call upon OCG for analytic assistance.

The Economic Development Secretariat contains forty professionals and about sixty support staff now serving a Cabinet-level committee. The secretariat was originally supposed to serve the Board of Economic Development Ministers, which was directed to:

- Define integrated economic development policy by industrial sector and region, review and concert submissions to the Treasury Board and the Cabinet in light of these, and improve program delivery
- Advise the Treasury Board on the allocation of government resources to economic development programs
- Lead and coordinate consultation on economic development with the provinces, business, labor, and other public and private organizations
- Conduct its own research and policy development.[40]

The Trudeau government thus had taken economic development, formerly a subsidiary concern of the Economic Policy Committee of the Cabinet, and dignified it with a Cabinet-level board and secretariat with sweeping mandates. As a result, tidal waves washed the shores of every other segment of the economic policy establishment. Under the Trudeau arrangement the Department of Industry, Trade, and Commerce lost its lead of other departments and agencies responsible for economic development. The Department of Finance expected much of microeconomic policy to slip gradually from its purview and

---

40 P. M. Pitfield, Privy Council, 1978-3803, pp. 2-3.

that of the Economic Policy Committee which it led. The Treasury Board was directed to accept estimates and expenditure proposals related to economic development only after they had been distilled by the Board of Economic Development Ministers. Industry, Trade, and Commerce, Labour, the Federal-Provincial Relations Office, and other departments and agencies which previously dominated consultation with their respective clients among economic sectors and the provinces were to share this function with the board. Even the Privy Council Office faced the horrifying fact that, except for dramatic departures from government policy, all initiatives in economic development policy were to proceed directly to the Cabinet, without passing through the Priorities and Planning Committee, after they were endorsed by the Board of Economic Development Ministers and their expenditure implications had been cleared by the Treasury Board.

Joe Clark further muddied the waters by merging the Board of Economic Development Ministers with the Economic Policy Committee in a Cabinet committee he dubbed Economic Development. To maintain some of the emphasis on microeconomics, which the board's creation was meant to heighten, he placed the minister of industry, trade, and commerce in the chair of the Economic Development Committee. Clark's government wanted to downgrade the status of the Finance Department in economic policy because the department was thought, somewhat unjustly, to be a hotbed of Liberal sympathizers. In any event, it now appears that his move was doomed to failure. The Finance Department still takes the lead in the formation of macroeconomic policy and the preparation of the budget—both the fiscal framework (expenditures) and taxation (revenues).

One Prime Minister, Several Incarnations

With an understanding of distribution of executive authority and power between the Prime Minister and Cabinet, and of the secretariats and departments which support the political executives, we can now turn to how the system actually worked under Trudeau. This section will examine the performance of the three Trudeau governments between 1968 and 1979 in four areas: international affairs and defense, economic policy, financial administration, and federal-provincial relations. Attention will focus on two questions: How well were issues managed by the Prime Minister and Cabinet in these policy sectors? And did structural adjustments to improve performance actually achieve this goal?

How to Become a Statesman without Even Trying. When Lester Pearson left the Prime Ministership in 1968 he brought to an end a period in which the Canadian international image was fading into obscurity. Ironically, the man who, as minister of external affairs, had won the Nobel Peace Prize for his work during the 1956 Suez crisis failed almost completely, while Prime Minister, to impress the world with his statesmanship. To be fair, Pearson was new at the game of domestic politics; he had to contend with two minority governments; he faced growing unrest in Quebec and, very much to his favor, committed tremendous energy to a package of Liberal social reforms which included comprehensive medicare. In retrospect, Pearson was to Pierre Elliott Trudeau on the domestic front what John F. Kennedy was to Lyndon B. Johnson: He put into gestation social programs which have become the high-water mark of the welfare state in North America.

Trudeau walked onto the Ottawa scene in 1965 with only one claim to expertise in international affairs—as a young man he had traveled widely throughout the world. By 1979 he had become the dean of the Atlantic community statesmen, even attending economic summits that included only the United States, the United Kingdom, France, Italy, Germany, Japan, and Canada. There is little doubt that this part of Trudeau's success as a statesman derived both from his relatively long tenure and his flamboyant personality. Indeed, foreigners often greeted with utter incredulity news from Canadians that Trudeau's popularity had slipped at home.

Immediately upon taking office Trudeau set out to establish himself as a statesman. He employed a twofold strategy. First, he kept his hand on the controls of the external affairs department. As a result, the position of secretary of state for external affairs lost its traditional status as the second most prestigious portfolio in the Cabinet. Ivan Head, a PMO adviser who started as a legislative assistant but soon was carrying out special missions for the Prime Minister in several hot spots, became his eyes, ears, and confidential agent in all things international. Second, Trudeau personally led a sweeping reevaluation of Canada's foreign and defense policies.[41] The upshot was the decision to decrease the size of the Canadian Armed Forces and scale down Canada's commitment to NORAD and NATO. In more positive initiatives, the Trudeau government recognized China; introduced a staged policy for increasing the proportion of Canada's gross national product (GNP) committed to foreign aid; and

[41] Bruce Thordarson, *Trudeau and Foreign Policy: A Study in Decision-Making* (Toronto: Oxford University Press, 1972).

concentrated defense planning on the sovereignty of Canadian territory. The latter policy, sparked by concern over international adjustments in offshore limits and heightened American interest in Arctic waterways, led eventually to the development of coastal surveillance vessels and aircraft.

Trudeau put in place most of his new foreign and defense policies, but in recent years the original plans have been considerably modified. NORAD and NATO have lobbied effectively to increase Canadian military personnel and equipment beyond the original plans. When the *Manhattan* voyage in 1969 proved a failure and altered American plans for Arctic shipping, the specter of U.S. dominance of Canadian waters and contamination of delicate Arctic ecology began to fade, and Canadian apprehensions diminished. Successive spending cuts, especially during the summer of 1978, led to delays in increasing the proportion of the Canadian GNP committed to foreign aid. None of these diversions drastically undermined Trudeau's policies, but the process by which they were carried out raises some serious questions because the new stress on sovereignty-related defense programs was not followed through by officials and ministers.

First, as early as 1970 a blue-ribbon panel of officials, some with previous links in the petroleum industry, had advised commitment of northern and Arctic oil and gas to the general North American resource grid.[42] The Cabinet endorsed this recommendation, even though many Canadians believe that these reserves, most of which are subject to U.S. companies' drilling and production rights, should be kept exclusively for Canadian use. Second, only with great difficulty was the Cabinet finally able in the summer of 1976 to commit the government to purchase aircraft capable of adequate surveillance of Canadian waters. At the time, officials observed that the sovereignty principle simply was not sufficiently enshrined in government defense policy to convince ministers that sophisticated surveillance was necessary. To avoid another such impasse, the government mounted a major study in 1977 focusing on selection of a new Canadian Armed Forces jet fighter. Defence, and Industry, Trade, and Commerce were the two departments with the most at stake in the process. The former wanted a fighter which could serve with NATO in Europe and also be able to fly far and high enough to patrol Canada's vast airspace—much of which is over frozen, unpopulated land. The latter wanted a contract with the largest possible proportion of construction in Canada. Just as the committee completed its

---

[42] Edgar J. Dosman, *The National Interest: The Politics of Northern Development, 1968-75* (Toronto: McClelland and Stewart, 1975), chap. 5.

analysis, the spending cuts of summer 1978 resulted in a recommendation which narrowed the choice to the two cheapest aircraft. Neither of these met the requirements of the two departments. Nevertheless, the Cabinet gave the green light for contract negotiations with the two cheapest contenders. The pursuit of stringency here meant that Canada would likely purchase an aircraft acceptable to NATO but of only marginal use to protect Canadian sovereignty.

Economic Policy: The Politics of Elite Accommodation. The political and business elite in Canada, as Porter, Presthus, and Clement tell us, live cheek by jowl.[43] Indeed, oligarchy even finds an institutional home in the Canadian Senate, where appointees, largely selected because of their standing in the business community and their success as party fund raisers, have exercised considerable influence over legislation that might harm big business.[44]

Many hoped that Trudeau would rise above the politics of elite accommodation. His 1968 government ended a string of three minority governments between 1962 and 1968 and provided an opportunity for the Liberal party to assert itself independently of support or resistance in the business community. Trudeau appeared to have no links with the country's business community and to owe it practically nothing for his ascendancy in the Liberal party. Yet Trudeau's handling of several successive issues proved these expectations wrong. He consistently has followed elite accommodation in pursuit of economic policy, all along giving disproportionate weight to business.

No more convincing support for this assertion is available than Trudeau's handling of tax reform. In 1966 a Royal Commission on Tax Reform (the Carter Commission), urged comprehensive reforms of Canada's income tax to make it more progressive—that is, less burdensome to the poor and more burdensome to the rich—and to introduce a capital gains tax.[45] A 1969 government white paper on taxation endorsed much of the report.[46] The tax bill was passed in 1971 with perhaps the stiffest review, both in the House of Commons

---

[43] John Porter, *The Vertical Mosaic: An Analysis of Social Class and Power in Canada* (Toronto: University of Toronto Press, 1965); Presthus, *Elite Accommodation;* and Wallace Clement, *The Canadian Corporate Elite: An Analysis of Economic Power* (Toronto: McClelland and Stewart, 1975).

[44] Campbell, *Canadian Senate*, pp. 10-19.

[45] Richard M. Bird, "The Tax Kaleidoscope: Perspectives on Tax Reform in Canada," *Canadian Tax Journal* (September-October 1970), pp. 444-73.

[46] A. D. Doerr, "The Role of White Papers," in G. Bruce Doern and Peter Aucoin, eds., *The Structure of Policy Making in Canada* (Toronto: Macmillan, 1971), pp. 179-203.

and the Senate, of any piece of legislation in the past decade.[47] Despite his healthy majority in both houses, Trudeau conceded many key white-paper recommendations to opponents. As one U.S. Treasury official remarked in a recent interview: "The Canadians shot for the moon and landed in the U.S." If anything, taxation became less progressive after reform than it had been before.

During the early 1970s economic arguments that pointed to the need for wage and price controls aroused a great deal of concern in Canada. Leaders in both the business and labor communities made it clear to the government that such controls would be unacceptable, and the 1974 election was fought largely on this issue. The Liberals, following the guidance of the strongly business-oriented Department of Finance, sought to ride out rising inflation. During the summer of 1975, even Finance officials became alarmed about simultaneous high unemployment and inflation.[48] At the same time, Liberal party organizers noticed growing public antipathy toward government because of its poor performance with the economy. Trudeau then imposed mandatory wage and price controls. This flip-flop further diminished Trudeau's credibility among voters, especially since it had only modest success with inflation and actually increased unemployment.

Financial Administration as a Regression Equation Run Wild. Those familiar with statistics will know that researchers use regression analysis to find out the degree to which two or more variables contribute to change in a dependent variable. Stepwise regression will discover which variable relates the strongest to the dependent variable and then will search for the variable which explains the greatest amount of the remaining variance. The process can continue indefinitely as long as a new variable is added to the equation at each step.

The history of financial administration in the past seventeen years reveals the degree to which the development of institutions has resembled a stepwise regression run wild. Rather than simply introducing new emphases to established approaches, the government has treated each new approach or technique as if it had the potential to account for all the undesirable variance in spending. Each analytic fad has merited full bureaucratic incarnation by the establishment of new branches, even secretariats. Trudeau presided over most of this

---

[47] C. E. S. Franks, "The Dilemma of Standing Committees in the Canadian House of Commons," *Canadian Journal of Political Science*, vol. 4 (December 1971), pp. 461-76; and Campbell, *Canadian Senate*, pp. 15-17.

[48] Radwanski, *Trudeau*, pp. 266-74; Campbell and Szablowski, *Superbureaucrats*, pp. 65-66.

regression run wild. He was guided by an apparently unfailing belief that if the right techniques could be found and institutions rationalized, financial administration would be adequate.

The process began in 1962 when the Glassco Commission canonized the principle that correct managerial techniques would bring about bureaucratic accountability.[49] To effect this change it recommended that financial affairs be divided into two distinct categories: (1) intragovernmental control over the allocation of expenditure budgets and management of all in-house resources; and (2) national, intergovernmental, and international strategy to regulate and influence the economy. Specifically, the commission proposed that the secretariat of the Treasury Board, at that time part of the Department of Finance, be hived off so as to take the lead in fostering greater accountability and skill among departmental managers. In 1966 Parliament created the Treasury Board Secretariat. The new central agency initially contained branches responsible for budget review, management improvement, and personnel policy.

Since 1966 various structural changes have reflected shifts of emphasis in TBS which increase the weight given to particular forms of analysis within finance and administration. In light of the recent creation of the Office of the Comptroller General, the development and growth of the units responsible for programmatic accounting is particularly interesting. In 1970 the Program Branch, the unit responsible for budgetary review, included one small division responsible for programmatic accounting. By 1973 the unit, still a division, moved to the Administrative Policy Branch, which is responsible for probity and prudence in the provision of material and supplies. By this time, Douglas Hartle, a University of Toronto economist, was preparing to leave town after installing mechanisms for management-by-objectives analysis, monitored by the newly titled Planning Branch of TBS. This branch included three divisions, Organizational Evaluation, Efficiency Evaluation, and Effectiveness Evaluation.

During the mid-1970s the auditor general, in successive reports, criticized TBS for not upgrading its programmatic accounting capability. By 1976 Financial Administration, the division responsible for programmatic accounting, became a branch with three divisions. But in the fall of 1976 the auditor general produced his most stinging criticism of the continued neglect of programmatic accounting and backed it up with a number of horror stories. These included evidence of a gross absence of probity and prudence in the operations of Atomic

---

[49] *Report of the Royal Commission on Government Organization*, abridged ed., vol. 1 (Ottawa: Queen's Printer, 1962).

Energy of Canada Limited. The government first attempted to defuse the issue by creating the Royal Commission on Financial Management and Accountability (the Lambert Commission). But the auditor general held his ground, and the Public Accounts Committee of the House of Commons launched an in-depth study of his report, the first ever conducted by Parliament. The government adopted the auditor general's principal recommendation by creating an office of the Comptroller General, independent of TBS and reporting directly to the president of the Treasury Board. This agency has now taken on the Financial Administration Branch and absorbed remnants of the Planning Branch. The latter had fallen out of fashion with the departure of Hartle from Ottawa and had become subordinate to the new buzz word, "financial administration."

Through all of this, the Program Branch maintained its status as the heart of TBS by virtue of the centrality of budget review and expenditure approval to TBS's mission. As already noted, however, its role is threatened by the newly established Economic and Social Development secretariats. In addition, the Lambert Commission report (March 1979) proposed that TBS and OCG be reorganized into two new autonomous secretariats reporting to a new Board of Management replacing the Treasury Board.[50] The two secretariats would be Financial Management and Personnel Management. Here the Program Branch would come under the comptroller general who would head the Financial Management Secretariat. Thus, the regression continues to run wild. Slants on financial management come into vogue and institutions go through metamorphoses. Meanwhile, few tangible improvements occur, as reflected by the fact that the Lambert Commission sought solutions to the same problems addressed by the Glassco Commission in the early 1960s.

Cooperative Federalism—Almost. When Trudeau took over from Lester Pearson the country was enjoying such tranquility in federal-provincial relations that the politics of the period was dubbed "cooperative federalism." Although considerable turmoil persisted in Quebec over linguistic divisions, progress was being made on several fronts. The government had committed itself to fostering bilingualism and improving Francophones' access to jobs and services; it had negotiated several new social programs, including medicare, through federal-provincial conferences; and it had made considerable progress toward a new constitution reflecting the current federal system.

---

[50] *Final Report of the Royal Commission on Financial Management and Accountability* (Ottawa: Minister of Supply and Services, 1979), chap. 7.

Trudeau's ethnic roots, which were decidedly French, and his articulate advocacy of a strong federalism suggested that he could serve as a much-needed bridge between Quebec and the rest of Canada. Indeed, he pressed bilingualism even more resolutely than Pearson and tried to accelerate adoption of a new constitution. His federal policies, however, yielded little improvement in his first eleven years as Prime Minister.

Trudeau faced his first setback in 1970 when the Liberal government in Quebec spurned the draft constitution, causing a hiatus in discussions which lasted until 1976. Later in 1970 the kidnapping of the British diplomat James Cross and the Quebec Cabinet minister Pierre Laporte, who ultimately was assassinated, triggered the October crisis during which Trudeau eventually invoked the War Measures Act. This step permitted authorities to detain suspected separatists indefinitely. Besides alienating a good number of innocent Québécois, this action tainted Trudeau's image among civil libertarians throughout the country.

Federal-provincial relations were relatively uneventful until 1973 when the events following the Yom Kippur war brought the energy crisis to Canada.[51] The federal government acted quickly by imposing export taxes on petroleum, which brought the price of Canadian shipments to the United States to the OPEC level. But these taxes simply underwrote subsidies for Canadians in Quebec and the Maritime Provinces, which import most of their petroleum from OPEC countries. The government began to press for further taxation of domestically produced and consumed petroleum in an effort to encourage conservation, stem windfall profits as companies raised domestic prices, and provide money for the development of alternate sources of energy. This move sparked a fight between petroleum-producing provinces, which also wanted to increase taxes, and the federal government, on one side, and the nonproducing provinces, on the other. Among the latter, Ontario, which both manufactures and consumes more goods than any other province, stood to lose the most from higher petroleum prices. In the end, the federal government and the producing provinces got their way. Thus, Trudeau accomplished in 1974 what three successive U.S. presidents attempted with only marginal success.

The whole episode could be viewed as a triumph of federal will over the recalcitrance of Ontario on economic issues that concern its

[51] Colin Campbell and Thomas Reese, "The Energy Crisis and Tax Policy in Canada and the United States: Federal-Provincial Diplomacy v. Congressional Lawmaking," in J. Richard Wagner, ed., *Border Problems of the United States and Canada: Issues of the Seventies*, a special issue of *Social Science Journal*, vol. 14 (January 1977), pp. 17-32.

dominance of Canadian finance and industry. It was followed in 1976 by a Supreme Court decision that strengthened the hand of the federal government in the regulation of the economy. Several provinces had contested the legality of the federal government's wage and price controls. The Supreme Court, however, styled the events leading to the imposition of controls as sufficient justification for invoking the emergency powers of section 91 of the BNA Act, the source of most of Parliament's legislative authority.[52]

Events since then have again weakened the position of the federal government. The Parti Québécois victory on November 15, 1976, gave leverage to all provinces as the federal government faced a very real threat of collapse of Confederation. On many policy fronts, the federal government has gained no ground, and its proposed constitution of 1978, largely a resuscitation of the one almost accepted in 1970, has only stiffened the provinces' resolve to reshape Confederation completely through the radical transferral of powers to their jurisdictions.

Trudeau failed to fulfill initial expectations on the federal-provincial front. He found in the 1979 election that his pledge to resolve the national unity crisis, which formed the key plank of the Liberal campaign, did little to rekindle Trudeaumania. But in the election of 1980, the relevance of issues shifted fortuitously for the Liberals. Polls convinced Trudeau that the separatist threat had ebbed in Quebec, and his campaign therefore downplayed the national unity issue. On the energy front, Joe Clark had not been able to work an acceptable compromise between the federal government and the provinces after events in the Middle East again introduced pressure for higher energy prices. Indeed, his budget placed such disproportionate burdens on Ontario that its voters shifted dramatically back to the Liberals after having given overwhelming support to the Progressive Conservatives in 1979. Trudeau's track record in the energy field contributed to this Ontario support and to the Liberals' victory on February 18. We should keep in mind, though, that the election results appeared to indicate more anti-Clark than pro-Trudeau feeling among the voters.

The Four Phases of the Trudeau Governments

The organization of political leadership may be viewed along two intersecting continuums.[53] The first represents the degree to which

---

[52] Peter H. Russell, "The 'Anti-Inflation Case': The Anatomy of a Constitutional Decision," in Schultz, Kruhlak, and Terry, *Canadian Political Process*, pp. 395-416.
[53] I owe a debt of gratitude to several scholars in the field of executive leadership

subfunctions of executive leadership fall into specific and highly differentiated units or come under the aegis of two or more units that often compete for influence; the second is the degree to which key policy decisions are actually delegated to peripheral units or ultimately made by bureaucratic or political authorities with direct access to the chief executive.

In this paradigm, we may posit four styles of executive leadership: (1) broker politics, whereby key policy decisions are made in the periphery but through negotiations between units with competing expertise and authority in a policy sector; (2) administrative politics, whereby decisions continue to be made in the periphery but the political leaders have tried to cut down on conflict at the Cabinet level by permitting single units to obtain virtual hegemony over specific subfunctions; (3) the planning and priorities style, whereby the government attempts to give greater direction and credibility to its mandate by challenging units to come up with policy alternatives and simultaneously attempting to bring these alternatives together in a comprehensive programmatic strategy; and (4) the politics of survival, whereby the government, under severe stress from the political environment—perceived or real—will attempt to gain control by sharply reducing the number of countervailing units and bringing many matters previously decided in the periphery to the center in highly differentiated units.

One is struck by how clearly these four styles appeared at various stages of Trudeau's administration. The period of brokerage politics occurred from 1968 to 1972, roughly Trudeau's first government, when the complex system of Cabinet committees emerged. It was argued that such a system would increase the effectiveness of individual Cabinet ministers in coordinating government policies. As it turned out, the roles of central agencies and operational departments became more countervailing than ever before. On the one hand, the Prime Minister's Office, especially under the direction of Marc Lalonde, began to influence the development of strategic plans by the government—a function which previously had been totally controlled by the Privy Council Office. Meanwhile, both the Finance Department and PCO had to contend with the pervasive role of the Treasury Board

---

for insights that served as the basis of this paradigm, especially Hugh Heclo and Aaron Wildavsky, *The Private Government of Public Money: Community and Policy Inside British Politics* (Berkeley: University of California, 1974); Stephen Hess, *Organizing the Presidency* (Washington, D.C.: Brookings Institution, 1976); and Richard Rose, *The Problem of Party Government* (Harmondsworth: Penguin, 1976), and "The President: A Chief but Not an Executive," *Presidential Studies Quarterly*, vol. 7 (Winter 1977), pp. 5-20.

Secretariat in the review of expenditure budgets and programmatic proposals with expenditure implications. On the other hand, operational departments that had formerly taken the undisputed lead in policy sectors now faced competition by virtue of the strengthening of the Cabinet committee system and the creation of new departments. For instance, the Department of Industry, Trade, and Commerce, which formerly held the high ground in all matters concerning industrial development, now had to share it in committees not only with departments such as Labour, which traditionally had been in the sector, but also with new departments, including Regional Economic Expansion, Consumer and Corporate Affairs, Science and Technology, and Communications.

The years 1968–1972 fell short of expectations—especially in light of the government's very healthy majority. Electoral unrest in 1972 almost led to a defeat of the government. Trudeau, from 1972 to the next election in 1974, retreated to administrative politics. The policy role of PMO became virtually nonexistent, and Gordon Robertson, by then clerk/secretary in PCO for more than ten years, stayed more than ever aloof from politics. No new central agencies or departments were created during this period. More important, these years marked the golden era of Cabinet fiefdoms. Gerard Pelletier and Jean Marchand, two "wise men," who along with Trudeau decided in the mid-1960s that it was time for Francophone federalists to go to Ottawa and work for the cause, both found solid bases in departments which they were building to positions of prominence. Pelletier had just finished a stint as secretary of state, during which he masterminded implementation of Trudeau's bilingual and bicultural policies, and was building up the Department of Communications; Marchand had just finished heading the Department of Regional Economic Expansion, with control over the considerable funds earmarked for Quebec, and had become head of the prestigious Department of Transport. Both loomed almost as large in the minds of Québécois as Trudeau. During this period, several Anglophone Cabinet ministers won prominence in the public eye. John Turner established himself as the principal Anglophone minister by taking over the Finance Department, which he ruled with greater authority than any incumbent in memory—even fighting off proposals for mandatory wage and price controls; Charles Mills "Bud" Drury, a distinguished parliamentarian and crucial figure in maintaining confidence in the Liberal party within the Anglophone-dominated Montreal business community, lent his considerable clout to the Treasury Board by serving as its president; Otto Lang used two key portfolios, Justice and the

Canadian Wheat Board, to consolidate his position as czar of the Prairie Liberals; and Mitchell Sharp, a former finance minister, maintained since 1968 his post as secretary of state for external affairs, which perpetuated his standing as dean of Ontario ministers.

After the election of 1974 gave him another healthy majority, Trudeau went through his priorities and planning phase, which lasted until fall 1975. He established in the Prime Minister's Office a policy unit to monitor the Cabinet policy process and relate key decisions, initiatives, and overall strategy to a definite schedule which would optimize the achievements of the mandate and the prospects for a big majority in the next election. For the first time the Privy Council Office became explicitly attuned to political considerations. Michael Pitfield, a close confidant of the Prime Minister, replaced Gordon Robertson as clerk/secretary; the Plans division joined energetically with PMO in getting ministers to sort out their priorities and in prodding the departments to respond to them. Gordon Robertson kept some of his power by creating a third central agency, the Federal-Provincial Relations Office, which reports directly to the Prime Minister, and by retaining ultimate advisory authority to the Prime Minister both for development of senior personnel policy and recommendation of appointments. The Treasury Board Secretariat found itself in a tussle with PCO, which it eventually won when it gained authority to request all Cabinet documents as they entered the committee system rather than only shortly before consideration by the Cabinet. During the 1975 economic crisis, Finance found itself submitting to PCO's lead in DM-10, an assortment of deputy ministers which hammered out the details of a mandatory wage and price control program.

The upshot of the priorities and planning exercise was profound disillusionment on several fronts. The fall 1975 departure of Finance Minister John Turner triggered a critical attrition process, in which even Trudeau's most trusted Cabinet colleagues, such as Gerard Pelletier and Jean Marchand, departed. Departments largely evaded the priorities exercise by inundating Cabinet committees with mounds of paper saying essentially: "This is how our plans for the next five years fit into your projections." The economic crisis drained any remaining PMO and PCO energy which could have salvaged the task. PMO disbanded the policy unit in 1976; PCO retreated to its more conventional practice of servicing the day-to-day work of the Cabinet and providing ad hoc policy advice to the Prime Minister. TBS found its credibility undermined by a succession of highly critical auditor general's reports and faced a Royal Commission study focused largely on the effectiveness of its work. Finance still sought to recover from the stigma of being wrong on wage and price controls and losing its most prominent minister in years.

By 1976 Trudeau leaned irrevocably toward survival politics. He had turned the PMO almost completely into a switchboard for political operations and relied almost entirely on PCO for policy advice. Thus, his 1974 campaign sidekick, Jim Coutts, geared up the Liberal election machinery while serving as principal secretary in PMO, and Ian Stewart worked in PCO to provide Trudeau with his own economic advice independent of that proffered by the Finance Department. Michael Pitfield, still clerk/secretary in PCO, was having weekly sessions with Albert Breton, a University of Toronto economist, to upgrade his knowledge of economics. At the same time, Pitfield took over the policy development side of Robertson's responsibility for senior personnel and greatly upgraded his machinery of government unit. Both moves significantly eclipsed the traditional roles of the Treasury Board Secretariat. The center was drawing more functions to itself.

A provincial election, rather than a federal one, confirmed Trudeau in survival politics. The Parti Québécois victory on November 15, 1976, posed an unprecedented threat to the survival of Confederation. Trudeau responded by creating another unit in the Federal-Provincial Relations Office to coordinate the government's response to separatism. In addition, a retiring deputy minister of the Department of Justice and constitutional expert, Donald Thorson, moved to FPRO as special adviser. Trudeau responded to other crises in a similar way. He created the Office of the Comptroller General in response to the auditor general's fall 1976 attack on financial administration in government; upon returning from a 1978 economic summit where Helmut Schmidt, the West German Chancellor, had exhorted sharp expenditure cuts, he ordered $2 billion slashed from the 1978 allocations without even consulting the heads of his two fiscal policy departments, the minister of finance and the president of the Treasury Board; and he created the Board of Economic Development Ministers in December 1978 in a dramatic attempt to salvage the foundering consultations of regions and sectors on issues related to economic development. Increasingly, differentiated secretariats working at the center, serving either the Prime Minister or Cabinet committees, became the remedy for chronic political ills.

Such dramatic gestures had little impact on the electorate, however. For instance, in October the Liberals found that their dramatic expenditure cuts and their emphasis on national unity had little effect on voters in fifteen by-elections in which they won only two seats. At this time, members of the Liberal campaign committee appeared to have decided that it was time for the Prime Minister to resign so that the party's image could be rehabilitated before the end of the mandate in 1979. Trudeau, sensing what was in the air, forced the committee's hand by saying at the start of the strategy meeting immediately after the by-election defeats, "Well, I suppose you are going to fire me." The committee lost its resolve to bell the cat and thereby consented to the scorched earth policy which led to the defeat of the government in the 1979 election. Survival politics, with its overcentralization and bureaucratization of the government's response—even its response to electoral results that pointed to sure defeat—began to run its full and inevitable course. From fall 1978 to the May 22, 1979, election, not only was machinery more a preoccupation than politics, but the future of Pierre Elliott Trudeau took precedence over that of his party.

For Everything There Is a Season

Those who know the Bible will recall that it contains a series of books known as "wisdom literature," collections of sayings about life. Within the literature two extremes coexist. On the one hand, in books such as Proverbs, one finds the optimistic view of the connection between good works and rewards in this life: "For the upright will inhabit the land and men of integrity will remain in it" (2:21). Among specialists in the machinery of government the equivalent of this view as applied to executive leadership is: "If only we get the structure right this time . . ." On the other hand, in books such as Ecclesiastes, one finds a cynical view of the link between justice and one's earthly condition: "Vanity of vanities! All is vanity. What does man gain by all the toil at which he toils under the sun? A generation goes, and a generation comes, but the earth remains for ever" (1:2-4). Among political scientists and other students of government, the application of this view to executive leadership is that administrations go through cyclical phases brought on by changes both in the political environment and in the perceptions and morale of the political leadership. Structural adjustments, rather than influencing how the administration weathers the storm, are, in fact, products of cyclical shifts. In brief, the Proverbs view of organizing political leadership holds that structural change can improve executive leadership; the Ecclesiastes view holds that structural change simply provides the illusion of control by reflecting the status quo or, worse, what would have been appropriate months, even years, before.

Perhaps in Jesuitical fashion, my final remarks examine the degree to which both views apply to the organization of political leadership. On the Ecclesiastes side, the moralistic tone and open style of the Carter administration has not eradicated the phenomenon of corruption among some highly placed officials; Her Majesty's Treasury faced the unpleasant task of having to inform the new Thatcher government in Britain that the country's economic ills sharply constrain the maneuverability of Conservative innovators; and Joe Clark found that preoccupation with the machinery of government can fritter away a honeymoon without producing the tangible results by which voters evaluate a party's ability to govern. On the Proverbs side, career officials in the Carter Office of Management and Budget enjoy heightened morale because from time to time they actually have the privilege of discussing budgetary matters personally with the President, whereas Richard M. Nixon once boasted that he had spent twenty minutes on the entire budget; units such as the Central Policy Review Staff and Bernard Donoughue's policy unit have at times led to appreciably better policy decisions on the part of the British Prime Minister; and under Pierre Elliott Trudeau, Canadian officials developed machinery and analytical techniques which have become models for innovation in central agencies throughout the world. On matters concerning the organization of political leadership, the wise person tries to find the balance between optimism and pessimism.

The case for changes in machinery suggests ways in which government might be restructured to optimize executive leadership under a specific set of circumstances. A government that campaigned on promises of dramatic departures from the status quo and won the legislative majority to enact these promises should channel its efforts into areas where popular expectations are clear. Part of this task should involve prodding the bureaucracy by means of a core group of partisan advisers. Such advisers should have both sufficient analytical ability to grasp the substance of the issues and adequate knowledge of the bureaucratic process and machinery to monitor policy development and implementation. Trudeau preordained his lack of success on several policy fronts by emphasizing structure rather than priorities and partisan direction during his first government. In other words, traditional brokerage politics might have been appropriate from 1968 to 1972 if Trudeau had not raised expectations so high and on so many fronts.

Without a clear mandate from the electorate or in the face of intense popular disaffection, a government should probably keep a low profile. Especially under the Westminster model, a government that lacks clarity in its mandate must be discreet in its use of partisan advisers. Creation of a Royal Commission or a new central agency can help defuse issues such as accountability or national unity by appearing to find solutions, even though government can no longer treat the problem effectively because it has lost sway over bureaucrats, citizens, or other governments who could bring about real change. In other words, the government can buy time and ease nerves even if it lacks the authority to bring about real change. But these tactics can be overdone. During the last three years of Trudeau's 1974–1979 government, the dismantling of PMO's policy unit and the creation of central agencies (not to mention offices within them) in response to just about every major political problem produced a density of bureaucratic claims on the Prime Minister's time unsurpassed by previous governments. Thus, Trudeau held on to the leadership and fought an election even though the political Cabinet knew in spring 1978 that all the signs pointed to sure defeat and that the only hope was for Trudeau to resign and for the party to pick a new face. In addition, the Prime Minister continued to pour most of his energy into the national unity issue, even though the Parti Québécois faced severe problems of its own, and in countless polls for more than a year before the election Canadians listed national unity far down a list of grievances led by concerns about the economy. The Clark government made Trudeau a phoenix, but he still bears much of the responsibility for the Liberal defeat in 1979.

Trudeau's eleven years as Prime Minister suggest four notes of caution to other organizers of political leadership:

1. No matter how much it is thought that governmental machinery, either in operational departments or in central agencies, is inadequate, resist wholesale attempts to restructure and reorganize, and, above all, avoid being identified as a systems-oriented administration.

2. Limit priorities at the outset to a few issues with which the electorate has identified your government, and eschew comprehensive exercises aimed at developing a point-by-point game plan for the entire mandate.

3. Always keep on hand a group of partisan aids who report directly to the Prime Minister and provide policy analysis and intelligence on the operations of the bureaucracy. Keep this group separate as much as possible from other partisan units responsible for the day-to-day operation of the Prime Minister's Office and organizational work in the party. The unit should assume a reactive partisan role, facilitating transmission of caucus, party, and electoral views

to the Prime Minister and evaluating advice from the civil service in light of these criteria, as well as selling the Prime Minister or marshalling support for his programs. Resist at all times the temptation to reduce the size of the unit or its differentiation from the Prime Minister's Office in the face of major defeats of government initiatives by bureaucratic inertia or criticism from the press that the partisan advisers have "presidentialized" the system.

4. Bring only the most crucial control functions to the center and, in these areas, make especially certain to have countervailing sources of advice. Strategic planning of the mandate should be led by officials reporting directly to the Prime Minister, while senior personnel matters could conceivably by handled by a committee of the Cabinet and its officials (in Canada, by the Treasury Board and TBS). Especially in areas where countervailance is stressed, the partisan adviser should look at priorities from the standpoint of the mandate and the future of the government, while career officials should coordinate interdepartmental decision making and make certain that executive priorities and initiatives are actually being followed by departmental managers.

3

Presidential Government in France

Ezra N. Suleiman

Any chief executive elected by universal suffrage is assumed to have vast powers that emanate from the office he holds. Except during periods of national emergencies, however, rare is the case in a parliamentary regime in which the chief executive can exercise his power free of some constraint, be it political, bureaucratic, or constitutional. John Morley once said that although the British Prime Minister is only *primus inter pares*—the "keystone to the cabinet arch," as he described him—the Prime Minister's powers are always great "and in an emergency not inferior to those of a dictator."[1]

In a parliamentary democracy, where the concern of government is to deal with everyday routinized matters of politics and not with wars, the exercise of political leadership rests on the chief executive's ability to use the political or constitutional powers of office and to escape from, or circumvent, the web of constraints that surrounds his freedom of action. The extent to which he can do both determines his success or failure as a political leader.

This chapter deals with executive leadership in contemporary France, whose constitution has been interpreted by a number of analysts as an expression of the "purest" form of executive leadership in modern democratic societies. Without doubt, the 1958 Constitution of

NOTE: The author wishes to thank Valerie Rubsamen for the help she rendered as a research assistant in the preparation of certain parts of this chapter. Acknowledgment is also made of the Spanish-American Committee's support for a comparative study of bureaucracies in Europe and the United States. Some of the preliminary findings of the larger study have been used in this chapter. This chapter was written under the auspices of the Center of International Studies, Princeton University, whose support is gratefully acknowledged.

[1] Cited in Harold Wilson, *The Governance of Britain* (London: Weidenfeld and Nicolson, 1976), p. 5.

the Fifth Republic accorded the President of the Republic powers that had not been given to any chief executive of the earlier Republics. This essay endeavors to explain the *process* by which such a chief of state *exercises* his leadership. Notwithstanding the importance of the constitution, it alone cannot explain the nature of Presidential government in France. We must also consider the sources of the President's authority, the functions that he performs, the organization of his political leadership, and the context within which his political power is exercised, that is, the types of constraints that effectively check the wide-ranging powers that the constitution—and the absence of checks and balances—accords him. In short, Presidential government in France will be examined within the context of the political system.

The Character of the Fifth Republic

The drafting of the Constitution of the Fifth Republic was haunted by political squabbles that had weakened executive authority in the state. This situation was the theme of de Gaulle's Bayeux speech in 1946. Three days before agreeing to form what was to be the last government of the Fourth Republic, he explained to General Salan's deputy, who had come to see him on a mission at Colombey-les-Deux-Eglises, "I want to be summoned as an arbiter coming at the demand of the whole country, to take over direction of the country so as to spare it useless rendings. I must appear as the man of reconciliation and not as the champion of one of the factions currently confronting each other."[2] The Fourth Republic collapsed because the executive was incapable of taking decisive action in the face of an external crisis at the height of the Algerian war. Like Marshal Pétain in June 1940, General de Gaulle was called in May 1958 to take over the reins of the French government when the constituted authorities avowed their incapacity to govern the nation. "The regime failed," Philip Williams has noted, "because it was incapable of providing a government with authority."[3]

Historians and analysts of the Fourth Republic's political system have disagreed about the reasons for its collapse which has been attributed to the constitutional provisions, to the ideological divisions, to the party system, to the electoral law, and to the personal ambitions

---

[2] Alistair Horne, *A Savage War of Peace: Algeria 1954-1962* (New York: Viking Press, 1977), p. 296.

[3] Philip M. Williams, *The French Parliament: Politics in the Fifth Republic* (New York: Praeger Publishers, Inc., 1968), p. 15.

of politicians desiring to enter the government.[4] In fact, the Fourth Republic's lack of authority stemmed from the party system and from Parliament's powers over the fate of governments. Every government of the Fourth Republic was made up of a coalition of diverse political families (socialists, radicals, and liberal Catholics). Because the parties were internally divided and because every government, even when united, was often subjected to assaults by the nongovernmental forces of the extreme left and right, no government could survive a struggle with Parliament. Between 1946 and 1958, twenty-five governments were formed and of the fifteen Prime Ministers who led them only two (Henri Queuille and Guy Mollet) lasted more than a year. Parliament's powers to consume governments that had fragile foundations explain why France lacked a strong and stable executive. Vincent Wright correctly notes that "The problem of the Fourth Republic was not that it was dominated by the parties but rather that those parties which formed successive coalition governments were so internally divided and so undisciplined in their parliamentary behavior."[5]

The functioning of the party system within the kind of parliamentary regime that the Fourth Republic provided gave the regime its dominant feature: weak government. There was, to be sure, a considerable continuity in the personnel that filled the key governmental posts, but this did not alleviate the weakness of individual governments, whose expectation of staying in office beyond a few months could be fulfilled only by following a most cautious course. The expectation of governmental instability endowed every new government with a basic weakness.

The Constitution of the Fifth Republic reacted to the regime's inability to act authoritatively. The three principles that were not accepted in 1945—and that caused de Gaulle to enter twelve years of self-imposed exile at Colombey-les-Deux-Eglises—were to find

[4] For varying interpretations of the Fourth Republic, see Philip M. Williams, *Crisis and Compromise: Politics in the Fourth Republic* (New York: Doubleday, Anchor Books, 1966); Jacques Fauvet, *La France dechirée* (Paris: Fayard, 1957); Nathan Leites, *On the Game of Politics in France* (Stanford, California: Stanford University Press, 1959); Herbert Luethy, *France Against Herself* (New York: Meridian Books, 1954); Duncan MacRae, *Parliament, Parties and Society in France, 1949-1959* (New York: St. Martin's Press, 1967); Georgette Elgey, *La République des illusions, 1945-1951* (Paris: Fayard, 1965) and *La République des contradictions, 1951-1954* (Paris: Fayard, 1968); Paul-Marie de la Gorce, *Apogée et mort de la IVᵉ République* (Paris: Grasset, 1979); and Jacques Julliard, *La IVᵉ République* (Paris: Calmann-Lévy, 1968).

[5] Vincent Wright, *The Government and Politics of France* (London: Hutchinson & Co. Publishers, 1979), p. 14.

approval in 1958 with the drafting of the new constitution. Michel Debré, the main author of the 1958 constitution, has described these principles:

> For the stability and authority of the executive I used an idea that found favor later, the idea of a republican monarch. In the second place, what was needed was a genuine parliamentary system, that is, a cabinet that directs the actions of the government and the work of parliament whose activity is organized and whose will is not all-powerful. And finally, a method of election which, while ensuring as cohesive a majority as possible, permits solid cooperation between the cabinet and parliament, and thus greater government stability.[6]

In the Fourth Republic the President was elected indirectly by an electoral college. In October 1962, however, the French people approved a referendum that required the French President to be elected by universal suffrage. His mandate came from the people and his term of office neither coincided with that of Parliament nor could it be affected by Parliament. The freedom from the Assembly and from the vagaries of the party system that the constitution granted the President coincided with a transformation in France's party system. The multiparty system of the Fourth Republic gave way to a bipolarization of political divisions during the Presidencies of de Gaulle and Pompidou, which has since given way to a quadripolar structure in which the left and the right are divided into two almost equal parts. The significant point is that the new powers that the Constitution of the Fifth Republic gave the President were buttressed by a change in the party structure.[7]

The regime of the Fifth Republic has seen not only the establishment of a strong executive and a weak Parliament, but also important changes in the party system that have strengthened the authority of the President and his government. In the Fifth Republic the President has been backed by a political party controlling a majority of seats in the National Assembly. This was the case in the de Gaulle and Pompidou Presidencies, and it is the case in Giscard d'Estaing's current Presidency, even though the relative strength of the partners

---

[6] Michel Debré, "The Constitution of 1958: Its Raison d'Etre and How It Evolved," in William G. Andrews and Stanley Hoffman, eds., The Fifth Republic at Twenty (New York: State University of New York Press, forthcoming 1980).

[7] See J. R. Frears, Political Parties and Elections in the French Fifth Republic (New York: St. Martin's Press, 1977); and J. R. Frears and Jean-Luc Parodi, War Will Not Take Place: The French Parliamentary Elections of March 1978 (New York: Holmes & Meier Publishers, Inc., 1979).

that form the present majority has changed.[8] Although in the early years of the Fifth Republic the new constitution was credited with changing the French political system, it now seems clear that changes in the party system have been equally as important, if not more important than the constitutional changes, because the President has been able to form relatively cohesive governments that have been able to count on a majority in the National Assembly. As William Andrews notes, "The increased control of the executive over parliamentary legislation in the Fifth Republic, 1959–1974, resulted less from new constitutional devices than from the unanticipated emergence of a cohesive and stable parliamentary majority."[9]

Party Management. To win the office of the Presidency, a candidate needs the backing of a political party or of a coalition of parties. To facilitate the task of governing, a President needs to secure a majority in the National Assembly. To win the next elections, a President needs the support of one or more parties. All this means that no President can ignore other forces that form the majority in the Assembly. Even though he is elected for a seven-year term, he cannot consider himself free of party politics as soon as he has entered the Elysée Palace.

General de Gaulle's well-known disdain for political parties has given the mistaken impression that a President, once elected, need not care about his party or about preparing for the next (legislative) elections. Although de Gaulle's particular conception of the Presidency originally included opposition to the creation of a Gaullist party to support him, he gradually came to modify—at least in his actions— this view. He campaigned for candidates of his party in legislative and local elections and he kept abreast of developments within the Gaullist ranks. Most important, his politically loyal aides represented him in the management of what he regarded as the "low side" of politics. A President need not become personally involved in the management of his party in the way that a British Prime Minister does, but he must recognize that deep involvement, whether direct or indirect, is a prime task of his office.

---

[8] Giscard d'Estaing has always been part of the Gaullist majority, although he has never been a Gaullist. In fact, he often kept his distance from the Gaullists, as he did when he voted against the April 1969 referendum that led to de Gaulle's resignation. His own small Republican Party was needed by the Gaullists before 1974, whereas it is Giscard who now counts on the support of the much larger RPR (Rassemblement pour la République) Gaullist party.

[9] William G. Andrews, "Executive Control of Parliamentary Legislation in Gaullist France," unpublished paper, 1977, p. 1.

Both of de Gaulle's successors were astute party politicians before they were elected to the Presidency. Once elected, Georges Pompidou continued to stress his party role, and he gave considerable attention to strengthening the party behind his Presidency. Giscard d'Estaing has to pay even greater attention to party politics than did Pompidou because his support comes from a relatively unstable coalition of two wings—the Union pour la Démocratie Française (UDF), a federation of parties that supports him, and the Gaullist (RPR) party that attacks his Presidency but is obliged, for the time being, to support him. These two wings have been forced into a coalition against the left-wing opposition. Given the complex nature of the Presidential coalition as well as the number of parties involved, Giscard d'Estaing has had to devote considerable time to managing his "parties." As one of his aides put it: "The president spends a lot of time thinking about how to keep the parties in the UDF together, how to drive a wedge between the socialists and communists, and how to drive a wedge between those in the RPR who support him and those who support his enemy, Jacques Chirac." If he does not actually do all the thinking himself, his strategists and tacticians work on these goals and keep him informed; however, he makes crucial tactical decisions himself.

The nature of the parliamentary majority that Giscard d'Estaing relies on and the opposition's growing dissatisfaction with the regime mean that the President is almost always constrained by the political forces that he faces. His policies have been designed either to win over the noncommunist wing of the left (socialists and radicals) or to drive a wedge into the Gaullist camp, or to regroup the center-right and center-left parties behind him. "France must be governed at the center," Giscard often says. Nothing could infuriate the Gaullists and Communists more than seeing France "governed by the center."

The experience of all three Presidents of the Fifth Republic shows how critical has been the backing of a party (or parties) that could command a parliamentary majority. Even though de Gaulle did not want to be associated with any party, he recognized—as did Pompidou, who in contrast relished involvement in party politics—that the support of a political party would determine the success of the new presidential system. Giscard d'Estaing lacks a major party of his own, but he, too, has recognized the necessity of gathering a parliamentary majority, and he acted accordingly the moment he was elected President when he chose Chirac to be Prime Minister over Michel Poniatowski.[10] No President,

---

[10] See Robert Schneider, "Giscard-Chirac: histoire d'une rupture," *L'Express*, August 18-24, 1979, p. 78.

therefore, can afford to consider himself an "arbiter" who is "above politics."

Because a President may face not only the hostility of the opposition parties but also that of the coalition that backs him, Giscard, unlike his two predecessors, has attempted to restructure the support base of the Presidency so that it does not rest on a single political force. His conception of the kind of political support that the French Presidency needs is one of changing majorities and different alliances in Parliament formed in line with the issues that come up.

The Constitution of the Fifth Republic reversed the relative powers of the executive and legislative branches. "Under the new regime the Parliament of France, once among the most powerful in the world, became one of the weakest," [11] and the executive, once one of the weakest, now became one of the most powerful. "Parliament was diminished because the main source of policy was not the Premier, but a President who was not responsible to it." [12] As de Gaulle, the architect, if not the author, of the new constitution, explained in his press conference of September 20, 1962, which was held one month before the referendum that approved the election of the President of the Republic by universal suffrage: "The Keystone of our regime is the new institution of a president of the Republic designated by the reason and sentiment of the French people to be chief of State and leader of France. Although until recently the president was confined to the role of advisor and representative, the Constitution now places on him the outstanding responsibility for the destiny of France and of the Republic. . . . In sum, one of the essential characteristics of the Constitution of the Fifth Republic is that it provides a head for the State." The French President would no longer occupy what Sir Henry Maine, writing of Third Republic Presidents, had called a "pitiable position." [13]

Parliamentary Function. The President of France is not a member of the Assembly, and Cabinet ministers are obliged to relinquish their seats in the Assembly upon assuming their ministerial posts (article 23). The Constitution of the Fifth Republic has curtailed parliamentary power by defining the areas under Parliament's jurisdiction in such a way as to give the government considerable control over any areas

---

11 Williams, *The French Parliament*, p. 51.

12 Ibid., p. 42.

13 A. Lawrence Lowell, *Governments and Parties in Continental Europe*, 1 (Port Washington, N.Y.: Kennikat Press, 1970), p. 29. This work was first published in 1896.

in which it does not want Parliament to have legislative authority. The government controls Parliament's timetable and agenda and allows it little time to study the numerous bills that the government presents because the constitution has substantially reduced the length of parliamentary sessions. Moreover, Parliament's power over financial legislation has been reduced to such an extent that the government is able to impose the budget by ordinance—as it attempted to do in December 1979—if Parliament refuses to vote on it within a specified period.

Despite the curtailment of Parliament's powers, the President cannot ignore what goes on inside what used to be described under the Fourth Republic as "the house without windows," because he needs to find a majority in the Assembly to support the government's legislative proposals. The President has to circumvent constraints that both the majority and the opposition place in his way. Therefore, his staff keeps a close watch on party maneuvers within the chamber, as does the staff of the Prime Minister. The President seeks to obtain the greatest support on all sides of the hemicycle even if at times he has to go against part of his own coalition. For example, when Giscard d'Estaing supported Chaban-Delmas's candidacy for the Presidency of the National Assembly in 1978 while the Gaullists supported Edgar Faure, the President needed to score this victory over his reluctant supporters in order to have his "own" man as President of the Assembly. De Gaulle and Pompidou could count on loyal majorities, but Giscard has only the tenuous support of the RPR and therefore has sought to widen his majority beyond his Republican party and beyond the RPR. This clearly suggests that Presidential power is ineffective without the support of Parliament. Jean Charlot's analysis of executive-legislative relations under de Gaulle concluded that the "system is complex, but it works well as long as the Presidential and parliamentary majority coincides."[14] Of course, the President does not have to live with a hostile parliamentary majority for the duration of a legislature's term since he can dissolve Parliament and call new elections. The power of dissolution is his key weapon against a hostile parliamentary majority.

The President needs to manage successfully his relations with Parliament, however, even when the majority of its members are allies. Giscard d'Estaing, for example, learned rather bitterly that he could not use Parliament as a rubber stamp. Because the President of France may not have to convince or compromise with the legislative

---

[14] Jean Charlot, *The Gaullist Phenomenon* (London: Allen & Unwin, 1971), p. 146.

body in the way that his American counterpart is obliged to do, some observers have mistakenly concluded that he can do just about whatever he pleases when he pleases:[15]

> The Georges Pompidou Center: a billion to construct it, 130 billion to run it in 1977. Its construction, desired by the then President of the Republic, was undertaken "outside of the budget." In other words, without control. . . . The financial supervisor whose job was to regulate expenditures also received the word to keep quiet. As in the case of the *Concorde* . . . the President of the Republic said "I want." And it was done.[16]

This highly simplistic (or imperial) view of the French Presidency ignores the manifold *political* constraints to which the President of France is subject. Unlike the President of the United States, the President of France must have a majority in the National Assembly and therefore needs the support of a political party or of a majority coalition. Concessions must constantly be made to this majority. Even if, as in the present case of Giscard d'Estaing, a President attempts to escape from under the net of a political party by creating a more fluid majority in Parliament—a *majorité d'idées* as opposed to a *majorité des partis*—some type of majority that will support the government in Parliament nonetheless has to be found. As a result, many reforms are not undertaken because prior consultation reveals the lack of a majority, while some projects are presented in diluted form to make them palatable to the majority on which the President counts. Action, in other words, is often aborted, so that effective Presidential leadership remains confined to issues that have already undergone serious compromise. Consequently, the real forces of opposition in such a case are often bureaucratic and not political in nature.

What happens when the President becomes determined to ignore the political opposition among his own allies? When Giscard d'Estaing was elected President in 1974, he set about introducing a series of reforms that, as one of his advisors put it, "will change the face of this country over the next seven years." The fate of one of these projects—the reform of the capital gains tax—tells us a great deal about the political constraints that the President of France confronts.

---

[15] A number of students of French politics have used certain articles of the constitution as a way of describing the actual political process in France. Typifying this view is Henry Ehrmann's *Politics in France* (Boston: Little, Brown & Co., 3d ed., 1976), which speaks of "Presidential omnipotence" (p. 267). For a more realistic assessment of Presidential power in France, see Wright, *The Government and Politics of France*.

[16] Françoise Giroud, *La Comédie du pouvoir* (Paris: Fayard, 1977), p. 107.

On June 1, 1976 the government's bill proposing the taxation of capital gains was submitted to the National Assembly for discussion. Giscard had first suggested the institution of a capital gains tax twenty-two months earlier. The bill focused on speculative gains, but included other operations which, once inflation was accounted for, permitted a certain number of real capital gains. Its introduction to the Assembly marked the first time in many years that a fiscal reform of such magnitude was examined by the deputies. The difficulties that the bill encountered in the previous two years and the subsequent concessions made by the government foretold the troubled path it was to follow in Parliament. Before the project was introduced to the Assembly, it had been the subject of six long sessions in which the Finance Committee, headed by Maurice Papon (RPR), and the government, led by the Minister of Finance, Jean-Pierre Fourcade, attempted to render the bill more palatable to the RPR majority. In the end, the Gaullist majority succeeded in forcing Giscard to withdraw all the principal measures of the bill.

From this stunning defeat Giscard learned that (1) the President cannot count on his allies because they have their own constituencies; (2) Parliament is a political force that has to be manipulated or cajoled; and (3) the President takes serious risks when he supports a highly controversial measure.

Constitutional and Political Power of the President

The President of France is, in many respects, probably the most powerful executive in the western world. His constitutional powers are as important as those of the President of the United States, yet he does not face the same constraints on his power. He does not have to strike bargains for votes with deputies at Elysée breakfasts nor does he have to deal with unpredictable majorities in Parliament, with legislators whose base of power is separate from that of the President, with parliamentary commissions that question his policies and ask his aides and policy makers to account for their actions, with a committee system that allows deputies to accumulate the power to alter a bill beyond recognition if they do not lock it up in a drawer, with a powerful lobby group system (private groups as well as state and local governments) that acts directly on the President or indirectly through their representatives, or finally, with the institutional constraints of federalism or of a Supreme Court.

If the term "imperial presidency" can be applied with any degree of validity, one might choose to apply it to the President of France rather than to his counterpart in the United States. Not only does the President of France not face the same constraints as the President of the United States but he also has the advantage of not engaging in what appears to be a perpetual electoral campaign. He is elected for seven years, and he needs only one reelection to remain in office for almost a generation. This does not, however, spare him the political considerations that preoccupy the President of the United States the moment that he enters the White House.[17]

Although the President of France does not find himself hemmed in by the same constraints that surround the President of the United States, it does not follow that he is the prototypical "imperial" President or that he has little in common with the latter. Chief executives everywhere share the same problem in directing the vast structures of government that operate under them: How to exercise the authority and power that derive from the constitution? Upon taking office, the head of the executive branch organizes his leadership in a manner that he believes will make him an effective leader. The organization of power resources and authority will determine his success or failure in winning approval for his projects and in implementing them.

In assessing Presidential power in France we want to arrive at an understanding of the extent to which the constitutional provisions are, or are not, an accurate reflection of the power exercised by the President. The constitution enables the President to take important actions at certain times: article 16 grants him emergency powers; article 12 grants him the power to dissolve the National Assembly; and article 11 grants him the power to bypass Parliament and to submit certain important issues to a referendum. These prerogative powers, which can be used only in times of national crisis, allow the President to take decisive steps when an emergency arises. These provisions therefore reflect a breakdown in the way things are "normally" done. The decision to bypass Parliament and to submit an issue to the people would have to be the result of a serious rift in executive-legislative relations,[18] just as dissolution of the National Assembly would have to be the result of a grave political crisis.[19] Constitutional provisions

---

[17] For a comparison of the powers of and constraints on the Presidencies in the United States and France, see Ezra N. Suleiman, "The Chief Executive in the U.S. and France," paper prepared for delivery at the conference on L'Administration et la Politique en France, held at the Fondation Nationale des Sciences Politiques, Paris, November 30-December 1, 1979.

[18] Jean-Luc Parodi, Les Rapports entre le Législatif et l'Exécutif sous la Ve République (Paris: Presses de la Fondation Nationale des Sciences Politiques, 1972).

[19] De Gaulle dissolved the National Assembly during the crisis of May 1968.

that grant the President extensive powers are generally used when other efforts have failed to control or shape events. These provisions may be decisive at critical moments, but they have no bearing on the everyday conduct of Presidential authority. What does influence everyday conduct is the way in which the President organizes his power so as to reduce the constraints on his activities.

This applies to the Presidents of France and the United States as well as to the Prime Minister of Great Britain. But where the President of the United States is constrained by the checks and balances of institutions the President of France is constrained by a political check on the exercise of his leadership. Although constitutional provisions and the bureaucratic structure in France work in the President's favor more so than in other countries, the realities of the political system limit what might otherwise have become an "imperial" Presidency.

Whatever other role the constitution has assigned the President as "the protector of national independence, of territorial integrity," and as the official responsible for seeing that "the Constitution is respected" and for ensuring "the continuity of the State" (article 5), he nonetheless plays a vital role in the politics (both low and high) of the nation. The President, as Vincent Wright notes, has three major political roles: "He is the general spokesman of the Government and its principal pedagogue; secondly, he is the guardian of the unity of the coalition that supports him; finally, he is the coalition's principal electoral guide and agent."[20]

All the Presidents of the Fifth Republic have seen themselves as heads of the executive. Pompidou and Giscard recognized or accepted more readily than de Gaulle did that being the head of the executive is a partisan role and that therefore the President is a political figure who must use political and electoral means to escape the constraints that surround him.

Presidential Image. Despite his deep interest in party politics, the President must give the impression that he stands above petty quibbling, that he in fact arbitrates conflicts rather than participates in them. De Gaulle probably orchestrated this image of the Presidency more fully than anyone else could. In his press conferences, television interviews, speeches, and the manner he adopted, he projected himself as a President who was not in the least concerned with or involved in political conflicts.

Giscard d'Estaing has recognized that projecting a Presidential image does not conflict with a keen interest in party conflicts. To the

[20] Wright, *The Government and Politics of France*, p. 32.

extent that the two roles are an indispensable part of a President's function, they are complementary. Giscard's speeches are calculated to project the image of a President who looks after the French people and the French state *and* who at the same time is perfectly capable of engaging in conflicts. As one of Giscard's political advisors put it:

> This makes him seem human, and so he is able to strike a chord in the French people because he has the demeanor of a president while being, if you will, capable of being petty like them. . . . He has actually improved on de Gaulle's method because whereas de Gaulle was really a sort of unbelievable character, someone who was regarded as something of a caricature, Giscard is both "above it all" and human. People perceive this and they can identify with him more easily.

The ways in which a President presents himself to the people, to the coalition of parties that supports him, and to the media, can help him to exert influence on others. This projected image is, in short, a weapon in the exercise of his political power. If he is not perceived to be in command, he is likely to lose support and allies.

President and Prime Minister

The President sits at the top of the political structure in France. He is not *primus inter pares*. He is elected by popular vote and has the constitutional authority (article 8) to name the Prime Minister, and on the recommendations of the latter, to name the ministers of the various departments. The constitution, however, accords the Prime Minister considerable powers. Article 20 states that "The Government shall determine and direct the policy of the nation," and article 21 adds that "The Prime Minister shall direct the operation of the Government." It happens that no Prime Minister in the Fifth Republic has sought to challenge the primacy of the President by challenging the President's reading of the constitution because the Presidents who have so far held office have belonged to the same political coalition controlling a majority of the seats in the National Assembly. A left-wing majority in the National Assembly would probably lead the President to call a Prime Minister from the left to form a government. A Prime Minister from that quarter would likely take a different view of articles 20 and 21 of the constitution. For the time being, we can accept Charles Debbasch's description of the authoritative position of the President in relation to the "other" arms of the executive: "Thus, the Prime Minister is not the head of a political group capable of opposing the Chief of State. He is hierarchically subordinated to the

President. Although the Constitution designates the Prime Minister as the leader of political affairs for the nation, his role has been narrowly subordinated to the Chief of State under the Fifth Republic."[21]

The preeminence of the President in the French political system, both constitutionally and in practice, has given rise to considerable debate, but the fact that the President is the pivot of the political system can scarcely be questioned. The typical view of the President's position was expressed in a recent survey on France conducted by *The Economist*:

> Theoretically, the French power structure lies somewhere between the British parliamentary system and the American presidential system. In practice, given a beholden assembly, the Elysée Palace can outdo the White House for power and patronage. . . . The President is a republican monarch. He makes policy in every sphere, domestic and foreign, and makes sure it is carried out by a government he names. He can send his prime minister packing at will. Mr. Raymond Barre, the current premier, has made a name for himself as "Monsieur Economy" but when the time comes for him to go, his stature will sink. There are a lot of old prime ministers in France. On top of that the president runs cabinet meetings, can call referendums, dissolve parliament and rule by emergency decree. The senior members of his palace guard may not outrank but they can certainly outflank cabinet ministers.[22]

Like most analyses of executive power in France, the one expressed in *The Economist*, while broadly correct confuses "political" and "prerogative" power. Although it is true that the President names and can fire the Prime Minister, and that he dominates Cabinet meetings and sets the tone for the kinds of policies that he wishes to see initiated, he cannot afford to quarrel continually with his Prime Ministers and to keep changing them. His authority depends on durable governments that can govern, or that at least seem to be governing.

In theory, the government that the President names is a collegial institution acting as a collective unit. In reality, it is nothing of the sort. In the Chirac government[23] formed in May 1974 after Giscard's

[21] Charles Debbasch, *La France de Pompidou* (Paris: Presses Universitaires de France, 1974), p. 38.

[22] "Outdoing the White House," *The Economist*, January 27, 1979.

[23] The term "government" is used in the more limited sense to refer to a Cabinet. I have avoided using the American designation of Administration because the French use "Administration" to refer to the bureaucracy and not to a Cabinet.

election to the Presidency, several members were scarcely on speaking terms with one another. After the government had been in power for a year, serious divisions having to do with internal policies became evident. It was the Prime Minister's task to contain the differences that had arisen among the ministers.[24] Collegiality in the government has a symbolic importance in parliamentary democracies, for it indicates that the nation's affairs are being well conducted. In reality, however, it is either nonexistent or, where it exists, it is probably unimportant since the head of the government is likely to run the show.[25]

In France, constitutional arrangements have created a dual executive: a President elected by popular vote and a Prime Minister responsible to Parliament. The choice of a Prime Minister and the installation of a government are important elements in the way that a President organizes his power. The President and the Prime Minister have one thing in common: both are free from departmental interests. What, then, explains the relatively unsuccessful relations that developed between the three Presidents of the Fifth Republic and their Prime Ministers? To answer this question we must first understand how Presidents choose their Prime Ministers.

In choosing a Prime Minister, the President raises the appointee's political status. He expects loyalty from his Prime Minister, loyalty both to his policies and to him personally. Although a Prime Minister can use his office to challenge the authority of the man who appointed him, he is certainly expected to resist the temptation. If he does not, then the President removes him forthwith: de Gaulle removed Pompidou for engineering the astounding success of the UDR (Union des Démocrates pour la République) in the legislative elections of June 1968; Pompidou removed Chaban-Delmas after the latter had made his "liberal" speech attacking the rigidities of French society in the National Assembly; and Giscard removed Chirac for repeatedly disagreeing with the President on a number of issues. In each case the President sensed that his authority, or primacy, was being challenged by his Prime Minister. Each President responded in the same way: by first disavowing and then removing his Prime Minister. This response is perhaps best illustrated by the incident that occurred while de Gaulle was President and Pompidou was his

---

[24] See André Passeron, "Le 'Patchwork' Ministériel," *Le Monde*, May 29, 1975.

[25] For the manner in which Cabinet meetings are usually run in France, see Françoise Giroud, *La Comédie du pouvoir*; Philippe Alexandre, *Le Duel De Gaulle-Pompidou* (Paris: Grasset, 1970); Pierre Viansson-Ponté, *Les Gaullistes* (Paris: Editions du Seuil, 1963).

Prime Minister: In the heat of the events of May 1968, de Gaulle considered holding a referendum. Pompidou dissuaded him by telling him, "If you lose the referendum, *mon général*, the regime is lost. If I lose the elections, I will be the only one to have lost them." De Gaulle replied: "Yes, but what if you win the elections?"[26] As it turned out, Pompidou did win the elections, was ousted from the Premiership and became even more of a threat to de Gaulle *after* his ouster.

The relationship between the President and the Prime Minister has built-in structural difficulties, for even though all the actors acknowledge the primacy of the President, members of the government consider the executive to be composed of two teams: the President's and the Prime Minister's. The Prime Minister may believe that his authority is undermined when he no longer controls his ministers. This is how Chirac explained to the ministers of his government his reasons for resigning:

> Against the wishes of most of my friends, I supported Valéry Giscard d'Estaing twenty-four months ago because he was the only one capable of preventing a communist victory. For the past twenty-four months I have repeatedly requested the necessary means to confront what I have considered a difficult situation. I continue to believe that according to our Constitution the Prime Minister must have authority over the ministers of the Government, and possess a certain autonomy. I was not granted the means nor the liberty that I requested.
>
> The Prime Minister should not judge the actions and decisions of the Chief of State. Several among you have complicated my task. Weakening governmental cohesion with their statements, they have weakened the majority.[27]

In fact, the Elysée did all it could to undermine Chirac's control over the government. Even Françoise Giroud, who served in the Chirac government and who harbors no sympathy for the former Prime Minister, notes that when the Prime Minister's power to arbitrate between the minister of finance and other ministers over budgetary disagreements was transferred to the Elysée for the 1975 budget, the Prime Minister "lost the little personal power that he used to have over his ministers and the appearance of his preeminence over the minister of Finance."[28] If the Elysée sought to undermine the actions

---

[26] Alexandre, *Le Duel De Gaulle-Pompidou*, p. 259.

[27] Giroud, *La Comédie du pouvoir*, pp. 234-35.

[28] Ibid., p. 48.

of Chirac, it was because his actions did not conform to what the President wanted his Prime Minister to do. A President cannot govern effectively if he is locked in conflict with those who are ostensibly governing in his name. Hence, a conflict between a President and a Prime Minister always leads to the removal of the Prime Minister.

The case of Chaban-Delmas is not different from that of Chirac or even of Pompidou. Chirac believed that the Prime Minister should have "a certain autonomy" from Presidential power, and Pompidou secured a strong political base in Parliament. Both posed a challenge to Presidential authority and both were removed. Chaban-Delmas, who was removed shortly after he had secured an independent base for himself, not only made a famous speech in the National Assembly (on September 16, 1969), against the "société bloquée" without receiving the accord of the Elysée, but also issued policy directions that were clearly out of line with those of President Pompidou.[29] His appointment of "liberals" like Simon Nora, Pierre Desgraupes, and Jacques Delors was resented by Pompidou's key advisors.[30] Indeed, Chaban-Delmas claims that his ouster from Matignon, the office of the Prime Minister, was caused by Pierre Juillet, who together with Marie-France Garaud, were Pompidou's most influential advisors and who strongly influenced Jacques Chirac subsequently, both while he was Prime Minister and after his departure from Matignon.[31] The Elysée resented Chaban-Delmas's attempt to obtain a massive vote of confidence in Parliament in support of his policies. "It was when he was massively given the confidence of the Assembly, that he was broken."[32]

The President of the Republic tries to choose a Prime Minister whom he can trust and who will be loyal. Yet, as the examples show, that relationship is likely to become conflictive. Before being named Prime Minister in 1962, Pompidou often visited the Elysée, occasionally to inform de Gaulle of what the business and financial community was saying and thinking. So close were the two men that Pompidou's name seldom appeared on the list of persons having an official audience with the General.[33] Later, this intimacy disappeared:

> As soon as Pompidou was named Prime Minister, his relations with the General changed. Before, he would come to

---

[29] See Pierre Rouanet, Le Cas Chaban (Paris: Robert Laffont, 1974), and Pompidou (Paris: Grasset, 1969).

[30] See J. Bunel and Paul Meunier, Chaban-Delmas (Paris: Stock, 1972), pp. 203-13.

[31] Jacques Chaban-Delmas, L'Ardeur (Paris: Stock, 1976).

[32] Giroud, La Comédie du pouvoir, p. 46.

[33] Alexandre, Le Duel De Gaulle-Pompidou, pp. 86-87.

the Elysée once a month, having nothing to request or to say. With his visitor, de Gaulle could abandon himself to personal confidences and jokes about a minister. Being with a free man, he expressed himself freely.

Now, Pompidou was part of the State. Nor was his a minor post. Whatever his mood, the General had to meet four times a week with the Prime Minister. All these meetings, however, no longer allowed for philosophical discussions; they concerned the daily tasks of the government.[34]

The change that occurred in the de Gaulle–Pompidou relationship indicates that structural constraints exist in any President–Prime Minister relationship. One of de Gaulle's close advisors aptly described that change: "Between them there exists now only a 'functional' relationship. The President of the Republic has his domain, the Prime Minister has his. The border between them is well established."[35] Of course, the President will always try to choose someone who can be expected to remain subordinate, but this rule is not always followed. As Giscard d'Estaing explains: "When I took office, several political friends came to warn me, saying: We advise you not to nominate Mr. Chirac as Prime Minister. And I had the wisdom not to follow their advice."[36] And Françoise Giroud adds: "One does not give a sword to the man who made you king."[37]

Whether or not the President delegates considerable authority to his Prime Minister, in the final analysis he regards the Prime Minister as the executor of his own policies. De Gaulle, having just shouldered responsibility for all the major decisions in the Algerian crisis, said with a straight face to one of his collaborators: "What is a Prime Minister, if not the *directeur de cabinet* of the President of the Republic?"[38] Although de Gaulle's remark about the President's relationship to the Prime Minister is somewhat blunt and exaggerated —for a Prime Minister is able to take considerable initiative on his own if that initiative is approved, or at least not disapproved, by the President—his point is that the Prime Minister cannot act against the wishes of the President.

The relationship between the President and the Prime Minister cannot be analyzed merely in terms of personalities and ambitions,

---

[34] Ibid., p. 111.

[35] Ibid. One should add that the "border" was well established because Pompidou accepted the supremacy of the President.

[36] Giroud, *La Comédie du pouvoir*, p. 41.

[37] Ibid.

[38] Alexandre, *Le Duel De Gaulle-Pompidou*, p. 103.

even though personal ambitions do play a role if only because the elevation to high office itself nurtures ambitions. Neither Chaban-Delmas nor Chirac ever made any secret of their ambition to become President. The same was true of Pompidou, who asserted, "From the moment I arrived at Matignon, I knew that I would be President of the Republic. I prepared myself for it."[39] What other office can one aspire to after having been Prime Minister? As Pompidou put it: "Now I understand the tragedy that my predecessor Michel Debré experienced. When one has stayed a long time here in this post, with all its responsibilities, what is there left to do? It's impossible to go back to being a simple minister."[40] If a Prime Minister aspires to succeed to the highest office, that ambition may be ascribed to human nature and does not assume importance unless the Prime Minister loses sight of his function—that is, to serve at the will of the President.

> The conclusion is clear: the President of the Republic is the real head of the Government even though a necessary division of labor grants the Prime Minister certain "frontline" tasks such as responding to parliamentary criticism and coordinating the work of the different ministerial departments. To repeat once again, there is no diarchy.[41]

President–Prime Minister–Government

The complexity of the relationship between the President of the Republic and the Prime Minister is exacerbated by the ambiguity of the relationship between the government and its two superior chiefs. The experience of the three Presidents of the Fifth Republic suggests that, whatever the constitution says, the President has the final say in the choice of ministers. Françoise Giroud, recounting how she came to be chosen as a minister in the Chirac government of 1974, refers to the theory according to which the Prime Minister chooses the ministers as just one more farce.[42] Chirac, like Chaban-Delmas when the latter was asked by Pompidou "to present proposals with a view to forming a government,"[43] knew that the President can accept or reject suggestions, just as he can choose particular men or women for particular posts.

---

[39] Ibid., p. 110.

[40] Ibid., p. 24.

[41] Jean Massot, *La Présidence de la République en France* (Paris: La Documentation Française, 1977), p. 123.

[42] Giroud, *La Comédie du pouvoir*, p. 64.

[43] Jack Hayward, *The One and Indivisible French Republic* (London: Weidenfeld and Nicolson, 1973), p. 93.

If the President is able to form precisely the sort of Cabinet that he seeks, it does not follow that this body becomes a deliberative or even an advisory group. Rarely has it been a body that actually makes decisions: "The room where, every Wednesday morning, the Council of Ministers meets is one of the privileged places where the 'comédie du pouvoir' takes place."[44] Françoise Giroud maintains that no proposal made to the Council of Ministers is ever rejected, although occasionally the President objects. Since the important decisions have all been made, or will be made independently of the Council of Ministers, the Cabinet meetings are, according to Giroud, without much significance. The procedure of collective decision making is observed as it was even under de Gaulle's Presidency.[45]

Whether under the Fifth Republic there has in fact developed what Chaban-Delmas referred to as the President's "domaine reservé" (foreign and defense matters) is doubtful in light of what we now know about the extent of involvement in domestic matters of all three Presidents. Certainly de Gaulle was more interested in foreign than in domestic matters. Even his coming to power in 1958 was the result of a major crisis beyond France's borders, and all the crucial decisions he made during his first years in office were in the realm of foreign affairs. It is a mistake to conclude from this, as most analysts of de Gaulle's Presidency have, that he was uninterested in economic, administrative, and other matters touching on domestic policy.[46] He was, to be sure, selectively interested in domestic issues and he saw himself as being responsible for all of the government's actions. As one of his advisors noted, "The General considers himself the chief of the executive, assisted by the Prime Minister whom he chooses to direct the actions of the government and of the administration in his name."[47] De Gaulle, in fact, was perceived by politicians to dominate the executive in all spheres. Before naming Pompidou as his Prime Minister, he had this revealing conversation with Guy Mollet:

De Gaulle: Pompidou has always been faithful to me. Of course he was at the Banque Rothschild, but I believe him capable of establishing good relations with the members of

---

[44] Giroud, *La Comédie du pouvoir*, p. 25.

[45] Alexander Werth, *De Gaulle: A Political Biography* (New York: Simon and Schuster, 1965), pp. 361-62.

[46] See the book written by de Gaulle's former collaborators, *De Gaulle et le service de l'Etat* (Paris: Plon, 1977). See also the contributions to Gilbert Pilleul, ed., *"L'Entourage" et De Gaulle* (Paris: Plon, 1979).

[47] Jacques Boitreaud, "L'Exercise de l'autorité," in *De Gaulle et le service de l'Etat*, p. 81.

Parliament. You know very well that Debré cannot work with a Parliament.

Mollet: You are constituting a de Gaulle government, with your "directeur de cabinet" responsible for relations with other ministers. Pompidou will be nothing but your intermediary. Already you have become your own Minister of Foreign Affairs. . . .

De Gaulle: But look! Everything is decided in the Council of Ministers. My role is simply to provide the necessary orientation. That is my role.[48]

De Gaulle's involvement in foreign and domestic affairs can be seen from the use he made of Interministerial Councils (*conseils restreints*): "De Gaulle gathers together the main figures and high-ranking officials to study all important business which can't be handled at the lower levels."[49] Initiated by de Gaulle to circumvent Debré during the Algerian Putsch, the *conseils restreints* became the primary focus of policy making within the executive, and the range of activities that they covered continued to expand; in 1966 and 1967, for example, *conseils restreints* were held on international monetary problems, economic and financial matters, key industries, administrative organization of the Paris region, reform of the police, social security, and European agricultural prices.[50] Consequently, noted Pierre Avril:

There is no longer a "private preserve," as the expression would imply that the President left other matters to the Government: he now takes it upon himself to handle everything, from the reorganization of the Paris area to color television or Common Market agricultural policy. The result is a presidential cabinet in which the Prime Minister, to quote a prominent Gaullist, the jurist René Capitant, serves only as a sort of "civilian staff officer" for the President.[51]

Jacques Chirac's definition of the respective roles within the executive is not an unrealistic one: "Une orientation est donnée par le président. Une volonté politique existe au Gouvernement. Une mise au point

---

[48] Cited in Alexandre, *Le Duel De Gaulle-Pompidou*, pp. 103-104. After recounting this conversation, Alexandre adds that unrelentingly de Gaulle would repeat to all those he came in contact with, "Il faut une tête á l'état." (p. 104).

[49] Pierre Avril, *Politics in France* (Middlesex, England: Penguin Books, 1969), p. 114.

[50] Etienne Burin Des Roziers, "Relations de travail avec le premier ministre," in *De Gaulle et le service de l'Etat*, p. 360.

[51] Avril, *Politics in France*, p. 114.

technique est effectuée par les ministres."[52] Yet, the "orientation" of the President may differ from the *volonté* of the government, or, at any rate, of the Prime Minister. When this occurs a clash develops. The *conseils restreints* are an element in this clash, for the Elysée uses them to go its way and the Prime Minister seeks to go his way with the creation of Interministerial Committees. While de Gaulle was holding his numerous *conseils restreints* at the Elysée,

> At Matignon, Pompidou gathered certain colleagues together in the form of an Interministerial Committee just about every other day. The questions they dealt with were so diverse that it would be a vain attempt to enumerate them here. It is interesting to note, however, that the matters treated under the direction of the Prime Minister, independently of particular problems which his cabinet handled in collaboration with individual ministers, overlapped more often than not with questions that de Gaulle had at some point raised with him. During the period under consideration, the relations between the President of the Republic and the Prime Minister assumed the form of a cooperative effort rather than a separation of tasks.[53]

It is possible to draw a different conclusion from this description of Interministerial Committees presided over by the Prime Minister and of *conseils restreints* presided over by the President at the Elysée on the same matter—namely, conflict over a particular policy question. Why, otherwise, should there be two sets of meetings, each of which may come up with different decisions? Is this work *en commun?*

Under the Presidency of Giscard d'Estaing, the holding of separate meetings in the Elysée and at Matignon was a clear sign of a conflict. One close advisor to Giscard noted that when Chirac was Prime Minister, "he was always up to something. The tip-off would be when he called meetings at Matignon. I would find out what was going on and I would usually tell the President that he should hold a *conseil restreint* at the Elysée on the same matter." When this occurred, it merely indicated that the President and the Prime Minister were not working in harmony. This same Presidential advisor also noted that "we were spending a good part of our time in the Elysée holding these *conseils restreints* and, frankly, we were often openly at war with the Prime Minister's staff." Indicating the changed climate that has come about between the President and his second Prime

---

[52] Giroud, *La Comédie du pouvoir*, p. 97.
[53] Etienne Burin Des Roziers, "Relations de travail avec le premier ministre," p. 361.

Minister, Raymond Barre, the Elysée official noted that, "with Barre things are altogether different and it's rare that there is a *conseil* and a *comité* on the same subject. The President doesn't distrust Barre; he doesn't feel that Barre is always plotting to go against his wishes, which is how he felt with Chirac; so we no longer waste our time holding *conseils* merely for the purpose of using them as a weapon against the prime minister."

The conflict between Giscard and Chirac was immediately mirrored in a conflict between their respective teams. Several of Giscard's advisors echoed one who said, "My interlocutor at Matignon was my enemy. There was simply no way for any meaningful collaboration to take place." Conflict between the President and his Prime Minister has several consequences: it undermines the coordination process; it disrupts the policy-making process; and it weakens the authority of the President.

When the President and his Prime Minister are locked in conflict, the normal day-to-day work of ministerial departments goes on, as it did in the United States at the height of the Watergate scandal.[54] The coordinating mechanisms between different departments, difficult enough in the best of circumstances, break down. Under these conditions the absence of political leadership is felt most strongly. The President attempts to circumvent his Prime Minister by having direct contact with the ministers, whereas the Prime Minister, who views himself as the head of the government, seeks to maintain his authority over the ministers. The ministers respond to one or the other but try to appear loyal to both. The former head of de Gaulle's Elysée staff observed how easily a conflictive situation can arise:

> Effectively fulfilling the role of head of the government, General de Gaulle maintained direct, prolonged and regular relations with each of his ministers. His cabinet was open to them at all times. He asked his staff to arrange his appointments in such a way that each head of a ministry could periodically inform him of the state of affairs within his purview. This systematic practice ran the risk of establishing an appeal process from Matignon to the Elysée, and the Prime Minister might have considered it an affront if the General, steeped in the sense of hierarchy, had not kept him abreast of the exchange of viewpoints he had with the other members of the government.[55]

---

[54] Hugh Heclo, *A Government of Strangers: Executive Politics in Washington* (Washington, D.C.: The Brookings Institution, 1977), pp. 8-9.

[55] Etienne Burin Des Roziers, "Relations de travail avec le premier ministre," p. 356.

This picture of de Gaulle's working methods is probably incomplete and exaggerates the openness of his relations with the members of government. "In every case, the General wants to make clear that the responsibility for action, for direction, and for the government belongs to him."[56] On several occasions de Gaulle took decisions of which he informed his Prime Minister only after having first informed other ministers. Citing one such case, when de Gaulle refused to stay General Jouhaud's execution, Philippe Alexandre records, "At Matignon, Pompidou was reliving Debré's nightmare. To Christian Fouchet, who came to see him, he said: 'The General treated me atrociously. I can't accept this. I offered him my resignation.'"[57]

When Pompidou became President of the Republic, his view of the Presidency scarcely differed from de Gaulle's. "The fundamental difference between the Fourth Republic and the Fifth," Pompidou declared in 1972, "is that the government no longer depends on the National Assembly and the agreements or disagreements between groups, but on the President of the Republic who appoints the Prime Minister and the members of the government."[58] Pompidou, in effect, acted as the head of the government, exercising control over the ministers and, like de Gaulle, circumventing the Prime Minister.[59]

Whereas de Gaulle's position as President had been strengthened by the historical role he had played earlier, Pompidou's Presidency found security in his personal control of affairs: "From the moment he entered the Elysée, Georges Pompidou acted differently from de Gaulle. He was intent on reserving for himself the possibility of intervening in every domaine."[60] His distrust of his Prime Minister was even greater than de Gaulle's had been.[61]

A President's mistrust and suspicion of a Prime Minister may lead him to bypass the Prime Minister and to exercise authority directly over the ministers. Chirac, Chaban-Delmas, and Pompidou all had this experience and were resentful of it when they became Prime Ministers. It is perhaps not surprising that when Pompidou became President he relied heavily on a few key advisors who were adroit in bypassing the Prime Minister.[62] When Messmer was named

---

[56] Alexandre, *Le Duel De Gaulle-Pompidou*, p. 115.

[57] Ibid., p. 122.

[58] Debbasch, *La France de Pompidou*, pp. 39-40.

[59] Ibid., p. 40.

[60] Gilles Martinet, *Le Système Pompidou* (Paris: Editions du Seuil, 1973), p. 89.

[61] Pierre Rouanet, *Le Cas Chaban*, p. 243.

[62] Martinet, *Le Système Pompidou*, p. 90.

by Pompidou to replace Chaban-Delmas, he was not allowed to choose any ministers or even his principal collaborators.[63]

Despite the Prime Minister's wholly subservient position, now and then a serious disagreement over policy direction separates the Prime Minister and the President. Pompidou who did not fully trust Chaban-Delmas found Chaban's "blocked society" speech to be totally out of line with his own image of France. Yet when he had been Prime Minister, Pompidou disagreed openly with de Gaulle. In the last meeting (before the dissolution of the National Assembly) of the Council of Ministers in April 1968, the ministers present witnessed what Alexandre refers to as "an astonishing scene."[64] De Gaulle began to speak of the social reforms to which he had always attached great importance.[65]

> Then, Pompidou spoke. But instead of merely bristling, he clearly affirmed his opposition to all these grandiose dreams. He spoke as the man responsible for the well-being of France, for internal peace, and for the treasury. It was the first time that he dared to be in disagreement with the General, and to express his disagreement in front of witnesses. For political and strategic reasons, the Prime Minister was no longer afraid to affirm, on this occasion, his differences with de Gaulle. Indirectly, he even boasted of it in front of some of his confidants.[66]

The conflicts between Presidents de Gaulle, Pompidou, and Giscard d'Estaing and their Prime Ministers can be related to the structural characteristics of a twin-executive: the Prime Minister's need to define a sphere of authority; disagreements over policies; the President's need to have full and uncontested authority over the government. The rare cases of a smooth relationship between the President and the Prime Minister—for example, between de Gaulle and Couve de Murville, and between Pompidou and Messmer—can be attributed to the Prime Minister's willingness to accept the view that authority resides in the Elysée. When Couve de Murville, who had been minister of foreign affairs for ten years, became Prime Minister, he accepted as Premier what he had taken for granted at the Ministry of Foreign

---

[63] See Ezra N. Suleiman, *Politics, Power, and Bureaucracy in France* (Princeton: Princeton University Press, 1974), p. 360.

[64] Alexandre, *Le Duel De Gaulle-Pompidou*, p. 231.

[65] "Capitalism must be condemned," said de Gaulle. "Totalitarian communism must be condemned. We must find a new way: participation." Alexandre, *Le Duel De Gaulle-Pompidou*, p. 229.

[66] Ibid., p. 231.

Affairs—namely, that instructions, policies, and initiatives came from the Elysée.

Regardless of individual circumstances, however, the President must find a *modus vivendi* with his Prime Minister if he hopes to exercise any measure of authority. If he has to devote himself to establishing his political and constitutional superiority, he will be consumed by his battles. If he has to resort to the ultimate power of dismissal too often, he can consider that he has failed.[67] If he delegates considerable authority to his Prime Minister, he runs the risk of losing control over the administrative structures that govern in his name. If he delegates too little authority, the Prime Minister will feel constrained and may try to break out of his confining situation.

In the relationship between President Giscard d'Estaing and Prime Minister Raymond Barre, the President has managed to maintain his predominance over the Prime Minister while allowing him a considerable measure of responsibility. One advisor to Giscard explained the difference between Barre's and Chirac's relationship to the President in this way:

> When Chirac was Prime Minister, everything had to come from the President. In fact, for most of the time Chirac showed no initiative at all. I know that this doesn't square with his combative image, but he actually accepted the fact that he was a simple executor. But between taking no initiatives, that is, proposing no reforms, and being a faithful executor of presidential policies, there is a long road. Barre, on the other hand has been a faithful Prime Minister. But that doesn't mean that he is a weak Prime Minister. The President has delegated much more responsibility and authority to him than he ever delegated to Chirac.

The Giscard-Barre relationship is different in that the President has preserved his authoritative position even though he has granted Barre a certain autonomy. One of Giscard's aides noted:

> Curiously enough, Barre has much more power than Chirac had. With Chirac, the President's advisers used to give orders and then they spent most of their time seeing to it that the orders were carried out or that they weren't being twisted. In Barre's case, the President has simply given him considerable leeway so that the president's advisers have

---

[67] See Richard E. Neustadt, *Presidential Power* (New York: The New American Library, 1964), pp. 15-21.

to negotiate with the Prime Minister's staff. We can't just give orders now.

Another advisor has observed:

The President is aware that it is only in avoiding conflicts with his Prime Minister that things get done. He actually increases his power when he avoids conflicts. This also means that when the Prime Minister is absolutely determined about something, the President does everything to avoid a conflict, which means that he will give in.

Knowing that the President might give in, the Prime Minister and his staff have found that on many issues, they have considerable room for negotiation. One of Barre's aides noted that:

When the Prime Minister is really convinced about something, he is very stubborn and he communicates this to the President. Of course, he knows how to pick his fights with the Elysée, so when he does pick a fight, the Elysée knows that he is serious. He doesn't go out on a limb for anything. He also knows when the President will not give in on an issue, so his own stubborness is tempered by a keen political instinct.

The stage was set for the Giscard-Barre relationship when Giscard first asked Barre to form a government. At that time Giscard was looking for a way to save his long-time friend, Michel Poniatowski, the minister of interior. Although he was quite willing to sacrifice Olivier Guichard (the Gaullist) and Lecanuet (the Centrist), he wanted to find a way to keep Poniatowski in the government. Barre refused to accept Poniatowski in the government and remained adamant. Giscard was forced to give in.

If a dual-executive form of government imposes such constraints on the exercise of Presidential power, why then does a President need a Prime Minister at all? Whether a President needs or does not need a Prime Minister is no longer questioned, for the dual executive system is now an accepted, and unchallenged, part of France's constitution. As a result, Presidents have come to accept the constraints that this system creates for them. The constitution provided two offices because it attempted, as Wright notes, "to fuse two ultimately incompatible notions: on the one hand, the separation of powers with a strong Head of State (which smacked of presidentialism) and on the other, the principle of governmental responsibility to Parliament (which implied a parliamentary regime)."[68] As Presidents have dis-

---

[68] Wright, *The Government and Politics of France*, p. 23.

covered, however, there are also certain functional advantages to the dual executive system.[69]

The President chose Barre to be his Prime Minister in 1976 in the hope that Barre could solve France's economic crisis, and he has allowed Barre to take the measures deemed necessary. At present France has serious economic problems—high unemployment, inflation, declining industries aggravating regional problems—and the Prime Minister has been given a mandate to solve them. Because national elections will not take place before 1981, the Prime Minister has been allowed to initiate whatever measures he considers to be necessary.

The present Prime Minister thus has approximately two years to solve France's economic problems. Giscard has chosen to stress his concern with France and the world in the year 2000 and has left it to his Prime Minister to deal with the current economic crisis. In so doing, Giscard minimizes the chances of losing face: he reinforces his "Presidential" image; he takes the credit for any substantial improvement in the economy; and, finally, he can sacrifice his Prime Minister if the government's economic policies aggravate the crisis. The dual executive system, therefore, has the advantage of shielding a President from trouble.

The President's Staff

A President cannot organize his political leadership without the help of a committed staff. The Prime Minister and the ministers are, in one sense, part of a different "staff." Since the individual ministers represent bureaucratic agencies, the President has to rely heavily on an inner circle of advisors who are free from departmental interests but who have, as much as possible, interests similar to his own.[70]

In principle, the President of France and the President of the United States have a similar problem: how to direct and control their respective bureaucratic structures. The means at their disposal differ.[71]

The Selection Process. Although every newly elected American President who enters the White House says that he will appoint the best people to fill the top positions, there is really no system for selecting the best people. In France, however, the selection of administrators

---

[69] I am indebted to Richard Neustadt for pointing this out to me.

[70] Neustadt, *Presidential Power*, p. 21.

[71] Heclo's discussion, in *A Government of Strangers*, of an American President's problems in controlling the federal bureaucracy has been suggestive for this discussion.

has long been facilitated by the existence of a pool of recruits to which all chief executives and political leaders turn. In supporting the pool, the state has created its own elite, and in subsidizing the political careers of the members of its administrative elite, it guarantees itself the service of a highly trained, loyal, and competent group of officials.[72]

The politico-administrative system functions to the advantage of both the executive branch and of a small group of highly successful civil servants. The Ecole Nationale d'Administration (ENA), like the Ecole Polytechnique, has become a school for identifying and certifying an elite rather than a school for training the state's future administrators.[73] As François Bloch-Lainé put it: ENA "is a machine for mixing and ranking. It is hardly a machine for teaching."[74] More so than in the past, those who gain admission to ENA consider it to be the gateway to a political career. There is little doubt that, as a stepping stone to politics, it offers distinct advantages over the "apprenticeship" career pattern of the Third Republic, which was a slow climb up the political ladder from local office and local party service to national office.

Foremost among ENA's advantages is the rapid advancement of the graduates to offices such as a mayorship, a seat in the National Assembly, or a ministerial portfolio, for these political heights are attainable without spending many years developing a constituency in the provinces. Instead, the political career pattern is gradually becoming reversed: success at the national level (for example, becoming a minister or secretary of state) leads to success at the local level, whereas prior to the Fifth Republic, a political career progressed from the local to the national level. The civil servant who wishes to take his chances in the political arena does not even have to contend with the elements of insecurity normally associated with a political career, because he is free to return to his administrative corps at any time without penalty. It is not surprising, therefore, to find that 20.9 percent of the deputies currently holding seats in the National Assembly are civil servants and of this number half are members of

---

[72] The discussion that follows on this point is derived from a more extensive analysis of the ways in which the state subsidizes the forays of civil servants into the political arena. See my "Administrative Reform and the Problem of Decentralization," in William G. Andrews and Stanley Hoffmann, eds., The Fifth Republic at Twenty.

[73] Ezra N. Suleiman, Elites In French Society: The Politics of Survival (Princeton: Princeton University Press, 1978).

[74] François Bloch-Lainé, Profession: fonctionnaire (Paris: Editions de Seuil, 1976), p. 236.

TABLE 3–1

DISTRIBUTION OF CIVIL SERVANTS IN FIFTH REPUBLIC GOVERNMENTS
(percentage)

Government	Non-Parlia-mentarians	Civil Servants[a]	Higher Civil Servants	Members of Grands Corps	Members of Technical Grands Corps
Presidency of de Gaulle (Fourth Rep.)	41.5	50	37.5	33.5	22
Presidency of de Gaulle:					
Debré	39.5	46	34.5	55.5	21
Pompidou I	31	41	31	33.5	N.A.
Pompidou II	37	42.5	31	44.5	N.A.
Pompidou III	25	50	32	44.5	N.A.
Pompidou IV	18.5	55.5	40.5	45.5	N.A.
Couve de Murville	3.5	48	38.5	50	N.A.
Chaban-Delmas	0	43.5	36	50	N.A.
Messmer I	0	53.5	40	58.5	N.A.
Messmer II	7.7	61.5	51.5	40	N.A.
Messmer III	3.4	65.5	55	44	N.A.
Chirac	18.4	53	45	41	N.A.
Barre I	34	58	47.5	28	17.5
Barre II	28	61.5	43.5	23.5	N.A.
Barre III	20	57.5	42.5	23.5	23.5

NOTE: N.A. = not available.

[a] Includes Parliamentarians and Non-Parliamentarians.

SOURCE: Jean-Louis Quermonne, "L'Autorité du pouvoir exécutif sur l'administration en France sous la Ve République," paper presented at the conference on *L'Administration et La Politique en France Sous La Ve République*, Paris, November 30-December 1, 1979, p. 21.

the *grands corps de l'Etat*.[75] Table 3–1 confirms the importance of civil servants and of members of the *grands corps* in governments.

The law in France is very accommodating to a civil servant who wishes to enter politics. He need not resign from the civil service either while he is a candidate for office or when he is elected. Not having to resign or take a leave of absence, a candidate for an elective office continues to draw his salary just as though he were performing

[75] See Jean Bourdon, *Les Assemblées Parlementaires sous la Veme République* (Paris: La Documentation Française, 1978).

his normal duties. If elected to a local office, he continues to exercise his function as a civil servant. Legally inadmissible in many other western countries, the *cumul* of two positions—administrative and political—is sanctioned by law in France. This form of *cumul* not only does little to separate the political from the administrative domain, but it allows the state to subsidize, in one way or another, the political career (or the attempt at such a career) of its privileged civil servants.

The higher civil servants, particularly those who belong to the *grands corps de l'Etat*, benefit from state subsidies in numerous ways. First, the state subsidizes the entry of its officials into ministerial cabinets. Although the minister is free to pick his aides from any sector, all ministerial cabinets (personal staffs of ministers) are made up almost exclusively of civil servants. The ministerial cabinet has become an indispensable step to rapid promotion within and outside the administration.[76] The ministerial cabinets give the officials who serve in them both a taste for a political career and an opportunity for entering such a career. What is less evident is that civil servants who enter a ministerial cabinet—who, in other words, serve a minister belonging to the government and, generally, a political party—continue to be paid by the corps to which they are attached. A public institution thus continues to pay the salary of a civil servant who no longer works for it and who is taking some form of political apprenticeship. In a juridical study of the French Presidency, a member of the *Conseil d'Etat* noted with respect to the President's advisors:

> The state of these collaborators is precisely that of members of ministerial cabinets: (1) they remain, administratively, in a position of active service in their corps, which is evidently a pure fiction, but which allows for their remuneration by their corps; (2) they are chosen freely by the President of the Republic who names them by decree bearing only his signature.[77]

Institutions that train, nurture, and legitimize an elite to serve the political class and to become the political class facilitate considerably the task of the President. From this ready pool, the President, like his ministers, can fill top positions. The assured dedication and loyalty of this state-created elite cannot be matched by any other institution, so that no other institutions are needed to supply political

---

[76] Jean-Luc Bodiguel, *Les Anciens élèves de l'E.N.A.* (Paris: Presses de la Fondation Nationale des Sciences Politiques, 1978), chap. 4.

[77] Massot, *La Présidence de la République en France*, p. 167.

executives. Thus, in selecting political executives, the President of France does not experience the dilemmas that confront an American president.

Transience versus Permanence. In the United States, "the single most obvious characteristic of Washington's political appointees is their transience,"[78] which has developed because there are no institutions to provide executive leadership with a potential pool of public servants. In France, however, the state has made possible the "production" of an administrative elite, so that it has created a certain permanence both in personnel and in work methods. The problem in Washington—that "public executives will be strangers with only a fleeting chance to learn how to work together"[79]—has been avoided in France because the training of these officials has been tied to their careers. Consequently, they come to form a community that is self-assured, tightly organized, and politically heterogenous.[80] The permanence, then, refers not just to stability of personnel, although that certainly exists, but to a general commitment to institutions.

In the United States there is neither the loyalty to institutions nor the stable recruitment of public executives. The "president's men" rise to the top rapidly, not because of previous accomplishments (as in Britain or France), but because of their attachment to a politician who was elected president. The lack of resignations on matters of principle in American public life is remarkable in that:

> In selecting a cabinet, subcabinet, and White House advisors, each newly elected President must choose among a large, random assortment of eager, more or less qualified candidates. In Britain, such choices are limited to a small number of eligibles who have already reached the requisite rungs of the ladder. The very randomness of the American process inevitably puts a high premium on the cultivation of close personal contacts by the young with a few senior members of the upper-class Establishment. While Englishmen advance politically by steps, Americans vault upward in leaps, usually catapulting off the tall, broad shoulders of a patron.[81]

The President of France, on the other hand, is surrounded by people who owe their careers to their institutions, because their institutions

---

[78] Heclo, *A Government of Strangers*, p. 103.

[79] Ibid., p. 104.

[80] This is discussed in detail in Suleiman, *Elites in French Society*, chaps. 5, 6, and 7.

[81] Edward Weisband and Thomas M. Franck, *Resignation in Protest* (New York: Grossman Publishers, 1975), p. 161.

have given them legitimacy. One of President Giscard d'Estaing's closest advisors recently described how he came to work with Giscard several years ago quite by accident. "When Giscard was Minister of Finance, he thought he ought to have someone from the Cour des Comptes in his cabinet. The head of my corps asked me if I was interested in entering the cabinet of the minister of Finance, and I said yes. So I came to work for Giscard without ever having met him personally." Another of Giscard's advisors in the Elysée said he came to work for the President in the Elysée without having met him. "I was hired by the Secretary-General and not by Giscard. It happened that Giscard wanted someone from the *ponts et chaussées* corps on his staff. I was recommended to the Secretary-General and that's how I got the job."

The United States has no equivalent to France's training of public officials, which creates an institutional base and serves as the recruiting ground for the top posts in the executive branch. The President can therefore surround himself with competent advisors, who are legitimate in the eyes of the community that they serve, who belong to a permanent and stable set of institutions, and, finally, who are linked to a wide network in the public sector and beyond.

Loyalty to the President. The method of choosing Presidential advisors and the other public officials in France takes for granted the loyalty of these men. The President's advisors will not only see eye to eye with him on various issues, as is to be expected, but they will also have a loyalty to institutions that is seldom known in the United States because of the selection process there. Where the President of France is allowed to choose public officials from an available community and is free of outside pressures, the American President has no such community from which to select officials nor is he free from the outside pressures of Congress and other lobbies. Worse still, he must try to influence the appointment of officials in the departments in much the same way that a lobby does. In effect, he becomes one more element of a large network of competing lobbies trying to influence a nomination in his favor.

The method of selecting political executives in the United States does not assure the allegiance of these officials, most of whom owe their appointment to lobbies that are wholly independent of the President. Thus, President Nixon attempted to "take over" the bureaucracy over which he felt he had lost total control.[82] In view

---

[82] This attempt is detailed in Richard P. Nathan, *The Plot That Failed: Nixon and the Administrative Presidency* (New York: John Wiley, 1975).

of the selection process, the American President is in a weak position when it comes to eliciting the loyalties of public officials on whom he depends to get things done.

Networks. Unlike his American counterpart, the President of France can count on a stable and loyal network in organizing his political leadership. Not subject to pressures from political or interest groups, he can appoint like-minded persons who feel that they belong to the same network.[83] Furthermore, the President not only appoints all the public officials to the top posts in the administrative apparatus, but his own advisors are linked in a stable and permanent way to those who run this administrative apparatus. As a result, all three Presidents of the Fifth Republic have shown a particular interest in appointments over which they have control. The President either names his own man to a post or he accepts the recommendation of someone else. He can, however, exercise a veto when an appointment is proposed to him, and here his personal staff plays an important role; if a member of his staff thinks that the person being proposed for a particular post will not be cooperative, he advises the President to block the appointment. In this way, the network into which the Presidential staff fits is continually enlarged.

The chief executive of France meets few obstacles in organizing his power because all appointments to the top politico-administrative positions are made from the civil service. Hence, all officials have a similar professional and educational background that allows them to form a network. Although some conflicts appear in the network, they never go beyond the point of threatening to break down the system. In Washington, on the other hand, "political appointees . . . are substantially on their own and vulnerable to bureaucratic power."[84] Washington may have more of a network than Heclo suggests here, but the *cursus honorum* of its members is different, and they remain subject to greater external pressures than do members of the network in France.

The Organization of the President's Team

The President of France appoints his staff exclusively from the civil service. The secretary-general is "the highest ranking civilian official of the Presidency of the Republic."[85] His functions are as follows:

---

[83] Suleiman, *Elites in French Society*, pp. 134-49 and 162-88.

[84] Heclo, *A Government of Strangers*, p. 112.

[85] P. Verrier, *Les Services du Président* (Paris: Presses Universitaires de France, 1971), p. 31.

First of all, he is the privileged counselor of the President of the Republic with whom he has frequent meetings; in this capacity, he is constantly called upon to give his advice on all the decisions the President must make, and which he has prepared for the President; then, following logically from his first duty, he insures in the name of the President the execution of presidential decision through the intermediary of his personal collaborators, the *conseillers techniques* and the *chargés de mission* of the General Secretariat. He is, in addition, the "ears and mouth" of the President in all meetings in which the President is absent, usually the interministerial committees at the Hotel Matignon. Together with the General Secretary of the government, he participates in the preparation of the agenda of the weekly meeting of the Council of Ministers before informing the President of the Republic, in whose name he keeps up with the preparation of legislative and regulatory texts. Finally, he is often the personal representative of the President, whom he replaces when the latter is absent or cannot or does not want to personally appear.[86]

The secretary-general, being the central figure in the Elysée, has even been described as a "surreptitious Prime Minister."[87] His powers are considerable because he performs important advisory functions and because he has the President's ear. Under his direct authority are fifteen or so *conseillers techniques* (advisors), each of whom has a specific sector (or several sectors) to follow.

The task of each advisor is to keep the President informed of what is going on, to let him know what should be done, and to see that what he wants done is done. As one advisor of Giscard explained:

It is critical in this job to gather all the information that a President could possibly want. But it is equally critical to give him ideas, for the President needs imaginative people around him since his job does not allow him to think up ideas on the thousands of things that he has to deal with. This is what I call the advisor's motivating or "driving" role toward the President. Once the President wants to push an idea or a project, then we have to play the motivating role toward the bureaucracy.

---

[86] Ibid., pp. 31-32.
[87] Pierre Viansson-Ponté, "Les Pouvoirs parallèles," *L'Evènement*, no. 2, March 1966, ibid.

Another advisor observed that "some of the President's advisors are mediocre and so they tend to spend their time gathering information. They don't give the President any ideas. Others place their emphasis on the 'ideas' function and so tend not to leave themselves much time to acquire information."

An advisor's devotion and loyalty to the President must override all other loyalties. One of Giscard's closest advisors noted that "to be truly successful in this position, you must have no personal politics of your own. You have to be ready to do what the President wants." The President, he noted, cannot afford to be bypassed by the bureaucracy once he has decided on a policy, so that

> We have to keep tabs on what is going on in the ministries. We have to be able to tell the President that this or that minister is doing such and such and that he should be warned about it. We have to be able to warn the President any time that a civil servant, a minister, an advisor to the Prime Minister, or the Prime Minister himself are up to something that is not in line with his policy.

How can all this information be obtained by the *conseiller technique*? A President generally instructs his ministers to work closely with the civil servants in their ministries and, consequently, to have small personal cabinets. In addition, he generally tells his own collaborators not to circumvent the ministers. Giscard has told his staff on several occasions that they should not consider themselves ministers. The procedure has clearly been observed by the President's staff:

> We never call the ministers—the President can do that directly. We go through the minister's *directeur de cabinet*. . . . In order to be efficient in this job, you have to have an information network. You have to know who to go to and I always go to the person who has all the information I need. Mind you, it's not difficult to do this. We've all had an administrative career and we all have contacts throughout the bureaucracy. But you have to cultivate these contacts, and you have to extend them, and this is why as the President's term wears on and as he names more and more people that he knows or approves of, his information network gets larger.

The highly centralized method of nominating staff ignores outside pressures; yet, it is considered to be a legitimate procedure even though it gives the President of the Republic full control over his own staff and over all the top posts of the bureaucracy, as well as the para-administrative institutions and the nationalized sector. "It's the power of appointment that a President has," noted an official in the Elysée, "that allows him to get things done, and that allows him to name, more or less, the directors of ministries himself. This is also where his advisors have some power because if one of them says to the President: 'Be careful, this chap can't be counted on' then the President really listens." As we noted earlier, Presidential appointments in France are not influenced by pressure from deputies or interest groups as they are in the United States, and this insulation of the bureaucracy gives it the kind of coherence that appears to be lacking in the United States or in Italy. Moreover, because the President draws on a pool of civil servants who belong to the major administrative and technical corps, his choice, which in any case does not have to be ratified, is rarely questioned. Members of this pool are presumed to be highly qualified and are presumed to play technical roles. Yet, it seems necessary to deny the political functions that these officials fulfill. A recent authoritative study of the French Presidency concludes: "Finally, in support of the view that presidential collaborators do not constitute a super-executive, although their influence is sometimes considerable, we can note this fact: a member of the general secretariat never presides over a meeting if politicians are present: politics must take precedence over administration."[88]

Although the common professional background of the "politico-administrative" executives may hinder them from transcending their administrative attachments,[89] it creates considerable unity among the executive staff, especially as the President begins to name more and more of "his" people to key posts. One former advisor to Giscard, who now is a director in a ministry, commented on this point as well as on the differences between his present job and his previous one at the Elysée:

> The President put me in this position because he really wanted to see this reform put into effect. He knew of all the obstacles it would encounter in this ministry and he thought that by placing me here he would get it through. I think we'll succeed because my authority is much greater in the ministry having just spent four years at Giscard's side. In this job, I have to motivate a whole administration and I have to argue and persuade constantly. At the Elysée, I never had to do that. It was an easier job.

---

88 Massot, *La Présidence de la République en France*, p. 173.
89 Suleiman, *Politics, Power, and Bureaucracy in France*, pp. 209-38.

Once having the consent of the President, the advisor continued, it is a matter of giving instructions. And the President asks for only one thing: "Gauge the wind and do not be mistaken about its direction."[90]

The President thus uses his personal staff as a source of information, as a brains-trust, and as a watchdog—functions that are complementary as long as his staff is bound to a larger network in control of the bureaucracy. The almost exclusive use of civil servants for political executive positions in fact strengthens the hand of the President when he is committed to a particular policy, because all political executives, having a solid base in terms of status and of career, can be moved in and out of their career posts as the need arises.[91] Many members of this network eventually fill a variety of prestigious and remunerative posts, even if a serious disagreement arises between the President and one of his aides.[92]

The stability of this network encourages its members to "play the game," so that resignations on matters of principle are just as rare as they are in the United States despite France's characteristic ideological divisions. The persons who sit at the top are extremely flexible about their political views, as the following example illustrates. In 1974, shortly before the Presidential election that brought Giscard to power, one socialist official in a technical ministry said that it would be a disaster for France if Giscard were elected and that he was supporting Mitterrand. Two months later Giscard was elected President and this same official turned up as one of his advisors.[93] Pierre Rouanet, commenting on another aspect of this political flexibility, notes that the "New Society" theme so dear to Chaban-Delmas when he was Prime Minister owed much to the pen of Yves Cannac:[94] "In sum, a speech writer with an inquiring mind. . . . The prototype of the boys educated at ENA between 1948 and 1968. Irrevocably, there is an element of the speech writer there. Yves Cannac is at ease only

---

[90] Josette Alia, "Les Hommes du président," *Nouvel Observateur*, July 3, 1978, p. 34. On the extensive use that Giscard has made of his patronage powers, see the extremely revealing article by Yves Agnès, "L'Etat-Giscard," *Le Monde*, March 3, 1980.

[91] The Hamilton Jordans and the Jody Powells are an unknown species in France.

[92] When Giscard and his Secretary-General, Claude Pierre-Brossolette, could no longer work together, the latter was named president of France's largest state-owned bank, the Crédit Lyonnais.

[93] Some years later he told the author in another interview that he hadn't known Giscard personally before coming to work for him at the Elysée. He had been recommended to the secretary-general by a minister that he had worked for.

[94] Cannac became second in command in Giscard's Elysée staff. A year ago he left the Elysée to become president of the Agence Havas.

with superiors who have passed through the same mold: their political orientation remains secondary."[95]

Although the networks into which the President's people fit are the chief means by which the President organizes his political leadership, the effectiveness of this leadership derives more from personalistic than from bureaucratic factors. The congruence between authority and power—a feature of patrimonial administration—can be found in modern bureaucratic organizations and can in fact "help to overcome bureaucratic pathologies."[96] In the case of France, Presidential authority is largely attributable to the patrimonial features that remain embedded in what is otherwise a highly bureaucratic structure.

The President and the Policy Process

The President, then, can organize his staff so as to overcome bureaucratic resistance to particular projects and to overcome in most instances the structural constraints that obtain in the dual executive system established by the Constitution of 1958. We can now ask whether the President is involved in the policy-making process, and if so, whether his involvement is marginal or whether he initiates and supervises the implementation of policies.

The President obviously bears some responsibility for all government policies, for on his shoulders falls the credit and the balance for actions taken by the Cabinet over which he presides. Although he might try to take credit for successful policies and might blame some failures on individual ministers, he cannot escape the final responsibility for what happens to his party (or parties) at the polls. Hence, the President uses his team to monitor what is happening in the various sectors of government, rather than to initiate policies.

President Giscard d'Estaing, for example, has tried to give the impression that his proper concern is the condition of France in the next century, whereas the resolution of today's problems fall within the purview of the Prime Minister. In so doing, he has not abdicated his authority; the President has merely given the Prime Minister the necessary support for dealing with the present crisis—the successful handling of which can only help to secure the President's reelection. Because the president has to keep in mind his reelection in 1981, he tries to be above everyday political squabbles. For this reason, he

---

[95] Pierre Rouanet, *Le Cas Chaban*, p. 289.

[96] Lloyd I. Rudolph and Susanne H. Rudolph, "Authority and Power in Bureaucratic and Patrimonial Administration: A Revisionist Interpretation of Weber on Bureaucracy," *World Politics*, vol. 31, no. 2 (January 1979), pp. 195-227.

has become more involved in foreign policy issues. Nevertheless, he is still deeply involved in any political strategy that might help him to be reelected. The Prime Minister's role is to initiate and implement measures of economic austerity (it is no accident that these measures have been named after the Prime Minister—*le plan Barre*), for which the President will claim credit in the event that the measures succeed. If they fail, the Prime Minister will be held responsible and will be removed from office. De Gaulle, too, recognized the advantages of having a Prime Minister on whom he could throw "all that would not add to his dignity."[97]

In looking ahead to his reelection or to the victory of his party in the legislative elections, a President needs, in Richard Rose's words, to "keep out of trouble." Rose explains this task that the President sets for himself:

> In order to have time and capital to pursue his positive priorities, a President must give equal weight to a negative priority: keeping out of trouble. A President must decide in given circumstances whether the best way to keep out of trouble is by establishing institutions to keep trouble away or by refusing to establish institutions that can deliver to his doorstep more troubles than he can handle."[98]

The area of greatest Presidential involvement is foreign affairs. Ever since de Gaulle's Presidency, foreign affairs have been concentrated in the Elysée. Neither the Ministry of Foreign Affairs, which has completely lost ground to the Elysée, nor the Prime Minister has much say in international affairs. This was the case with Pompidou, and it has not changed with Giscard. Although Giscard might have been expected to show less interest in foreign affairs in view of his previous ministerial experience elsewhere and his early Presidential initiatives after 1974 toward social issues, he has become increasingly concerned with foreign affairs.

This attention to foreign affairs is not difficult to understand because it creates a more prestigious presidential image than do other roles that he assumes. Here the President represents France, and not merely a political party. What he fights or bargains for at international conferences are French interests. "France's position in the

---

[97] Alexandre, *Le Duel De Gaulle-Pompidou*, pp. 219-20.

[98] Richard Rose, "The President: A Chief But Not Executive," *Presidential Studies Quarterly*, vol. 7, no. 1 (Winter 1977), p. 11. Rose quotes, as the epigraph to his article, Theodore C. Sorensen, to the effect that "any chief executive of a private business corporation has greater power over his subordinates than does the President of the United States."

world" is a theme that runs throughout Giscard's speeches, as it did in de Gaulle's. Foreign policy can also have great impact on the President's domestic political goals. De Gaulle's foreign policy, for example, won him the support of the Communist party and so prevented, until 1972, a left-wing alliance. Giscard has not hesitated to use foreign policy issues (his European policy is the clearest case of this) to split his opponents and to divide his Gaullist allies.

In addition, a President now and then scores victories on international issues more easily than he does on domestic issues. The considerable publicity that attends such victories can be exploited immediately by the President. For substantive reasons, however, today's Presidents have to be deeply involved in international affairs. The military threats to international security that prevailed up to the early 1970s have been supplanted by threats to the economic interdependence of the world's industrial nations and by economic crises such as inflation, oil shortage, and unemployment, all of which demand genuine Presidential concern. Thus, his role in setting the agenda for foreign policy issues is more important than any other policy role he plays.

Of course, the President cannot be concerned with all social and economic issues, and he is obliged to select only those that may involve a conflict with opponents or allies, and that promise ample rewards in the event of success. This is the kind of "symbolic" politics that Giscard has practiced. He has, for example, shown little concern for issues such as the reform of the heavily indebted social security system, or for problems of transportation or housing. He saves a housing site in a particular urban area when it helps to enhance his image as an "environmentalist," or he cancels a project for a highway along the Seine river that his predecessor strongly desired when he wishes to gain the favor of the ecological movement. He pushes through a law allowing women to have abortions when he wishes to have the support of the feminist movement.

There is no systematic agenda for domestic issues. Nor is such an agenda possible since there would be no way of adhering to it. The party configurations are unstable, which is precisely how Giscard wants them to be because that is the only way he can manipulate them. To adopt some type of doctrinaire agenda would be to ignore the political world in which he lives. As one of Giscard's advisors has noted: "The President must above all have a very finely tuned ear. He must always be ready to do this or that if it supports some ultimate goal of his. Of course, there are contradictions in his policies.

He is a political animal who wants to get reelected and not some dogmatic ideologue."

Giscard's interest and involvement in economic matters have been less than expected in light of his previous background as a civil servant in the Ministry of Finance and as a finance minister for almost a decade. Instead, he chose Raymond Barre, whom he introduced as "France's best economist," to solve France's economic crisis. He does not himself formulate economic policies, but he will judge the success or failure of Barre's policies; therefore his involvement in this area is indirect but not unimportant. First, Barre has been allowed to formulate economic policy and starting in 1976, to take strong measures because there were no elections on the horizon. The President at first was not overly concerned with the political "fallout" of these policies. In the long-run, however, Giscard has everything at stake in these policies, for if unemployment remains at its present level, if firms continue to go under at the present rate, if industrial restructuring fails to alleviate the serious regional problems, if the so-called move toward a liberal economy results only in a higher inflation rate, then Giscard and the center-right majority that now supports him may not survive the next presidential and legislative elections. Giscard's approach is to monitor through his staff the political effects of Barre's economic policies.

The President of France, then, plays a critical role in international affairs and in formulating foreign policy. He is less involved in domestic social or economic affairs, not because he lacks "power" in the sense that an American President does—he lacks neither constitutional powers nor power over the bureaucracy—but because his political life depends on successful policies, which must therefore be considered an adjunct of "political realities." In this sense, although the President of France is not subjected to the same number or variety of forces experienced by the President of the United States, he shares this critical constraint with him.

Changing Structure of Leadership

We suggested at the outset of this essay that, constitutionally at least, the President of France operates under fewer constraints than his counterpart in the United States. He does not have to worry about congressional lobbies, congressional committees, or private lobbies; furthermore, the relative docility of the press shields him from public scrutiny and helps to augment his power. His control over the government is assured by his authority to name the Prime Minister and the ministers in the government, as well as by the constitutional provision requiring ministers to abandon their seats in the National Assembly once they take up their ministerial portfolios.

The Constitution of the Fifth Republic and the power it bestows upon the President are no longer questioned by any significant political force in France. Presidential power is now accepted as a legitimate aspect of the political system. Hence, any President, whether he belongs to the left or to the right, will enjoy the powers granted him by the constitution. So long as the President can count on a majority in the National Assembly, his powers will not be questioned by his government.

Twenty years is a short time in the life of a constitution. Since 1958, France has been governed by relatively cohesive governments that have been able to deal with major external and internal crises, to preside over the transformation of the French economy, and to undertake domestic and foreign policies that have left a strong imprint on the society. Each successive President has taken on greater powers and responsibilities. The President's involvement in budgetary matters has even cracked the power of the Ministry of Finance. The team that surrounds him and that governs for him is linked through an extensive network—in marked contrast to the American pattern—with the entire administrative structure. Despite the power at the President's disposal and despite his hand in organizing that power, it does not follow that the system is without constraints. The President is constrained in the exercise of his power partly by the constitution, which provides for a twin-executive, and partly by the political system.

Although the President rules both over and with the Prime Minister—a relationship that has numerous advantages when the two belong to the same political majority—serious cleavages can arise when they belong to different political forces, for the French constitution, like all constitutions, is open to different interpretations. Consequently, a Prime Minister belonging to a majority party who faces a President belonging to a minority will probably demand all the powers that he is entitled to in the constitution.

On the other hand, when the President comes from a majority party that is well disposed to support him, he has to preserve that majority, for without it he cannot act as a chief legislator. To preserve the support of the parliamentary majority, the President becomes obliged to tailor his programs to that majority whether or not he approves of them. Giscard, for example, has sought to free himself from the Gaullist majority that he depends on because he does not always agree with its "conservative" or antireformist views, and yet he might not succeed in obtaining a majority if he stressed reformist policies. Unless he can secure some kind of parliamentary majority, his policy initiatives must remain restrained. If Giscard no longer suffers defeats of the type he experienced with his capital gains project, it is because he has learned to dilute his projects himself before making them public. Indeed, Giscard has learned that the constraints on Presidential actions in France make it important for him to project himself as a leader; that means he must be attentive to the concerns of the people, he must play the political game but at the same time be above it, and he must not create or exacerbate divisions in the society. As one of Giscard's advisors put it:

> The President has come to the conclusion that real reforms are impossible to achieve because of the division that their proposal leads to in the society, so he concentrates on throwing ideas that people discuss, on speaking about reforms on this or that. My job here, for example, is to help the President develop his image in the environmental area. We've tried very hard to make him an *ecologiste*.

In his Verdun-sur-le-Doubs speech, delivered shortly before the 1978 legislative elections, Giscard himself stated the difficulties of governing:

> France . . . must be governed. You have observed with me how difficult it is to lead a country politically divided into two equal parts. Nobody could hope to govern a country divided into four. Today, the voters are separated into four big groups. Two in the majority, two in the opposition. None of these groups will receive more than 30 percent of the votes. None of them is capable of governing alone. Many among you . . . would like the party for which they vote to be able to govern alone. They must understand that this is impossible. No government will be able to confront France's difficult problems with the support of 30 percent of the electorate.[99]

Giscard has recognized the difficulties of governing his society, and is under no illusions about the President's powers if the left should become victorious. As he warned in the speech at Verdun-sur-le-Doubs: "You may choose to put into effect the Common Program. That is your right. But if you do choose it, it will be put into effect. Do not believe that the Constitution grants the President the means

---

[99] *Le Monde*, January 29-30, 1978.

to oppose it. And I would have shirked my duty had I not warned you." [100]

The President of France, then, has at his disposal the means to organize his leadership in a way that may well be envied by his counterpart in the United States.[101] If his real powers do not coincide with those provided in the constitution, it is because the Constitution of 1958 was primarily concerned with creating a safety-valve for times of crisis. Nonetheless in comparison with the President of the United States, he enjoys substantial political power and is subject to few constraints. The political world in which he operates has given him not the position of a "clerk," in which the American President finds himself, but that of a political manager. Ultimately, however, his major concern is no different from that of an American President—to govern without antagonizing his enemies or his friends. Giscard's slogan during his 1974 campaign for the Presidency indicated that Giscard had already understood what a President must do: "I want change without risks."

---

[100] Ibid.

[101] This strength may also in certain circumstances be a weakness, for it means that the President has to work within clearly established patterns that are set by the administrative milieu on which he comes to depend heavily. So long as he does not threaten this milieu, those who belong to it will be willing to serve him.

4

Executive Leadership in Germany: Dispersion of Power or "Kanzlerdemokratie"?

Renate Mayntz

In analyzing political leadership one can concentrate on the top office holder and the extent of his power, or view government as a collective enterprise in which a variety of actors and institutions play their parts. Given the complex nature of modern political-administrative systems, the second perspective must be chosen if the purpose of the analysis is to understand the policy process. In modern states government is not a one-man job. Ministers who head vast bureaucratic structures will necessarily enjoy considerable influence on the choice and implementation of policy, even though the constitution may view them merely as aides to the top executive. Yet there are important differences between countries in the structure of collective leadership and in the extent to which the powers of leadership are concentrated in one top office or dispersed among several actors. Government in the Federal Republic of Germany seems characterized by a considerable dispersion of executive power, especially if contrasted to the constitutional model of Presidential leadership.

There is a basic similarity in the functions which the government of modern states must fulfill. Besides the classical executive function of directing the implementation of legislation, governments develop policies and make decisions in their own right. A function of increasing importance is coordinating the policies of the various agencies of the executive branch. The relative merit of a specific pattern of executive leadership depends in part on the extent to which it facilitates or inhibits the performance of the various governmental functions.

The Constitutional Framework of Executive Leadership

A newly made constitution is likely to reflect distinctive functional considerations. This is particularly evident in the German constitution of 1949. The Basic Law (*Grundgesetz*) clearly reflects two dominant concerns: to safeguard the country against the totalitarian inclinations of power-hungry political leaders by a careful separation and distribution of powers, and to facilitate the stability of national government. The Weimar Republic, it was felt, had been deficient in both respects; the bitter lesson learned from history inspired the new constitution.[1]

The intended decentralization of power is reflected in the choice of a federal system for the new republic. Federalism has strong historical roots in Germany, but this tradition had been weakened in the course of the Weimar Republic, and especially under Hitler. A special political motive was therefore needed to reestablish federalism as the formative principle of the new state. The constitutional distribution of powers between the federal level and the *Länder* (states) makes for a rather clear-cut vertical division of functions: Most legislation is federal, while policy implementation is largely the task of the Länder. This general principle has a number of exceptions. The Länder have a few primary and many concurrent legislative prerogatives. On the other hand, defense, taxation, rail transport, and postal services are directly under the federal government.[2] Some government activities not delegated to the Länder are managed by federal agencies that operate largely free of departmental control; for example, the Federal Labor Agency (*Bundesanstalt für Arbeit*) administers federal labor market policy, including unemployment insurance. The fact that the federal government depends on the Länder and extra-Cabinet federal agencies for the execution of most of its policies has important consequences. The federal government has relatively little to do with controlling the vast bureaucratic apparatus, and relatively more to do with policy development. This fact particularly influences the role of German federal ministers.

The Länder have their own direct representation at the federal level in the Bundesrat. These representatives are not publicly elected, but are the prime ministers and other cabinet members of the Länder governments. The number of votes that each Land has is roughly related to its population, and on any issue all its votes must be cast in a bloc. The Bundesrat may develop legislative initiatives of its

---

[1] Karl Dietrich Bracher, "Die Kanzlerdemokratie," in Richard Löwenthal and Hans-Peter Schwarz, eds., *Die zweite Republik: 25 Jahre Bundesrepublik Deutschland—Eine Bilanz* (Stuttgart: Seewald, 1974), pp. 179-86.

[2] For more detail, see Klaus von Beyme, *Das politische System der Bundesrepublik Deutschland* (Munich: Piper and Co., 1979), pp. 196-214; and Nevil Johnson, *Government in the Federal Republic of Germany* (Oxford: Pergamon Press, 1973), pp. 98-137.

own, but has made sparing use of this power. Its main influence rests in the fact that it must approve not only constitutional amendments but also all federal legislation which directly affects the Länder, especially their finances and the activities of their administrative offices.[3] The viewpoint of Land governments is thus taken into account in central government decision making, where it constitutes an important constraint on the power of the federal executive.

The concern with political stability is reflected in the clear priority given to the Chancellor over the President.[4] The office of the President has lost most of the power it had in the Weimar Republic. The President today is largely a figurehead, with no independent power base such as direct election would give him. He is elected by the Bundesversammlung, a constitutional organ meeting especially for this purpose, half of whose members are federal MPs while the other half come from the Länder parliaments. The political decision-making powers of the President are minimal. He must countersign bills ratified by parliament and can refuse to do so only if they are unconstitutional. He has only formal power in the appointment of higher civil servants and officers, and his functions in the formation of government are minor as long as there is a clear parliamentary majority. He plays no role in the day-to-day business of political decision making and may in fact even feel out of touch with what happens in government.[5] If he has some political influence, this is personal and indirect. Though nominated by a political party (or party coalition), the President is expected to remain nonpartisan, and there are strong pressures against his taking sides on partisan issues.

The desire to assure political stability can also be seen in the constitutional norms determining the relationship between Chancellor and parliament. The Chancellor is elected by the Bundestag, which means that the choice is made by the parliamentary majority party or coalition. The President may nominate a candidate, but *must* appoint whomever the parliamentary majority elects. Once elected, the Chancellor is relatively protected from changing parliamentary moods. He

---

[3] For more detail, see Thomas Ellwein, *Das Regierungssystem der Bundesrepublik Deutschland* (Opladen: Westdeutscher Verlag, 1973), pp. 298-308.

[4] Reference works for the following analysis are von Beyme, *Politisches System der Bundesrepublik*; Ellwein, *Regierungssystem*; Johnson, *Government in the Federal Republic*; and Kurt Sontheimer and Hans H. Röhring, eds., *Handbuch des politischen Systems der Bundesrepublik Deutschland* (Munich: Piper and Co., 1977).

[5] See, for instance, Eppler's remarks about Heinemann in Erhard Eppler, *Das Schwerste ist Glaubwürdigkeit* (Reinbek bei Hamburg: Rowohlt, 1978), p. 95.

can be ousted by parliament only on the basis of a "constructive vote of no confidence," that is, if a majority not only is willing to depose him but also has agreed on an alternative candidate. This particular constitutional rule led to the defeat of the one attempt by a parliamentary opposition to oust a Chancellor (Willy Brandt) whose majority had eroded. It permitted Brandt to continue governing in 1972 until he himself wanted the dissolution of parliament and new elections to take place.[6]

Though the constitution assures the Chancellor of security in office, it does not grant him particularly strong powers. In fact, the constitutional framework of executive action hinges on three principles of leadership, none of which is given clear priority in the constitution: leadership by the Chancellor, by the Cabinet, and by the departmental ministers. All three principles are based on section 65 of the constitution and on by-laws in the procedural manuals of the government and the federal departments. The leadership functions accorded the three main political actors—the Chancellor, the Cabinet as a group, and the ministers individually—constrain each other mutually, thus making for an apparently dispersed power structure at the top.

The leadership function of the Chancellor (*Kanzlerprinzip*) has as its base three powers: to make ministerial appointments forming the government; to organize the executive branch, that is, to establish and change the number and jurisdiction of the federal departments; and to formulate general policy guidelines. In fulfilling his tasks the Chancellor is aided by the Chancellor's Office, which at present has close to 500 employees, including more than a hundred higher civil servants. The Chancellor commands the services of the Press Office, and the federal intelligence service is also under his formal supervision. But the Chancellor lacks certain powers which other top office holders may have. He may assume military command only in the case of war; he can dissolve parliament only if he has first failed in a vote of confidence; outside the budget of his own office, he has no special power to make spending decisions; and his autonomous power of appointment is restricted to the ministers. Other important appointments (such as the president of the federal bank) are made by the government collectively, some posts (such as the judges of the Constitutional Court) are filled by the Bundestag and Bundesrat, and the ministers name all the leading civil servants in their departments. Not even in the case of a national emergency does the Chancellor

---

[6] Eckhart Busch, "Die Parlamentsauflösung 1972," *Zeitschrift für Parlamentsfragen*, vol. 4 (1973), pp. 213-46.

enjoy special powers, since the constitution vests these in the government collectively.

The second of the three leadership principles is Cabinet government (*Kabinettsprinzip*). All proposals submitted to parliament by the federal government must pass through the Cabinet. Limited by the Chancellor's right to formulate general policy guidelines on the one hand, and by the independent jurisdictions of the departmental ministers on the other, the Cabinet is expected to function as a collective decision-making body. This is also manifested in the norm that holds ministers to abide by Cabinet decisions and not oppose them publicly even when in a minority in the Cabinet. The apparent conflict between this norm and the mandate of ministers as members of parliament is generally solved in favor of the former, both in legal theory and in actual practice.[7] While the government formally includes only the federal ministers, the few ministers of state[8] and the chiefs of the Chancellor's Office and the Press Office also participate in Cabinet meetings. State secretaries participate by invitation and generally serve as deputies if the ministers cannot attend. The Cabinet meets once a week while parliament is in session, and more frequently in case of a crisis. Though relatively small (most Cabinets have between fifteen and twenty-five members), the Cabinet is too large and too unspecialized to deal effectively with all issues coming up for decision. For this reason, Cabinet committees have developed over time, even though neither the constitution nor the procedural manuals mention such bodies.

The third principle of executive leadership is that every minister is personally and fully responsible for the activities of his department (*Ressortprinzip*). Within his sphere of jurisdiction, he cannot be given specific orders, not even by the Chancellor. The Cabinet may reject a minister's proposal if he asks for Cabinet approval, but it cannot issue specific directives in his area of jurisdiction. This departmental autonomy is jealously guarded by all ministers.

The number of federal departments has varied over time; at present there are sixteen, of which two are managed by the same minister (Transport and Postal Services). Departments differ considerably in size and importance, and have a much less complex structure than their U.S. counterparts. All are organized along the same general lines: Hierarchically arranged divisions, subdivisions, and sections

---

[7] Edzard Schmidt-Jortzig, *Die Pflicht zur Geschlossenheit der kollegialen Regierung (Regierungszwang)* (Stuttgart: Kohlhammer, 1973).
[8] The title of minister of state *(Staatsminister)* was introduced only in 1974; essentially the position and rights are those of a parliamentary state secretary; see Sontheimer and Röhring, *Handbuch*, pp. 83, 439.

143

are overlaid by a matrix of resource and personnel management, organizational functions, and, recently, planning and information services. The departmental leadership is a relatively small group, consisting of the minister and the state secretaries, usually aided by a small secretariat, one or two personal assistants (normally junior civil servants), and maybe a special official for press relations. There exists no ministerial cabinet as in France. The next highest rung of civil servants, the divisional leaders, are less powerful than their counterparts in more highly centralized political systems. In contrast to, say, a French director general, the German *Abteilungsleiter* does not head a large bureaucracy reaching down to the local level and therefore lacks executive power reaching beyond the federal office in Bonn.[9]

The picture of executive leadership which emerges is of a focused network rather than a pyramid. Executive power is shared. While this may well increase overall leadership capacity, and is in fact designed to do so, it also poses obvious problems such as a great need for consensus among the politicians involved.

The Pattern of Influence

The Power of the Chancellor. The way in which Konrad Adenauer, the first Chancellor of the Federal Republic, chose to interpret his role and make use of his constitutional powers is sometimes said to have made that position so predominant that the postwar political system of West Germany can be described as a *Kanzlerdemokratie*. Others such as Bracher argue that a predominant role for the Chancellor is in fact built into the constitution. He points in particular to the Chancellor's strong position vis-à-vis parliament and his ministers, who he not only chooses but also can dismiss at will.[10] Similarly, Hennis emphasizes that the Chancellor has at his disposal all the necessary legal instruments to assume a dominant role: "The powers of his office leave nothing to be desired. At the moment of his election his stallion is bridled and saddled; he only needs to be able to ride it."[11]

But the truth of such statements is relative. The Chancellor's potential power is considerable, especially if measured against the expectation that he might be no more than first among his peers in the government. He is constrained, however, even in the exercise of his limited formal powers, by such factors as the need to form an

[9] For more details, see Renate Mayntz and Fritz W. Scharpf, *Policy-Making in the German Federal Bureaucracy* (Amsterdam: Elsevier, 1975), pp. 63-94.

[10] Bracher, "Kanzlerdemokratie," pp. 180-86.

[11] Wilhelm Hennis, *Richtlinienkompetenz und Regierungstechnik* (Tübingen: Mohr, 1964), p. 27 (translated from the original German).

interparty coalition, the existence of political dissension within his party, and the autonomy which federal ministers enjoy.

The Chancellor has relatively little scope to appoint a Cabinet entirely of his own choosing. In a one-party government he must listen to the wishes of his party's executive committee and above all to the leader of the parliamentary party group, since he will subsequently depend on their support. Individual politicians with a strong following in the party and among deputies can successfully demand to be included among ministerial nominees. Thus, in the process of forming a Cabinet, important factions within the party organization are represented. In retrospect it is clear that even Adenauer, who often dealt with his party in a rather highhanded fashion, was bound by such constraints in forming his governments.[12] In a coalition government the Chancellor's freedom of choice is even more severely restricted since, short of a costly veto, he has no influence on the selection of candidates for offices allotted to the coalition party.[13]

The Chancellor's authority to establish and abolish federal departments and to reshuffle their jurisdictions can be used only when forming a new government. Most departmental reorganizations have in fact taken place precisely at this time. Once a minister has assumed office (or is returned to office for another term) he will usually oppose strongly any attempt at reorganization that would curtail his department's jurisdiction. As a result, substantively necessary reorganizations are sometimes not undertaken. At other times such reorganizations—especially the establishment of a new department—have been motivated more by the need to represent some group than by the needs of policy development. The one major reorganization took place after the 1969 election, when the first Social Democratic–Free Democrat coalition under Brandt was formed. This reorganization had been prepared by a special task force for the reform of government and administration.[14]

The authority to formulate policy guidelines has been used by all Chancellors in a highly selective and rather informal way. It is rare that a decision is formally designated as a policy guideline according to section 65 of the constitution. In most policy fields, Chancellors ex-

---

[12] Franz Alt, *Es begann mit Adenauer* (Freiburg in Bresgau: Herder, 1975), pp. 116-25.

[13] For the first government of Willy Brandt this is discussed by Hartmut H. Brauswetter, *Kanzlerprinzip, Ressortprinzip und Kabinettsprinzip in der ersten Regierung Brandt, 1969-1972* (Bonn: Eichholz Verlag, 1976), pp. 6-16.

[14] Projektgruppe für Regierungs- und Verwaltungsreform, "Erster Bericht zur Reform der Struktur von Bundesregierung und Bundesverwaltung" (Bonn, August 1969, unpublished); see also Arnd Morkel, "Die Reform des Kabinetts," *Politik und Zeitgeschichte*, vol. 43, no. 70 (October 1970), pp. 15-19.

press their opinion after rather than before the fact; that is, instead of formulating policy goals to be subsequently translated into legislation, they react to legislative proposals as they are submitted by the federal ministers. The main reasons for this are the unavoidable selectivity of a Chancellor's interest and expertise, the jealously defended autonomy of the federal departments in setting policy in their areas of jurisdiction, and the special difficulties of maintaining government consensus in a coalition government. The resulting pattern of leadership might be characterized as "selective voluntarism," meaning that Chancellors will actively set policy goals and formulate directives only in one or a very few selected fields, limiting themselves to managing the process of collective decision making. Adenauer as well as Brandt had a selective interest in foreign policy, the first more directed to the West, the second to Eastern countries. In this field both had strong convictions, formulated goals, and used all their influence to bring Cabinet and parliament in line with them. Erhard had and Schmidt has a similarly selective interest in economic questions. Schmidt does not wait for a Cabinet consensus to form but takes a stand on economic issues (including the controversial one of nuclear energy) on the basis of his personal knowledge and convictions, trying to sway dissenters by use of his personal authority. In matters beyond their selected areas, Chancellors are content to play a more reactive role within the framework of collective Cabinet deliberations.

Whether or not it is his personal priority, every Chancellor is of course involved with foreign policy. Attending summit meetings and negotiating with other heads of state are unavoidably the Chancellor's tasks, and the basic questions of international relations fall clearly within his authority to formulate guidelines. The Chancellor of the Federal Republic has long had an added reason for paying close attention to foreign relations; to regain international status was important for Germany after the war, so that to be accepted internationally strengthened the Chancellor's position at home.

To consider how a Chancellor exercises his major formal powers gives only an incomplete picture of what his job entails. The Chancellor is very little involved with executive tasks in the strict sense. Outside his own office, he cannot give specific orders to anybody, but must get others—mainly the ministers—to do this. Since policy implementation is largely the prerogative of the Länder and of special agencies, even the federal ministers are in fact not much engaged in executive tasks. Decision making is the dominant concern of the federal executive in general and the Chancellor in particular.

As decision maker, the Chancellor is always more actively involved in crisis management than in routine governing. Most decisions concern routine sectoral matters and fall within the scope of a particular minister. Only when a sectoral problem—such as terrorism, unemployment, or the energy shortage—becomes so acute as to produce a threat to the system in general does government as a whole, and hence necessarily the Chancellor, deal with it. The Chancellor is usually less concerned with making substantive decisions himself than with managing the decision-making process. This is a function that no one but the Chancellor can perform. Only he can set priorities among policies, since each minister would rank his own departmental policies first. The Chancellor must also see that the often diffuse and fragmented process of opinion formation eventually crystallizes into a concrete decision. Consensus building and coordination (in a nontechnical sense) thus become activities of major importance for the Chancellor. In fact, priority setting and coordination may have become more important than substantive decision making over time, because of changes in the problems faced by successive German governments and in the complexity of the system to be managed.[15]

The real power of a Chancellor depends largely on the support he gets from his party and the parliamentary party group (and often also from his coalition partner), and on his popularity with the electorate. Relatively little depends on his performance as a leader in relation to parliament as a whole. This stands in obvious contrast to the case of the British Prime Minister and is related to the character of the German Bundestag, which is more a working than a debating parliament. Of course there are debates in the Bundestag,[16] but they have relatively little effect on the final decision. The stable party system and the internal cohesion and disciplined behavior of the parliamentary party groups make the outcome of parliamentary votes highly predictable. The Chancellor is therefore not normally faced with the problem of insecure and shifting majorities and need not seek support in the open arena, as an American President must do in Congress. Parliamentary debates serve mainly to register and argue in public the positions already determined. The German Chancellor therefore speaks in parliament mainly on major occasions: the presentation of the budget, the state of the nation debate, the discussion

---

[15] This is suggested by Jürgen Reese, "Autorität und Macht des Bundeskanzlers," *Neues Hochland*, vol. 65 (1973), p. 332. The primacy of consensus building is also emphasized by Rolf Zundel, "Normale Zeiten—Schlechte Zeiten," *Die Zeit*, no. 13 (1979), p. 1.

[16] In the 139 sessions of the eighth legislative period until February 16, 1979, the parliamentary service had registered 609 hours and 23 minutes of debate.

of the government's program, and special debates on important current issues. The institution of question time was copied from the British model and introduced in 1951, but it does not play the same role as it does across the English Channel. The number of questions asked is very large and has steadily increased, but the answers are normally not given by the ministers themselves, let alone by the Chancellor.[17] Neither the public nor the media are much interested in what happens in question time, and no member of the government need feel that his reputation depends on his performance.

The most important basis of the Chancellor's power is his position within his political party. The relation among the offices of Chancellor, party chairman, and chairman of the parliamentary party group (*Fraktionsführer*) is especially critical. Both these chairmanships are potentially of great influence. The chairman of the parliamentary group can exert substantial influence on the process of opinion formation that determines the effective reaction of the legislature to government proposals. This office is much sought after, commands great prestige, and is usually filled by an eminent politician who has a substantial personal following among party members. The offices of Chancellor and parliamentary party group chairman are constitutionally separate, and the loyal support and the effectiveness of the latter is of decisive importance for the Chancellor. A strong party group chairman who can assure the Chancellor of parliamentary support can relieve him of the burden of managing such consensus by himself. The dependence of government action on the parliamentary party (or parties) is particularly pronounced in the German system, where government proceeds largely through legislation, rather than administrative programs and spending decisions.

German political parties have rather clearly structured organizations and staffs of their own. The offices of Chancellor and party chairman are separate in principle, but the constitution does not forbid the same person to hold both simultaneously. In the Christian Democratic Union (CDU), Adenauer seemed to have established an informal rule that the Chancellor should also be party chairman. Heidenheimer, writing in 1961, took this to be a lasting feature of the German as of other political systems,[18] but Adenauer's immediate successor, Ludwig Erhard, was already an exception to the apparent

---

[17] Gerhard Loewenberg, *Parlamentarismus im politischen System der Bundesrepublik Deutschland* (Tübingen: Rainer Wunderlich Verlag, 1969), pp. 481-90; the ministers did respond before the introduction of parliamentary state secretaries.

[18] Arnold J. Heidenheimer, "Der starke Regierungschef und das Parteiensystem: Der Kanzler-Effekt in der Bundesrepublik," *Politische Vierteljahresschrift*, vol. 2 (1961), pp. 241-62.

rule. His failure as Chancellor was at least in part attributed to the fact that he had no control over the party. This served to support the view that simultaneous incumbency of the two offices by one person is an advantage, and even a necessity.[19] But the successful cooperation between Brandt as Social Democratic party (SPD) chairman and Schmidt as Chancellor has shown that a division of labor can work to advantage. There is an economy of time: Chancellor and party chairman are both full-time jobs, if each job is to be done well. The separation of the two offices shields the Chancellor from the direct impact of his party's opinion on his own decision in a given issue and opens up new possibilities for conflict management. The separation of offices works well in this particular case because Brandt as party chairman is unique; he has been Chancellor himself and is obviously without any ambition to seek this office again. The case of Brandt and Schmidt, therefore, is not conclusive proof that the Chancellor can forgo the active leadership of the party without risking his power and position.

Popular support is also of evident importance for a Chancellor. The parties try to win votes by putting up attractive candidates, and it has become common practice for the major political parties to designate publicly their candidate for the office of Chancellor before a general election. A candidate who wins elections for his party finds his dependence on the party organization is attenuated. By achieving the popular image of a national leader, a Chancellor secures a certain autonomy for himself. It is of course difficult to assess the precise impact of the so-called Chancellor effect in elections.[20] In a careful analysis of survey and election data, Norpoth concludes that while party identification remains the dominant factor in election decisions, the attractiveness of a candidate has an indirect effect on party identification and accounts directly for around 10 percent of the variance in voting decisions.[21] Differences in the popularity of specific candidates are mainly due, Norpoth shows, to personal traits and to their presumed experience and leadership potential. The latter works to the advantage of the incumbent, and in the five elections between 1961 and 1976 the acting Chancellor has always been the more popular candidate.[22]

---

[19] Werner Kaltefleiter, "Die Kanzler-Demokratie," in Helmut Unkelbach, Rudolf Wildenmann, Werner Kaltefleiter, eds., *Wähler, Parteien, Parlament* (Frankfurt: Athenäum, 1965), p. 49; Bracher, "Kanzlerdemokratie," p. 196.

[20] Heidenheimer, "Kanzler-Effekt," p. 253-57.

[21] Helmut Norpoth, "Kanzlerkandidaten—Wie sie vom Wähler bewertet werden und seine Wahlentscheidung beeinflussen," *Politische Vierteljahresschrift*, vol. 18 (1977), pp. 551-72.

[22] Ibid., p. 563.

Popular support is of greatest importance to a Chancellor for winning office. But for maintaining a hold on office, the party rather than popular support becomes crucial. This is clearly demonstrated by the fact that three of the five Chancellors of the Federal Republic— Adenauer, Erhard, and Brandt—resigned in between elections when they became a burden rather than an asset to their parties and hence lost their active support. The case of Erhard is of particular significance, since he was neither too old, as was Adenauer, nor involved in a scandal, as was Brandt; he was prevailed upon to resign because his leadership was judged to be ineffective.

Federal Ministers as Sectoral Executives. German federal ministers are constitutionally defined as sectoral leaders who exercise executive authority in their own right and not merely in the Chancellor's name. In fact, their responsibility for and interest in their department restricts their potential function as generally disinterested political counselors. This was recognized in one of the several proposals for Cabinet reform, which called for a Cabinet composed of genuine counselors, ministers without portfolio.[23] This proposal was never seriously considered because the effectiveness of a political executive that excludes the heads of powerful bureaucratic departments is highly doubtful.

Federal ministers are politicians, not bureaucrats. The career ladder of the higher civil service does not lead to these political offices. Of course civil servants can and increasingly do enter parliament, but to aspire to the office of minister they would normally have to renounce their civil service career and become professional politicians. Nearly all federal ministers have been members of the federal parliament and have usually served for more than one legislative period before becoming minister. Many had leading positions in the parliamentary party group. The vast majority of federal ministers have also had leadership positions in their political party.[24] A minister who at the time of his appointment did not even belong to a political party is a rare exception. The functional importance of these two selective criteria is evident, for a minister must convince the parliamentary majority to support his legislative initiatives. Yet, it is probably the

[23] Morkel, "Reform des Kabinetts," pp. 8-11.

[24] Recruitment criteria of federal ministers have been analyzed by Loewenberg, *Parlamentarismus*, chap. 5; Rolf-Peter Lange, "Auslesestrukturen bei der Besetzung von Regierungsämtern," in J. Dittberner and R. Ebbighausen, eds., *Parteiensystem in der Legitimationskrise* (Opladen: Westdeutscher Verlag, 1973), pp. 132-71; Klaus von Beyme, "Regierungswechsel 1969," in Gerhard Lehmbruch et al., *Demokratisches System und politische Praxis der Bundesrepublik* (Munich: Piper and Co., 1971), pp. 255-85.

visibility of these leadership positions rather than the experience they provide that makes them important for a ministerial career.

While the catchment area for the recruitment of federal ministers is primarily at the federal level, there is also a certain influx from leading positions at the regional level. Lange mentions that of eighty-three federal ministers appointed up to 1972, thirty-six had previously been members of a regional parliament, twenty-three had held executive positions at this level, and twelve had been high Länder officials.[25] There is also a general tendency, though not an explicit rule, that ministers should come from the different regions roughly in proportion to the political weight of the different Land organizations in the party. Religious affiliation has increasingly lost importance, and only a few ministers held leading positions in interest organizations previous to their appointment. The most relevant organizational affiliation for federal ministers, especially those from the SPD, has been labor union membership.

A significant characteristic of German federal ministers is that the majority are experts in the fields for which they are appointed, whether by virtue of education and training or by virtue of professional experience and organizational affiliations. Most ministers of finance and of economic affairs have been economists, while the department of labor tends to be headed by a union official. This is not inconsistent with their being professional politicians, since a successful political career is typically started after having learned a profession, and expertise continues to be important for advancement.[26] Rotation among departments is consequently rather rare. Only a small minority of federal ministers has headed two or more different departments.[27] Potential Chancellors, however, seek to rotate among ministries in order to broaden their knowledge. Thus, when Schmidt asked the SPD finance minister Apel to become minister of defense, it was interpreted as a sign that the Chancellor considered him a potential successor.

Whether or not they change departments, federal ministers tend to stay in office for more than one legislative period. Loewenberg analyzed the reasons federal ministers are not returned to office or lose it prematurely. He found that of forty-nine cases the majority (thirty-two) had lost the support of their party and were therefore not nominated again or prevailed upon to resign, thirteen resigned of their

[25] Lange, "Auslesestrukturen," p. 155.

[26] Dietrich Herzog, *Politische Karrieren* (Opladen: Westdeutscher Verlag, 1975).

[27] Frank Armbruster, "Ressort-Rotationen in Grossbritannien und in der Bundesrepublik Deutschland: Minister—Fachmann oder Politiker?" *Zeitschrift für Parlamentsfragen*, no. 1 (1973), pp. 95-110.

own account or had died, and only in four cases had the Chancellor dismissed a minister or refused to nominate him again.[28] The chance of dismissal, though formally a legal instrument of the Chancellor, is very slight indeed.

An analysis of ministerial careers shows a dual base of power: party support and departmental jurisdiction. Party support is needed to obtain and maintain office, and to get parliamentary approval for departmental programs. Ministers who cannot count on a relatively secure following in their party and parliamentary party group easily suffer defeat with their proposals and in their careers. An extremely clear illustration of this point is the fate of the nonpartisan minister of science and education, Hans Leussink, who was unable to find political support for his policies and therefore resigned from office. Much the same fate may befall a minister coming from a regional party or parliament who has not yet built up his own following at the federal level.

An important determinant of a minister's standing within government is the jurisdiction of the department he heads. A department such as Finance or Foreign Affairs provides its chief more occasion to present and make decisions on weighty issues than a department dealing with youth and family affairs or with relations to underdeveloped countries. Within these jurisdictional constraints, the unpredictable development of problems often determines the potential influence of a minister. If questions of internal security and terrorism suddenly become pressing, the minister of the interior will have his hour; if unemployment threatens, the voice of the minister of labor assumes added weight. Only within this twofold set of external constraints is an individual's departmental leadership of importance for the real executive power of a minister.

The process of leadership in the federal departments has been described extensively elsewhere.[29] The pattern of ministerial influence is basically not unlike that of the Chancellor, though in a different context. Ministers do not function as supreme policy makers within their department's area of jurisdiction. Their attention to issues and legislative initiatives is selective. In many cases they formulate opinions only by reacting when proposals developed by the sections are submitted to them. Intradepartmental policy making evolves from an implicit dialogue between the political leadership at the top and the civil servants at the base of the organization. This process, which is mediated by the divisional leadership, articulates two criteria of ratio-

---

[28] Loewenberg, *Parlamentarismus*, p. 281.
[29] Mayntz and Scharpf, *Policy-Making*, pp. 95-106.

nality, the expert opinion of civil servants and the political consider-ations of the department's leaders. To hold his own in this process, it is important for a minister to be able to counter the expert arguments of his officials and to have sources of information outside the depart-ment. These are often provided in a seemingly haphazard way through contacts at party meetings, public hearings, scientific con-gresses, and informal chats on a great variety of occasions. A minis-ter's hold on the development of his department's program is firmer, the greater his personal weight in government and in his party. If a minister is able to get Cabinet and parliamentary approval for his policy proposals and financial demands, he also enjoys high prestige in his department, because in the eyes of his officials, that is, civil ser-vants, that is precisely his function.

In contrast to the British case, ministers do not form a cohesive social group.[30] German ministers seem to be loners who have to fight on all fronts: against at least some of their officials, of their colleagues, and of the factions within their party. Their ties of loyalty and friendship appear to be determined more by their particular back-ground and party career than by the position in which they find them-selves, so that no clear pattern emerges. While this may make their individual lives more uncomfortable, it decreases the danger that wrong decisions are made or right ones dropped because they might chill the collegial atmosphere.

Collegial Decision Making in the Cabinet. The influence structure of the federal government described so far calls for specific complemen-tary functions to be fulfilled by the Cabinet as collective actor in the policy-making process. For the Chancellor, Cabinet meetings should provide the platform to articulate his policy guidelines and to exercise leadership in direct interaction with his ministers. The second major Cabinet function derives from the relative autonomy of the federal departments. It is to coordinate and integrate departmental policies and to resolve conflicts between ministers. The Cabinet should also evaluate policy proposals from different departments in terms of a common frame of reference. If this does not happen collectively, the policy process will be fragmented, disjointed, and bear the seeds of conflict, which will emerge only later when programs with discordant effects are implemented.[31]

---

[30] Hugh Heclo and Aaron Wildavsky, *The Private Government of Public Money* (London: Macmillan, 1974).

[31] This section is partly based on interviews which the author was able to conduct with a number of ministers.

The agenda of Cabinet meetings is only partly determined by formal rules stipulating the matters subject to its decision. Legislative proposals of the government must receive Cabinet approval before going to parliament, as do government decrees (*Regierungsverordnungen*, § 80 I 1 GG). A number of emergency decisions are also constitutionally reserved for the collegial decision of the Cabinet. Whether the government's answer to a formal parliamentary request for information (*Grosse Anfrage*) must be considered by the Cabinet is open, and has been handled in different ways on different occasions and by different Chancellors.[32]

The Cabinet regularly discusses certain matters that often do not involve a formal decision. They are the current state of foreign affairs, the Bundesrat's reaction to legislative proposals, and decisions prepared by the European Community on which the German government has to take a position. There are also departmental matters which ministers may, but need not, submit to the deliberation and judgment of the Cabinet. Inexperienced ministers and those seeking Cabinet support against opposition within their department make use of this opportunity more often than do powerful and experienced ministers.

Many of the proposals that are formally submitted to the Cabinet never appear on the agenda of its meetings after they are circulated among the departments (*Umlaufverfahren*). Analyzing the performance of Brandt's Cabinet, Brauswetter estimated that fully 75 percent of the proposals formally submitted to the Cabinet were circulated and approved without discussion.[33] The ministers and the Chancellor often sign the proposals as formally requested without even reading them, because they rely on the judgment of their officials. Most of the papers circulated either need no substantive decision, or, if they do, informal agreement among all concerned has been reached beforehand, so that Cabinet approval can be a mere formality.

Matters which actually get on the agenda of Cabinet meetings are those of great political or financial importance and urgency. Even then, proposals coming up for a formal decision have mostly achieved an informal consensus in negotiations between the departments. In this process of coordination, the Chancellor's Office decides what is to be circulated and what will be discussed by the Cabinet. To be able to plan the agenda of Cabinet meetings in advance, the Chancellor's Office sets dates and deadlines for the submission of proposals coming from the different departments. It therefore plays a central role in structuring the governmental decision-making process. Since timing

---

[32] Brauswetter, *Kanzlerprinzip*, p. 132ff.

[33] Ibid., p. 51.

and the choice between circulation or direct discussion can make a difference in the substance of a decision, procedural management is a source of much influence for the Chancellor's Office.

Cabinet decisions may be prepared beforehand in three different ways. The first involves the sections or divisions of the departments which are directly or indirectly affected. The agreement or compromise they work out among themselves is acknowledged by their ministers, mostly without much discussion, and subsequently submitted for Cabinet approval.

The second way is through one of the Cabinet committees, where the ministers and departments affected meet directly to negotiate an agreement and prepare a recommendation for Cabinet approval. Cabinet committees are problem-oriented and mostly, though not always, cut across ministerial jurisdictions.[34] Thus, Cabinet committees exist for security, finance, economic affairs, nuclear energy, and science and education. Formally, the Chancellor chairs the meetings of Cabinet committees, though in practice it is mostly the responsible minister. Depending on the importance of the issues, ministers who are members of a committee may in turn send a deputy, so that the actual attendance of ministers becomes an indicator of a committee's importance. Importance varies with the general political and economic situation; at present, nuclear energy and finance seem to be the two most important committees. Brauswetter estimates that 20 percent of all Cabinet proposals, especially the important ones and those with a high conflict potential, pass through a Cabinet committee.[35]

A third route is through bilateral contacts between the Chancellor and various ministers, or discussion in one of the informal groups that are more or less institutionalized. At present, for instance, there is a regular breakfast meeting of the Free Democratic (FDP) members of the Cabinet before each meeting (the SPD deliberately renounces doing the same), and the weekly luncheon of the so-called Schaumburger Runde, a meeting of the SPD and FDP coalition partners, in which the parliamentary party groups are also represented.

Where decisions (and especially legislative proposals of importance) have been prepared in this fashion, a new view seldom emerges in the Cabinet meeting. But occasionally an apparently agreed-upon proposal meets unexpected criticism or is even rejected by the Cabinet, and all interested parties are then reminded to take this hurdle seri-

---

[34] Arnd Morkel, *Kabinettsausschüsse als Instrumente interministerieller Koordination*, Report for the Projektgruppe Regierungs- und Verwaltungsreform (Bonn, December 1973).

[35] Brauswetter, *Kanzlerprinzip*, p. 152.

ously and to anticipate carefully the possible arguments and decision criteria of the government acting as a collective. Not all issues coming up at Cabinet meetings have been prepared in this way, so that discussions are usually lively. One of the informal rules that guides discussion is that the smaller coalition partner is not to be outvoted on points defined as essential by him. Another convention (which Heclo and Wildavsky have also found in Britain[36]) restrains ministers from criticizing the proposals of a colleague in Cabinet if their own department, its tasks and jurisdiction, are not affected. This convention can also be reflected in the briefing a minister gets from his officials, which may simply state "No substantive comment—this department is not affected." This restraint is sometimes ignored, especially if the Chancellor himself insists on a critical evaluation in the course of a Cabinet discussion.

These conventions and procedures serve to lower manifest conflict in Cabinet deliberations. If the full conflict latent in the issues submitted were to erupt in Cabinet discussions, the consensus-building capacity of this group would be seriously strained and the process of policy making blocked. Conflicts which do become manifest in Cabinet discussions are rarely of a purely partisan nature (for instance, FDP ministers against SPD ministers); more often they are structurally determined, reflecting the conflicting interests and orientations of the departments and their clientele. Independent of the party affiliation of their ministers, conflicts thus come up with a certain frequency between Labor and Economic Affairs, Health and Agriculture, Interior and Justice, and between Finance and all departments affected by major spending decisions. Aside from such structurally determined clashes of interest, intense Cabinet conflicts are triggered by issues with a great degree of cognitive uncertainty, since these leave wide scope for interpretation and lack any evident best solution.

Conflicts of opinion in the Cabinet can be resolved by putting the issue to a vote, but formal voting is relatively rare. The Chancellor normally attempts to formulate what he perceives to be the majority view, and if there is no formal opposition, this becomes the Cabinet decision. This procedure gives the Chancellor a particularly good chance to bring his own view to bear on the matter. As already mentioned, Cabinet members are formally held to support the collegial decision of the Cabinet or at least not to oppose it publicly. Though this rule has sometimes been violated, it is usually adhered to.[37] Of course not all acute conflicts within the Cabinet can be resolved.

---

[36] Heclo and Wildavsky, *Private Government*, pp. 141ff.

[37] Schmidt-Jortzig, *Geschlossenheit der kollegialen Regierung*, pp. 31-43.

The situation takes a dramatic turn when a minister faces the opposition of the rest of the Cabinet, including the Chancellor, on a point he deems essential. In a situation like this the well-known economics minister Karl Schiller resigned under Brandt, and recently Erhard Eppler resigned under Schmidt.[38]

The relative influence of individual ministers in Cabinet deliberation varies with the issue, their political weight, and the esteem in which they are held by the Chancellor. Only the finance minister enjoys formally a special position: He has the power of veto in all decisions of financial importance, including all legislative proposals with implications for public spending, provided that the Chancellor sides with him. The power position of the finance minister is supported by the fact that his department must be consulted at an early stage in the development of policy proposals that call for government expenditure. Yet the German finance minister may well be relatively less powerful than his British or his Italian counterpart. Not only does the annual budget itself have the status of a law, but legal norms restrain his handling of the budget during the fiscal year.[39]

The analysis of its internal dynamics suggests that most Cabinet decisions should be described as decisions *approved* rather than *made* by government collectively. But the anticipated need to obtain Cabinet approval influences all policy formation and decision processes that occur before the issue comes before the collective organ. The integrative force of this mechanism should not be underestimated, though it is true that the process is indirect. To the extent that decision making does take place in Cabinet meetings, much depends on the role played by the Chancellor. By his own behavior and contributions he can select the points to be discussed, and whether these discussions lead to some concrete result or peter out without a decision depends on his chairmanship. The management of the decision-making process on critical issues which have yet to be fully agreed on is a basic function of the Chancellor, and nobody can substitute for him. At this point, the personal leadership style of a Chancellor becomes important.

The leadership style of the various federal Chancellors has varied considerably.[40] The strong, at times even authoritarian performance of Adenauer as Chancellor has often been noted. He tended to make decisions on important matters himself—the often criticized "solitary

---

[38] Eppler, *Das Schwerste ist Glaubwürdigkeit*, pp. 97-103.

[39] Sontheimer and Röhring, *Handbuch*, p. 276.

[40] See Alt, *Es begann mit Adenauer*; Brauswetter, *Kanzlerprinzip*; Loewenberg, *Parlamentarismus*, especially pp. 299-316; and Bracher, "Kanzlerdemokratie," pp. 186-201.

decisions," which implied a decidedly reduced role for the Cabinet as an organ of collective decision making. Adenauer's successor, Erhard, recognized the importance of the Cabinet as a decision-making group, but his personal leadership style lacked decisiveness; the expert on economic matters proved unable to provide the general leadership expected of a Chancellor. Kurt-Georg Kiesinger, the Chancellor of the Grand Coalition between SPD and CDU, was forced to engage in constant maneuverings because the substantive consensus between the two governing parties was small. Furthermore, Kiesinger came to office from one of the Länder and lacked a strong personal following at the party's federal level. These external constraints and his personal inclination not to force an issue but always to seek a compromise produced a situation in which the focus of the policy process shifted away from government.

Willy Brandt's performance as Chancellor is particularly interesting because of the pronounced difference in leadership style between his first and his second term of office. Brandt was intensely interested in foreign policy and wanted the Cabinet to look after domestic policy. During his first term of office his leadership was perceived as strong, though decidedly nonauthoritarian. He used all his considerable personal authority to convince his government of his foreign policy, and he listened patiently and with little interference to long Cabinet discussions on domestic issues. Over time Brandt seems to have become less willing or less able to direct these discussions to a conclusion. In Brandt's second term of office, the intense and often heated Cabinet discussions often failed to produce a decision and were viewed as increasingly pointless, and Brandt was more and more accused of being a weak leader (*Führungsschwäche*). Brandt's successor, Helmut Schmidt, emphasizes the role of the Cabinet in governmental decision making but exercises his leadership functions unhesitatingly. Observers remark that Schmidt is extremely well prepared in Cabinet meetings, that he has read the proposals in detail and has a knack of picking out critical details and implications. From his ministers he expects equally well-considered opinions, which he willingly hears out, but he monitors the discussion firmly and directs it toward a concluding decision.

The dynamics of executive decision making vary considerably with the Cabinet's party composition. It seems particularly easy for a Chancellor to assume a predominant role in Cabinet deliberations when there is one clear majority party. A Grand Coalition seems to make for a rather diffuse pattern of decision making; here the government has no firm hold on the parliamentary party groups, and the importance of small informal groups in the decision process grows.

At the time of CDU-SPD coalition, the so-called *Kressbronner Kreis*, a circle of top representatives of the two coalition partners in government and in parliament became a more effective decision center than the Cabinet. A coalition government that jointly enjoys a small majority in parliament provides a different context in which the discipline of the parliamentary party groups is more decisive and their consent more sought after. At the same time this situation forces policy compromises which may make relations with his own political party difficult for the Chancellor.

Conflicts and Constraints in Executive Decision Making

By their very nature, powerful organized interest groups advocate conflicting policies, and these conflicts are reflected in the government. Here we shall look at the conflicts that arise between government and two other major actors in the political system, the political parties in parliament and the Länder.

Ironically, the most serious constraints for government action lie not in the opposition party but in the governing parties. The opposition can be outvoted; support of the government's own party group(s) is essential. It is therefore useful to see on what grounds parliamentary members of the governing coalition may refuse to go along with the expressed wishes of their own Chancellor and government.[41] An interesting example is provided by the decision on old age pensions in late 1976.

In the Federal Republic, old age pensions are paid out of a special fund and adjusted at regular intervals to changes in average per capita income; the decision must be formally taken by parliament (*Rentenanpassungs-Gesetz*). In the 1976 election campaign, the coalition parties had promised to increase pensions by 10 percent on July 1, 1977 (SPD), or at least in the course of 1977 (FDP). When the new coalition government was being formed after the election in September, new calculations that posited a higher rate of expected unemployment made it clear that the financial basis for such a pension increase was lacking. In a meeting on December 7, the top political leaders of the FDP and SPD therefore decided to postpone the promised upward revision of pensions until January 1978. Neither the Cabinet nor the parliamentary party groups had been consulted before this decision. Within the SPD party organization and its parliamentary party group, this provoked immediate and strong opposition, since party politicians

---

[41] The following is based on two case studies especially prepared for this purpose by Lothar Klaes. He analyzed in detail the extensive press coverage of the two issues.

felt personally committed to the promise they had made to voters at numerous campaign meetings, and they felt their credibility would be questioned. Within the FDP, opposition was less vociferous since its campaign promise had been less precise than that of the SPD, and old age pensioners are not an important group of voters for this party. The SPD called its parliamentary party group to a special meeting on December 8. Schmidt, who was to be formally reelected Chancellor on December 14, and the designated (SPD) ministers of finance and of labor defended the decision as financially unavoidable and socially just (the average net income of the working population had in fact risen less than 10 percent in the period of comparison), but they failed to sway the majority opinion of the parliamentary members. By the end of the meeting Schmidt gave in, motivated possibly by the realization that the defection of only five parliamentary members of the coalition parties could endanger his election, even though apparently no such threat had been made.

A small commission was set up to investigate financial alternatives and was convened under the Chancellor's chairmanship that same evening. A compromise solution was found during the first meeting, and that same night Schmidt and the chairman of the SPD parliamentary group met with the prospective Vice Chancellor Genscher (FDP) and the FDP parliamentary group's chairman to agree on the new proposal. This was formally accepted the following day at the meeting of the coalition parties. The compromise permitted the coalition parties to save face (the increase *was* to take place on July 1, 1977), but took the existing financial strictures into account by laying the ground for decreasing expenditures later.

A second well-publicized case shows basically the same dynamics, though this time it was the party group that had to compromise. The case involved a decision on whether to build a nuclear power plant in Kalkar. The decision had been shifted upward to the federal parliament by the Land parliament of Northrhine-Westfalia, which did not want to take full responsibility in view of the protest of citizen groups. A vast majority of the members of parliament in Bonn were actually in favor of the power plant. When it became clear that some of the FDP members were opposed, however, the CDU and Christian Social Union (CSU), the parliamentary opposition, saw the possibility of inflicting defeat on the coalition government and came out against building the plant. The real problem was that six FDP members of parliament, following a recent resolution of the annual FDP convention, said they would vote against the project. This opposition took the coalition government by surprise, probably because the FDP resolution against nuclear energy had not been discussed at the highest level between the two governing parties. No early indication of what was about to happen had come to the attention of the executive branch, nor had precautionary measures been taken. The conflict was solved only when Chancellor Schmidt put strong pressure on the FDP leaders, threatening to make the issue the object of a vote of confidence, whereupon the FDP ministers and the parliamentary party group's chairman made it clear to their parliamentary members that they in turn would consider a negative vote as a vote of no confidence against themselves. The issue about nuclear energy had thus been turned into a question of the government's survival, and this extreme pressure finally brought the opposing members of parliament back in line. Taken together, these two cases illustrate well the complex interdependence between the executive branch and its parliamentary group, and the special nature of issues that can arouse the latter's opposition to government action.

Conflicts between the federal government and the Länder arise largely in connection with legislation, although other problems may arise in the execution of a program that requires the active cooperation of the Länder. Some programs, such as regional economic development, have been constitutionally established as Joint Tasks, while others, such as finding deposits for nuclear energy waste or combating terrorism, require ad hoc agreements. We are here concerned only with legislative conflict, however, and with the Bundesrat as a public forum.

The Bundesrat meeting in plenary session is a decision-making body only within limits. Legislative initiatives of the federal government are first discussed in the appropriate Bundesrat committee, where the expertise of leading administrators guides deliberation. The initiatives are then passed on with the committee's recommendation to the Länder cabinets, where each Land decides how it will vote. In the plenary meetings of the Bundesrat these decisions are registered and justified, but normally are not subject to change. Until 1969 the CDU and CSU dominated both the Bundestag and the Bundesrat. The Bundesrat was then considered an institution in which partisan views were of little importance and considerations of administrative practicability prevailed. Even then, however, it often modified bills submitted by the federal government. When the SPD became the major governing party in 1969, the Bundesrat was for the first time dominated by Länder governments led by the federal opposition party.

Since 1969 the Bundesrat has gained political power, which it uses to impose the federal opposition party's view on legislative matters; the Bundesrat can thus defeat the intentions of the parliamentary majority. The extent of this obstructive potential is clear from the fact that since 1969 the proportion of federal bills needing Bundesrat approval has increased to more than 50 percent.[42] The federal government can diminish the influence of the Bundesrat by using certain strategies, for instance, having bills introduced by one or both of the majority parties (in which case it is passed to the Bundesrat only after it is first discussed in parliament).[43] To some extent legislative initiatives can also be formulated in such a way that Bundesrat approval is not needed, but there are definite limits to this strategy if substantive issues are at stake. In the 1970s the Bundesrat imposed significant modifications on a number of federal legislative initiatives. In 1976, for instance, it rejected the new vocational training law (*Berufsbildungsgesetz*), making itself the spokesman of industry and the craft organizations that opposed the law. Parliament later passed a very truncated version of this law, which no longer needed Bundesrat approval, but which also no longer contained the provision that would have made a substantive difference to the quality of vocational training.[44]

It could be argued that the Bundesrat no longer regards legislation from the point of view of an administrative body charged with implementation, nor is it simply defending the constitutional autonomy of the Länder; its criteria have instead become more political. The general motive of defeating the governing majority in Bonn is linked in complex ways with the desire to advocate partisan ideology (for instance, in favor of private property and against nationalization) and to represent specific social groups in the formation of policy decisions. But even if the Bundesrat does engage in political opposition to the federal government and parliament, neither its inclination nor its power to do so should be overemphasized. The Länder Executive in Saarland, for example, though dominated by the CDU, includes one of the governing parties in Bonn in a coalition (FDP), a circumstance that obviously attenuates the willingness of this group to oppose federal government proposals. And some of the smaller, CDU-dominated Länder feel particularly dependent on federal support and therefore do not tend to oppose it in the Bundesrat. On many issues, however, the structurally determined, common interest of the Länder is still more important than partisan politics in determining the attitude toward federal government proposals. The role of the Bundesrat as a

---

[42] von Beyme, *Politisches System der Bundesrepublik*, p. 200; data cover the period until 1976.

[43] Heinz Laufer, "Der Bundesrat als Instrument der Opposition?" *Zeitschrift für Parlamentsfragen*, vol. 1 (1970), p. 339.

[44] See *Entwurf eines Gesetzes zur Förderung des Angebots an Ausbildungsplätzen in der Berufsausbildung*, Bundestagsdrucksache 7/5236 (May 20, 1976).

political opposition to the federal government is therefore limited, and most legislative proposals do in fact achieve Bundesrat approval without major difficulties.

Changes in the Exercise of Executive Leadership

It is difficult to set an intelligent baseline date for changes in the pattern of executive leadership. I shall consider here the period reaching back to the middle of the 1960s, which marked the end of the postwar phase of reconstruction and the "economic miracle." It was the time when student rebellion and extraparliamentary opposition created unwonted unrest and when the need for effective executive action assumed a new urgency. Closely connected with the attendant changes in the problem of governing were two significant developments that have affected the pattern of executive leadership. There have been attempts to set up institutional and procedural machinery for government-wide planning, and there have been changes in the relationship between government on the one hand and party organizations and parliamentary party groups on the other hand.

Attempts to increase the planning capacity of the federal government started in the field of resource management.[45] A system of medium- and long-term financial planning was introduced, the main function of which is to improve the information base of the budgetary process, since it is an instrument of an indicative rather than a prescriptive nature. The financial planning system, however, has not been integrated, either procedurally or substantively, with the process of policy planning.

A second attempt to strengthen planning capacity focused on individual departments. Special units for planning (group, staff, or division) were set up, since it was felt that existing divisions were already overburdened by the demands made on them and were unable to tackle future-oriented and complex planning tasks. Efforts were also made to improve the data base and data processing capacity as a prerequisite for planning. By and large, these innovations have become an integral part of federal departments, though it is difficult to establish with any certainty how much this has improved departmental policy making.[46]

---

[45] Heribert Schatz, "Auf der Suche nach Problemlösungsstrategien: Die Entwicklung der politischen Planung auf Bundesebene," in Renate Mayntz and Fritz W. Scharpf, eds., *Planungsorganisation* (Munich: Piper and Co., 1973), pp. 21-26, 48-57.

[46] Mayntz and Scharpf, *Policy-Making*, pp. 107-16.

The third and most significant effort aimed at creating a government-wide planning system managed by the Chancellor's Office. This office has traditionally fulfilled several functions besides serving as the secretariat of the Cabinet, organizing the inflow of proposals, and setting up the agenda of Cabinet meetings. It aids the Chancellor in developing and formulating his policy decisions. To this purpose the internal structure of the Chancellor's Office mirrors the program structure of the government at large, that is, it covers all areas of policy making and can therefore provide the Chancellor with expert knowledge, information, and advice on all major problems, independently of the expertise concentrated in the federal departments. In this function the office enjoys a near monopoly, since the Chancellor has no other institutionalized sources of policy advice—not even the famous Economic Advisory Council (*Sachverständigenrat*) reports directly to him. The Chancellor's Office can also be used to carry the Chancellor's point of view into the federal departments, whose state secretaries meet every Monday with the office's chief to discuss current policy issues. Last and not least, the Chancellor's Office is expected to coordinate the activities of the federal departments. In the early years of its existence, such coordination was mainly technical; on substantive issues it remained rudimentary. This changed dramatically when the new planning system was introduced.

Faint beginnings of this system reach back to the time of Erhard, when a section for political planning was first established in the Chancellor's Office.[47] Under Erhard's successor, Kiesinger, this grew into a special staff for planning tasks. But it was only with the advent of the coalition of SPD and the liberal Free Democratic Party (FDP) and the appointment of Horst Ehmke (SPD) as its chief that the Chancellor's Office was transformed into the central planning unit of the federal government. Ehmke—ambitious, apparently a technocrat and a believer in modern planning procedures—was given large scope for action by Chancellor Brandt, who wanted him to develop initiatives and direct the office without much need for his own intervention.

Under Ehmke the office nearly doubled in size; the planning staff was changed into a regular division and assigned important directive and coordinative tasks. Brain-storming procedures and the

---

[47] The following paragraphs are based on Brauswetter, *Kanzlerprinzip*, pp. 16-52; Heiner Flohr, "Planungstätigkeit der Planungsabteilung im Bundeskanzleramt," *Politische Vierteljahresschrift*, vol. 4 (1972), pp. 54-69; Mayntz and Scharpf, *Policy-Making*, pp. 116-19; Jürgen Reese, "Eine Strategie zur Erhöhung der 'relativen Autonomie' des politischen Systems?" *Politische Vierteljahresschrift*, vol. 6 (1975), pp. 265-80; Schatz, *Auf der Suche*, pp. 34-67; Klaus Seemann, *Entzaubertes Bundeskanzleramt* (Landshut: Verlag Politisches Archiv, 1975).

task force principle were widely used. To increase the government-wide planning capacity of the office, a system of planning commissioners was created; these were departmental officials of senior rank who met every fortnight at the Chancellor's Office to discuss policy matters and who were to tighten the links with the departments. At the same time, rotation of personnel between the departments and the Chancellor's Office was urged. The next step was the introduction of a reporting system which obliged each department to inform the Chancellor's Office in a standardized form of all projects which at some later time would come up for Cabinet or Bundersrat approval. This system was also meant to inform the other departments, but primarily it was to enable the Chancellor's Office to coordinate projects and fit them into a timetable of government activities over the whole legislative period. This in turn implied the chance to set priorities and the opportunity, even the obligation, to urge departments to meet established deadlines. Finally, an attempt was made to set up groups for long-term planning, which were to spot policy-making needs on the basis of analyses of prospective developments in selected fields.

The nature of these innovations, the time pressure with which they were introduced, and Ehmke's personal leadership style all provoked increasing resistance, both within the Chancellor's Office and, more important, from the federal departments. The long-term planning effort did not produce any tangible results, partly because of the lack of an adequate information base and of analytical capacity. The new information and coordination system was perceived as a disguised attempt at central control and as a threat to departmental autonomy—not that the need for coordination between departments was disputed, but there was already a host of interdepartmental committees, varying greatly in size, duration, and importance.[48] The number of these committees is not exactly known, but the estimates have ranged from 60 to 150, depending on how they are defined. These committees exist at the departmental, divisional, and sectional levels and are composed of civil servants.

A violent clash finally occurred when the Chancellor's Office presented—without consulting with or even informing the departments—a medium-term program of government activities which it had based on information received through the new reporting system. Dissatisfaction became so widespread that Brandt himself withdrew

---

[48] Manfred Lepper, "Die Rolle und die Effektivität der interministeriellen Ausschüsse für Koordination und Regierungspolitik," in Heinrich Siedentopf, ed., *Regierungspolitik und Koordination* (Berlin: Duncker and Humblot, 1976), pp. 433-50.

his support. After the 1972 general election, Ehmke was not re-appointed, and the role of the Chancellor's Office was redefined in a more traditional, instrumental way that did not antagonize the departments.

What has remained as useful is the reporting system and an increased coordinating capacity in the Chancellor's Office. Schmidt uses the office today as a secretariat and a source of advice and information on various policy matters, but he definitely reserves for himself the leadership function and for his Cabinet the function of government-wide coordination. This development does more than reflect the pragmatic attitude of Schmidt; it compensates for a basic defect in rational-planning approach to politics by acknowledging the increasing demand for strategic ad hoc intervention and crisis management in the midst of growing economic and political pressures.

The nature of the problems confronting government today has also changed the relationship between the executive and the majority party or parties. In the period under consideration here, this relationship has become one of growing mutual dependence as well as increasing tension, leading to closer linkages. One reason for this is the growing organizational strength and self-assurance of the parties as political actors. To a certain extent this is a natural development, given the fact that today's political parties had to be created or reestablished at the beginning of the Federal Republic and needed time to consolidate. For the CDU this was particularly difficult, not only because of its initially loose structure, but also because it was so clearly dominated in the beginning by Adenauer as Chancellor, and not party chairman! In time, the CDU gained force (and demonstrated it by prevailing first upon Adenauer and later upon Erhard to relinquish office), and when it finally had to pass into opposition, concerted efforts were made to strengthen the party organization. The SPD, a coalition governing party since 1966 and the dominant partner since 1969, has always had a stronger and more coherent organization than the CDU and its party program had traditionally an ideological basis.

In the meantime, the parties' relationship to the executive has also been influenced by the signs of political mobilization in the face of new social and economic problems. The problems faced by the Federal Republic in its early years—satisfying basic material needs, rebuilding the economy, finding acceptance internationally—could command a widespread consensus. Since then there has been an erosion of the agreement on exactly what the major problems are now, what major goals are to be pursued, and how to go about doing so. This erosion was manifested in the student movement and later in political terrorism, massive citizen protest against nuclear power, and the sprouting of ecologically minded quasi parties which have started to take votes away from the established parties, particularly the SPD. This development has posed a challenge both to government and to the major parties. More than ever the executive needs effective support from political organizations able to function as mediators between it and the politically vocal population. At the same time, the parties try to keep abreast of the changes in popular mood by making themselves the advocates of new hopes and desires. There has therefore been a general trend for political parties to formulate not just election platforms, but policy goals which they expect their representatives in parliament and in government to take as guidelines for action. Party conventions today pass resolutions on specific policy issues such as nuclear energy, investment control, or public housing. These resolutions are clearly directed at the representatives in parliament and especially at government, which the majority parties increasingly perceive as *their* executive arm.

The impact of this development on government is the stronger because of a parallel growth in the power of parliamentary party groups. Since the middle of the 1960s, it has been the rule rather than the exception that governments have held relatively narrow majorities, which makes them dependent on the disciplined behavior of the parliamentary party groups. Meanwhile, the policy-making potential of the parliamentary politicians has increased, in part because an improved infrastructure provides members of parliament with expert assistance, information, and scientific advice. The recruitment and career patterns of members also contribute to the policy-making potential of the present parliament. Members can be characterized as professional politicians who normally have not only a solid occupational background but also experience in a series of increasingly important elective offices, both within their party and within local or regional authorities.[49]

The greater potential of parliamentary party groups to influence governmental policy making is now activated by party organizations. The parties and their parliamentary groups are closely linked, since the party organization largely controls the reelection chance of parliamentary members through its nominating procedures. This not only inspires individual loyalty to the organization, but also ensures that the different party wings, factions, and informal groups are repre-

---

[49] Herzog, *Politische Karrieren*, pp. 62-160.

sented among the elected members of parliament. In this way the view of the party on policy issues is directly transmitted to the parliamentary party group. If a Chancellor or minister antagonizes some important segment of his party with one of his decisions, it will provoke immediate criticism from the parliamentary party group.

To avoid clashes, ways have to be found to improve links between party politicians and the executive decision process at an early point. The most important institutional response has been the establishment in 1967 of a new executive role, the parliamentary state secretary. In contrast to the tenured state secretary, who has traditionally been a career civil servant responsible for the continuity of departmental administration, the parliamentary secretary must be a member of parliament. His term of office ends with the legislative period, and his role is to strengthen both the political element in the department and, in particular, its relations with parliament and the political parties.[50] In fact, this new role was largely perceived as the "parliamentarization of the executive."[51] Although the parliamentary secretary functions as ministerial deputy in Cabinet meetings and parliament, he does not merely relieve his minister of some duties and substitute for him. The parliamentary secretary *adds* to the previous pattern of executive interaction, especially by maintaining closer contact with various party groups than the minister could do by himself.[52]

As a second, less formal response to the need to maintain closer links with the relevant political groups, procedures were set up for the joint deliberation of policy questions *before* executive decisions are made. In one way or another—bilateral contacts, informal meetings, cooptation to existing committees—the leaders of the parliamentary party groups are included in the preparatory discussion of proposals that will be submitted to the Cabinet.[53] In this connection, semiformal political groups play an important role. As Rudzio has argued, the function of such groups is not merely that of a traditional coalition committee, a necessary forum to regulate preliminary conflict in coalition governments. The regular inclusion of party or

---

[50] Heinz Laufer, *Der Parlamentarische Staatssekretär: Eine Studie über ein neues Amt in der Bundesregierung* (Munich: Beck Verlag, 1969).

[51] F. Nuscheler, W. Steffani, "Umfrage zum Selbstverständnis der Parlamentarischen Staatssekretäre," *Zeitschrift für Parlamentsfragen,* vol. 1 (1970), pp. 25-29.

[52] Friedrich Karl Fromme, "Die Parlamentarischen Staatssekretäre," *Zeitschrift für Parlamentsfragen,* vol. 1 (1970), pp. 53-83.

[53] Gunter Hofmann, "Rücksicht auf viele Stimmen: Beim 'Macher' Schmidt haben die Parlamentarier ein Wort mitzureden," *Die Zeit,* no. 9 (1979), p. 4.

parliamentary party group leaders and the existence of similar institutions in the case of one-party governments show clearly that they serve to integrate the political sector into the process of executive policy making.[54]

The ambivalence of relations between executive and party becomes evident in the critical observations made before the general election due in 1980. In contrast to Brandt, who maintained close ties to his party and could be seen as executor of its will in a domestic reform program, Schmidt aspires to relative autonomy as Chancellor and national leader. Sober and pragmatic, he has shelved the failing reform program which became too costly, both financially and politically. To him, the programmatic views of his party are often a hindrance rather than a help to effective problem solution. The SPD knows there is no alternative to Schmidt to win the 1980 election. But if the party were to support him unconditionally it would decline as a political actor in its own right and thus maybe lose the allegiance of certain groups of voters among the young, the environmental protectionists, and the left-wing union members.[55] The present signs of unrest and discontent, especially at the level of regional SPD organizations,[56] foreshadow increasing conflict between the party and the Chancellor, and an increasingly difficult integrative task for the party chairman Brandt and the parliamentary party group's chairman Herbert Wehner.

The distribution of power among the major political actors is not a zero-sum game. In some ways both the executive and the political parties, including their parliamentary groups, have become more powerful by growing in functional importance, in organizational strength, and in planning capacity. The same general point can be made about Chancellor, Cabinet, and the ministers. A strong Chancellor does not employ ministers who are weak in their own sphere. A Cabinet able to resolve conflicts successfully and bring decision processes to a conclusion will not be found where the Chancellor lacks personal authority and leadership. While there are variations in the internal balance of power in the executive branch, the dominant pattern is one of checks and countervailing powers. The need for consensus building and conflict resolution is correspondingly high; the result can be the neutralization of initiatives and a loss in govern-

---

[54] Wolfgang Rudzio, "Mit Koalitionsausschüssen leben?" *Zeitschrift für Parlamentsfragen*, vol. 1 (1970), pp. 206-22.

[55] Gunter Hofmann, "Die SPD soll wieder Flagge zeigen," *Die Zeit*, no. 27 (1979), p. 4.

[56] "SPD: Blüten in der Provinz," Spiegel-Report, *Der Spiegel*, no. 10 (1979), pp. 44-54.

ment effectiveness. The pattern of executive leadership in the Federal Republic of Germany seems therefore to make more for a stable than for a very powerful government.

5

Is There a Government in Italy? Politics and Administration at the Top

Sabino Cassese

The Italian case is particularly challenging to those seeking to understand the relationship between politics and administration at the top. Whereas in other European countries problems of government are said to be intensifying,[1] Italy, according to recent studies by Percy A. Allum and by Giuseppe Di Palma,[2] has reached the point of having no government at all. Di Palma suggests that political leaders cannot even agree on decision rules or the question of who is in charge. Another of Italy's problems is that the central government has to deal with most issues, even though regional government has been in existence since 1970. Few problems are solved at the local level because communes, provinces, and regions are weak; because Italy

---

[1] See Richard Rose and Guy Peters, *Can Government Go Bankrupt?* (New York: Basic Books, 1978), p. 4; and Richard Rose, "Governo e autorità nelle democrazie occidentali," *Rivista Italiana di scienza politica*, no. 2 (1978), p. 213 ff. Of the four important points explaining the crisis of "governability," only the second one (growing complexity of the organization of government institutions) is analyzed in this article.

[2] Percy A. Allum, *Italy: A Republic Without a Government* (London: Weidenfeld and Nicholson, 1973), Italian translation: (Milan: Feltrinelli, 1976). Giuseppe Di Palma, *Surviving without Governing: The Italian Parties in Parliament* (Berkeley: University of California Press, 1977), Italian translation: (Bologna: Il Mulino, 1978).

More prudent is the judgment of Gianfranco Pasquino, "Recenti trasformazioni nel sistema di potere della democrazia cristiana," in Luigi Graziano and Sidney Tarrow, eds., *La crisi italiana*, vol. 2 (Turin: Einaudi, 1979), p. 609 ff., which speaks of government "weakness" in Italy.

It should be pointed out that, while everyone speaks of Italy as a country without a government, Italians who know about government from firsthand experience are mute. There are no memoirs or biographies of politicians or of public administrators. It would be difficult in Italy to write a book such as the one by Bruce Headey, *British Cabinet Ministers: The Roles of Politicians in Executive Office* (London: Allen and Unwin, 1974), which drew upon memoirs of ministers and civil servants.

has a centralized financial structure (the regions, provinces, and communes have spending powers, but their income derives from the central treasury); and because parties are effective mediators between local demands and the central government. These characteristics of the Italian system place excess strain on the central government and cause the lack of government action about which there are so many complaints.

In order to understand Italy's political situation today, we need to define government and to determine where and how it operates. We can define government in at least three ways: (1) as a group of political leaders or a political class, (2) as an institution defined by a constitution (for example, the Council of Ministers in Italy), or (3) as the executive, that is, the administrative machinery. In current usage, the term may refer to any or several of these meanings at one time, for example, in referring to the Council of Ministers and the public administration. A possible fourth meaning is government action and its results. Some people, for example, point to the innovative action of government following World War II, as reflected in the economic boom of the 1950s, the expansion of welfare institutions in the 1960s, and the great reforms of the 1970s (the regional reform of 1970, the fiscal reform of 1971, and the public health reform of 1978). Other people stress the negative consequences of government as reflected in the current inflation, increased public expenditure, and public disorder. This aspect of government is difficult to evaluate and is therefore excluded from the discussion.

If we first consider the political class, we are struck by the stability and continuity of the leading political groups in Italy. Since the end of World War II power has been in the hands of one party, the Christian Democrats, governing alone or in alliance with other parties. Since December 10, 1945, all the Premiers have belonged to the Christian Democratic party, and since June 2, 1946, the Ministry of the Interior has been in the hands of Christian Democrats. In only four out of thirty-four postwar governments has the Treasury not been controlled by the Christian Democrats.

Despite frequent crises (on average, there have been about five governments between every general election), the same persons have remained at the head of government: Alcide De Gasperi presided over eight governments; Aldo Moro, Mariano Rumor, and Giulio Andreotti over five; and Antonio Segni and Giovanni Leone, two each. The number of times individuals have held the key office of minister of the interior, calculated on the basis of the number of governments, were: Mario Scelba, seven times; Emilio Paolo Taviani, six; Franco Restivo, five; Ferdinando Tambroni and Rumor, five each; and **Amintore Fanfani**, two. At the Treasury, Emilio Colombo was minister eleven times; Giuseppe Pella and Silvio Gava, four each; and Taviani, twice. The saying that ministers pass while the bureaucracy remains can, in the Italian case, easily be reversed,[3] for ministers show great durability in certain posts.

Second, if we consider government in the sense of constitutional authority, today the government and the Council of Ministers (Consiglio dei Ministri) are synonymous. The 1948 Constitution of the Republic states that the Council of Ministers is charged with the function of government. The earlier constitution of 1848 mentioned neither the Council of Ministers nor the government; it was concerned only with ministers of the Crown. In the hundred years since the union of Italy in 1861, the role of the Council of Ministers has changed four times. Twice government has resided in the Council of Ministers, and twice elsewhere. During the first forty years after the union of Italy, government was in the hands of the Crown party under royal initiative, and in the late Fascist period after 1930, Mussolini "governed with the heads of departments," but the Council of Ministers rarely met and supremacy rested with Il Duce.

The Council of Ministers was the seat of government during the era of Giovanni Giolitti and during the first phase of Fascism. Giolitti recalls in his *Memorie* that the nationalization of the railways, legislation on religion and on public health, and the nomination of Riccardo Bianchi to be first director general of the railways were the result of collegial activity, which was influenced by Giolitti's choice of many technicians to be members of his second cabinet. During the first phase of Fascism the Council remained strong because it still had numerous politicians and technicians from the preceding period: for example, Gino Sarrocchi and Gabriele Carnazza in the Ministry of Public Works, Alberto De Stefani and Vincenzo Tangorra in the Ministry of Finance, and Alfredo Rocco in the Ministry of Justice. Mussolini himself needed their support.

The Constitution of 1948 must be evaluated with the history of the Council's changing function in mind. The constitution represented a revolution, because for the first time the function of government was

---

[3] Ezra Suleiman, *Politics, Power and Bureaucracy in France* (Princeton: Princeton University Press, 1974), pp. 112, 161 ff., similarly points out that the instability of governments in France was accompanied by considerable stability among ministers and parties. See Suleiman, *Elites In French Society: The Politics of Survival* (Princeton: Princeton University Press, 1978).

formally vested in the Council of Ministers. Whereas the constitution of 1848 permitted government functions to be carried out from various offices, the Constitution of 1948 introduced constraints that have led to a discrepancy between actual practice and what is prescribed in the constitution. Since 1948, government has once more moved away from the Council of Ministers: some governmental functions have been acquired by the governor of the Banca d'Italia and presidents of several public corporations; the minister of the Treasury has become stronger in comparison with his colleagues; and the Premier has acquired primacy over the committees of ministers in charge of different sectors of administration. Before 1948, government tended to function outside the Council of Ministers because greater power lay in other hands; today the phenomenon is the result of difficulties within the Council of Ministers.[4]

These difficulties, which have caused the function of government[5] to move outside the Council of Ministers, stem from several causes, one of which is the expansion of the bureaucracy in Italy. Today there are twenty ministries and their ministers, as well as several offices headed by ministers without portfolio.[6] With respect to the number of ministries, Giulio Andreotti has remarked:

> I remember among the things that scandalized me most in life (and . . . I have seen a good many), that at a meeting, for the changeover from the Badoglio ministry to Premier Bonomi, it was necessary to establish how many ministries there should be. It was not a question, then, of establishing if it was a good thing to have only one Ministry of Communications or a Ministry of the Economy; no, as there were six parties, each one should get three ministries, six by three is eighteen, eighteen ministries were agreed upon.[7]

---

[4] Sabino Cassese, *Burocrazia ed economia pubblica—cronache degli anni '70* (Bologna: Il Mulino, 1978).

[5] On government functions, Luigi Preti, *Il governo nella Costituzione italiana* (Milan: Giuffrè, 1959) and Fausto Cuocolo, *Il governo nel vigente ordinamento italiano* (Milan: Giuffrè, 1959), as well as "Consiglio dei ministri," in *Enciclopedia del diritto*. For an example of widespread criticism of "sick government" and "vacuum of power at the summit of the State," see Vezio Crisafulli "Partiti, Parlamento, Governo," in *La funzionalità dei partiti nello Stato democratico* (Milan: La Nuova Europa, 1967).

[6] See the items "Ministro," "Ministeri (dir. cost.)," and "Ministeri (dir. amn.)," respectively by Gian Franco Ciaurro, Onorato Sepe, and Lorenzo Carlassare in *Enciclopedia del diritto*.

[7] *I Conferenza nazionale dei trasporti*, vol. 1, Ministero dei trasporti (Rome: Istituto poligrafico, 1979), p. 56.

The Council of Ministers, thus swollen, does not function as a collegial organ.[8] There has even been talk of "government by ministries."[9] Frequently, bills are brought to the Council of Ministers without being indicated on the agenda, and subsequently are sent to Parliament in a text different from the one approved by the Council; meetings are convened suddenly and without an agenda; incomplete or even fictitious texts are approved by the Council; minutes of Council meetings are incomplete and are kept secret; meetings are held infrequently (at intervals of more than a month during the Rumor governments); the Council exercises its veto power in *concerti* (agreements obtained from some ministers, especially from the minister of the treasury concerning spending); there is poor coordination among ministers in initiating parliamentary legislation, and so on. Recently, however, Council meetings of the Andreotti governments returned to the weekly sessions introduced under De Gaspari; under Moro and Rumor, meetings had taken place monthly.

Ministers are chosen not only on the basis of their party and faction, but also, as in Canada, on the basis of their region, in order to ensure a balanced representation of the various territories. Government programs are formulated by the Premier in consultation with a few ministers and subsequently communicated in summarized form to the Council of Ministers before they are presented to Parliament. If the Council fails to function collectively, ministers and their offices operate in its stead, and even propose legislation that the Council then ratifies. It is enough, however, for one of the ministers or their offices to fail to ratify the legislation for the procedure to stop.

Another reason that the Council finds it difficult to function collectively is that the ministries, which on paper are equal, do not all have an equal weight of responsibility. Some have minor administrative tasks (Tourism and Entertainment, Merchant Navy, and Public Works), whereas others have important directive functions. The number of staff in each ministry also varies. For example, the Ministry of Education has more than a million employees, whereas ten minis-

---

[8] On this point, there is the important essay by Enzo Cheli and Vincenzo Spaziante, "Il Consiglio dei ministri e la sua presidenza dal disegno alla prassi," in Sergio Ristuccia, ed., *L'istituzione governo—analisi e prospettive* (Milan: Comunità, 1977), p. 41 ff.

[9] On the poor functioning of the Council of Ministers, especially in promoting legislation, see Nicola Greco, "Carenza di coordinamento, policenrismo e contrattualismo nell'attività di governo—Esame critico delle 'direttive' della Presidenza del consiglio, *Studi parlamentari e di politica costituzionale*, vol. 2 (1969), p. 23 ff. and Stefano Rodot, "La circolazione delle informazioni nell'apparato di governo," in Ristuccia, *L'istituzione governo*, p. 63 ff.

tries have fewer than 5,000 employees each, of which five have under 500.

Furthermore, ministerial appointments are not based on any standard qualifications for office, except that most ministers are members of Parliament. In the past many ministers had previous administrative experience, especially as councilors or mayors of local bodies. Others such as Colombo or Andreotti entered Parliament when they were still very young and therefore had ministerial experience in their early thirties. Now, however, few ministers have had any administrative experience. Whether or not they become good administrators depends on their individual ability and sensitivity. Many effective members of Parliament when put in charge of a ministry do not prove a success. Although many members of Parliament take an interest in the work of particular sectors of government, some may do so for reasons of self-interest. About a third of the presidents and vice-presidents of parliamentary committees subsequently receive ministerial or undersecretary appointments in the same sector of the executive.

A similar pattern can be observed among technicians who became ministers. Those who had previous administrative experience—for example, Gaetano Stammati, who had held positions of responsibility in ministries such as Finance, State Holdings, and the Treasury, and Rinaldo Ossola, who had been a manager at the Banca d'Italia— became successful administrators in government. Others, however, did no better than the ministers chosen from among members of Parliament. The few nonparty ministers nominated, especially since 1975, have not had to be concerned about their electoral supporters, as is usually the case for partisan ministers, who must maintain weekly contacts with their particular electoral constituency and who must help party leaders formulate party policy.

The overall structure of ministries can be weakened when outside interests gain entry into the organization, or when the responsibility of ministerial office becomes unimportant in the minds of the individual ministers. The Council of Ministers is organized to include administrative heads; that is, the heads of the ministries are present as the official representatives of their departments. The responsibility of office, however, is being neglected by more and more Council members, who are giving higher priority to their role as representatives of factions or parties outside their departments than to their governmental role. A study of the distribution of circulars issued to the ministers by the Premier's office from 1950 to 1968 has shown that in the 1950s these circulars were sent to all heads of departments, but that subsequently they were directed to ministers in their capacity as members or representatives of parties or factions.[10] Interministerial committees have also helped to drain power from the Council of Ministers, especially between 1948 and 1967, when they were numerous. In 1967 some of these committees were absorbed in the Committee for Economic Planning, but since 1970 their numbers have increased once again.[11]

The Council's role as the governing body has been reduced further by the shifting of functions to higher and lower levels. For example, the minister of agriculture theoretically has given up jurisdiction over certain issues to the European Economic Community and to the regional governments in Italy. In fact, however, this is true only of his department and not of the minister himself, whose position has actually strengthened in terms of his membership in the council of ministers of the European Economic Community and his new position as president of the collegial organization that represents all the regions of Italy. In other words, he now exercises his powers in these two groups rather than in the Council of Ministers.

The job of directing government, therefore, has been slipping away from the Council of Ministers. Aware of this phenomenon, the political leadership several times has proposed a cohesive cabinet government with only the more important ministers as members, like the government in Britain. It was tried out in 1944 by the second Badoglio government and by the first Bonomi government until the constitution came into force in 1948. The idea of having secretaries of the coalition parties in the government was actually tried unsuccessfully by Amintore Fanfani in 1970 and by Ugo La Malfa in 1972. The idea of establishing four superministries—economy, defense, foreign affairs, and public order—to coordinate government measures was suggested by Antonio Giolitti in 1974.

Government in its third meaning of executive machinery cannot be analyzed in detail here. In general, Italy's administrative system can be described as a heterogeneous network consisting of twenty ministries having more than a hundred departments (*direzioni generali*). Within the departments there are more than a thousand divisions called careers, posts, and classes (*carriere, ruoli,* and *categorie*). The sections into which these organs are divided, when multiplied by the number of personnel therein, add to the complexity of the system.

---

[10] Greco, "Carenza di coordinamento," p. 26-27.

[11] For a chronicle of the matter, see Giuliano Amato, "Il governo," paper presented at the Italo-German meeting, Rome, May 18-19, 1979.

Mobility across sections is uncommon, if nonexistent. The system resembles a beehive.

Within this system, the careers of civil servants are governed by mechanical routines and respect for precedence. Because of the numerous regulations pertaining to the civil service, the fear of political intervention in the career of the civil servant, and the egalitarianism and routine advancement stressed by the trade unions, promotion in the civil service is a slow process of gradual elevation as vacancies occur in the next level above (*ruoli*). The civil servant first spends about three years as a councilor (*consigliere*); (*a ruolo aperto*) he then proceeds to the position of section manager (*direttore di divisione aggiunto*). If posts are vacant and if he passes a competitive examination, he then advances to the position of first manager (*primo dirigente*), who is commonly head of a division. Subsequently, he can reach the position of senior manager (*dirigente superiore*), from which he can advance to the highest position, that of ministerial director, or head of department (*direttore generale*). Unlike the promotions that precede it, the last one is not governed by civil service regulations, but is based on a decision of the Council of Ministers following the recommendation of the minister in charge of the department in question. Even so, this decision respects, in most cases, the civil service rule of seniority.

The routine way in which the administrative system operates makes it particularly impervious to outside influence. Significant in this respect is the testimony of a leading Communist official responsible for contacts with the Premier during the period 1976–1978, when the government had Communist support. This official noted that the inadequacies of the administrative system were largely outside the control of the Christian Democratic party even though it had been in the government since 1944.[12] If we consider that the administrative system is a weak instrument of government, partly because the system itself is difficult to control, the possibility for interaction between the administration and the political leadership decreases. Up to about 1923, there was considerable assimilation of the high levels of bureaucracy and the Council of Ministers: in fact, a number of higher civil servants were appointed ministers. With the rise of Fascism, this contact ended. Since the end of World War II few politicians (or ministers) have been recruited from the upper ranks of bureaucracy; for example, Raffaele Pio Petrilli, a member of the Council of State, became undersecretary at the Treasury in the fourth De Gasperi

---

[12] Fernando di Giulio, Emmanuele Rocco, *Un ministro ombra si confessa* (Milan: Rizzoli, 1977), pp. 133, 151-53.

government and then minister in the sixth De Gasperi government, and Aldo Bozzi, Tommaso Morlino, and Gaetano Stammati, who had been in the Council of State, the State Legal Advisory Office, and the Central Accounting Office, respectively, all became ministers.[13]

The relationship between political parties and the administration has changed to the point that only a few politicians have recently been nominated to high civil service positions: Giorgio Ruffolo (Socialist) in the Ministry of the Budget; Ferdinando Ventriglia and Ammassari (Christian Democrats) in the Ministry of the Treasury and in the Ministry of Industry, respectively; and Vittorio Barattieri (Republican) in the Ministry of Foreign Trade. As for other offices, the number of political nominations for state councilors (*consiglieri di stato*) has never exceeded 20 percent of the total, and even fewer such nominations have been made at the Audit Office. A factor that partly accounts for this changing relationship is the growing influence of the large extra-state public sector, also called *parastatale* (state-controlled) sector, which employs about 2½ million persons, as compared with about 2 million employed directly by the state. This sector comprises very different entities: local bodies and regions employing slightly more than half a million people, public economic corporations employing many people, and other corporations such as regulatory or service agencies. Excluding the smaller corporations and bodies with elected heads, the boards of directors of these corporations and their presidents are chosen without restriction (since 1978 there is a parliamentary scrutiny of appointments in some corporations) by individual ministers or by the Council of Ministers, who frequently appoint party men.

Furthermore, recent studies have shown that higher civil servants (the bureaucracy in the strict sense, which consists of about 40,000 persons) do not come from an elite group. They come from the middle classes, and the vast majority (60 to 70 percent) come from southern Italy. Their values are characteristic of a static society; that is, in general they do not pursue other prospects of employment, and they tend to have a defensive rather than an innovative approach to life. Public administration has been a channel for the upward mobility of the southern middle classes. This movement toward a preeminently

---

[13] Gian Paolo Storchi, "Materiali per una analisi del ruolo politico del Consiglio di Stato. Gli 'incarichi esterni' dei magistrati amministrativi," *Rivista trimestrale di diritto pubblico*, vol. 2 (1977), pp. 583, 597, highlights the fact that an average of two to three members of the Council of State (members of the Parliament or not) took part in all governments from 1911 to 1922 (there were then about fifteen ministries). Their mere parliamentary presence in the period 1948-1976 never exceeded five.

southern administration at the higher levels[14] began around 1900–1920, just when the differentiation between the political class and the administrative class started to increase. Now a defensive attitude toward politics has emerged in the administration, in that those in the higher ranks of the administration—precisely because they are on the path of routine promotion—reject all external intervention in favor of egalitarianism and the attachment to impersonal, neutral, and automatic rules. Any attempt to disturb these bureaucrats is taken to be interference not only in the work of public administration but, even more, in the social system from which they have emerged.[15]

The higher levels of the Italian bureaucracy differ from the French bureaucracy. Italy does not have an administrative elite, for its bureaucracy is widely accessible to nonelite groups, and it is in close touch with the middle class. The continuity of the bureaucracy is also strong. Although the political leadership has changed, up until the late 1960s the bureaucratic elite was still composed of persons who had entered service and had been trained in administration during the Fascist period. This continuity is due partly to the limited application of laws allowing the ranks of the bureaucracy to be "purged" after the change from a Fascist dictatorship to the democracy of the Republic.

The Primacy of the Premier

Thus far, the analysis tends to support the suggestion that Italy's administrative system lacks a head. What, then, of political leadership? We need to consider its role in government in order to identify the distinctive features of the Italian experience that affect the way in which the institutional and the political elements interact.

The thesis of this chapter can be summed up as follows: Italy's system of government has hinged on the exceptional continuity and stability of political leadership, which has not found it necessary to identify a permanent institution in order to carry out the function of government. On the contrary, the political leadership has preferred to preserve the existing complex web of governmental institutions and to use them to its own advantage. Italy, therefore, does not have merely one center of government and one type of relationship between the political leadership and the administrative system, but many governments and many types of relationships. Because of its extreme

---

[14] I have tried to develop these points in the book *Questione amministrativa e questione meridionale—dimensioni e reclutamento della burocrazia dall'unità ad oggi* (Milan: Giuffrè, 1977).

[15] On the French situation, see Suleiman, *Politics.*

fluidity, this system of politico-administrative relations has eventually found it necessary to have an institutional center to give the system a degree of coherence. Thus the Premiership has emerged in a key role, uniting the disparate elements of the system. As a result, the government in Italy is not to be found in the body specified by the constitution (that is, the Council of Ministers), or in any other collective body. Following the changes that have taken place particularly in the last five years, the seat of government can be found in the Premier's Office, for it has acquired a unique status. The Premier is able to assume the necessary powers and to control the necessary jurisdictions in order to give some central direction to the government.[16]

The predominant characteristics of Italy's system of government, then, are the fluidity of its institutions and the increasing importance of the Premier, not because the Premiership has specific powers but because the office is strategically situated to influence and coordinate the various fragmented systems. There is no doubt that the center of government has shifted as a result of political instability (due to struggles among factions within the Christian Democratic and Socialist parties).

At the same time, the developing fluidity of governmental institutions allowed a new class of persons—who traditionally do not become members of the Council of Ministers—to take positions in the "real" government. These individuals are the *grand commis* (a French expression frequently used in Italy for the administrative elite), such as state councilors, the governor and other members of the *direttorio* (governing body) of the Banca d'Italia, presidents of public corporations, ministerial directors and other senior civil servants, and the head of the Central Accounting Office.

In considering the way in which senior civil servants are coopted into government, we have noted that the Council of Ministers (and therefore the parties), in nominating ministerial directors, generally respects professional administrators and ends up nominating persons belonging to the administrative machinery. In many cases, it also takes into account seniority, so that the next head of a particular directory in a ministry can frequently be forecast.

---

[16] In Italian, the Premier is called the *Presidente del Consiglio dei Ministri*. To avoid confusion with the Head of State elected by Parliament (the *Presidente della Repubblica*) and with directly elected Presidents in France and the United States, the position of the Presidente del Consiglio, analogous to that of Prime Minister, is translated here as Premier. The institution supporting the Premier (the *Presidenza del Consiglio dei Ministri*) is here referred to as the Premier's Office.

During the 1960s, before and during the center-left governments, ideas favoring greater autonomy of the administration with respect to politics gained ground.[17] Although the upper bureaucracy certainly did nothing extreme to "sabotage" government policies, it helped to curb party activity. The administration also expanded its political role with the delegated legislation decree of 1972, granting special powers to about 6,000 to 7,000 higher civil servants.

Italy's government obviously needs the administrative system as much as governments in other countries do. But Italy created a special relationship between the political system and the administrative system to ensure respect for the rules of the game according to which each body has gained certain advantages, and to establish a kind of competition that would foster loyalty to the government through these expectations. That is why the methods of recruitment are respected by political leaders. Political intervention is considered unacceptable and is interpreted as intervention in the social system, for the southern middle class, which has few other professional outlets, counts on the administrative system as a vehicle for upward social mobility. This attitude was evident in the 1977 protests voiced by the Treasury's administrative sector when it was proposed that a ministerial director be chosen from outside the ministry.

The support is won by politicians in other ways, particularly by introducing competition into the agencies or bodies from which people are recruited for government. In this way, the political leadership can count on a supply of high-level administrative personnel.

The other element of this distinctive form of government, the growing influence of the Premier, is the result of a long process involving the evolution of government institutions in Italy.[18] In the first forty years of a united Italy, there were two unsuccessful attempts to give the Premier primacy over other ministers: Bettino Ricasoli in

---

[17] See the effects of this attitude in juridical science, in particular, in Aldo M. Sandulli, "Governo e amministrazione," *Rivista trimestrale di diritto pubblico* (1966), p. 752 ff., followed by Nico Speranza, *Governo e pubblica amministrazione nel sistema costituzionale italiano* (Naples: Jovene, 1971), which tries to find in the constitution the foundation of the split between administration and politics and the relative autonomy of the former with regard to the latter. A critical point of view on the separation between politics and administration is expressed by Leopoldo Elia, *Problemi costituzionali dell'amministrazione centrale* (Milan: Giuffrè, 1966), particularly p. 36 ff.

[18] See Ettore Rotelli's historical work, *La Presidenza del Consiglio dei ministri* (Milan: Giuffrè, 1972), and Maria Paola Viviani Schlein, "La Presidenza del Consiglio dei ministri: storia di un fallimento," *Giur. costituzionale* (1973) fasc. 6, p. 2729 ff. (which, however, upholds the widespread thesis of the weakness of the Premiership) and Alberto Predieri, *Lineamenti della posizione costituzionale del Presidente del Consiglio dei ministri* (Florence: Barbera, 1951).

1867 and Agostino Depretis in 1876. From 1900 to 1915 Giovanni Giolitti provided strong leadership for the government without the support of any law, although he did avail himself of the Zanardelli decree of 1901, which at least defined the jurisdictions of the Council and the functions of the Premier in relation to these jurisdictions. His central position was a result of, among other things, his long career and experience in the bureaucracy and the astute way in which he used some high civil servants as ministers. The 1925 law passed under Fascism subsequently established the preeminence of the head of government in Italy, but this changed following the Liberation. The Constitution of 1948 represented a compromise between the strengthening of the Council of Ministers and the strengthening of the Premiership.

It should be remembered that the Constitution of 1948 was influenced by Italy's Fascist experience and by Mussolini's rise from Premier to head of government. Because a concentration of power in the central government was feared following the Fascist experience, it was considered more acceptable to say that the Premier merely "directs" (*dirige*) the policies of the government.

Although the role assumed by the Premier in the last few years is the result of a long historical process, it is not merely a continuation of the process. The long and laborious pursuit of a dominant role for the Premiership in the past was undertaken by politicians who were *also* Premiers. In fact, it was common for the Premier to be also the head of a major ministry. First Giolitti and then Mussolini—except from June 17, 1924 to November 6, 1926, when Luigi Federzoni was home minister[19]—were at the head of the then most important ministry, the Home Ministry. Similarly, in the first years after World War II, Bonomi also held the Home Ministry during his first and second governments, as did Ferruccio Parri and later De Gasperi in his second government. Badoglio in his second government and De Gasperi in his first and second governments also held the Ministry of Foreign Affairs.[20] Up to the mid-1950s, the Premiership was almost an appendage of the Home Ministry, for the offices of the Premier up to then were still in the Viminale, a building that Giolitti had

---

[19] To be precise, in all governments, since the beginning of the century, the Premier was also minister of the interior, except for three cases: Zanardelli (1901–1903), Boselli (1906–1917), and Facta (1922). The same had happened in governments of the nineteenth century, but only in thirteen out of thirty-five governments.

[20] Giulio Andreotti, *De Gasperi e il suo tempo*, 3d ed. (Milan: Mondadori, 1974), p. 444, speaking of 1951, makes it understood that it was then considered exceptional for the Premier not to be also at the head of an important ministry (Home Office or Foreign Affairs).

constructed in 1912 for the purpose of housing the Home Ministry. The Premiership and the Home Ministry were linked because this ministry contained both the Ministry of Police and the intelligence department, and also had contacts with local notables through the prefects. The Home Ministry also controlled the local authorities. When these last two functions were lost between 1960 and 1970, the need for such a link disappeared.

An attempt to establish the superiority of the Premier over other ministers made in the decades after 1900 met with success. In the period since 1945, the Premier has both gained and lost some powers. He cannot impose his will on the ministers, but only "direct" their activities (according to article 95 of the Constitution of 1948). His sphere of power, however, *was not confined* to the Council of Ministers, for it reached beyond it, directly to various agencies of the administrative system. The only precedent in this direction occurred during the second period of Fascism when Mussolini disregarded the ministers and governed with the administrative heads of departments, as well as through direct contacts with the high bureaucracy of public corporations.

The Premiership, then, has come to be recognized as the focal point of government today, not because of its links with the Home Ministry, nor because the Premier might be able to impose his will on individual ministers, but because the holder of this office has a free hand in mediating between the various key powers of the political system.

Organization and Functions of the Premier's Office

We should now examine more closely the Premier's Office and its relationship with other parts of the political system. The way in which the Premiership has interacted with other parts of the system has allowed the government to function successfully since 1945.

The Premiership reflects a general characteristic of Italy's government, that is, the gap between real structures and those existing only in the statutes. The office has no formal structure, and it has limited functions provided by law. It has no personnel or budget of its own, although it has always had some organizational apparatus of varying magnitude. The organizational apparatus carries out numerous functions codified by practice, and it has attached to it personnel loaned by ministries and public corporations.

The Premiership includes under its jurisdiction a number of units that do not directly serve the Premier. Since from time to time the

Premiership takes advantage of its connection with these offices, they are of some interest. Depending on the particular Premier, they are first the Council of State, the regional administrative courts, the Audit Office, and the State Legal Advisory Office. These structures have a high degree of autonomy. Their association with the Office of the Premier (previously they were under the Home Office) has at least facilitated the use of the Council of State as a nursery of *grand commis*.

The information and copyright service is another part of the Premiership; it is a general directorate having its own central accounting office. Its functions—press documentation, radio programs, financial contributions to newspapers, publications, defense of copyright, and so forth—could be carried out more efficiently by other ministries, for example, by the Ministry of Cultural Property (*Ministero dei beni culturali*), set up in 1975 and to which only the state record library and the first division of the information service and copyright were transferred. This office adds work to the Premiership but at the same time it allows the Premier to exercise influence over the mass media.

A third institution encompassed by the Premiership is the Office for Public Administration, which includes the council, and the Advanced School of Public Administration, and which until recently was headed by a politician. In the past, this office worked out the job descriptions and the wage scale of civil servants, and also bargained with them about wages. These functions, however, have been slowly absorbed by the inspectorate for personnel regulations (*Ispettorato Generale per gli ordinamenti del personale*) of the Central Accounting Office in the Treasury. Ministers without portfolio, such as the minister for extraordinary interventions in the south, and the minister for scientific research, also come under the Office of the Premier. For these ministers, the Premiership is only a point of support. Other offices that enhance the Premier's mediating powers are the following: (1) the *head* of the Premier's Office (*Capo di Gabinetto*), (2) the *deputy head* of the Premier's Office (*Vice Capo di Gabinetto*), and (3) the Legislative Office (*Ufficio Legislativo*). Of these, the first two also carry out administrative functions for the Council of Ministers, which does not have a secretariat of its own.

The organization within which the Premier functions can be summed up as follows: the Premiership is not a ministry and therefore has no machinery of its own except for certain offices that have become attached to the Premier's as a result of the division or abolition of other ministries, the creation of new ministries, the failure to bring together offices with the ministries responsible for an overall administrative function, for organizational reasons, or for historical or political reasons.[21] A maximum of 855 officials of ministries can be attached temporarily to the Premiership. These offices have no bearing on the Premier's task of directing government policy. Only a small part of the ongoing organization of the Premier's Office ties in with the Premier's own activity.

Constitutionally, the Premier's powers appear to be few. Ministers are nominated by the Premier and are appointed to office by the President of the Republic. The Premier cannot remove ministers. If the Premier resigns, however, the Council must leave office. He directs government policy and is responsible for it, for the unity of political leadership. In general, the constitution is concerned with the Premier's activity *within* the Council of Ministers and not with roles that he might have outside it, except, of course, in his relationship with Parliament, in that the government must maintain Parliament's confidence.[22] The limited powers that the constitution grants the Premier are reflected in the budget and in the personnel at his disposal. The Premier's Office has no budget of its own, but uses funds assigned to it in the budget of the Ministry of the Treasury. Unlike the ministries, the Premier's Office does not have a central accounting office of its own; a section of the Central Accounting Office of the Ministry of the Treasury controls the expenditures of the Premier's Office.

If we examine the actual organization—as opposed to the constitutionally authorized organization—and the functions and personnel of the Premier's Office, the situation looks different. First, we note that three types of offices not provided for in any regulation are filled by politicians: vice premier, minister without portfolio, and under secretary to the Premier. The Office of Vice Premier has existed in

---

[21] Centro italiano di ricerche e di informazione sulle imprese pubbliche e di pubblico interesse (CIRIEC), "Legislazione vigente e schemi organizzativi della Presidenza del consiglio e di alcuni ministeri," unpublished manuscript, 1978, p. 7.

[22] On this point Predieri, *Lineamenti* and Giovanni Rizza, *Il Presidente del consiglio dei ministri—posizione poteri e attività nell'ordinamento costituzionale italiano* (Naples: Jovene, 1970), and Maria Paola Viviani, *La Presidenza del Consiglio dei ministri in alcuni Stati dell'Europa occidentale e in Italia* (Milan: Giuffrè, 1970), p. 109 ff. and Pier Alberto Capotosti, *Accordi di governo e presidente del consiglio dei ministri* (Milan: Giuffrè, 1975), particularly p. 185 ff., which gives an interpretation that leads to widening the Premier's powers, since it considers them a function of the Premier's more general power of political guidance. For the sake of completeness, mention should also be made of Emilia Baldini's short note, "Alcuni aspetti della figura del Presidente del Consiglio dei ministri nell'ordinamento italiano," *Studi politici* (January-March 1960), p. 57 ff. and all the articles on government in general.

twenty-one of the thirty-four governments of the Republic. Up to 1957 the vice premier's functions were assigned to a minister without portfolio, but subsequently he came to have a place of his own. Not being declared a minister, however, the vice premier has an anomalous position since the Council of Ministers, according to article 92 of the constitution, is "composed of the Prime Minister [Premier] and the Ministers who, together, constitute the Council of Ministers." He acts especially in coalition governments as the representative of a minority party. The post has been filled by Communists, Socialists, Liberals, Social Democrats, and Republicans, and for short periods by Christian Democrats. Only twice, in 1952, did the vice premier actually replace the Premier and in both cases the vice premier (Attilio Piccioni) belonged to the same party as the Premier (De Gasperi).[23]

The powers of the majority party (or of the major factions) are also counterbalanced by the ministers without portfolio, offices that have become numerous even though there is no legal provision for them. They were rare in the De Gasperi governments and limited in number in the Fanfani governments, up to four or five, but their number increased up to nine in the Moro and Rumor governments. They have had either general political functions (for example, the vice premier is a kind of minister without portfolio) or specific political or administrative functions delegated to them. An exception is the minister for scientific research, who does have specific jurisdictions established by law.

The under secretary to the Premier (*sottosegretario alla Presidenza*—not to be confused with the under secretary of the Premier's Office, the *sottosegretario presso la Presidenza*) is a different figure. According to an old practice but contrary to law, he acts as secretary of the Council of Ministers. Furthermore, he is the real head of the administrative machinery of the Premiership. More important, the under secretary to the Premier is the Premier's chief political advisor and spokesman. One need only recall that this office has been filled by such prominent politicians as Andreotti in the fourth to the eighth De Gasperi governments and in the Pella government; Angelo Salizzoni in four Moro governments, Antonio Bisaglia in the first three Rumor governments, and Franco Evangelisti in the five Andreotti governments.

---

[23] On the position of the vice premier and ministers without portfolio, Enzo Cheli, "Consiglio dei ministri," *Enciclopedia forense* (Milan: Il Foro), vol. 2, pp. 2-3 of the abstract; for a chronicle of the events, Rocco D. Passio, "La Presidenza del Consiglio dei ministri nel sistema politico-costituzionale. Gli organi della Presidenza del Consiglio," *Stato e regioni*, no. 3 (1978), pp. 44 and 50 ff.

Turning to the administrative organization of the Premier's Office, we find the same type of informal arrangements. The only organizational chart was drawn up in 1964, but since then much has changed. Some of the changes, however, were made without written instructions, but on the verbal orders of the head of the Premier's Office. The Premier's Office, therefore, is an informal political and administrative organization that nonetheless has a relatively high degree of stability, as can be seen from a record of the number of individuals occupying this office in relation to the number of governments. In the thirty-four governments of the Republic, there have been only fourteen heads of the Premier's Office. This means that even among the most direct collaborators of the Premier—whom the law permits to be chosen freely—there is greater stability than is generally supposed.

If we consider the principal administrations, we see that the prefect Francesco Bartolotta was head of the Premier's Office in the De Gasperi governments (in addition to the governments of Pella, the first Fanfani government, and that of Scelba), the councilor of the Audit Office Marcello Valentini (who had been inspector-general at the Ministry of Labor when Fanfani was minister and who was nominated councilor of the Audit Office to facilitate his appointment as head of the Premier's Office) was head of the Premier's Office in the three successive Fanfani governments (as well as in the first Leoni government); the Councilor of State Giuseppe Manzari was head of the Premier's Office in the Moro governments; the Councilor of State Franco Piga in the Rumor governments and the head of the Central Accounting Office in the third, fourth, and fifth Andreotti governments.

The stability increases among the vice heads and the other personnel of the Premier's Office. For example, there have been only four heads of the vice premier's office since 1948. It has also been pointed out that "the changes that actually take place when the Prime Minister [Premier] changes concern, in addition to the personnel of the Prime Minister's [Premier's] secretariat . . . very few persons (some ten at most out of a total of nearly six hundred)."[24] When a new Premier enters office, only the direct collaborators of the Premier change whereas the great majority of staff remain in position. There are two explanations for this continuity. Politically, great changes in personnel are not required if the party from which a Premier comes remains in power; technically, it is preferable to

---

[24] Vittorio Mortara, "Prima ipotesi per un assetto organizzativo degli uffici della Presidenza del Consiglio," unpublished manuscript.

retain most of the personnel to benefit from their experience in the routine duties they have to perform.

Further evidence of the growing importance of the Premier's Office lies in the great increase in its size since 1945. Immediately after the war it had about fifty staff, not counting the personnel of offices nominally its concern. By 1963 the number had reached 300, and today it is 800.

This description of the personnel has not taken into account the bipartite structure of Italy's administrative system, for public corporations operate alongside the ministries. Personnel of the Presidency are also seconded from these corporations and there is no statutory limit to the number of people employed.

The functions of personnel in the Premier's Office go far beyond what the law specifies. Article 95 of the constitution states that "the Premier directs the general policy of the Government and is responsible for it. He maintains the unity of political and administrative policy, promoting and coordinating the activity of the ministers. . . . The law provides for the organization of the Premier's Office." Now, a legal definition of the organization of the Premiership has never been issued, even though numerous bills have been proposed, of which three at least were presented by various governments. Moreover, questions have been raised about the applicability of some of the articles of the Zanardelli decree, which goes back to the beginning of the liberal-democratic era and of the 1925 decree, which strengthened the head of the executive, right from the first years of Fascism.

The legislative vacuum has allowed the powers of the Premier to increase gradually in a number of ways. First, the office of administrative and interministerial coordination was strengthened, mainly through the increasing numbers of councilors of state brought in during the Moro and Rumor Premierships. Directives issued by the Premier suggest that purely administrative activity far outweighs political activity. Second, the Premier's Office has come to control government expenditure and the spending of public corporations. Under Andreotti the control of public expenditure was placed under the supervision of the Premier since the head of his office had been the head of the Central Accounting Office. Since that time, the public corporations have slowly passed under the influence of the Premiership to such an extent that it has been said:

> At the head of the public economic corporations there are, and have followed one another, men of the Premier and not of the Minister of State Holdings, or of the Treasury, or of the Budget and Economic Planning. Since . . . the corpora-

tions are instruments of implementing economic strategy, the Premier is seen to intervene directly in the working out of economic policy and, through an intermediary, in the phases of choice (through the ministers or within the Council of Ministers) and of implementation (through the administrators of the corporations) of economic strategy.[25]

A newly established office within the Premiership provides the following three services, which are subdivided into other functions: it watches over some corporations under the direct control of the Premiership; it monitors operations for the reorganization and abolition of corporations, as laid down in the statutes of 1975 and 1977.

The corporations also include offices representing the twenty regions, which have become economically important too, for one-fifth of the total public expenditure passes through the regions. A special office for the regions, directed by a prefect and divided into nine services, exists under the Premiership; it is concerned primarily with reviewing the constitutional legitimacy of regional laws and with coordinating the activity of government commissioners in the regions. But the Premiership has another significant connection with the regions. Regulations introduced in 1970 require regional corporations to abide by the state's guidance and coordination, which are normally to be implemented by ministers in the various sectors. To avoid confusion, it was laid down that such directives should be implemented along with acts drawn up by the Premier or acts given his approval. According to article 3 of Law 382, July 22, 1975, the function of guidance and coordination "is carried out . . . by means of deliberations of the Council of Ministers on the proposal of the Premier in agreement with the competent Minister or Ministers." The exercise of this function can be delegated from time to time by the Council of Ministers to the Premier, who operates together with the competent minister.

Another way in which the Premier's power has expanded is that the office has taken control of security and public order. A regulation passed in 1977 has placed the secretariat (now directed by a prefect) of the Executive Committee for News and Security under the Premiership. This secretariat facilitates the Premier's coordination and guidance by handling data supplied by two security services. The Premier, in fact, is president of both the Interministerial Committee for News and Security and the Executive Committee for News and Security.

[25] Rocco Di Passio, "Le funzioni amministrative del Presidente del Consiglio dei ministri," *Rivista trimestrale di scienza dell'amministrazione*, no. 2 (1977), p. 243.

With the control of these vital sectors—public expenditure and security—the Premiership has in the last few years taken a step outside its traditional sphere of activity, which was previously *within* the Council of Ministers. That is, the Premier acted through the Council and not by instruments directly under his control. Recent institutional innovations have allowed the Premier to act *outside* the Council, where the constitution, however, had wished to confine the Premiership for fear that Fascism might be repeated. It was no mere chance that a decree passed in 1944 immediately after the fall of the Fascist regime hastened to replace the expression "head of government" (*Capo del Governo*), which had been introduced by the 1925 law, with "Premier" (*Presidente del Consiglio dei Ministri*).

Whether the extension in the functions of the Premier will continue in the years ahead remains to be seen. It should be noted that in the past the presidency of interministerial committees was entrusted to the Premier even though he did not actually exercise this function. For example, since it was established in 1967, the Committee for Economic Planning has been presided over by the Premier only twice; in other cases, it has been presided over by the vice president of the committee itself, who is the minister of the budget and of economic planning. Two developments indicate, however, that this trend may accelerate. In 1977, for the first time, the staff office of a committee (the Secretariat for News and Security) was placed in the Office of the Premier, and direct contact—rather than contact via ministers—between the Premier and the major departments has become so commonplace that these departments now consider it desirable to have their own "representatives" in the Premier's Office itself, and all the important departments now have some officials there.[26] The fact that the Premiership has no personnel of its own and therefore must rely on employees of individual ministries lends itself very well to this purpose.

---

[26] Halfway through 1979, the personnel detached temporarily from other departments came from the following departments: Interior, 78; Post Office, 60; Finances, 48; Defense, 38; Treasury, 37; Education, 32; Telephones, 18; Audit Office, 11; Transport, 9; Cultural Goods, 8; Foreign Affairs, 7; Public Works, 6; Agriculture, 6; Labor, 6; Justice, 5; Council of State, 5; State Legal Advisory Office, 3; Industry, 3; Foreign Trade, 3; Merchant Navy, 2; and Health, 1.

The relative weight of the "representation" of the various machineries in the Premier's Office must, however, be evaluated also in relation to rank. It should be kept in mind that while councilors of state are few in number, they are superior in rank to the directors general (the highest level of civil servants). The data given are taken from an unpublished essay on the Premiership by Rocco Di Passio.

Bureaucratic Politics and the Premier

Thus far we have considered the growing importance of the Premier's role in Italy, but we have also noted that the Italian Premier has considerably more decision-making centers to coordinate or to mediate among than do heads of state in other countries. How, then, has this office managed to become more important in the last few years, despite the constitutional limitation on its powers and the high degree of political and administrative fragmentation? This probably happened because the instability of Italian politics allowed the Premier to establish relations with particular authorities and bodies and to take advantage of the conflicts among the various governmental units.[27] In a word, the government succeeded in transforming itself by keeping the essential components of the political system under the direction of the Premier's Office. In spite of personnel changes, it also succeeded in maintaining a high degree of stability and continuity.

Changes occurred, for example, in the departments from which the head of the Premier's Office (*Capo di Gabinetto*) were chosen. The head of the Premier's Office first came from the Home Office, then from the Council of State, and subsequently from the Treasury. Such shifts occurred not only in the high offices of government. As long as the Premiership was bound to the Home Office, personnel in the Premier's Office were mainly prefects. When the councilors of state arrived, they brought so many colleagues with them that some complained that they were overrunning the Premier's Office. The same thing happened with the head of the Central Accounting Office, who brought with him officers of the Treasury.

Despite these waves of change, a delicate balance has been established between the new and the old components of the system, so that even today, some sections of the Premier's Office retain prefects and councilors of state even though the individuals are not the ones who occupied the posts originally. Thus, until 1961, when the Premiership was transferred from the Viminale—the seat of the Home Office—to Palazzo Chigi, the entire staff consisted of about fifty persons,

---

[27] The thesis of the "functional elasticity" and of the "many-sidedness" of the Premier, "which can be expressed in a very wide form: direction of the general policy of the Government; and which can also be reduced to a mere activity of stimulus and coordination of ministers' activity," is sustained, though only on the basis of exclusive juridical data, by Iole Buccisano, "Premesse per uno studio sul Presidente del Consiglio dei ministri," *Rivista trimestrale di diritto pubblico* (1972), fasc. 1, p. 31 ff. The thesis is taken up again, but in a negative and critical sense, by Vittorio Mortara, "Prime ipotesi per un assetto organizzativo degli uffici della Presidenza del Consiglio," unpublished manuscript.

thirty in the Premier's Office and twenty in the Premier's secretariat. All the support services of the Premiership, including the legislative office, were supplied by the corresponding bureaus of the Home Office. Even among the Premier's most direct collaborators, some came from the Home Office: the head and deputy head of his office (a prefect and a vice prefect), and some members of the private secretariat (two vice prefects).

Prefects prevailed up to the 1960s not only because of the link between the Home Office and the Premiership, but also because of the Home Office's central role in the administrative system. Prefects were generalists with experience in the field. Then, too, the personnel of the Home Office was, traditionally, the servant of politicians; their role was paramount in Giolitti's system as well as in the Fascist one. Finally, the fact that local public order depended on the prefects and that up to very recent times the head of the police was a prefect, must not be overlooked. Certainly throughout the 1950s public order represented one of the central problems confronting the government, so that to win the alliance of the bureaucracy concern with order was important.

Councilors of state became necessary when a crisis arose in the Home Office, making it today almost exclusively a police ministry, and when the technical and political problems of government increased. Many councilors of state have not only good technical administrative qualifications (entry into the group remains very selective even today), but also good administrative experience. Positions on the Council of State are open only to those who have had some years of experience as officials or as judges, or to those who have worked as a head of a legislative office or a minister's office. Another qualification that has become acceptable is experience as a "knight of industry" (that is, president of a public bank or member of the board of directors of companies controlled by public corporations), owing to the important role played by such officials at the Office of the Premier.[28] In order to understand the new role of the councilors of state, it is important to remember that they are recruited by competitive exams (only a few are appointed by the Council of Ministries, usually from among ministerial directors). They number fewer than 100, and on average about one-fifth of them normally function as heads of ministers' offices. The growing role of councilors of state can be seen from a comparison of the number of heads of ministers' offices who were councilors of state in various periods. From 1928 to 1942 there

---

[28] Storchi, *Materiali,* p. 593 and 601.

were never more than three; from 1942 until the third Rumor government in 1970 there were about six; and from 1970 to the present there have been more than ten.

The first serious attempt to exercise powers of coordination through the Premiership was made precisely by councilors of state, but it was destined to fail even though they had a thorough knowledge of the administrative system and had established a network of councilors of state in the ministers' offices. Owing to decreasing importance of the Home Ministry and the growing weight of the Treasury, prefects lost control of the administrative system and only financial personnel were capable of taking over, but they took control in a particular way. Thus arose the significance of the nomination of the head of the Central Accounting Office as head of the Premier's Office.

Two factors account for the power of the financial bureaucracy.[29] First is the increase in public expenditure and the increase in public activities that have occurred in all industrial societies and that are determined by allocations of money rather than by laws and administrative regulations. The second factor is peculiar to Italy, that is, the growing role of the state's Central Accounting Office ever since the Cavour law of 1852. Particularly as a result of the De Stefani reform of 1923, the branches of the Central Accounting Office operating in the ministries were placed under the State Accounting Office in the Ministry of the Treasury. Today, a large network of central, regional, and provincial accounting offices depends on this office in Treasury, which, because of its omnipresence and its importance, constitutes the central nervous system of public institutions.

Whereas the guiding role of the Home Office used to be exercised with a kind of supremacy over other ministries, the Central Accounting Office wields its power in a less conspicuous but more penetrating way—through scrutiny of financial procedures and administrative activity. The matter is so important that Emilio Colombo, who was minister of the Treasury longer than anyone else, said, on celebrating the centenary of the Central Accounting Office, "Alongside the harmonization and coordination that the Council of Ministers and the Premiership carry out on the political plane, a similar and substantial

---

29 The theses set forth in the text have already been developed by me in "Controllo della spesa pubblica e direzione dell'amministrazione," now in Sabino Cassese, *La formazione dello Stato amministrativo* (Milan: Giuffrè, 1974), p. 241 ff. and in the introduction to Sabino Cassese, ed., *L'amministrazione pubblica in Italia*, 2nd ed. (Bologna: Il Mulino, 1976), p. 34.

role is exercised by the minister of expenditure on the administrative plane through the Central Accounting Office."[30]

This coordination, however, is of a rather particular type. Because it is exercised through the control of public expenditure, priority is given to the allocation and the outlay of expenditures, before the aims of administrative activity are determined. In other words, the aims are determined on the basis of the amount of money that the Central Accounting Office assigns and asks the various public offices to spend.

Even though Italy's administrative system is so divided that it appears fragmented, this drawback is offset by the omnipresent Central Accounting Office. The only area outside its control is the financial expenditure (but not the allocation of resources) of the public corporations. This is understandable because it is the only area in which the patronage powers of the political class can be exercised, albeit in ways that vary from corporation to corporation. Because of its dominant role, the Central Accounting Office will be at the center of any conflicts between the Treasury, on which it depends, and the Ministry of the Budget, which it has tried to take over. The control that it and the Ministry of the Treasury exercise is bound to diminish, however, because there are internal limits on its possible action. Since the guiding principle of this office is financial control, it has never managed to rationalize administrative action.

Other examples of a "policy of mobile alliances" are found in the field of economic policy. In 1947, the first government without Communists and Socialists set up the Ministry of the Budget so that its new holder, the Liberal Luigi Einaudi, could control revenue and expenditure, as a kind of superminister informally controlling both the Ministry of Finances and the Ministry of the Treasury. The Ministry of the Budget subsequently became the center of new aspirations: an attempt to strengthen the position of Pella, minister of the budget in 1951, against Piccioni, and a decision to present a law—which had bogged down in Parliament—that would restore its directive and coordination function.[31] There were further such attempts by Tambroni (1960) and Pella (1961). Attempts to establish the preeminence of the Budget Ministry led to conflicts between Socialists on one side

---

[30] The passage by Colombo quoted in the text is in *Saggi in onore del centenario della Ragioneria generale dello Stato* (Rome: Poligrafico dello Stato, 1969), pp. 8, 10, and 14.

Already in 1950 the Rocco Commission, nominated by De Gasperi to define the institutional order of the government, had evaluated the importance and the power assumed by the Treasury as able to exercise a kind of veto power over other ministries.

[31] The episode is recalled by Andreotti, *De Gasperi*, pp. 446 and 454.

and Republicans and Christian Democrats on the other that were settled with the 1967 law strengthening the Ministry of the Budget, but the law was not put into practice much.[32]

A similar attempt was made by the fourth Moro government (1974–1975), in which the Republican Ugo La Malfa was nominated vice premier and was given the task of coordinating the economic policy of the government. His assignment was criticized by those[33] who maintained that the task of coordination was the proper function of the Ministry of the Budget, for since 1962 it had also been the Ministry of Economic Planning. Strangely enough, these critics opposed the vice premier's assignment on the same grounds that the Ministry of the Treasury had defended itself against the interventions of the Ministry of the Budget: that the Ministry of the Budget did not have a technical machinery and was without institutional ties with the departments.

Most institutional conflicts over the direction of the economy concern the relative roles of the Ministry of the Budget and the Ministry of the Treasury. Typically, the clash is between conservatives interested in financial balance and Socialists interested in development, the former defending the Treasury, the latter defending the Ministry of Planning. The clash is not much different from that which took place in France, both in the Blum government in 1936 and during the postwar period, and in Britain during the period 1964–1969. The Ministry of Planning and the Socialists have been on the losing side in all of these cases.

A different attempt to strengthen the Ministry of the Budget was made by the so-called troika of the fourth Rumor government (July 17, 1973 to March 2, 1974). The economy was entrusted to the Socialist Antonio Giolitti, minister at the Budget, the Christian Democrat Colombo, minister at Finance, and the Republican La Malfa, minister at the Treasury. This trio was called the *noyau dur* (hard core) of government, for to begin with it operated in a particularly effective way. At least in the first phase, the three ministers met nearly every day. Often the Premier was not even informed of the questions dealt with, but other ministers interested in the subjects discussed (agriculture, public works, employment, and so on) were invited in turn to the meetings. A practice was established whereby the sessions of the Committee for Economic Planning and of the Council of Ministers

---

[32] Donatello Serrani, "Il ministero del bilancio e della programmazione economica," *Rivista trimestrale di diritto pubblico*, no. 1 (1973), p. 54 and Manin Carabba, *Un ventennio di programmazione 1954-1974* (Bari: Laterza, 1977).

[33] Manin Carabba, interview in *Panorama*, October 30, 1975.

were preceded by informal meetings between the troika and the Premier. The result was a close mesh of measures inspired by the principle of state control and aimed at obtaining rapid and tangible results in the short term. For the first time, the Central Accounting Office was given political directives to draw up the budget and even the prefectures seemed more active in controlling prices (locally, the provincial price committees come under the prefectures). After the first phase, in autumn 1973, the meetings became less frequent and La Malfa (Republican) and Giolitti (Socialist) became opponents, the former concerned about inflation and the latter about unemployment. As their disagreements grew, despite the Premier's attempts to mediate, the experience of collegial direction of economic policy was virtually over by the end of the year.[34]

In Italy, then, the actual center of policy making can shift from one place to another. Alongside a weak Council of Ministers, which carries out mainly the functions attributed exclusively to the Council by the constitution (especially legislative initiative), there is a Premier's Office having no statutory provision that is unstable and flexible in composition, for it consists of the Premier and—according to the balance of power in the political and the administrative systems—one or more ministers and representatives of the principal administrative bodies.

This description of Italy's bipolar type of government would be incomplete, however, without brief mention of the governor of the Banca d'Italia. As in many European countries, the head of the central bank has an unquestioned role as adviser to the government. In Italy, however, the governor has a wider role in that the Banca d'Italia is not only the central bank, but it also controls the banking system. The governor of this institution does not have a fixed term in office. Moreover, the machinery of the Banca d'Italia is quite autonomous and has not been subjected to party influence. Its relative independence offsets the political role of the governor, who has been involved with the government several times. One thinks of the role of Guido Carli in the 1974 negotiation with the International Monetary Fund, which concerned the La Malfa-Giolitti conflict and

---

[34] See Carabba, *Un ventennio*, p. 301 ff. and Pippo Ranci, "Cronaca di un biennio," in *La congiuntura più lunga—materiali per una analisi della politica economica italiana 1972-74* (Bologna: Il Mulino, 1974), p. 192 ff., as well as articles in *Mondo economico*, "Il nocciolo duro del governo," 1973, p. 3; "La Malfa e le riforme," 1973, p. 5, "Due documenti," 1973, no. 46, p. 1; "Il 'riciclaggio' della credibilita," February 23, 1974, p. 9. See also the articles of Cesare Zappulli on the "troika," published on the third page of *Corriere della sera* (Milan) on July 24, July 28, and August 5, 1973.

led to the resignation of La Malfa as minister of the Treasury, or even before that, of Carli's part in the nationalization of electricity in 1962 and of Donato Menichella's earlier role in the liberalization of trade in 1951. In making decisions about the liberalization of foreign trade, La Malfa recalled:

> I had prepared my plan and had informed De Gasperi, Vanoni and Menichella about it. We brought the question to the Council of Ministers and everything was decided in a few minutes. This is to tell you that certain fundamental reforms do not need years of discussion. I had reached agreement with the Premier, the Governor of the Banca d'Italia, and the most intelligent and capable minister and off I went.[35]

On matters of money and credit, the governor of the Banca d'Italia can act outside his strict jurisdiction, entering areas that normally fall under the control of particular ministries.

Each branch of this "mobile" government acts in its own style. The style of the few ministers who count and of the representatives of the Council of State and Central Accounting Office corresponds to the cliche of the politician and the administrator. But we must take care not to believe that the *actual* relations are those of minister and civil servant. The case of the governor of the Banca d'Italia is different. His autonomy allows him to oscillate between participation in the government and critical detachment. But there are signs that this oscillation is about to decrease and that participation in government will prevail over detachment.[36]

---

[35] On these episodes, see Ugo La Malfa, *Intervista sul non governo*, ed. A. Ronchey (Bari: Laterza, 1977), pp. 42, 57, and 94.

[36] On the governor-judge, see Guido Carli, "Problemi odierni di un istituto di emissione," *Burocrazia* (June 1966). Other developments are discussed in Cassese, "Introduzione," *La amministrazione pubblica*, p. 31.

The Banca d'Italia has given several collaborators of the government: Luigi Einaudi, who was first governor and then minister; Donato Menichella, who was unsuccessfully proposed by De Gasperi for the government in 1946 (Andreotti, *De Gasperi*, p. 312) and who always had a great weight in government economic policy; Guido Carli, who was minister of foreign trade in 1957-1958; and in recent times, let it be enough to mention Rinaldo Ossola, minister for foreign trade.

A further recent trend is the rise in importance of the Ministry of Labor. With the coming into force of laws that emphasize the safeguarding of employment (for example, laws on industrial reconversion and on the employment of young people) in a period of economic crisis, the ministry, which had hitherto had mainly a function of mediation in relations between employers and employees, has acquired new and important functions for government economic policy.

The preceding remarks concerning the interchangeability of administrators and politicians in the key roles of government presuppose a "minister-civil servant relationship as a constant."[37] In some cases this relationship has gone through a crisis as a result of the preeminence of the head of the Premier's Office over the ministers. In one such case the head of the Premier's Office became concerned exclusively with the Premier's political relations and, in a complete reversal of roles, left administrative matters to the care of the under secretary to the Premiership. During the Rumor government even the traditional politico-administrative relationship was reversed.

> In these cases, the attempt is made to deprive the government of its powers, in actual fact . . . to the advantage of the Premier's powers, exercised, actually, by the head of the Premier's Office. The technique adopted in the ousting process is as follows: surprise meetings, short and at long intervals, of the Council of Ministers; the lack of or sudden preparation of the agenda; a large volume of business submitted to the examination of the Council with the relative measures already defined; failure to keep the ministers updated about the work of the Council. In practice, the Council of Ministers reduces its functions, in these cases, to approval of measures already prepared and defined by the Premier's Office.[38]

To complete the picture, it should be mentioned that a different model of relations emerges—at least as an attempt—in the fourth and fifth Andreotti governments, which were particularly restricted in composition (Christian Democrat one-party government) in contrast to that of Parliament (Communists, Socialists, Social Democrats, Republicans, and Christian Democrats), and which paid more attention to administrative activity than had past governments. That model depends both on the style of the Premier (in this case Andreotti) and on the request of Parliament for the actual implementation of the policies of the majority. In such a situation, the link between the parliamentary coalition and the government coalition tends to become less strong, for the second cannot reflect the first, even it it wants to. Consequently, the Premier tries to become the sole intermediary between the government and the parliamentary majority. The action of the ministers is, in one sense, limited to the political sphere, but it gains new importance in the administrative field. The ministers are asked first and foremost to be the heads of their departments rather

---

[37] Headey, *British Cabinet Ministers*, p. 17.
[38] Di Passio, *Le funzioni amministrative*, no. 5, p. 225.

than warring heads of party factions. Since ministers are chosen (for example, Vincenzo Scotti, Filippo Maria Pandolfi, and Gaetano Stammati) for key posts such as Public Works and the Treasury because the programs demand technician politicians rather than pure politicians, the matter becomes even plainer. Understandably, this model (which must have been greatly influenced by the De Gasperi experience for Andreotti was under secretary to the Premier's Office and an assiduous lieutenant of De Gasperi) allows the Premiership to reach the height of its powers, because the Premier becomes an arbiter between the politico-parliamentary system and the administrative system.

Although this model is probably closest to the one laid down by the constitution, its flexibility and fluidity make it impossible to predict whether and how long it will last, whether the tendency of the last few years to give the Premier greater freedom in choosing at least some of his ministers will be accelerated, or whether he will have to leave the matter to parliamentary groups (and, therefore, to parties and factions), in accordance with the practice that has prevailed since the De Gasperi governments.

A more careful analysis of this point would require a detailed analysis of government-Parliament-party relations, which is outside the scope of this chapter. It should be noted, however, that the Premier in Italy has usually been leader of his party, but that once he becomes Premier, he gives up that leadership and his successor as secretary of the party becomes his most formidable rival for the Premiership.

The four persons who served longest as Premier (De Gasperi, Fanfani, Moro, and Rumor) have all been secretary of the Christian Democratic party. De Gasperi and Fanfani were for some time both secretary of the party and Premier, but since these experiences, the secretary has not been simultaneously Premier. There is no statutory provision preventing this, only de facto behavior, mainly due to the distribution of roles among factions (that is, if a faction "controls" the party, it cannot "control" the government at the same time). Moro and Rumor each became Premier when they were secretary, but then resigned from their party post. In accordance with the statute of the Christian Democratic party (which, of course, has been in power in Italy since 1945) the Premier is a de jure member of the main national body of the party, the Directorate.

As for relations among parties in coalition governments, complaints are often heard that the Premier merely "records" party agreements. Within the Council itself, although conflicts among parties may be evident, such disagreements have never led the ministers to vote against the government. Parliament, meanwhile, is occupied mainly with passing laws—in one year it passes four times as many laws as does the British Parliament. Policy discussions occur infrequently and parliamentary control of the activity and results of government action is almost nonexistent.

Conclusion

Italy's system of government can be said to be written on water, for it is a highly fluid system. This feature is, perhaps, its principal strength, even though some lament that the organization envisaged by the constitution has failed to work out in practice, with respect to the organization of the Premiership, the determination of the number of ministers, or the assignment of responsibilities and organization of the ministries. The standard historical work on the Premiership has observed that "Generally, the subject of the definition of the Premier and also that of the organization of the Premiership, are brought up during situations marked by the political weakness of the Premier in office."[39]

The system has obvious weaknesses, the first of which derives from the fact that the leadership exercised is more the result of mediation among factions, pressure groups, and parties, than the result of elaboration, promotion, and planning by responsible and expert ministry officials. There is an insufficient collection and circulation of data, an absence of policy analysis, and a lack of persons and offices capable of formulating and comparing policies. The inadequacy of information is illustrated by the still relevant 1951 experience of De Gaspari, who "wanted to create a statistical office, to publish data collected every two weeks, in order to involve all the ministries concerned through the publicity given to documents and fulfillments of obligations. Opposition from all the ministries soon caused the initiative to be dropped."[40] The Italian system is more suited to reaching agreement about problems as they gradually emerge than to ensuring positive guidance and direction. Consequently, coordination has been replaced by institutionalized political bargaining, of which the interministerial committees, in particular, are an expression. The number of committees was high before the 1960s and since then has been reduced only slightly. In the economic sector alone there have been committees for the nationalized electricity corporation, for state

---

[39] Rotelli, *La Presidenza*, p. 452.
[40] Andreotti, *De Gasperi*, p. 431.

holdings, for nuclear energy, and for the Mezzogiorno. There is still the price committee, the credit committee, the planning committee, the committee for industrial policy, the committee for agricultural and food policy, and the committee for foreign policy. Because all these committees are composed of ministers, there has been talk of a "government by interministerial committees," and complaints that they proceed with particularistic policies.[41]

Here, too, the "complaining" tendency of Italian political science and juridical criticism becomes evident. This negative Italian attitude stems not so much from a government by committees as it does from the disorder with which the committees were introduced into Italy and the fact that, instead of being instruments for the coordination of the ministries, they are a way of projecting into the government the particular interests of individual ministries: every minister has wanted "his" interministerial committee.

Although Italy's governments may be unstable, its political leadership is very stable. This leadership, however, does not exercise its power in the Council of Ministers. This function of government is exercised through an informally organized office that can and does change with time. It hinges on the Premiership and is composed of the politicians and higher civil servants who are, in turn, indispensable for the requirements of the moment. The Premier's collaborators at first came from the Home Ministry and subsequently from the Council of State and finally from the Ministry of the Treasury. Even the ministers' committees can change with time. Even though the relationship between politics and administration at the top is highly adaptable to changing situations, it has many drawbacks, the principal one being that it lends itself more to mediating conflicts than to providing positive guidance in the direction of government.

---

[41] Stefano Merlini, "Struttura del governo, centri separati di potere e indirizzi di politica economica," in *Il governo democratico dell'economia* (Bari: De Donato, 1976), p. 83 ff.; Fabio Merusi, "I comitati interministeriali nella struttura di governo," in Ristuccia, ed., *L'Istituzione governo*, p. 161 ff. on interministerial committees; and Greco, *Carenza di coordinamento*, pp. 29-30.

On the multiplication of spheres of political competence and on committees as organs not so much for coordination as for the sectorial decentralization of the guiding power, see Enzo Cheli, "Il coordinamento delle attivita di governo nell'attuale sistema italiano," *Studi parlamentari e di politica costituzionale*, no. 4 (1969), p. 7 ff.

On the insufficiency of coordination, Guglielmo Negri, "In tema di coordinamento delle attività amministrative dei ministri," *Rassegna parlamentare*, nos. 3-4 (1963), p. 214 ff. and "Il ministro in repubblica," *Studi parlamentari e di politica costituzionale*, nos. 5-6 (1969), p. 25 ff.; and Giulio Correale, "Spunti in tema di attività di coordinamento del Presidente del consiglio dei ministri," *Cronache parlamentari siciliane*, nos. 5-6 (1974), p. 5 ff.

6

Governing Norway: Segmentation, Anticipation, and Consensus Formation

Johan P. Olsen

The Norwegian Constitution of 1814 was written in the spirit of Montesquieu. Functions and powers were separated. The king was given executive leadership, with the right to select his advisers, the Cabinet, and to appoint his servants, the administrators. The introduction of parliamentary government in 1884 gradually converted the Cabinet into an executive committee of the Storting (parliament) and the king into a ceremonial leader. All power was to be assembled in the hall of the Storting. Since the executive derived its authority from the representatives of the people, it was to be dependent in large part on national elections and on laws, budgets, and other instructions from the Storting. Transactions with the administrators and those affected by governmental interventions would be dominated by legal-rational authority.

The concept of a parliamentary chain of governance has been—and is—the prevailing interpretation of executive leadership in Norway. But there are alternatives. Interpretations oscillate between theories that assume the fate of the nation is decided by a powerful executive elite and the view that executive leaders are the prisoners of and bookkeepers for broad technological, economic, demographic,

NOTE: The author has benefited from the advice, comments, and help from several friends and colleagues. I want to thank the editors Richard Rose and Ezra Suleiman, and the other participants in the Ross Priory Conference on Organizing Political Leadership: Carlos Alba, Colin Campbell, Sabino Cassese, John Helmer, Sheila Mann, Thomas Mann, Renate Mayntz, Richard Neustadt, and Lord Trend. Thanks go also to the participants in the 1979 International Political Science Association World Congress on Political Administration in Moscow, where a version of this chapter was presented, and to Morten Egeberg, Per Laegreid, James G. March, Paul G. Roness, Harald Saetren, Reidun Tvedt, Mariann Vågenes, and Berit Wagtskjold for their help and support. Finally, I want to thank the Norwegian Council for Research and Societal Planning, which has financed the project.

and cultural forces. A single metaphor is unlikely to capture the complexity of modern political systems. This chapter offers an interpretation of Norwegian executive leadership based on ideas and observations from empirical studies of decision making in and between formal organizations.

Executive Leadership and Problems of Political Capacity, Understanding, and Authority

Leadership may refer to formal roles, to types of activities, or to the results of those activities. The executive leaders discussed here are selected on the basis of their formal roles. They are politically appointed leaders—including the Prime Minister, the other Cabinet ministers, the under secretaries of state, and the political secretaries—all of whom have to leave office when a Cabinet resigns. To what degree such politically appointed leaders actually lead is the crucial empirical question: whether they run the ministries, make the most important policy decisions, and affect the course of history. This chapter considers the relations within the executive branch of central government. They key questions here are the *degree* to which politically appointed leaders are able to give direction to the large administrative apparatus acting in their name and *how* they give this direction.

The point of departure is the common observation that public agendas have changed dramatically in recent decades. An enlarged and more complex agenda may produce a strong executive, or a demand for one, making the executive the organizational center of the political system.[1] Yet the increased volume, complexity, and interrelatedness of governmental tasks have in important ways reduced the opportunity of executive leaders for rational calculations and political control. The expanded agenda strains executive capacity because of limitations on time and energy; makes it difficult for executives to understand their own goals and the relations between means and ends; and raises problems of executive authority in relation to other elected or appointed political leaders, to administrative staffs, and to organized interest groups.

An interpretation of executive leadership must take into consideration that time, energy, and attention are scarce resources. It is also necessary to acknowledge that the expanded public agenda

---

[1] Lester G. Seligman, "Leadership: Political Aspects," in David L. Sills, ed., *International Encyclopedia of the Social Sciences* (New York: Macmillan and Free Press, 1968), vol. 12, pp. 107-13.

makes assumptions about omniscient rationality problematic. Executive leaders often have to act in an ambiguous and uncertain world, without a consistent, well-defined ordering of preferences. Government cannot refuse to deal with problems to which no one knows the answer. Finally, the expanded public agenda is closely interrelated with increased demands for representation and participation. The Cabinet is at the top of an electoral hierarchy, but it cannot expect other actors to accept its policies for that reason. And it can rarely force through policies solely on the basis of its electoral power. Thus it is necessary to ask how much power and authority results from winning elections and entering executive positions.

Executive institutions, their structures, personnel, procedures, and policy making will be viewed as organizational responses to the expanded agenda of public policy and as attempts to cope with the problems of capacity, understanding, and authority.

What, then, are the major factors favoring executive leadership in influencing events and behavior? The exercise of leadership depends on whether other centers of power recognize the authority and power of executives as legitimate, and on whether these centers can be called in to back up executive decisions.[2] Executive leadership in Norway is based on party support, and it makes a difference whether the support comes from a majority or a minority party, a well-disciplined or a fragmented party, a single party or a coalition of parties. It also makes a difference whether executive leaders have a strong or weak position within their party or coalition. Executive leaders also need support from and legitimacy among organized interest groups. Thus the organization of the interest group system, like the organization of the party system, is important.

The recruitment of executive leaders and the way they function are expected to reflect executive dependencies and coalitions. While it has been difficult for social scientists to specify the effects of different recruitment processes on the functioning of executive institutions,[3] organized interests want their people, or people sympathizing with their interests, in executive positions. They also want to monitor and influence executive processes. Thus, one expects well-developed

---

[2] Arthur L. Stinchcombe, *Constructing Social Theories* (New York: Harcourt, 1968), pp. 158-60.

[3] Bruce Headey, *British Cabinet Ministers* (London: Allen and Unwin, 1974), p. 269; Anthony King, "Executives," in Fred I. Greenstein and Nelson W. Polsby, eds., *Handbook of Political Science*, vol. 5, *Governmental Institutions and Processes* (Reading, Mass.: Addison-Wesley, 1975), p. 184; and Hugh Heclo, "Presidential and Prime Ministerial Selection," in Donald R. Matthews, ed., *Perspectives on Presidential Selection* (Washington, D.C.: Brookings Institution, 1973), pp. 19-48.

and fairly stable networks of communication between executives and their dependable allies.

In this chapter I consider the possibility that executive leadership depends on constitutional rights and that the number of politically appointed executives is important. Also considered is whether their ability to give direction to the administrative apparatus is affected by their experience, tenure, and unity. Experience in directing other large-scale organizations may also be valuable. The shorter the tenure of executives, the more likely that they will be guests instead of masters in the ministries. But it is also possible that the longer their tenure, the more likely ministers are to identify completely with "their" ministries, civil servants, and clients. Executive teams may be well or poorly organized. The less united they are, and the more energy they use to fight each other, the less likely that executive influence will be a dominant force. Finally, I study staff resources, their location, and the degree to which there are competing sources of expertise. The ability of the executive leaders to formulate goals and to initiate, implement, and assess policies depends on the size and competence of their staffs. But at the same time large staffs may take over, alienating leaders and making them prisoners of the pet projects of the staffs. I also ask to what degree the influence of executive leaders depends on their role perceptions and their philosophy of governance. Do they expect to make a difference, and how much?

The Anatomy of the Executive

Since November 1945 there have been ten Cabinets and seven Prime Ministers in Norway (table 6–1). The Constitution specifies a lower limit on the size of the Cabinet—a Prime Minister and at least seven other members. As of October 1979 there are sixteen members in addition to the Prime Minister, each heading a ministry.[4] Each ministry is divided into departments and divisions with a total of 2,730 positions, clerical personnel included. The Prime Minister has a small staff, but he does not head a ministry. Approximately fifty persons—ministers, under secretaries of state, and personal or political secretaries of the ministers—are party appointees and leave office

---

[4] Since 1977 (table 6-2) a Ministry of Petroleum and Energy has been added and a position as minister of the law of the seas has been discontinued. The latter, however, never had a separate ministry, only a small staff. In October 1979 Prime Minister Nordli reorganized his Cabinet and established a Ministry of Long-Range Planning, a fairly small unit, closely connected to the Prime Minister's office.

TABLE 6-1

Norwegian Cabinets since November 1945

Prime Minister	Duration	Party Base	Support in the Storting	Reason for Resigning
Gerhardsen	Nov. 1945–Nov. 1951	Labor party[a]	Majority	Personal decision by the Prime Minister who said he was tired
Torp	Nov. 1951–Jan. 1955	Labor party	Majority	Demand within the Labor party for stronger leadership
Gerhardsen	Jan. 1955–Aug. 1963	Labor party	Minority after 1961	Vote in the Storting related to accidents in the Kings Bay mines
Lyng	Aug. 1963–Sep. 1963	Conservatives, Liberals, Center party, Christian Peoples party	Minority	Vote in the Storting when the Cabinet presented its program
Gerhardsen	Sep. 1963–Oct. 1965	Labor	Minority	Elections giving nonsocialist parties a majority in the Storting
Borten	Oct. 1965–Mar. 1971	Conservatives, Liberals, Center party, Christian Peoples party	Majority	Internal problems in the coalition, especially related to the European Common Market issue; decision made in the parties

(continued on next page)

TABLE 6–1 (continued)

Prime Minister	Duration	Party Base	Support in the Storting	Reason for Resigning
Bratteli	Mar. 1971–Oct. 1972	Labor party	Minority	Resigned after a majority of the people voted against Norwegian membership in the European Common Market in a referendum
Korvald	Oct. 1972–Oct. 1973	Center party, Christian Peoples party, some Liberals	Minority	Resigned after the elections
Bratteli	Oct. 1973–Jan. 1976	Labor party	Minority	Decision within the Labor party, partly to solve general leadership problems in the party
Nordli	Jan. 1976–	Labor party	Minority	N.A.

NOTE: N.A. = not applicable.

[a] A Labor party Cabinet (Nygaardsvold) was appointed in 1935. In 1945 the Cabinet returned from London and retired June 25, 1945. From June to November Gerhardsen led a Cabinet in which all political parties were represented. The Labor party won a majority in the elections that fall.

TABLE 6–2
Norwegian Ministries: Number of Administrative Staff and Budget Proposals

	1939–40	1947	1957	1967	1977
Administrative staff					
Ministries[a]	10	11	14	14	14
Departments	31	47	55	64	81
Divisions	105	184	212	216	304
Civil Service positions	765	2,159	2,010	2,047	2,730
Politically appointed positions	10	22	29	33	50
Budget proposals (millions of Norwegian kroner)[b]	381	1,268	3,624	10,825	47,877

[a] Prime Minister's office excluded.

[b] Refers only to budget proposals from the ministries. Expenses for the royal family, the Cabinet, Storting, auditor general, Supreme Court, state banks, state firms, pensions and insurance, and extraordinary appropriations are excluded.

Source: Paul G. Roness, *Reorganisering av departementa* (Bergen: Universitetsforlaget, 1979), pp. 41, 58, 65, 74.

when the Cabinet resigns (table 6–2). The under secretary is next in command to the minister, while the political or personal secretary is a personal helper of the minister with no authority over the career civil servants.

The Prime Minister: Political Organizer but No Superstar. The rights and the duties of the Prime Minister are not well specified in the Constitution or in any other laws and instructions. The countersignature of the Prime Minister is required on Cabinet decisions. He has one extra vote if the king is not present in the Council of State, a rare event. He has a right to have any information from all ministries. But the Prime Minister has no hierarchical authority over the other members of the Cabinet. He cannot issue orders or change their decisions; neither can he dissolve the Storting or call elections.[5]

Clearly a Prime Minister cannot base his leadership on constitutional prerogatives. The key to authority and power is a strong position in a political party, as reflected in the tasks of the Prime

[5] Kristian Bloch, *Kongens råd* (Oslo: Universitetsforlaget, 1963); Frede Castberg, *Den utøvende makt* (Bergen: Grieg, 1945); Jan Debes, *Statsadministrasjonen* (Oslo: NKS-forlaget, 1978); Innstilling om Den sentrale forvaltnings organisasjon, Otta, 1970.

Minister, his contact patterns, his recruitment of personnel, and the selection process.

A very important responsibility of a Prime Minister is to lead the process of transforming a party platform—or, in the case of a coalition government, party platforms—into policy proposals and programs. Norwegian parties take their platforms seriously. The development of new platforms may take more than two years and activate the party organization throughout the country. It is the Prime Minister's job to remind the ministers of items on the platforms for which they are responsible and to tally the proposals submitted to the Storting and the programs implemented.[6]

Another important part of the Prime Minister's job is to gather the necessary political support or acceptance for proposals inside as well as outside the Cabinet. A Prime Minister has to be an expert on the political effects of policies. He has to foresee and warn against political difficulties, to clarify areas of disagreement, and to cool the intensity of conflicts. His job is more often to identify solutions that are politically feasible than to discover the "correct" or "right" solution. He should also discover and make others aware of areas of political gains. The Prime Minister's attention will focus on maintaining a viable coalition, on preserving and strengthening Cabinet and party unity, as well as on reinforcing the larger coalition with organized interests in society. These tasks and dependencies are reflected in a series of weekly meetings.

Norwegian Cabinets usually meet three days a week. The most important decisions are made in Cabinet meetings on Mondays and Thursdays. These meetings last for two to three hours. Most often there are eight to ten issues on the agenda—sometimes as many as twenty—but a special Cabinet meeting may be called on a particular issue. Present are the ministers, the under secretary of state in the Prime Minister's office in charge of public relations, and a director general in the Prime Minister's office who prepares the meetings.[7]

---

[6] The argument here is based on interviews with all the ministers, under secretaries of state, and political secretaries of the Bratteli government (1975). During the fall of 1978 the five former Prime Ministers still alive were invited to Bergen to give lectures on their experiences. All accepted, and they also commented on Cabinet work in more informal talks. Later they were interviewed—some for several hours, others more briefly. The Minister of the Law of the Seas, Jens Evensen, had a special mission and was not head of a ministry; he was excluded from this study, and so was his under secretary of state.

[7] Other persons may be called in, especially in budget matters. The Borten Cabinet introduced a new routine in 1970 whereby under secretaries of state met regularly as alternates in the absence of their ministers. This practice was not continued by the Korvald Cabinet or the Labor party Cabinets (NOU 1974:18, *Statssekretaerordningen* m.m., p. 16).

Also of importance politically is an informal luncheon on Fridays.

The preparatory Council of State meets for a half to one hour on Thursdays after Cabinet meetings to consider informally the agenda of the Council of State. Brief discussions occasionally occur, especially if issues have not previously been presented at a Cabinet meeting. The Council of State, chaired by the king, is primarily ritual and lasts for half an hour to forty-five minutes.[8] Several attempts to reduce the number of decisions that must be made formally by the Council of State have so far met with limited success.[9]

The role of the Prime Minister in Cabinet decision making is closely linked to his participation in an external political network. These networks are different for Prime Ministers from the Labor party, which has never taken part in a coalition government, and for nonsocialist Prime Ministers, who since 1945 have always led coalition governments.

A Prime Minister from the Labor party has four separate weekly meetings with the party faction in the Storting, with the governing board of that faction, with the party directorate, and with a coordinating committee between the party and the federation of trade unions (LO). The political importance of these meetings is emphasized.[10] The routine meetings are followed up by daily personal and informal contacts and by formalized cooperation on important single issues. An example is that when the Cabinet prepared its platform for 1978 to 1981, the process was closely coordinated with the preparation of similar platforms for the party and for LO. A coordinating group was established, chaired by the Prime Minister, with repre-

---

[8] In 1905 the king and his cabinet would sit together for four to five hours; in 1920 for one and a half hours (Olav Solumsmoen, "Regjeringens arbeidsform i Sverige og Norge," *Administrasjonsnytt, Oslo: 1962-63,* pp. 4-10). In one important respect the meeting is not a ritual. In order to avoid responsibility for Cabinet decisions a minister has to dissent in the Council of State. This, however, seldom happens. From 1945 to 1961 there were thirty-two votes of dissent, primarily on decisions related to treason during the war (Per Stavang, *Parlamentarisme og maktbalanse* [Oslo: Universitetsforlaget, 1964]). During the Borten Cabinet the number increased, but has since dropped again to a couple a year.

[9] Bloch, *Kongens råd,* p. 129. Some decisions have been delegated to the ministries, but after a certain decrease in the first part of the 1960s the number has increased again to 3,645 in 1978. That includes 1,526 issues from the Ministry of Justice alone because applications for pardon (1,287 in 1978) have to go to the Council of State (Statsministerens kontor, *Kontorstatistikk for året 1978*).

[10] The coordinating committee meets for one hour every Monday. Since 1965 these meetings are alternately led by the party chairman and the chairman of LO. The meetings are advisory only. A division of labor and of responsibilities is recognized, and the party, LO, and the Prime Minister are all on guard against violations of their autonomy (according to an interview with Trygve Bratteli, who has been a member of the committee since 1945).

sentatives from the party, the youth organization of the party, the party faction in the Storting, and LO.[11]

The Prime Minister's role in the Cabinet may be strengthened by his external contacts, but he does not have a monopoly on interpreting the views of other power centers. Other Cabinet members also have close relations with the party, with LO, and with the party faction in the Storting. The centrality of the Prime Minister in these networks has varied.

For Prime Ministers in coalition governments the situation has been different. The parties protect their autonomy and have not developed a unified communication system between the Cabinet and the Storting. The party factions have seldom had joint meetings, and each minister, the Prime Minister included, has met only with his own party faction in committees. After 1969, when several coalition party leaders left the Cabinet to return to the Storting, parliamentary leaders participated more actively in the Cabinet's preparation of cases. But then again in the Korvald period leaders of party factions in the Storting were more seldom activated.[12]

Thus, there are important differences in the organizational frameworks within which Prime Ministers operate. But there are also similarities. A Prime Minister is the chief spokesman for the Cabinet in important debates in the Storting. He will consult with the Standing Committee on Foreign Affairs on major foreign policy or security decisions, and perhaps with the leaders of the party factions.[13] So far, however, the opposition has not used the question period in the Storting to challenge the Prime Minister. He is seldom questioned, and very rarely by other party leaders.

In addition, all Prime Ministers are in touch with organized interest groups in society. Incomes policies are discussed in a committee of representatives of the Cabinet and of the major economic (producer) interests. The Federation of Norwegian Industries, the Federation of Norwegian Commercial Associations, and the Norwegian Shipowners' Association have special contacts with the Cabinet, even when the Labor party is in office. Generally, however,

---

[11] Odvar Nordli, "Regjeringens virkemåte," unpublished lecture, University of Bergen, 1978, p. 16.

[12] John Lyng, *Fra borgfred til politisk blåmandag* (Oslo: Cappelen, 1978), p. 92; Arve Solstad, "The Norwegian Coalition System," *Scandinavian Political Studies*, vol. 4 (1969), pp. 160-67; Per Vassbotn, *Lekkasje og forlis* (Oslo: Cappelen, 1971), pp. 124-25.

[13] When the Labor party lost its majority in 1964, the nonsocialist party factions in the Storting showed an increasing unwillingness to accept their leaders' informal consultations with Cabinet members (Tim Greve, *Det norske Storting gjennom 150 år: Tidsrommet 1908–1964*, vol. 3 [Oslo: Gyldendal, 1964], p. 405).

economic organizations have been reluctant to accept integrated participation in policy-making processes at the Cabinet level. Instead, they have preferred integration at the ministry level.[14]

We may conclude that a Norwegian Prime Minister has to act in an environment dominated by formal organizations such as parties, the Storting, ministries, and organized interest groups. Though he is unlikely to achieve a position as superstar in these networks, it is possible for him to affect policy making through political organizing and brokerage. The degree of success depends upon many factors, especially his political career.

All Norwegian Prime Ministers have been party leaders, but some have had a more dominant position than others. Einar Gerhardsen, who was born in 1897, fits the Weberian ideal of a political generalist with politics as a vocation.[15] He had only elementary schooling and was a road worker from the age of seventeen to twenty-four. From then on his career was related to politics. He was Prime Minister for seventeen years and chairman of the Labor party for twenty years. Gerhardsen was not an expert on issues and never headed a ministry. His strength lay in organizing political choice situations, an ability acquired through practice. His major organizational affiliation was the party.

The strong party base and the learning-by-doing aspects are shared by two other Labor party Prime Ministers. Oscar Torp (born in 1893), an electrician with no higher education, was Prime Minister for three years and the head of four different ministries over a twelve-year period. For twenty-two years he was the chairman of the Labor party. Trygve Bratteli (born in 1910) also started as a worker with no higher education and was Prime Minister for nearly four years. Bratteli was a member of the Cabinet for a total of fourteen years heading the Ministry of Finance and the Ministry of Communications. He was deputy chairman of the Labor party for seventeen years and chairman for ten years. Bratteli, as of 1979, is the leader of the party faction in the Storting.

The biographies of these three Prime Ministers illustrate the continuity in the leadership of the party that has been in power for more than thirty-seven years since 1935. Since Cabinet members have to leave their seats in the Storting while serving in the Cabinet, the political work of these three Prime Ministers has been related pri-

---

[14] Johan P. Olsen, "Integrated Organizational Participation in Government," in Paul C. Nystrom and William H. Starbuck, eds., *Handbook of Organizational Design*, vol. 2 (London: Oxford University Press, forthcoming).

[15] Max Weber, "Politics as a Vocation," in H. H. Gerth and C. Wright Mills, eds., *From Max Weber* (London: Routledge and Kegan Paul, 1970), pp. 77-128.

marily to party and Cabinet functions. Their party base was stronger than that of the two pre–World War II Labor Prime Ministers (Hornsrud and Nygaardsvold), and stronger than that of the present (1979) Prime Minister, Odvar Nordli. Nordli (born in 1927) attended junior college and became an accountant. From his early twenties, Nordli was active in party politics and local government. But he has not been employed by the party and has not been chairman. He became a member of the Storting in 1961, was minister of labor and local government (1971–1972), and leader of the party faction in the Storting (1973–1976) before he was appointed Prime Minister.

None of the Prime Ministers from the Labor party has had a university degree. All the nonsocialists have, and their careers in the Cabinet and the parties are closely related to long tenure in the Storting. Per Borten (born in 1913) spent twenty-seven years in the Storting, was chairman of the Center (farmers') party for twenty-two years, and held positions in farmers' organizations. Lars Korvald (born in 1916) has been a representative in the Storting for eighteen years, chairman of the Christian People's party for ten years, and active in religious organizations. John Lyng (born in 1905) made a career in the court system. He was a member of the Storting for twelve years, representing the Conservative party, but was never chairman of the party. Lyng later became minister of foreign affairs for a five-year period and was appointed county governor.

Norwegian Prime Ministers have long party careers. They know their parties, and the party cadres know them. The biographies reflect the fact that political parties are the main arenas for appointing and removing Prime Ministers. Only twice has a Cabinet left after a defeat in a general election, once after a referendum, twice after votes in the Storting, and four times as a result of party decisions (table 6–1). The careers of the Prime Ministers show a tendency away from a one-sided emphasis on the party organization, however; party leadership is usually combined with a career in the Storting or a vocation outside politics. The selection and recall processes today reflect this broader base and involve a wider group of participants than in the 1950s.

In 1945 the Labor party made Gerhardsen Prime Minister, but the decision to withdraw in 1951 was his own. Many of the major participants have described the process, and they basically agree: The decision to leave was a personal choice by the Prime Minister and he more or less appointed his successor. The decision was described as a coup, a bomb, a shock, and a bolt of lightning; it was judged a disaster for the party. Gerhardsen was strongly urged to continue, but he refused. Central participants in the process have argued that if regular party procedures had been followed, Gerhardsen would not have been allowed to leave. Gerhardsen's argument was that he was tired and that changes in the Cabinet had to come suddenly. "I cannot leave little by little," he argued.[16]

Gerhardsen returned in 1955 after internal party criticism of the Cabinet under Torp, who did not want to leave.[17] Bratteli resigned in 1976 as a result of intraparty decisions. At the national conference of the Labor party there were two candidates for the position of chairman. The solution was to make one the chairman and the other Prime Minister in the next Labor Cabinet. A party committee was appointed to decide the time of the changeover.

The heads of the nonsocialist coalition Cabinets have been selected through interparty decisions, with the locus of influence in the party factions in the Storting. Borten was chosen by a formal vote in 1965, and his coalition was dissolved from within in 1971 when three of the four partners refused to continue. Parts of the struggle between the party leaders took place before open microphones and running TV cameras.[18]

Most Prime Ministers in Norway have been appointed on the basis of the candidate's position in his party and the party's position in the Storting.[19] The people selected are political generalists; they know Norwegian politics well and are expected to coordinate the work of their Cabinets. The ability to coordinate has been reduced, however, as one-party majority Cabinets have been replaced by minority or coalition Cabinets and as the tenure of Prime Ministers has become shorter. Also, the administrative resources of the Prime Minister are very modest. And the Prime Minister cannot expect the Cabinet members to form a unified group.

---

[16] Einar Gerhardsen, *Samarbeid og strid* (Oslo: Tiden, 1971), pp. 294-302; Olav Larssen, *Den langsomme revolusjonen* (Oslo: Aschehoug, 1973), pp. 99, 102; Haakon Lie, . . . *slik jeg ser det* (Oslo: Tiden, 1975), pp. 7, 53-59; Konrad Nordahl, *Gode arbeidsår* (Oslo: Tiden, 1973), pp. 32-34; and Olav Solumsmoen and Olav Larssen, eds., *Med Einar Gerhardsen gjennom 20 år* (Oslo: Tiden, 1967), pp. 97-99.

[17] Larssen, *Revolusjonen*, pp. 120-34; Lie, . . . *slik jeg ser det*, p. 72; and Nordahl, *Arbeidsår*, pp. 103-5.

[18] Olav Brunvand, *Fra samspill til sammenbrudd* (Oslo: Tiden, 1973); Hans Chr. Finstad, *Fra dragkamp til samspill* (Oslo: Lutherstiftelsen, 1970); Lyng, *Borgfred*; Herbjørn Sørebø, *Slik sprakk koalisjonen* (Oslo: Det norske samlaget, 1971); and Vassbotn, *Lekkasje*.

[19] Henrik Hermerén, *Regeringsbildningen i flerpartisystem* (Lund: Studentlitteratur, 1975).

The Prime Minister's Office. When Johan L. Mowinckel resigned in 1935 he had been Norwegian Prime Minister three times. In all three Cabinets he was also head of the Ministry of Foreign Affairs. Although as Prime Minister he had no secretariat, apparently he did not feel overloaded.[20] Today such a combination seems very unlikely.

Ever since 1945 the limits on the capacity of executive leaders have been on the political agenda, and many institutional changes have been made in response to this problem.[21] The Prime Minister still has little administrative assistance, however. A small office was established in the mid-1950s, with three under secretaries of state, one on economic planning, one on relations with the Storting, and one on relations with the media. Three positions of director general were also established, one of which was later transferred. In 1979 the Prime Minister's staff counted only nineteen persons, including clerical personnel and chauffeurs. Nor can he count on much assistance from committees. Out of a total of 1,155 public committees and boards, 905 permanent, with 7,200 members, only five permanent and three temporary committees are attached to the Prime Minister's office.[22]

When the idea of an office for the Prime Minister was raised, it was viewed—in Norway as in other countries—as an indication of the Prime Minister's desire for power. The office has clearly not become a superministry, however.[23] Rather, a public commission has argued that with the present administrative apparatus the Prime Minister is scarcely able to look after the activities of the ministries. Another committee expressed doubt, however, about whether it is "appropriate" to expand the Prime Minister's office into a coordinating department.[24]

---

[20] Per Bratland, *Hvem har makt i Norge?* (Oslo: Aschehoug, 1965), p. 109.

[21] Rolf N. Torgersen, "Flere departementer?" *Verdens Gang* (November 22, 1948) and "Regjeringsreformer: Konsentrasjon av den utøvende makt?" *Verdens Gang* (November 23, 1948); St.prp. nr. 121, 1955, *Tiltak for å lette den administrative arbeidsbyrden for statsrådene m.v.;* St.prp. nr. 111, 1970–1971, *Personlige sekretaerer for statsrådene;* NOU 1974: 18, *Statssekretaerordningen;* St.meld. nr. 58, 1975–1976, *Om statssekretaerordningen m.m. og om avskjed m.m. av embets- menn;* see also James G. March and Johan P. Olsen, *Ambiguity and Choice in Organizations* (Bergen: Universitetsforlaget, 1976).

[22] St.meld. nr. 7, 1977–1978, *Utvalg, styrer og råd m.v.*

[23] King, "Executives," p. 224; and Debes, *Statsadministrasjonen,* p. 53.

[24] Innstilling om Den sentrale forvaltnings organisasjon," Otta, 1970, p. 46; and NOU 1974: 18, *Statssekretaerordningen,* p. 28. Prime Ministers disagree among themselves about the administrative adequacy of the Prime Minister's office. For instance, Bratteli finds the present capacity adequate, while Korvald would like to strengthen the politically appointed staff, but not the group of tenured civil servants. Korvald would also like to have an under secretary of state who could follow the budgetary procedures in the Ministry of Finance and eventually in other ministries (interviews).

The lack of administrative resources under direct control of the Prime Minister is not compensated for by control of the selection of the heads of the ministries. Usually the Prime Minister is the central actor in the appointment of the executive team, but that does not mean that he can always pick the ministers he wants.

Selecting the Team. King has argued that while appointments to ministerial office in some countries are formally made by the head of state, in almost all countries the real decisions are made by the head of government.[25] This description is fairly accurate for Norway in the 1950s. It is less adequate for the later Labor party Cabinets and is wrong for the coalition Cabinets of the 1960s and the 1970s.

Prime Minister Gerhardsen comes closest to this description. Gerhardsen took the initiative and suggested a solution. He discussed it with a fairly small group: the deputy chairman and the secretary general of the party, the chairman of LO, the leader of the party faction in the Storting and the president of the Storting, and with the editor of the Labor party newspaper in Oslo. Changes were then discussed in the party directorate and in the party faction in the Storting. The Prime Minister listened, but the decision was his own.[26]

The process, which lasted for a short time only, was one of consulting, not bargaining. It was constrained by the expectation that different regions and organized interest groups—and to some degree women and the youth organization—should be represented. The Prime Minister also had to consider the need for able people to remain in the party faction in the Storting.

While both Gerhardsen and the present Prime Minister, Nordli, have argued that nominating a Cabinet is not a one-man job,[27] the process has changed in important ways. During the 1970s, Labor party Cabinets have been selected through a longer process, with more participants, more demands for group representation, and more publicity. It has become more difficult to govern through selecting Cabinet members. One result has been public demands within the Labor party for a stronger leadership. The argument is that "too much democracy" and quotas for various interests produce a Cabinet

---

[25] King, "Executives," p. 197.

[26] Larssen, *Revolusjonen*, pp. 59–60; Lie, . . . *slik jeg ser det*, p. 303; Gerhardsen, *Samarbeid og strid*, pp. 280-88; and Nordahl, *Arbeidsår*, pp. 33, 101.

[27] Gerhardsen, *Samarbeid og strid*, pp. 280-81; *Dagbladet* (Oslo), November 1, 1975.

characterized by mediocrity and lack of a clearly defined political orientation.[28]

Changes in selection procedures have been explained by the different styles of leadership of Gerhardsen and Bratteli.[29] While personal style may be important, changes in selection procedures also reflect more fundamental political and social trends. The Labor party, having lost its majority, needs ministers competent in interparty as well as intraparty bargaining. Because its traditional base—blue-collar workers, fishermen, and farmers—is declining in size, the party has to attract new groups, and in the process has become more heterogeneous. More interests have to be taken into consideration, including special interests more concerned with the choice of a specific minister than with the overall composition of the Cabinet. At the same time, a new generation is taking over leadership in the party, as well as in the Storting, the Cabinet, and LO—a change that is affecting the general style of decision making.[30]

Prime Minister Nordli is quoted as saying, "If you cannot get the ones you love, you have to love the ones you get." For the Prime Ministers of the nonsocialist coalition governments in the 1960s and 1970s this was even more true. They had to work with ministers unilaterally selected by each of the participating parties. Borten learned about changes in his Cabinet through the media.

The lack of Prime Ministerial control of the recruitment process is also illustrated by the remarkable stability in the four first years of the Borten Cabinet. The only minister who left (because of health

[28] The major reorganization of the Nordli Cabinet in October 1979 deviated from the pattern. The criticism against the Cabinet, the heavy losses of the Labor party in the local elections, and the demand for leadership and unity legitimized major changes. Nordli picked his Cabinet after consulting with very few people. It remains to be seen whether this was a return to the old pattern or a one-time event in a special situation. Nor is it clear that the Prime Minister was able to govern through the selection of his team. Because the Cabinet is very heterogeneous, the process of anticipated reactions seems to have been working, even though few people participated. It is also too early to say whether the new Ministry of Long-Range Planning will strengthen the Prime Minister.

[29] Larssen, *Revolusjonen*, pp. 98, 123; Lie, . . . *slik jeg ser det*, p. 57; and Egil Sundar, "Skifte bør skje brått," *Aftenposten* (Oslo), May 19, 1979.

[30] Prime Minister Nordli has argued that the party still has a lot to learn about how this change of generations should be tackled by the party organization (*Dagbladet*, December 23, 1978). And the president of the Storting says that in this new situation the right forms of communication and coordination between the power centers of the labor movement—the party directorate, the Cabinet, the party faction in the Storting, and LO—have not yet been found (Guttorm Hansen, *Bergens Arbeiderblad*, December 27, 1978). The president of the Storting concluded that the country cannot have more than one Cabinet, and that some decisions have to be made by the Cabinet and by the party faction in the Storting without intervention by the party or LO.

problems) was replaced by his own party. After winning the 1969 election, representatives of the coalition parties gathered for only two and a half hours to discuss the composition of the Cabinet. A status quo may indicate that no one dared to open up new, general discussion. When the Cabinet was later reorganized the Prime Minister did not take the initiative, but observed the process from a distance.[31] Again, the process has been explained by reference to the special leadership style of the Prime Minister. Things happened in a planless way because the Prime Minister was unable to assume leadership and take initiatives, because he was too concerned with details, and because he did not clearly signal to the ministers his own preferences and intentions. Yet this explanation has to be supplemented. In a coalition in which four parties were jealously protecting their autonomy and identity, and leading Cabinet members were publicly differing on major issues, strong initiatives and leadership would probably have been unacceptable.

To summarize, the potential for Prime Ministerial leadership is highly dependent on his position in the party and the strength of that party, as well as on his relations to major interest groups. The Prime Minister's constitutional prerogatives are few, his administrative resources modest, and the power to appoint ministers lies largely with the parties.

Gerhardsen comes closest to hierarchical leadership because of his long tenure, his leadership talents, and the support he received from a majority party facing a split opposition and from LO, which also had a stable leadership[32] with whom Gerhardsen had routine contacts. There was also a fairly high consensus about economic growth as a main goal and Keynesian economics as an instrument of governance. Gerhardsen had clashes with other major actors, such as the chairman of LO,[33] however, and the Labor party never implemented some of its most ambitious plans.[34] Still, Gerhardsen had a

---

[31] Brunvand, Samspill; Lyng, Borgfred, pp. 147-50; Solstad, "Norwegian Coalition"; and Vassbotn, Lekkasje, p. 103.

[32] Einar Gerhardsen, Trygve Bratteli, Konrad Nordahl (chairman of LO), Haakon Lie (secretary general of the party), and Halvard Lange (minister of foreign affairs) were all members of the party directorate from 1946 to 1965. The stability of the leadership, along with the fact that the party in most of the period had a majority in the Storting, provoked the comment that the Cabinet had become an executive committee of the party and that Norway had become a one-party state (J. A. Seip, Fra embedsmannsstat til ettpartistat og andre essays [Oslo: Universitetsforlaget, 1963]; Herbert Tingsten, "De norska regeringskriserna 1963," in Herbert Tingsten, Från ideer til idyll [Stockholm: Norstedt, 1966]).

[33] Larssen, Revolusjonen, pp. 71-73.

[34] Trond Bergh and Helge Ø. Pharo, eds., Vekst og velstand (Oslo: Universitetsforlaget, 1977), pp. 86-87, 116-22, 484.

greater leadership potential than any of his successors. The problems of political capacity, understanding, and authority have not been accompanied by a major expansion of the Prime Minister's ability to govern. He has to work through the ministers, and the administrative apparatus in Norway favors political specialization rather than co-ordination by the Prime Minister.

Ministers: Specialists or Generalists? How likely is it that the politically appointed heads will become leaders of the ministries in a world of expanding problems, where most orders are not self-executing[35] and where ministers have to act upon the advice of civil servants? How likely is it that ministers will identify with their roles as ministers more than with their functions in the Cabinet[36] and that they will promote the policies of their administrative staffs and of well-organized client groups more than party platforms?

The enlarged public agenda has been countered by a delegation of authority from the Cabinet to the individual minister, making him or her more independent. At the same time, some decisions have been moved from the ministries to other central administrative agencies or to local and regional authorities. The underlying ideology is that ministries should be the political secretariats of the ministers and that decisions covered by an adequate set of laws or rules should be delegated.[37]

While the number of ministries and of employees has changed modestly since 1945, the number of departments and divisions and the budget size have grown considerably (table 6–2). The functional differentiation is also illustrated by the fact that central administrative agencies outside the ministries have become relatively more important. In 1947 they employed 18.7 percent and in 1977, 27.7 percent of state administrative personnel.[38]

As in France, a Norwegian minister can expect civil servants to have strong loyalties toward their own institutions, tasks, and professions. Each ministry has a great potential for indoctrinating and disciplining its personnel[39] and for defending its territory and juris-

---

[35] Richard E. Neustadt, *Presidential Power* (New York: Wiley, 1976), p. 114.

[36] Renate Mayntz and Fritz W. Scharpf, *Policy-making in the German Federal Bureaucracy* (Amsterdam: Elsevier, 1975), p. 43.

[37] Bloch, *Kongens råd*, p. 56; Debes, *Statsadministrasjonen*; NOU 1974:18, *Statssekretaerordningen*; NOU 1974:53, *Mål og retningslinjer for reformer i lokalforvaltningen*; and "Innstilling om Den sentrale forvaltnings organisasjon," Otta, 1970.

[38] Paul G. Roness, *Reorganisering av departementa* (Bergen: Universitetsforlaget, 1979), p. 62.

[39] Ezra N. Suleiman, *Politics, Power and Bureaucracy in France* (Princeton, N.J.:

diction. Attempts at coordination across administrative boundaries are often viewed as unwanted intervention. The tendency toward parochial identification and local rationality is likely to be strengthened as the participatory rights[40] of employees and their organizations increase. The same tendency is likely to result from increased rights of participation in governmental processes for organized interests in society.

The concept of pressure groups is inadequate in the Norwegian context. Organized interests, especially economic (producer) groups, are highly integrated into the governmental process through a system of committees and boards, through a hearing system, and through daily, informal consultations.[41] Major economic organizations have, however, several times resisted governmental attempts to institutionalize participation in general economic policy making at the Cabinet level through a board of economic coordination. They are interested in representation and participation in policy-making processes at the departmental and ministerial level. The individual ministry has become *the* most important point of contact in the political system for economic interest organizations (table 6–3). With the exception of the Norwegian federation of trade unions (LO), most contacts are between administrators from both government and interest groups.[42]

Princeton University Press, 1974); Per Laegreid and Johan P. Olsen, *Byråkrati og beslutninger* (Bergen: Universitetsforlaget, 1978); "Innstilling om Den sentrale forvaltnings organisasjon," Otta, 1970.

[40] Per Laegreid, "Tenestemenn i norske departement," Discussion Paper no. 40, Maktutredningen, Bergen, and hovedoppgave i offentlig administrasjon, University of Bergen, 1975; and Harald Saetren, "Implementering: En studie av utflyttingen av statsinstitusjoner fra Oslo," Maktutredningen, Bergen, 1977 (mimeo).

[41] Tom Christensen and Morten Egeberg, "Noen trekk ved forholdet mellom organisasjonene og den offentlige forvaltning," in Leif Skare, ed., *Forvaltningen i samfunnet* (Oslo: Tanum, 1979); Abraham Hallenstvedt and Jorolv Moren, "Det organiserte samfunn," in Natalie Rogoff Ramsøy and Mariken Vaa, eds., *Det norske samfunn*, vol. 1 (Oslo: Gyldendal, 1975); Jorolv Moren, ed., *Den kollegiale forvaltning* (Oslo: Universitetsforlaget, 1974); and Olsen, "Integrated Organizational Participation."

[42] A conspiracy of the bureaucrats is sometimes aired as a hypothesis. The two groups of administrators represent different traditions, however, as illustrated by their attitudes toward a further institutionalization of the contacts between the state and organized interest groups: 28 percent of the civil servants, as against 64 percent of the administrators and 67 percent of the elected leaders in the economic (producer) organizations wanted more permanent, institutionalized cooperation in their own field. In the ministries people in lower positions and with short tenure were most in favor of a further institutionalization, while in the economic organizations opposition was most widespread among the representatives of weaker organizations. The percentage for the civil servants in the ministries is from a study of all employees from the executive level to the secretaries general who had been in the ministries for at least one year; the response rate was 72 percent (Laegreid and Olsen, *Byråkrati*).

TABLE 6–3

CONTACTS OF ELECTED LEADERS AND ADMINISTRATORS
IN ECONOMIC (PRODUCER) ORGANIZATIONS, 1976
(percentage)

	% Having at Least One Contact	
	Elected leaders	Adminis-trators
Contacts with Ministry	37	84
Contacts with Storting	15	33
Individual representatives in Storting	37	54
Contacts with Authorities		
County	22	39
Local	31	48
Contacts with political parties	24	26
Interviews by mass media	44	65
Publications about own work		
in newspapers and journals	40	72

NOTE: Data are for 475 elected leaders and 536 administrators in economic (producer) organizations; data are drawn from the sixty-three most resourceful economic (producer) organizations and a random sample of sixty-three of the remaining organizations. Questionnaires were sent to elected leaders and to administrative personnel; 72 percent responded.

Elected personnel in full-time, paid positions are counted as administrators; they belong primarily to trade union organizations. The larger and more resourceful organizations are more strongly represented in the sample of administrators than in the sample of elected leaders simply because many small organizations do not have full-time administrators. (See also Jostein Gaasemyr, *Organisasjonsbyråkrati og korporativisme* [Bergen: Universitetsforlaget, 1979]).

The tendency is that the higher the administrative status, the more contacts there are and the less likely it is that the contact is centered on routine matters.[43]

The result is that ministers face not only an administrative apparatus with a well-developed division of labor but also agencies with routine support from strong interest groups. The tendency toward segmentation of the political-administrative system is also strengthened by the fact that contacts with research and educational institutions are highly specialized, and most of the contact between ministries and the Storting goes through a specific committee.[44] Mem-

---

[43] Gaasemyr, *Organisasjonsbyråkrati*; and Laegreid and Olsen, *Byråkrati*.

[44] Laegreid and Olsen, *Byråkrati*; and Johan P. Olsen and Berit Wagtskjold, "Organisering av laeringshorisonter," University of Bergen, 1979 (mimeo).

bers of the Storting have traditionally shown a dualism. Though they may be concerned with the overall growth of budgets and administrative staffs, as members of committees they usually defend the ministry and institutions connected with their own committee, arguing that the Ministry of Finance has been too eager to cut budget proposals.[45]

Is it likely that a minister can match this kind of coalition? Is he or she likely to want to do so? Does he or she stay in the ministry long enough to do anything?

Ministers: Masters or Guests? Obviously ministers are sometimes strangers in the ministries. Since they represent a fragile and transient element in the executive process,[46] they easily become the prisoners of and the spokesmen for projects that have been in the pipeline long before they themselves were appointed.

The Norwegian situation is a blend of visitors and veterans. Since 1945, 63 percent of the ministers have been members of only one Cabinet, 27 percent have been in two, 5 percent in three, and 5 percent have been members in more than three Cabinets. The average number of years in office is 4.1, with ministers from the Labor party averaging 5.2 years and those in nonsocialist Cabinets 2.4 years. While 21 percent of the ministers have a tenure of less than one year, 14 percent have served one or two years, but 45 percent have served more than five years. When new Cabinets are appointed, the ministers already have an average of 1.9 years of Cabinet experience, and they serve one Cabinet an average of 2.6 years. The average minister leaves the Cabinet with four years of service and has five years of service when he or she leaves for the last time (table 6–4).

There is a difference between nonsocialist and Labor party Cabinets, and there is also a tendency toward less experience and shorter tenure for Labor party ministers over time. Still, these Cabinets include people who are obviously not strangers to the governmental process or the ministries. Nor are Norwegian ministers likely to stay so long in a ministry as to be totally indoctrinated in the ministerial culture.

Headey argued that if a minister stays too long, he ceases to be a minister and becomes a sort of second permanent secretary—a creature of the department. According to Headey, three years is the maximum time a minister should spend in one department, and about

---

[45] Stortingsforhandlinger 1950, *Antall statstjenestemenn 1. januar 1950*, p. 1647.
[46] Hugh Heclo, *A Government of Strangers* (Washington, D.C.: Brookings Institution, 1977).

TABLE 6–4

Tenure of Norwegian Ministers, May 1979

| | Years of Service | | | |
| | Before entering specified Cabinet | Within specified Cabinet | Including specified Cabinet | Total in |
Cabinet				Cabinets
Gerhardsen, 1945–51	0.9	4.4	5.0	8.1
Torp, 1951–55	4.5	2.2	5.3	7.7
Gerhardsen, 1955–63	2.8	4.1	5.2	6.7
Lyng, 1963	0.0	0.1	0.1	2.6
Gerhardsen, 1963–65	5.9	2.0	7.5	8.1
Borten, 1965–71	0.0	3.9	3.9	4.0
Bratteli, 1971–72	1.3	1.5	2.8	4.7
Korvald, 1972–73	0.8	0.9	1.6	1.6
Bratteli, 1973–76	1.3	2.0	3.2	4.8
Nordli, 1976–	1.7	2.8	4.1	4.1
Total average	1.9	2.6	4.0	5.0

NOTE: The data are for 190 ministers, except in the first column, which includes only ministers appointed when the Cabinet began its term of office.

the optimum too.[47] It is unclear what criteria or data Headey uses, and it is likely that the extent of indoctrination will depend on the strength and unity of the ministry, other affiliations of a minister, such as with the party, and the external networks in which he or she operates.

In Norway three-fourths of all ministers have served in only one ministry, while only seven persons have been in three or more ministries (the Prime Minister's office included). There is considerable variation across ministries, however. On the one hand, 73 percent of the ministers of finance have been in another ministry, as have more than half the Prime Ministers and ministers of defense, commerce, justice, and foreign affairs. On the other hand, only 10 percent of the ministers of fisheries have been the head of another ministry.

Ministers with long tenure tend to be political generalists who have headed at least two ministries. The most outstanding exception is Halvard Lange who headed the Ministry of Foreign Affairs for twenty years. Ministers with long tenure also have long party careers. In my judgment, therefore, it is unlikely that length of tenure will be

---

[47] Headey, British Cabinet, pp. 95-96.

TABLE 6–5

MINISTERS' TENURE IN THE STORTING WHEN FIRST
APPOINTED TO THE CABINET
(percentage)

Number of Years in the Storting	Period First Appointed				Total
	1814–84[a]	1884–1920[b]	1920–45[c]	1945–78[d]	
More than 15	7	11	21	11	13
11–15	11	20	12	7	13
6–10	14	16	23	11	15
1–5	23	18	12	19	18
None	44	35	32	52	42
Number of ministers	70	114	77	130	391

NOTE: Percentages may not add to 100 because of rounding.
[a] From the 1814 Collegium to Christian H. Schweigaard
[b] From Johan Sverdrup to Gunnar Knudsen II
[c] From Otto B. Halvorsen to Johan Nygaardsvold
[d] From Einar Gerhardsen I to Odvar Nordli

a major factor in forming the ministers into spokesmen of the ministry and its clients. But ministers may take that role if they are identified with a specific sector *before* they enter the ministry and if this identification is a major reason for their appointment.

Paths to the Ministries. "No Prime Minister could have recruited his ministers so consistently from the outside as Gerhardsen and Torp, had the party faction in the Storting been a really strong element in the political game."[48] If this reasoning is accepted, experience in the Storting really has lost significance as a path to a ministry since World War II compared with any other period since the parliamentary system was introduced in 1884 (table 6–5). Less than half the ministers have held a seat in the Storting, and only 11 percent have been members for more than fifteen years.

During the late 1960s and 1970s, experience in the Storting was again more important that it had been in the 1950s. At the same time, a seat in the Storting is less of a guarantee of a generalist orientation than it used to be. Parliamentary work focuses more and more

---

[48] Stavang, *Parlamentarisme*, p. 155; also, Bergh and Pharo, *Vekst og velstand*, p. 457.

TABLE 6–6

NORWEGIAN MINISTERS' EXPERIENCE IN LOCAL GOVERNMENT,
1814–1978
(percentage)

Participation in Local Government	Period First Appointed			
	1814–84	1884–1920	1920–45	1945–78
Mayor	10	39	42	22
Representative	11	22	34	42
No experience	79	40	25	35
Number of ministers	70	114	77	130

on committees, and members have to specialize in order to catch up with the expanded agenda.

The role of mayor, another political generalist, has also become less important as a springboard to the Cabinet. Since 1945 the number of ministers with experience as mayor is little more than half what it was from the time the parliamentary system was introduced until World War II (table 6–6). Still, nearly two-thirds of the ministers have experience in local politics, although local politics has also become more specialized and is no guarantee of a generalist orientation.

Party experience may partly counteract the tendencies toward specialization. Norwegian ministers have, with few exceptions, long party memberships. This is especially true of Labor party governments, as illustrated by the party background of the Bratteli government (table 6–7). Even when under secretaries of state and (the mostly young) political secretaries are included, a third have more than twenty-five years of party membership. Just a little fewer have held public office at the local level and 10 percent have held office at the national level for more than twenty-five years. None had less than four years of party membership. Even if party work has become more specialized, the working of a Norwegian Cabinet cannot be understood if the integration provided by the common party background is overlooked.

Political indicators of a specialist-generalist orientation vary across ministries, as do social indicators such as vocational background, education, and connections with interest groups. When the parliamentary system was introduced, Norway broke away from recruiting ministers largely from the higher civil servants in the

TABLE 6–7
PARTY BACKGROUND OF MINISTERS, UNDER SECRETARIES OF STATE,
AND POLITICAL SECRETARIES IN THE BRATTELI GOVERNMENT, 1975
(percentage)

Number of Years	Membership in Labor Party	Party Office at Local Level	Party Office at National Level
25 or more	33	27	10
10–24	42	46	31
6–9	16	12	9
5 or less	9	15	50

NOTE: Data are for forty-six government leaders.

ministries. From 1814 to 1884, 84 percent of the ministers had reached the top after a regular bureaucratic career. In the post–World War II period only 31 percent were higher civil servants before they became ministers; another 18 percent held various white-collar jobs in public service; 19 percent were independent owners; and 18 percent were employees in the private sector. Of the latter group (twenty-three persons) eleven came from economic (producer) organizations, four from other interest groups, and six from political parties. That is, employees from the rest of the private sector are virtually unrepresented. Not one person was a blue-collar worker when called to the king's table, because workers first become trade union or Labor party employees or members of the Storting before they are appointed ministers. Only 3 percent of the ministers had been fishermen and 8 percent farmers.

The same trend is reflected in the educational background of the ministers. From 1814 to 1884, 86 percent of the ministers held a university degree; half were trained in law, one fourth had a military education, and 7 percent were theologians. In the post–World War II period, 57 percent have had a university degree. Law is still the most common discipline (22 percent), but both military and theological education have disappeared from the ranks, while 9 percent have held a degree in economics and 7 percent in agriculture. The tendency in the Cabinet is toward increasing variation in educational background.

As should be expected from the selection processes used, the distribution of social backgrounds across ministries is far from random. In the post–World War II period the Ministry of Justice has had ten ministers, all educated in law, eight of them with jobs related to the administration of justice. Furthermore, the nine ministers who have left office all went to work in this sector. Only one of the heads of the Ministry of Fisheries has held a university degree, but nine out of ten have been connected with the fisheries either by vocation or through an interest group, although only two of the nine returned to jobs related to fisheries. Six out of twelve heads of the Ministry of Agriculture have held a university degree, but only five of them were in agriculture. Eleven had vocational or interest-group affiliation with the sector, and seven out of eleven went back to jobs in agriculture. Eleven of thirteen heads of the Ministry of Industry have held a university degree, seven of them in law. Seven have been affiliated with the sector through jobs or interest groups, and four out of eleven have gone back to the same sector. The lack of specialization is most clearly seen in the Ministry of Defense. No profession dominates, and of eleven ministers only three were affiliated with the sector and no one went back to jobs in that sector.

For some ministries patterns are hard to discern because there have been few ministers, and it is difficult to establish precise criteria for counting vocations and interest group affiliations as being within a sector. The numbers should therefore be considered as illustrative of a more general pattern. It is likely that ministers will have specialized knowledge and affiliations, but there is also great variation across ministries.

The Cabinet is no longer a college of bureaucrats, firmly anchored in their ministries through a lifelong career. Still, ministers are not alien to the values and points of view dominating the ministries they lead. Through education and experience from agencies and interest groups close to the ministries, many of them are already indoctrinated before they sit down for the first time in the minister's chair. Their links to powerful outside groups are reinforced through frequent contacts.

Organized interests and agencies in their own sector are (together with the civil servants in their own ministry) among the partners ministers say it is most important to cultivate.[49] There are of course variations. Meetings with organized interests take more time for a minister of agriculture or a minister of fisheries than for a Prime Minister or a minister of finance. But in general ministers agree with a committee on the organization of the central administrative apparatus: Today government can in many cases reach its clientele only through interest groups.[50]

---

[49] This section is based primarily on interviews with ministers in the Bratteli Cabinet (1975) and upon data about their use of time.

[50] "Innstilling om Den sentrale forvaltnings organisasjon," Otta, 1970, p. 20.

The same specialization is seen in the contacts with the Storting. All the ministers in the Bratteli Cabinet (1975) report daily or weekly contacts with "their" committee in the Storting but interact less frequently with the others. In fact, they never interact at all with most committees.

To summarize, ministers are heads of administrative units with a great potential to mold and discipline their civil servants. The administrative division of labor is reinforced through the civil servants' specialized external contacts. The ministers' ability to counteract administrative subcultures is not severely hampered by the shortness of their tenure. Ministers are not strangers to their ministries, and they do not stay long enough to be indoctrinated into the particular culture of the ministry. More likely they already possess the same values and viewpoints, which are reinforced through specialized contacts. The chances for a specialist orientation, with ministers identifying more with their roles as ministers than with their roles as Cabinet members, have increased because ministers are less often recruited from political generalist positions such as member of the Storting and mayor.

Growing functional differentiation and increased workloads have affected recruitment patterns and made it more difficult for ministers to assume leadership and to provide coordination across administrative sectors and levels. One remedy suggested has been to provide the minister with more politically appointed helpers. Another has been to fight fire with fire by introducing new types of civil servants.

Ambivalence toward Political Friends. When the Gerhardsen Cabinet took office in 1945 the question of strengthening the political leadership of the ministries was immediately raised. The task of rebuilding the country was overwhelming, and the number of civil servants had increased (table 6–2). In 1947 the first seven ministries added the position of under secretary of state. Today there are one or two in each ministry. This expansion has not been met with general enthusiasm. Some higher civil servants have opposed the idea that the highest tenured civil servant, the secretary general, should be subordinated to the under secretary of state. Increasing the number of political appointees is seen as confusing the lines of authority and responsibility, reducing the continuity in the work of the ministry, and making the positions of higher civil servants less interesting.[51]

---

[51] Karl Evang, "Får vi snart orden på statssekretaerene . . .?" *Aftenposten* (evening edition), October 21, 1974; continued October 22; "En 'sideregjering' uten knostitusjonelt ansvar," and October 23; "Embetsstandenes stilling truet,"

Many of the arguments of the higher civil servants have been accepted by the nonsocialist parties in opposition. In 1947 they voted against introducing the position of under secretary of state, basing their stand on a bureaucratic interpretation of the ministries formulated by the Ministry of Justice. According to this view, the role of the Cabinet is to take care of the common interests of the people, not to achieve party political goals.[52] Thirty years later nonsocialists, again in opposition, argued that an independent civil service could counteract a too powerful political leadership.[53] But in the meantime two nonsocialist Cabinets had increased the number of political appointees.

The arguments of the higher civil servants and the opposition may be interpreted as a struggle for power. The greater the number of political appointees in government, the easier for the political echelons to control the nonpolitical ones. This was the idea behind the Gerhardsen initiative. And the chairman of the Committee on Administration in the Storting thirty years later repeated that more politically appointed positions would strengthen political leadership against bureaucratic power.[54] But many do not accept this argument.

A Cabinet committee chaired by the minister of justice in 1961 had several reservations. To some degree the chairman accepted that the under secretary was a foreign element in the ministries, while the committee argued that the role had become too administrative and not political enough. Nearly half the under secretaries had an administrative background in the ministry to which they were appointed.[55]

More generally, ministers are somewhat ambivalent about inviting more political friends to the ministries.[56] Of the members of

---

Christian Brinch in *Aftenposten*, August 2, 1975. "Innstilling om reglementer og instrukser for departementene," Oslo, 1966; NOU 1974:18, *Statssekretaerodningen;* and Archives in the Ministry of Justice.

[52] Inst. S. nr. 147, 1947, *Innstilling fra den forsterkede utenriks-og konstitusjonskomité om opprettelse av statssekretaerstillinger i departementene.*

[53] Stortingsforhandlinger 1976-77, *Statssekretaerordningen m.m. og avskjed av embetsmenn,* pp. 3179-94.

[54] King, "Executives," pp. 196-97; and Stortingsforhandlinger 1976-77, NOU 1974:18 *Statssekretaerordningen,* pp. 3179-94.

[55] Tilråding fra utvalget til å drøfte statssekretaerordningen," 1961. In addition, a leading member of the Labor party and the president of the Storting were members of a committee that defined the role of the under secretary in a fairly restricted way. The committee wanted further to constrain the activities of the political secretary so that he should be merely assistant to the minister, not a second under secretary (NOU 1974:18, *Statssekretaerordningen*).

[56] This description is based on interviews with, and questionnaires to, the Bratteli government (1975). The same trend is found in NOU 1974:18, *Statsse-*

the Bratteli Cabinet (1975), only one-third thought that the political leadership needed to be strengthened, while 63 percent of the under secretaries and 92 percent of the political secretaries held this opinion. Actually the number of ministers who think that more political appointees will increase leadership problems match the number who think that problems will be reduced (table 6–8). Those who want to increase the number of political appointees do not want dramatic changes in the organization of the political leadership of the ministries.[57]

A main argument among ministers against inviting in more politically appointed helpers is that the lines of authority become more ambiguous. Civil servants, the Storting, and the public may be confused about who are the responsible leaders. Coordination among the leaders may be difficult. Furthermore, civil servants may not as willingly volunteer their services if the most interesting decisions are given only to the political leaders. Finally, ministers know that they are political symbols. Representatives of communities and interest organizations want to meet the minister. If they do not achieve substantive results, at least they have taken the issue to the top. Such symbolic functions cannot be taken care of by others.

Variations in attitudes reflect variations in the ways under secretaries and political secretaries function. Some under secretaries work as the minister's equal in special fields. Others are clearly subordinated to the minister. Some political secretaries function like under secretaries. Others primarily help the minister organize his agenda and correspondence.

Variations in attitudes may also reflect ministers' unequal control of the selection of under secretaries and political secretaries. Ministers in the Bratteli Cabinet (1975) got nine under secretaries and five political secretaries they themselves asked for. They got respectively eight and five assistants they did not know. Some were informed that they would get a specific person. Others were allowed to pick

---

kretaerordningen, pp. 59–64, where ministers and under secretaries from various governments comment on their experiences with, or as, under secretaries. Among the Prime Ministers interviewed by the author, one stated that he was happy each time a minister did not want an under secretary. Another Prime Minister argued that there should never be more than one under secretary in a ministry, and that political secretaries should be appointed only if there were a definite need and the right person could be found.

[57] One minister, however, claimed that the political organization around the minister is quite amateurish. And a former minister of finance has argued that the leadership in the major ministries is very weakly developed (Jon Norbom, "Den økonomisk-politiske beslutningsprosess," in *Økonomi og politikk, skrift til Ole Myrvolls 60 års dag* [Oslo: Aschehoug, 1971], p. 36).

TABLE 6–8

ATTITUDE OF MINISTERS, UNDER SECRETARIES OF STATE, AND
POLITICAL SECRETARIES TOWARD STRENGTHENING THE
POLITICAL LEADERSHIP OF THE MINISTRIES
(percentage)

Respondent	Number	Political Leadership Should Be Strengthened	More Politically Appointed People Will		Reorganiza- tion Will Help Solve Problems[a]
			Help Solve Present Problems	Increase Problems	
Ministers	15	33	27	27	53
Under secretaries of state	19	63	42	21	37
Personal or political secretaries	12	92	67	8	50

NOTE: Data are based on respondents' replies to this survey question: The wish to strengthen the political leadership of the ministries has been a central question for a long time. To what degree do you think there will be a need for a further strengthening in the future?

[a] Includes splitting up ministries, decentralizing certain decisions, changing salaries or selection procedures to recruit better people, defining tasks and rules better, and allowing the under secretaries of state to meet in the Cabinet.

from a list composed by the Prime Minister's office and the party office.

The selection process is not very different from the one used to recruit ministers. The Prime Minister and the top leaders in the party and in LO are important actors, and the party organization in different regions is activated. The higher the minister's position in the party or in LO, the more likely that he or she will be allowed to pick his or her helpers. But certain criteria have to be met. Regions should be represented; so should women, vocational and educational groups, and different factions of the party.

A minister does not get helpers he or she is strongly against, but political leaders have to be able to cooperate, and ministers may accept secretaries with whom they disagree on important issues. With few exceptions, however, disagreement is not a problem. The recruiting process does indicate that if the number of political appointees is increased, more heterogeneity may be introduced and problems of coordination may arise. In such situations it may be easier to achieve leadership through tenured civil servants than through political friends. At least, a few more political friends may not be worth the price of antagonizing higher civil servants.

Do under secretaries and political secretaries relieve ministers of some of their political overload? In intrasectoral work, yes; in intersectoral coordination, the political secretaries normally play a modest role. But under secretaries play a significant role in inter-departmental work. They have weekly meetings, and frequently important issues are turned over to committees of under secretaries. For example, over a two-year period a committee of nine under secre-taries, headed by the under secretary of the Ministry of Finance, had thirty-five meetings before presenting a proposal to the Cabinet for a four-year program. Another example is that decisions on commis-sions to be appointed by the Cabinet have to go through a committee of under secretaries.[58]

There are no studies of the decision-making process of these committees, but in general there is no reason to believe that they operate very differently from committees of ministers. Through social background and patterns of communication, under secretaries and political secretaries are as firmly linked to groups and agencies in their own sector as are ministers. Thus, they are equally likely to identify with the institutions and tasks for which they are responsible. Is there, then, reason to believe that coordination problems between sec-tors and levels are relieved by the other type of ministerial helpers introduced since World War II—the planners?

Fighting Fire with Fire. As in most Western European countries, post-war planning in Norway meant economic planning and was partly initiated by the Organization for Economic Cooperation and Develop-ment (OECD). The first fifteen years after the war was the great period for economists and economic theory. In Norway economic planning was located inside the ministries. "The Labor Party wanted planning, but did not know how"; the economists offered a solution.[59]

---

[58] Nordli, "Regjeringens"; and NOU 1973:52, *Administrative og økonomiske konsekvenser av lover m.v.*, p. 26.

[59] Trond Bergh, "Some Preliminary Notes on Quantitative Economic Planning and the Use of Economists in Government," Oslo, 1977 (mimeo); and Bergh and Pharo, *Vekst og velstand*, p. 93. Partly because of the absence of a traditional aristocracy, civil servants have historically been an important political and cultural elite. Their training has been in law; their code of conduct has been one of centralism, loyalty, professional competence, and neutrality in party politics, with the judge as an important role model (Debes, *Statsadministrasjonen*; K. D. Jacobsen, "Politikk og administrasjon," magister-dissertation, Institutt for statsvitenskap, University of Oslo, 1955; K. D. Jacobsen, "Lojalitet, nøytralitet og faglig uavhengighet i sentraladministrasjonen," *Tidsskrift for samfunns-forskning*, vol. 1 [1960], pp. 231-48; and Stavang, *Parlamentarisme*).

The result was a new philosophy of governance, a new administrative infrastructure with planning divisions, national budgets and long-term budgets, and many positions for economists. Planning was supposed to move the minister from a passive role as the final link in a long chain of bureaucratic decision makers, and to supplement the legalistic orientation of the Rechtsstaat with a goal and future-oriented policy making.

The heyday for economic theory and economists meant a central role for the Ministry of Finance. But during the late 1960s and the 1970s aspirations of hierarchical macroeconomic planning and governance based on financial criteria have become more problematic. Economic growth is no longer a generally accepted supergoal, and it is difficult to achieve. The Cabinet's program for 1978–1981 is more a political program than a traditional economic program.

Today there are planning units in all ministries and "planning" stands for many different things. For some it signifies the future use of financial resources. For others the management of natural resources is more important, or the concern with social welfare criteria, the effects on local government, foreign relations, and so on. The coordination of various planning centers has itself become an issue.

In many ways planners are different from the traditional rule-oriented civil servants. They are younger than other civil servants in the ministries and few are trained in law. Economics is the most common training, but several other professions are represented. Planners are more active in political parties, less constrained by rules, and seldom find similarities between their own role and that of the judge, like civil servants trained in law do. Planners perceive more conflict in their work than in other fields, especially conflicts between ministries, and they are change-oriented. At the same time, planners tend to leave the ministry more often than their colleagues with other functions.[60] Strong pressures, however, make planners conform with established subcultures. This conclusion, based on questionnaire data, is consistent with the picture outlined by a veteran planner:

> Planning to a great extent must deal with the relationship of one's own system to the environment. But we have also learned that in doing this, planners must never form alliances with parts of the meta-system in order to fight their own system . . . .
> I learned quite a lot about the conditions under which a new agency in charge of functions rather threatening to the rest of an organization can be subject to organizational im-

---

[60] Laegreid and Olsen, *Byråkrati*, pp. 116-18, 309, 320.

munity, isolating the agency and making it absolutely harmless. I also learned some of the rules of the game that will permit such units not only to survive, but to interact constructively with other parts of the organization.[61]

One interpretation is that (at least in the short run) adding political friends or friendly planners will not produce miracles or change an otherwise segmented structure. What has been described as governance by ministers conceals stable, functional coalitions of organized public and private interests. Given this structure, the resources gathered around the prime minister, and the types of persons filling the major roles, how likely is the Cabinet to take leadership?

The Cabinet: United Team or Sprawling Fence Posts? In a small country such as Norway, half a hundred political appointees may be a significant political force, *if* they can pull together, and *if* they are able to concentrate on important issues instead of being immersed in details. The two conditions seem more difficult to fulfill in coalition Cabinets, with their demands for interparty management, than in one-party Cabinets.

When Borten turned the keys to the Prime Minister's office over to Bratteli, he stated that the leader of the Labor party was lucky in being backed by a united party. To lead a coalition had been a difficult task, similar to carrying sprawling fence posts. Others have emphasized the long and dreary discussions in the Cabinet conferences that too often focused on mere details.[62]

The sprawling fence posts situation is usually explained by the fact that the coalition parties jealously protect their autonomy and by the lack of leadership shown by the Prime Minister. However, the difference between one-party and coalition Cabinets may be one of degree rather than of essence. Parties large enough to get a majority are themselves coalitions. As we have seen, there certainly are other structural bases for cleavages than political parties; consensus cannot be assumed by any Cabinet. Prime Minister Nordli points out that there often are strained situations in any Cabinet;[63] others say there are "free and lively discussions."

A major task of the Cabinet is to organize decision-making procedures in order to find politically acceptable solutions that "all in all

[61] Kjell Eide, "A Planner Looks Back," Oslo, 1978, manuscript, p. 18.

[62] Brunvand, *Samspill*, pp. 73, 89; Lyng, *Borgfred*, pp. 92-93, 106, 107; Solstad, "Norwegian Coalition"; Sørebø, *Slik sprakk koalisjonen*, p. 61; and Vassbotn, *Lekkasje*.

[63] Nordli, "Regjeringens."

can get the most support and that cause the least disappointment and feeling of defeat."[64] The Cabinet is an arena where political problems are discovered, clarified, and sometimes solved. Ministers test proposals and identify the important cleavages and the intensity of internal and external conflicts. Ministers get advice or moral support. What kind of resources does the Cabinet have to match the tasks of finding politically acceptable solutions in a segmented system?

The Cabinet as a college has few and weak constitutional powers and no planning capacity or administrative infrastructure of its own. The size of the Cabinet has increased, but the idea of establishing an inner Cabinet has received little attention or support. Dividing the Cabinet into an A and a B team "is not suitable for Norway."[65] There are few, though some important, Cabinet committees, but they have become less rather than more crucial over the last two decades.[66]

The procedures of the Cabinet have been formalized since Gerhardsen inherited a seniority system. There was then no organized preparation of Cabinet meetings, and the minister with the longest tenure would present his or her issues first. The youngest minister sometimes had to leave without a chance to present even the most urgent and important issues. The system also made it difficult to find time for general political talks.[67]

Today a minister lists with the Prime Minister's office, at least one day before a Cabinet meeting, the issues he or she wants on the agenda, and a two-page note is circulated to the other ministers. The Prime Minister's office prepares the agenda and provides minutes of the meetings. The streamlining of Cabinet procedures has been most significant in budgetary decisions. Priority debates before the process and the use of quotas for ministries have considerably reduced the number of budget conferences and the time spent. Ministers view these changes as improvements. Decision making is less time consuming, and they feel better informed because a two-page note is read whereas voluminous reports are not. There is less of a chance of a minister's being surprised that a decision is made while he or she is away or of being unprepared when an issue is presented in the Cabinet.

---

[64] Ibid., p. 12.

[65] Bloch, *Kongens råd*, p. 134; Nordli, "Regjeringens," p. 12; Solumsmoen, "Regjeringens arbeidsform"; and Torgersen, "Flere departementer?"

[66] Bloch, *Kongens råd*, pp. 112-24; "Innstilling om Den sentrale forvaltnings organisasjon." Otta, 1970, p. 36.

[67] Gerhardsen, interview; Einar Gerhardsen, *Mennesker og politikk* (Oslo: Tiden, 1978), p. 84; interviews with the Bratteli government (1975); Dag Berggrav, "Regjeringen i arbeid" (Oslo: Unpublished lecture, 1978); and Bloch, *Kongens råd*.

Still, the formal setting of Cabinet meetings is less consequential than informal roles, rules, and communication patterns. A Cabinet has a culture, a set of norms and viewpoints that reflect problems of capacity, understanding, and authority and that also reflect the need to balance an inevitable division of labor with the necessity to coordinate and operate as a team. There is an agenda problem: Which of hundreds of thousands of decisions made in the name of the government should a Cabinet attend to? And there is a problem of procedure: If all ministers are allocated equal speaking time, the average time per minister would be approximately one minute per decision in an average Cabinet meeting.

A ground rule is to keep decisions out of the Cabinet. If that is impossible, one or more possible solutions should be found before the issue is presented at a Cabinet meeting. Ministers are supposed to clear a decision by briefing affected parties and eventually finding a compromise.[68]

If consulting and clearing processes are ignored or a compromise is not achieved, so that dissenting views must be aired in the Cabinet, conflicts may be resolved during the meeting. More likely, however, some other course of action is followed. The responsible minister may be asked to consider the points of view presented by the opponents and to return with a new solution. The ministers in conflict may be assigned to make a new attempt to find an acceptable compromise. A problem may be sent to an interdepartmental committee of under secretaries or civil servants, or to a Cabinet committee. More likely there will be an informal group including the minister concerned, the parties in discord, and one or two leading Cabinet members. Often they will include the Prime Minister, the minister of finance, or Cabinet members with a high position in the party. In some cases it may be obvious that an acceptable solution cannot be found, and the decision is postponed. As one minister argued, the Cabinet, like other decision-making units, has its boiling point. It senses when it is impossible to reach an agreement.

In case of conflict, the Prime Minister is expected to take initiatives and to act as arbitrator. But he is also expected to be unbiased,

---

[68] Again, the description is based primarily on interviews with the Bratteli Cabinet (1975), but it is generally consistent with the points of view presented by others (Berggrav, "Regjeringen"; Bloch, *Kongens råd*, pp. 25-26, 85, 88-89; "Innstilling om Den sentrale forvaltnings organisasjon," Otta, 1970, p. 45; Lars Korvald, "Regjeringens virkemåte," unpublished lecture, University of Bergen, 1978; Larssen, *Revolusjonen*, p. 141; John Lyng, *Vaktskifte* [Oslo: Cappelen, 1973]; Lyng, *Borgfred*; and Johan Nygaardsvold, *Kong Haakon 7 i samarbeid og samvaer med Regjeringen* [Oslo: Den norske forleggerforening, 1947], p. 227).

except in budgetary matters, where the Prime Minister sides with the minister of finance. Ministers may have a significant impact on a decision outside their own sphere of interest, if intervention occurs only once. If it happens often, intervention is highly disliked. Ministers do not approve of others meddling in their business. A minister's position is strengthened, however, if it is supported by the party program or a decision at the national conference of the party.

For several reasons intervention in decisions not affecting one's own ministry is infrequent. Time is scarce; so is goodwill, and ministers do not want to antagonize colleagues whose help they may need soon. Furthermore, few ministers have the surplus energy to familiarize themselves with issues outside their own field so that they can have a reasoned opinion. They may write letters while the minister concerned, others directly affected, and a few generalists debate. Ministers realize that they become specialists, somewhat removed from general politics.[69]

The result is an informal leadership group, based partly on formal position in the Cabinet and partly on position in the party hierarchy. Communications between Cabinet meetings, often by telephone, primarily reflect functional interdependencies. When asked with whom of their colleagues they most often had contact, a majority of the ministers in the Bratteli Cabinet (1975) answered the Prime Minister, the minister of finance, and the minister of local government and labor. The ministers of commerce and shipping, of fisheries, and of defense were mentioned most seldom. But the communications network is primarily characterized by clusters of contact among three or four ministers, the functional equivalent to nonexistent formal Cabinet committees.

The Constitution requests that the Cabinet, or rather the Council of State, be concerned with important matters. To the Cabinet, importance is defined politically. The sampling of issues is only partly a function of their substantive properties. Small issues sometimes have significant political effects. And if they threaten the unity of the coalition, cause problems in the news media, or are important for important people, they are attended to by the Cabinet, whatever their substantive properties.[70]

---

[69] Tor Halvorsen, *Arbeiderbladet* (Oslo), July 30, 1979; Jens Haugland, *Aftenposten*, September 11, 1979; interviews, Bratteli Cabinet.

[70] A former minister of finance has complained about the unnecessary amount of detail in discussions in both the Cabinet and the Storting. Although no issue is so small that the minister of finance should not know about it, other ministers sometimes demand that he decide on such issues as the allocation of office space (Norbom, "Økonomisk-politiske beslutningsprosess," p. 37).

Ministers think the Cabinet is an important policy-making unit, and without doubt some crucial decisions are made there. More often, the Cabinet approves decisions made somewhere else, or the college of ministers gives direction to or constrains decisions to be made by other units. The Cabinet is a clearinghouse for information about what is politically possible; that is, what is preferred and what is acceptable in the ministries, parties, Storting, interest groups, and other countries, and among local and regional authorities, mass media, and the people in general.

At the same time it is not difficult to discern limitations on the coordinating capacity of the Cabinet. Lack of constitutional powers, of its own administrative resources, and of time and energy clearly reduces the Cabinet's ability to take hierarchical leadership and to counteract the tendencies toward segmentation. It now remains to be seen whether the picture of a specialized and segmented structure is supported when we move from analyzing agencies, roles, rules, and actors to studying executive processes.

The Executive in Action

Executives have long working days; they have gone from part time to full time to overtime. But what do they do when they govern? How do executive institutions work in practice; how are decisions made; and how great is executive authority and power? There is remarkably little academic literature on these subjects, in Norway as in most countries.[71] Here attention is focused on four themes: How does a Cabinet work in times of crisis? What is the importance and what are the limits of governing on the basis of a party platform? How do the most central actors themselves perceive the distribution of influence in public policy making? And what are the major forms of coordination used in executive decision making in Norway?

Cabinet Crises and the Importance of Routines. The Bratteli Cabinet gave permission for a detailed time study of the forty-five ministers, under secretaries of state, and political secretaries during the week of December 9–16, 1974. The political appointees agreed to give a detailed account of who they met, who took the initiative, what the purpose was, and what the results were. The office secretaries also registered incoming telephones and letters. At the end of the week, a questionnaire was administered to all the political appointees. They were also interviewed for one and a half to two and a half hours.

---

[71] King, "Executives," p. 113.

About one-third of the participants made available their calendars for the whole year (1974). Somewhat later another study was undertaken, in which the office secretaries registered those who tried to get in touch with the political appointees without an appointment.

When permission for the study was granted, no one knew that the week would be a special one, and that the Cabinet would have to face a major crisis in the Storting. The Bratteli Cabinet wanted to buy 25 percent of Canadian stock in an aluminum company, in order to achieve a 75 percent majority. Approximately two weeks before the debate it became clear that there was no majority for this proposal in the Storting. The Labor party had no stable support from any other party. Together with sixteen left-wing socialists the Labor party had 78 out of 155 votes. But the leftist socialists would not vote for the proposal. They wanted to buy all foreign stock in the aluminum industry within a few years. The nonsocialists found the transaction too costly and the terms not good enough for Norwegian interests.

When the debate started at 10 A.M. Friday, December 13, Bratteli made it clear that the Cabinet would resign if a majority voted against the proposal. When the Storting took a break at 3 P.M. a crisis seemed unavoidable. Speakers from all the major parties said they did not want a crisis, but a majority would not vote for the Cabinet's proposal.

When the meeting started at 6 P.M. the Center party—to the surprise of Bratteli, as well as of other participants and observers—declared that they would provide subsidiary support to the Cabinet's proposal if their own proposal were defeated. A fundamentally new situation had come into existence.[72] When a vote was taken at 9:45 P.M., a majority of 86 to 69 voted for the Cabinet's proposal.

The crisis was averted through a unilateral decision in the Center party, not through negotiations. In the Storting several speakers regretted that the opportunity for consultation had not been used.[73] The

---

[72] Stortingsforhandlinger 1974-1975, *Kjøp av aksjer i A/S Ardal og Sunndal Verk*, p. 2135.

[73] Especially former Prime Minister Korvald (Stortingsforhandlinger 1974-1975, *Kjøp av aksjer*, pp. 2115-116). One week before the debate took place the Prime Minister had informed the faction leaders of the Center party and the Christian People's party about the decision to resign (Stortingsforhandlinger, *Kjøp av aksjer*, p. 2152). The leader of the Labor party faction in the Committee on Industry had talked with two of the leaders of the leftist socialists, but one of them regretted that the Prime Minister had not made contact (Stortingsforhandlinger 1974-1975, *Kjøp av aksjer*, pp. 2143, 2152). Although there had been consultations between the leftist socialists and parts of the Labor party faction, the pattern of consultation has to be seen in the light of their competition for the votes of the workers, as well as the competition between factions within each party. The incident is described by one of the participants. Finn Gustavsen, *Kortene på bordet* (Oslo : Gyldendal).

Prime Minister said that the decision had been comprehensive, important, and difficult for the Cabinet, but not for a moment had it occurred to him that it could produce a crisis.[74]

The feeling of a very special week was spread by the mass media. A close look at the behavior of ministers, under secretaries, and political secretaries gives a somewhat different picture, illustrating the importance of the political division of labor and of routines even in times of crisis.

For the Prime Minister and for the minister of industry the week was unusual because so much time was devoted to a single decision. The procedures and networks used, however, were standard. The Prime Minister and the minister of industry were in contact with each other and with the party faction in the Storting, with the party faction in the Committee on Industry, and with the chairmen of the party faction in the Storting and of the responsible committee. Furthermore, the issue was discussed in the party directorate. The under secretaries at the Prime Minister's office took an active part in the process. There were frequent contacts with the LO unions affected. The potential crisis was discussed in two Cabinet meetings.

The activity within these networks was hectic. The Prime Minister took political leadership, accompanied by the minister of industry. Both also had other things to do. The minister of industry at 6:50 A.M. the day before the debate had to comment on the radio on plans for developing new power plants. The Prime Minister took part in a TV program on torture. Most of their time, however, was focused on the crisis.

The situation was quite different for the other ministers, the under secretaries, and the political secretaries. Most of their time was organized around commitments in their own sectors. Ministers took part in Cabinet conferences where the crisis was discussed, but the minister of finance was the only Cabinet member who joined the Prime Minister and the minister of industry in the debate in the Storting, where he talked about his specialty, the tax aspects of the deal. Other ministers and political appointees tried to attend the informal discussions in the Storting that week, but mostly they did not have the time.

Ministers were away in London, Brussels, Frankfurt, and Stockholm. The minister of fisheries spent most of the week with his Russian counterpart traveling in the western part of Norway. The minister of local government and labor was troubled by the threat of a strike. And the minister of agriculture used more time on issues

---

[74] Stortingsforhandlinger 1974-1975, *Kjøp av aksjer*, p. 2118.

such as the use of horsewhips at race tracks, the castrating of horses, sheep disease, the use of barbed wire, and policies on the future provision of food, than upon the crisis. In general, ministers and their political helpers were concerned, but their behavior was mostly directed by routine. For some, the crisis also receded into the background because of family events.

Of the forty-five political appointees, 3 percent described the week as quite normal, 27 percent as somewhat normal, 16 percent said both normal and abnormal, 35 percent said somewhat special, and 19 percent held the opinion that the week had been very special. About two-thirds of those who found the week abnormal mentioned the crisis. For some respondents private reasons—such as the birth of a child, the return of a spouse, or a car accident—were more important than the crisis. Others judged the week special because they had been away. More than half of those who mentioned the crisis also gave other reasons. Despite the fact that calendars were filled with appointments, only half a dozen meetings were canceled or postponed. These were all intraministerial meetings or meetings with political appointees in other ministries. In one case a meeting with a Danish under secretary of state was postponed, but because of problems in Denmark. The possibility that the Cabinet would resign caused only four deviations from the planned schedules, which seems a remarkably small number, even for a more normal period than the week studied.

The use of time is highly contextual. Substantial variation in attention stems from other demands on the participants' time rather than from the decision in focus.[75] Ministers are busy people. They meet with busy people, and routines provide viable solutions to a relatively complicated problem of coordinating time. This simple mechanism works because most of the duties and responsibilities of the ministers are sector-oriented, and ministers are solidly anchored in their sectors. The use of time in times of crisis is consistent with the view of a specialized and segmented structure. An alternative interpretation is that the ministers execute specialized programs in the party platform. The specialization may be part of a hierarchical structure, but the coordination takes place in party organs, not in the Cabinet.

Limits of Governing through Party Platforms. Norwegian parties have few full-time positions at the national level,[76] and the influence

---

[75] March and Olsen, *Ambiguity.*

[76] The Labor party reports nine full-time employees, two of them elected, at the national level. In addition, there are nine in the youth organization, one in

of the party apparatus on the daily work of the Cabinet tends to be limited. It is the party faction in the Storting that arrives at a decision on unexpected issues.[77] A party's major impact is through its platform, and a great deal of energy is spent building one.

The introduction of published political score cards has made platforms more realistic, but parties share a dilemma with legislatures. They may specify general principles and goals, but intentions are often distorted during the implementation. Or they may specify operational goals, rules, programs, and deadlines, only to discover that the conditions and assumptions under which the platform was written have changed. The increasing complexity of modern welfare states makes it increasingly difficult to write a set of substantive rules that covers future conditions. Leadership assumes a fine balance between consistency over time, on the one hand, and, on the other, the ability to correct the course to allow for variations in the social, political, economic, or natural environment.

Students of politics have been most interested in the fact that legislatures and parties are often unable to specify operational substantive goals or rules; they specify only the framework for future decision making, and civil servants and organized interests fill in these frameworks. Members of the Bratteli government faced many difficulties because the party program was too specific.

During the Borten period the Labor party was out of power for the first time in thirty years, with the exception of the four-week Lyng intermezzo. This caused hectic activity within the party. New programs were developed, in many cases with specified deadlines. Several future ministers, under secretaries, and political secretaries took part in the process. Later they had to tackle some problems that illustrate the limitations of governing through a well-specified party program. One minister commented:

> We [sometimes] run like a steam roller, independent of what is taking place around us. We implement policies that people have never been interested in and policies they have lost interest in. We are criticized for things we expected would give political credit. At the same time we are unable to react when new opportunities and problems come along because there is no surplus energy.

the women's secretariat, and forty full-time positions in the party's educational organization. The other parties have fewer employees, except the Conservatives who report 125 full-time positions, regional offices included, plus twelve positions in the youth, women's, and educational organizations (Jorolv Moren et al., *Norske organisasjoner* [Oslo: Tanum, 1976]).

[77] Gerhardsen, *Mennesker og politikk*, p. 10.

Others used different words, but many agreed that the platform had been too detailed. It had been too specific about what should be done, how it should be done, and when it should be done. The result was a lack of flexibility. "The party program should provide the Cabinet with working material and be a compass. Now it has become a straightjacket," another minister complained. "There is never adequate research behind each part of the platform. New aspects are discovered as the ministry starts working on an issue, but there is little we can do. We are afraid of not keeping our promises and of losing our trustworthiness."

Basically there was agreement that the party could never go back to winning an election on one single issue or one single slogan. But it was also agreed that in the future the program has to be less specific, taking the form of a manifesto and formulating principles without specifying the solution of a problem.

My interpretation of these experiences is that a party may take a stand on sample issues and have a crucial impact on the Cabinet's handling of these issues. But a party cannot specify substantive, conditional rules in enough fields to make the Cabinet an executive committee of the party. Specifically, that will not be possible when a Cabinet is supported by a minority party, which has to discover the politically possible through interaction with many other organized interests. The need to take other organized interests into consideration is clearly reflected in the perceptions of influence held by major participants in governmental processes.

The Limits of Hierarchy. A majority of the Norwegian people believe that the members of the Cabinet and the Storting are the most powerful participants in public policy-making processes.[78] Those who participate directly in government perceive politically elected and appointed leaders as having a less heroic role.

Rokkan argued that votes count in the choice of who will govern, but that other factors decide the actual policies pursued by the authorities.[79] He maintained that the bargaining and consultation processes between government and organized labor, business, farm, and fishery interests have come to affect the lives of the rank and file more than the formal elections. The Cabinet, he wrote, has increasingly had to take on the role of mediator between conflicting interests.

---

[78] *Aftenposten*, March 3, 1979.

[79] Stein Rokkan, "Norway: Numerical Democracy and Corporate Pluralism," in Robert A. Dahl, ed., *Political Oppositions in Western Democracies* (New Haven: Yale University Press, 1966), pp. 106-7.

I agree with Rokkan in many respects. But my interpretation suggests that civil servants are important participants, and that most of the bargaining and consultation between government and organized interests takes place at the ministerial, not the Cabinet, level. There are many bargaining tables and many policy-making arenas.

Civil servants in the ministries differentiate among three kinds of influence: taking initiatives in their own field, making formal choices, and affecting interpretations of how programs and policies are working in practice. In all three respects their own ministry is perceived as important by a majority of the respondents (table 6–9). The constitutional powers of the Storting and the Cabinet are viewed as influential in the formal choice process, but less significant in the feedback phase, and few civil servants think the constitutional powers are important when it comes to taking initiatives. In contrast to the significance attributed to the constitutional powers, economic (producer) interests are thought to be important in all three phases, whereas the mass media are viewed as essentially reactive, interpreting new programs but not taking many initiatives.

This response pattern supports the notion of a specialized system more than the idea of a hierarchical system based on a parliamentary chain of command and responsibility. That specialization is most developed in the initiative phases, an important observation because most participants believe it is necessary to get into policy-making processes at an early stage in order to affect the end result.[80]

The perceptions of the civil servants by and large coincide with those of another key group of participants, elected leaders and administrators in the economic organizations. They, too, view civil servants as important participants, and they view the ministries as highly influential in policy-making processes. What then are the perceptions of ministers, under secretaries, and political secretaries?

The ministers and their politically appointed helpers do not feel impotent, but they are aware of the limits of their powers. Time and energy is the constraint mentioned most often. Ministers know that they are responsible for thousands of decisions which they do not take part in or hear about. They know the limitations on their capabilities for taking initiatives. Ministers even perceive their roles as somewhat more reactive than under secretaries and political secretaries perceive

[80] In general there is a strong tendency to trust preparatory agencies or committees. If a consensus is achieved at the preparatory stage, the Storting or Cabinet is highly unlikely to intervene. Both will look for signals from one administrative agency before they intervene in the proposals from another agency. Administrative failures to have proposals accepted by the constitutional powers is highly dependent on the lack of success in convincing civil servants in other ministries (Laegreid and Olsen, *Byråkrati*, pp. 234-35).

TABLE 6–9

PERCEPTIONS OF CIVIL SERVANTS OF THE IMPORTANCE OF AGENCIES AND GROUPS IN INITIATIVE, CHOICE, AND FEEDBACK PROCESSES IN THE RESPONDENTS' OWN FIELD

Agency or Group	Percentage of Respondents Ranking Each Authority or Group as Very or Somewhat Important		
	Initiative	Choice	Feedback
Own ministry	69	96	69
Own national administrative agencies outside ministry	18	48	40
Own regional or local agencies	16	46	49
Other ministries and their subordinated agencies	17	59	38
Governmental boards and committees	15	46	27
Court system	1	0	11
Storting	12	68	34
Cabinet	16	75	30
Opposition parties	1	16	10
Regional and local authorities	7	33	28
Economic (producer) interests	13	49	35
Other interest organizations	4	16	13
Ad hoc actions and movements	1	3	6
Mass media	3	18	33
Research and educational institutions	7	24	28
Firms, companies	5	13	14
Single persons representing themselves or their families	5	8	9
International governmental organizations	9	15	16
Other countries	5	11	11
Total number of responses	768	764	757

NOTE: The questions asked for each process were:

Initiative: "When it comes to taking initiatives to new programs/policies in your workfield, how often are initiatives coming from each of the following authorities and groups?"

Choice: "Could you in general say how important the following authorities and groups are when important choices are made in your field? More specifically, will you indicate how important each of the following authorities/groups are?"

Feedback: "How do you keep yourself informed about the practical results of various programs/policies, that is, how important are each of the following authorities and groups when it comes to such information?"

For each question the respondents had five alternatives, ranging from very often or very important to very seldom or very unimportant.

theirs. Their descriptions of an ordinary working day are similar to those given by other organizational leaders. They have to respond to a steady stream of initiatives from others, to deadlines, and to the pressure of the moment. They act on options mostly framed by others.[81]

Ministers know that they need the cooperation of the civil servants, and that they need to release the energy potential of their administrative apparatus. The problem is not that civil servants obstruct ministerial effort but that they do not volunteer their initiatives and services. Ministers know that life becomes complicated when civil servants do not respond to the same signal given in different situations but demand specific orders in each case. At the same time, ministers know that civil servants need ministers who will sponsor their projects. If the minister is not willing to fight for them, success is very unlikely. Ministers are also aware that they are constrained by powerful, organized interests, by other administrative agencies and professions, and by properties of the economic system and of cultural traditions. Despite all these constraints, most ministers do not feel a gap between their influence and their responsibility.

One interpretation may be that ministers do not view civil servants and organized interest groups as opponents. Both politicians and civil servants perceive little conflict between politically appointed personnel and civil servants. In cases of confrontation ministers are likely to win.[82] But most of the time there is no need for confrontations, and ministers know that they cannot afford to win many confrontations. Similarly, ministers and representatives of organized interests most of the time do not perceive each other as opponents. It is more likely that a minister will represent "his" interest groups to the rest of the Cabinet or to the minister of finance.[83]

Finally, ministers perceive their under secretaries and in some cases also their political secretaries as influential. While they are not eager to get more political appointees, they do not view the influence of their secretaries as problematic. Only in one case was there a confrontation between a minister and an under secretary, with the result that the secretary had to leave.

---

[81] Michael D. Cohen and J. G. March, *Leadership and Ambiguity* (New York: McGraw Hill, 1974); Richard M. Cyert and James G. March, *A Behavioral Theory of the Firm* (Englewood Cliffs, N.J.: Prentice-Hall, 1963); James R. Glenn, Jr., "Chief Executive Time: An Empirical Study of the Time Allocation of American College and University Presidents," Ph.D. dissertation, Stanford University, 1975; Headey, *British Cabinet*; and Neustadt, *Presidential Power*, pp. 34, 223-24.

[82] Laegreid and Olsen, *Byråkrati*, p. 247.

[83] Norbom, "Økonomisk-politiske beslutningsprosess."

Of the under secretaries, 84 percent view themselves as influential, compared with 33 percent of the political secretaries. Both groups describe their jobs in terms of interesting experiences rather than in terms of influence. Significant phrases are: "We know each other pretty well" and "I know how far I can go." In my interpretation these phrases are a key to the more general processes through which the politically acceptable is discovered or defined in Norway.

Anticipated Reaction and "Sounding Out." Styles of collective decision making vary from the formal aggregation of preferences explicitly expressed by a vote, through the synthesizing of preferences which are expressed only indirectly through social interaction, to autonomous adjustment where actors keep an eye on each other, anticipate possible actions and reactions, and take them into consideration when they make decisions. In a small and fairly transparent political system such as the Norwegian one, it is not surprising that anticipated reaction[84] is a major form of coordination. Implicit criteria filter out most alternatives. Only a small number are left for explicit consideration. A majority of ministers, under secretaries, and political secretaries report that in most cases they have a fairly clear picture of what is acceptable and how others will react. While under secretaries report surprises more often than the other appointees, they are usually surprised because of the strength of the reactions or because the debate is focused on a specific detail in the proposal. The less time for consulting, the more often things turn out differently than executive leaders had expected. On the average it is easier to predict the reaction of others than the long-term substantive effects of new programs and policies.

Civil servants agree. Less than 10 percent of all the civil servants in the ministries report that it is very or somewhat difficult to know the goals and intentions of political leaders in their ministry; to know which decisions to present to the minister; to know which issues will attract a public debate and which positions different groups will take in such a debate; or to predict the effects of new programs. More people (20 percent) say it is very or somewhat difficult to be sure what the substantive effects really have been.[85]

The difference between the Norwegian and an international decision-making system is commented on by a director general in one of the ministries:[86] "I discovered that my mastery of Norwegian

[84] Carl J. Friedrich, *Constitutional Government and Politics* (New York: Harper, 1937).
[85] Olsen and Wagtskjold, "Laeringshorisonter."
[86] Eide, "A Planner Looks Back," p. 16.

research policy consisted of knowing exactly what reactions to expect from professor X and doctor Y, from institution A and agency B. In an international context such experience was without value, as nobody knew the individuals or agencies involved." If actors do not know what is politically possible, they know how to find out. They use a lot of energy to find acceptable solutions through careful discussions, adjustments, and negotiations, as a foreigner has observed.[87] A lot of work and willingness to compromise is needed in order to pull a decision to shore. A Prime Minister indicated that before presenting a proposal to the Storting, he has to have a reasonable feeling about what can be accepted.[88] And an under secretary argued that if there were more consultation than there is today, nothing would ever be done.

A major commandment in executive policy making is: Do not announce a position; do not commit yourself at an early stage. Instead a sounding out process is used.[89] Participants in the first phase try to reveal the direction of their thinking and preferences and attempt to move the final outcome toward the most highly valued end result, but they avoid specific indications of preferences and beliefs. They retain counterarguments and some degree of ambiguity, contradiction, or openness in their statements. The final outcome is a result of more and more participants accepting a certain solution as the best, while other choices fade away. The support for the chosen solution may vary from enthusiasm to abstention from obstruction. If it is difficult to establish unanimity, the participants avoid clear, stable, and joint arenas for the decision-making process. The choice is moved from joint meetings to discussions in smaller groups.

The process is quite different from planning procedures that first establish operational goals and then search for the best way to achieve them. Goals are formed as a part of the decision-making process and in close interaction with the development of alternatives and with the registration of political support.

Ministers describe Cabinet decision making as a process in which "agreement crystallizes" or "we talk ourselves into agreement." First, the responsible minister gives an orientation, then the others cautiously feel their way in order to register the different standpoints and

---

[87] Harry Eckstein, *Division and Cohesion in Democracy: A Study of Norway* (Princeton, N.J.: Princeton University Press, 1966), p. 159.

[88] Nordli, "Regjeringen," p. 19.

[89] Johan P. Olsen, "Voting, 'Sounding Out,' and the Governance of Modern Organizations," *Acta Sociologica*, vol. 3 (1972), pp. 267-82; James D. Thompson and William J. McEwan, "Organizational Goals and Environment Goal Setting as an Interaction Process," *American Sociological Review*, vol. 23 (February 1958), pp. 23-31.

divisions.[90] The Prime Minister may draw a conclusion, most often that an alternative is acceptable. He may argue that the decision has to be cleared with the party faction in the Storting, a committee, or the party directorate; or the responsible or affected minister may be asked to take a new look.[91]

Thus, the Prime Minister frequently intervenes in the procedure. In case of conflict his word is important, but even then he tries to have the responsible minister announce the agreement.[92] The same type of "talking ourselves into agreement" is used with the rest of the governing environment. Before positions are announced and become a matter of prestige, the Storting, the party faction, the responsible committee, or a representative from a district particularly affected will be informed and consulted. So will important, affected interest groups. One result is that the formal aspects of the decision-making processes, such as voting procedures, become less interesting.

Sounding out and consultation are certainly not the only forms of interaction and coordination in executive decision making in Norway, but they are important and not well understood. Some substantive benefits may be lost as a result of compromises, and sounding out is a time-consuming process. Using a large amount of time on a single choice means relinquishing time from other activities and decisions. Executive leaders also lose the ability to act quickly and to adapt to a rapidly changing environment. Why, then, does a potential majority sometimes not establish a minimum winning coalition, but instead uses a great deal of energy to establish general acceptance?

A decision process is not only a means of choosing between substantive alternatives and of economizing on time and energy, but also a legitimizing procedure. Sounding out is used when executive leaders are afraid of phyrric triumphs. It is used when the negative effects of the losses of legitimacy, loyalty, cohesion, friendship, and trust are more important than the potential benefits of substantive programs and time saved. It may also be used to express and develop goodwill and trust.

Sounding out will be most common in systems in which resources and sanctions are spread out among the participants. The smaller the decision-making system, and the more closely knit the decision makers are, the more likely that sounding out will be important. That is often the case in policy-making processes within a segment and a sector. The less certain the substantive effects of new programs, the more important it is to avoid uncertainty through negotiated environments.

---

[90] Also Berggrav, "Regjeringen," pp. 6-7; Bloch, *Kongens råd*, p. 74; and Solstad, "Norwegian Coalition," p. 155.
[91] Berggrav, "Regjeringens," p. 4.
[92] Bloch, *Kongens råd*, p. 24; and interview, Bratteli Cabinet.

Montesquieu Revisited

A central theme in Western political thought is how to reconcile the need for order—for a state strong enough to prevent anarchy—with the need to tame Leviathan and to prevent a monolithic, all-powerful state. In an anarchic or unsegmented system any participant can take part in any choice. Executive leadership changes continuously, as an informal, shifting aggregation of key individuals or as a shifting network of issues or coalitions. Issue or candidate enthusiasts take control.[93] An unsegmented, highly situational leadership is based on weakly developed political institutions and division of labor. There are many sources of authority and power, changing goals, and shifting cleavages and coalitions. Planning is weak, and almost any opportunity for choice may become a garbage can that gathers participants, problems, and solutions.[94] Leaders are those who are interested in choices and have the time and energy to spend. Choices are defined by the problems and solutions activated at the time. Unsegmented structures complicate political calculations and decrease predictability. Those charged with formal governmental leadership are under considerable strain and may come to play a ceremonial role loosely linked with substantive policy making.[95]

In a monolithic or hierarchical system policy makers and choices are arranged in a stable hierarchy so that important choices must be made by important policy makers and important policy makers can

---

[93] Colin Campbell and George J. Szablowski, *The Super-Bureaucrats* (Toronto: Macmillan of Canada, 1979); Hugh Heclo, "Issue Networks and the Executive Establishment," in Anthony King, ed., *The New American Political System* (Washington, D.C.: American Enterprise Institute, 1978), p. 375; March and Olsen, *Ambiguity*; Richard E. Neustadt, "White House and Whitehall," in Anthony King, ed., *The British Prime Minister: A Reader* (London: Macmillan, 1969); and King, "Executives," p. 375.

[94] Michael D. Cohen and others, "A Garbage Can Model of Organizational Choice," *Administrative Science Quarterly*, vol. 1 (1972), pp. 1-25; and March and Olsen, *Ambiguity*.

[95] Norwegian students of politics have given little attention to the fact that governing is a public drama in which the Prime Minister is a major character. Since the Prime Minister is a symbol to many people whom he does not know and will never meet, he functions primarily through his image (Orrin E. Klapp, *Symbolic Leaders* [Chicago: Aldine, 1964]). It is difficult to say how concerned Norwegian Prime Ministers are with their public image, how they strengthen or change it, and how this affects other aspects of their behavior. Typically, a Cabinet crisis will have dramatic aspects. When Borten resigned in 1971 he had much more support among the people than among political leaders. In a nationwide poll (Norwegian Social Science Data Service) 87 percent said they followed the development of the crisis, and more people wanted Borten to stay than to leave; 66 percent felt that the political parties did not handle the crisis correctly.

participate in any choice. In such a structure the Prime Minister is the superstar; alternatively, the Cabinet or some external unit (the legislature, party, or interest group) operates as the apex of the hierarchy. Standard answers to problems of capacity, understanding, and authority are to expand the Prime Minister's office or some other central agency and to introduce more politically appointed personnel as well as more analytical staff. An inner Cabinet or a hierarchical committee structure is developed. Command or confrontation are the major forms of coordination.

The Norwegian case suggests an alternative to monolithic and anarchic systems. The executives' environment is dominated by a complex network of interdependent and interpenetrated formal organizations. Executives are in a bargaining situation both within the governmental apparatus and with organized interests in society, but the main tendency is toward specialization. The major response to the problems of capacity, understanding, and authority has been a political-administrative division of labor. And administrative sectorization has increased because the various ministries, departments, and divisions have developed specialized external patterns of contacts and support. The result is a segmented system with stable, nonhierarchical functional coalitions.[96]

In a purely specialized or segmented system, each executive leader is associated with a single class of choices, each class having a single group of policy makers. Leaders specialize in the choices to which they attend, and the coordination of them is relatively weak. Ministers are recruited from the relevant sectors and professions. The Prime Minister's office is poorly developed. There is no inner Cabinet or hierarchical system of Cabinet committees. Political staffs are developed around each minister. Sectoral planning agencies are more important than analytical staffs directly related to the Prime Minister's office. Expertise is sector-defined, not general. There are few attempts to coordinate goals or to provide comprehensive analytical theories. Executive leaders operate under parochial perceptions and priorities. They are spokesmen for the institutions and the tasks for which they are responsible. They are accountable to specialized constituencies rather than to the head of the government.

Specialization in an executive system may be combined with a hierarchical organization within sectors. But more often specialization arises in a negotiated environment in which a minister's independence from a single coordinating center is based on support from organized

---

[96] Morten Egeberg et al., "Organisasjonssamfunnet og den segmenterte stat," in J. P. Olsen, ed., *Politisk organisering* (Bergen: Universitetsforlaget, 1978).

interests in his own sector. Executive leaders avoid uncertainty and negotiate authority through a series of tacit understandings and contracts with organized groups in society as well as with civil servants. Such functional coalition may encompass all levels from local to international. Consultation and anticipated reactions are more important forms of coordination than command. The role differentiation between politically appointed leaders and civil servants and between public and private groups is blurred.

The main tendency in Norway is toward specialization and segmentation. Still, there are counterforces. The surge in direct actions and movements in the last part of the 1960s and the early 1970s introduced elements of unsegmented leadership that were most conspicuous in the struggle for Norwegian membership in the European Economic Community and in issues such as environmental protection, energy policy, and women's rights.[97] But generally their impact on central processes of governance seems modest (table 6-9).

A more significant counterforce has been attempts at hierarchical coordination and leadership by political parties, by the Cabinet, and by the Ministry of Finance. The elements of hierarchy and central planning were probably strongest during the 1950s. Since then the Labor party has lost its majority in the Storting and has probably become more heterogeneous and less centralized. There is no longer any obvious party leader, and a change of generations is taking place among the top leaders. Economic growth is no longer a generally accepted goal, there are fewer slack resources, and the adequacy of economic theories and economic planning is questioned. Organized interests have become integrated into government, but they have preferred participation at the ministerial—not the Cabinet—level. Civil servants have obtained increased participatory rights, and usually they defend specific institutions and parochial interests.

The tendency toward specialization and segmentation and the tendency toward consensus and anticipated reactions partly counteract each other. The system is probably more segmented in its behavior patterns than in the substantive premises that enter into policy-making processes. The two tendencies may also be related to features of Norway affecting the generalizability of this study.

Norway is a small country where political actors often know each other personally. In the post–World War II period the country has changed from being comparatively poor to comparatively rich. Until recently this process has provided a fair amount of slack resources.

---

[97] Johan P. Olsen and Harald Saetren, *Aksjoner og demolerati* (Bergen: Universitetsforlaget, 1980).

Class cooperation in the service of economic growth has been more prevalent than class conflict. Political, economic, and cultural life is highly dependent on the trends in other countries, primarily Western societies. At the same time, egalitarianism is emphasized, and differences between people and the open use of power are much disliked.[98]

It may be that a homogeneous, unsegmented society is a condition for a segmented state. The fewer the major cleavages, the easier it is to accept a division of labor that allows those most interested to make the decisions. At the same time, the smaller and more homogeneous the society, the easier it is to develop a consensual policy-making style and to use anticipated reaction as a major form of coordination. The more efficiently coordination through anticipated reactions works, the easier it is to exploit the benefits of specialization and segmentation.

It remains to be seen how closely the consensual, specialized style is related to a slack resource situation, nationally as well as internationally, and whether it will work only as long as policy making is incremental and focused on distributing new resources. One guess is that when slack is reduced, Norway's well-organized and "responsible" parties and organized interest groups will make it more likely that a segmented system will move more toward hierarchy than toward anarchy—at least in the short run.

It may also be that a segmented system is related to the substance of major policies. The more selective the benefits and the constraints of public policies, the more likely that intensive minorities will demand special attention or participation. The idea of one center of authority and power, and one chain of accountability, is related to the making of general policies that have an impact on society as a whole.[99] Thus, if the government reduces the use of selective incentives and constraints, as it did in Norway in 1979, it may make hierarchical decision making more likely.

It is most likely, however, that major aspects of the segmented state will survive through pragmatic adaptations to local problems. The metaphor of a segmented state is thus an alternative to the classical, Montesquieu-inspired interpretation of Western democracies. Montesquieu's suggestion was to separate legislative, executive, and

---

[98] Bergh and Pharo, Vekst og velstand; and Ulf Torgersen, "De politiske institusjonene," in N. Rogoff Ramsøy, ed., Det norske samfunn (Oslo: Gyldendal, 1968).

[99] Morten Egeberg, "Politisk organisasjon og politisk innhold," University of Bergen, 1979 (mimeo); E. E. Schattschneider, Politics, Pressures and the Tariff (New York: Prentice-Hall, 1935); and Sheldon Wolin, Politics and Vision (Boston: Little, Brown, 1960).

judicial powers. In the segmented state, powers are also separated, but contacts and cleavages do not follow the institutions Montesquieu trusted. Instead they cut across these institutions. The government is separated into functional, nonhierarchical coalitions, a fact reflected in executive institutions, their personnel, and their operation.

7

The Organization of Authoritarian Leadership: Franco Spain

Carlos R. Alba

There is as yet no adequate theoretical framework into which the Franco regime can be placed and through which it can be understood. The most common categories into which it has been placed have been too general to be of much use: "fascism," "conservative dictatorship," "despotic absolutism," "Catholic corporativist dictatorship," "military dictatorship," "paternalistic dictatorship," "national syndicalist regime," "organic democracy," "caudillaje," and "authoritarian regime."[1] None of these categories contributes a great deal to our understanding of the organization of executive power under a regime such as General Franco's. Indeed, much of the literature on Spanish politics concentrates on the pre-civil war era, on the civil war itself, and on the rise to power of General Franco. The death of Franco has led to a preoccupation with the problems of establishing a democratic regime in contemporary Spain. As a consequence, there is a paucity of knowledge about the process of governing under Franco's regime.

NOTE: The author wishes to thank the March Foundation and Yale University for their support in the preparation of certain parts of this chapter. Acknowledgment is also made of support from the Spanish-American Committee for Cultural Affairs for a comparative study of Spanish, Western European, and American public bureaucracies.
1 Juan Linz, "An Authoritarian Regime: Spain," in E. Allardt and Y. Littunen, eds., *Cleavages, Ideologies and Party Systems,* contribution to *Comparative Political Sociology* (Helsinki: The Westermarck Society, 1964). Juan Martinez Alier, "Critica de la caracterizacion del franquismo como regimen autoritario de pluralismo limitado," *Cuaderno de Ruedo Iberico,* vol. 43-45 (1975). pp. 67-75. Eduardo Sevilla Guzman et al., "Despotismo Moderno y Dominacion de Clase para una Sociologia del Regimen Franquista," *Papers Revista de Sociologia,* vol. 8 (1978), pp. 103-141. This journal has a very good bibliography on Franco's Spain. A good discussion of the sociological literature on *Franquismo* is given in Jose Felix Tezanos, *Estructura de Clases y Conflictos de Poder en la España Postfranquista* (Madrid: Edicusa, 1978), pp. 35-126.

Whereas constitutions of the United States and Western European democracies impose great constraints on political leaders, in Spain the position was reversed for more than a generation. The government of Franco Spain is an example of a dictatorship in which authority was formally and legally vested in a single individual, General Franco. Hence, an understanding of the government of Franco Spain can illuminate the problems of political leadership that arise even in a constitutional dictatorship.

The purpose of this paper is to understand how General Franco governed Spain and succeeded in staying in power for over thirty-five years. We shall proceed by describing the three main levels of the executive structure: the top office of Franco as Head of State and President of the Government during a period already known as "the forty years"; the Council of Ministers and the ministers; and finally the group of bureaucratic leaders who have occupied the highest positions under the minister in the ministerial departments, and who constitute a universe of some 700 persons.[2]

Franco: The Foundation

In order to understand the functioning of the post-1939 political system and, specifically, the executive apparatus and organization of political leadership, it is of fundamental importance to make a detailed analysis of the person who monopolized the top executive position and who appears to us with so many peculiarities in his effective functioning. Several biographies of Franco have been written in recent years and almost all concentrate on his personality.[3] It is important to understand his origins and ideological outlook.

Ideology. One of Franco's official biographers maintains that "until the arrival of the Republic in 1931, the political ideology of Franco was relatively elemental; a diffuse populism, the traditional values of the Spanish middle classes, the indisputable preponderance of the military over the civil and, it scarcely needs to be said, over the intel-

---

[2] I have based my analysis on histories of the Franco regime, especially the two volumes of R. de la Cierva, *Historia del Franquismo* (Barcelona: Planeta, 1975-1978), memoirs of key personalities in the regime's history, press reports, and interviews.

[3] For good biographies of Franco, one can consult Brian Crozier, *Franco, Historia y Biografía*, 2 vols. (Madrid: Magisteaio Español, 1969), English edition: (London: Syre & Spottiswoode, 1967); G. Hills, *Franco, el hombre y su nacion* (Madrid: San Martin, 1968), English edition: (London: Hale, 1967); J. W. D. Trythall, *Franco* (London: Hart-Davis, 1970); and R. de la Cierva et al., *Francisco Franco: un siglo de España* (Madrid: Editorial Nacional, 1972-73).

lectual, the primary analysis on the regenerational virtues and on the imprudent and avoidable errors of the first dictatorship. But the authentic and, moreover, definitive crystallization of the political ideology of Franco developed between 1933 and 1939, during the crisis of the Republic and the traumas of the civil war."[4] The new elements that were incorporated into the preexisting ideological framework are: the radicalization of Franco's rightist schema and the reinterpretation of these ideological values on the basis of a religious formulation, which can be understood in its most aggressive aspect as "a religious crusade."

Francisco Franco was born in a typical middle-class Spanish conservative family of military traditions and was educated in an interpretation of Spanish history whose models were the Catholic monarchs and the politics of the golden century, and whose demons were the attempts at establishing liberal or democratic regimes throughout the nineteenth and twentieth centuries. His experiences as a soldier in Africa, as director of the General Military Academy in the period of the dictatorship of General Primo de Rivera, and subsequently as a conspirator after the advent of the Second Republic, led him to formulate a set of political principles to which he remained faithful all his life.

These principles consisted of loyalty to historic leaders or caudillos, to the idea of national unity in the face of separatism, of political unity in the face of political parties, and of social unity in the face of the class struggle. Viscerally opposed to communism and freemasonry, he despised the intellectuals and the classic politicians; he relied instead on a populism tending toward fascism, on a corporatism in a Catholic mode, and on the support of technicians and experts. He derived all his lessons from the army and from his frozen memory of the civil war, which in his old age he would nostalgically recall again and again.

These values, which constituted his ideological universe, were to be propagated and made "permanent and unalterable." He accordingly set up the educational, political, and legal-constitutional mechanisms for ensuring their permanence. As dictator he was determined "to hold on to the helm of the State for as long as God granted him life and clarity of judgment" (as he proclaimed in the Plaza de Oriente on October 1, 1971). His position as Head of State was, despite certain legal ambiguities, always perfectly clear; it consisted of a power that was exceptional, arbitrary, and without limits in its exercise, except those deriving from his own will.

---

[4] de la Cierva, *Historia del Franquismo*, vol. 1, pp. 99ff.

Legal Structure. The Franco regime was born in a civil war. Franco, as one of the military leaders who rose against the constitutional government of the Popular Front of the Second Republic, became the supreme commander of the nationalist side. It was from this position that he set about organizing the legal and political framework of what at that time was called the "New State."

The first stage in the reorganization of the state came with the creation, on July 24, 1936, of the National Defense Junta. It consisted of rebel generals, headed by the oldest among them, General Cabanellas. This body was limited in its activity to military matters (the conduct of the war) and, although it assumed the powers of the state in areas controlled by the rebels, it lacked the necessary apparatus for carrying out the tasks of the government or its administration. As the war advanced it became clear that there was a need for a single command, which could control both the military and the civil spheres and which could set into motion the administrative machinery of the state. The need for such a command, magnificently illustrated by Sainz Rodriguez and Serrano Suner in their memoirs,[5] led to the transfer of power to Franco by means of the famous decree of the Junta, which institutionalized the position of General Franco as an omnipotent dictator. The decree, dated September 29, 1936, is, however, ambiguous. It does not make clear whether the members of the Junta were appointing a military leader, a head of government, or a dictator with unlimited power for an unlimited time.

Constitutional scholars have offered various interpretations of this decree. Without entering into an exegesis of the legal text, we can get at the clear intention of the decree by paying particular attention to the important role that the decree assigned to General Franco. The preamble of the decree noted the goal to be "the establishment, consolidation and development of the new State." The task of ensuring the attainment of this goal was given to General Franco. Article 1 stated that "his Excellency, General Francisco Franco Bahamonde is appointed Head of the Government of the Spanish State, and he shall assume all the powers of the new State." It is easy to see that the apparent limitations of the first part disappear in the second, in such a way that the second article of the decree seems redundant when it appoints him "generalissimo of the national forces on land, sea and in the air, and he is granted the post of General in Charge of the Armies of Operations." The General was definitively granted

---

[5] P. Sainz Rodriguez, *Testimonio y Recuerdos* (Barcelona: Planeta, 1978); and R. Serrano Suner, *Entre el silencio y la propaganda, la historia como fue. Memorias* (Barcelona: Planeta, 1977).

the "constituent power."[6] The identification of the position of Head of State and that of President of the Government with the person of General Franco has been so strong that the framers of the Law on Succession included the name of the General in the articles of the legal text itself. Article 2 stated that "the Office of the Head of the State is held by the Caudillo of Spain and of the Crusade Generalissimo of the Armed Forces, Don Francisco Franco Bahamonde." Professor Sanchez Agesta has described the position of the Head of State in the final moments of his mandate by the following features: (a) power is attributed specifically to the person of Franco; (b) extraordinary powers are given to him; (c) he is to enjoy his exceptional personal position for life; (d) his powers are either undefined or defined negatively, which means that any powers that are not specifically granted to another institution belong to the Head of State.[7]

Although Franco consolidated his power gradually with the help of fascism, terror, the civil war, and repression, one must not underestimate the legal framework that was set up and within which his regime functioned. For it was through legal mechanisms that Franco concentrated considerable political power in the newly created position of the Head of State. What Franco effectively did was to regulate his own power and then to authorize the acquisition of new power through legal means.

This can be seen from the introduction of three important legal texts. First, the Law of October 1, 1936, created the Junta Tecnica del Estado which had control over all civil and military matters. It was, effectively, the government, and it was headed by General Franco.[8] Second, the Decree of Unification of April 19, 1937, united Falange Española and Requetes in a single organization that was to be called FET y de las JONS (Falange Española Tradicionalista–Juntas Ofensivas Nacionales Sindicalistas). Its chief was the Head of State who, from that moment, was also head of the National Movement.[9]

---

[6] R. Fernandez Carvajal, *La Constitucion Española* (Madrid: Editora Nacional, 1969). I am using "constituent power" as something that Franco had, but a more realistic approach would be to consider that the authentic "constituent power" was embodied in the victorious side in the civil war and Franco was the, although not the only, spokesman for those interests.

[7] L. Sanchez Agesta, *Derecho Constitucional Comparado* (Madrid: Editora Nacional, 1971), pp. 489-96.

[8] R. Entrena Cuesta, "La Jefatura del Estado" in *La España de los años 70.III: El Estado y la Politica* (Madrid: Moneda y Credito, 1974), pp. 975-1026.

[9] In order to understand the unification see: Stanley G. Payne, *Falange: A History of Spanish Fascism* (Stanford: Stanford University Press, 1961). A very partial account, but interesting because it shows how the people in government saw the creation of the party, is given in R. Serrano Suner, *Entre Hendaya y*

Third, the Law of January 30, 1938, constituted the most important step in the institutionalization of power. By means of this legal instrument the administration of the state was organized into ministerial departments, and the post of the President of the Government was instituted. The new post was to be combined with that of Head of State. In terms of the organization of the political leadership, the importance of this law resided in the fact that Franco received the power to dictate legal norms that were translated into laws whenever there was a question of the organic structure of the state, to determine the principal norms governing the legal system of the country, and to issue decrees in numerous spheres (article 17).

In July 1939, the statute of FET y de las JONS was approved. It declared that the National Chief (Franco) was "Supreme Caudillo of the Movement" and that he "personifies all the values and all the honours of the Movement. As author of the historic era in which Spain acquires the possibilities of realizing its destiny, and with it the desires of the Movement, the Head assumes, in full plenitude, the most absolute authority. The Head responds before God and before history." (article 47). The legal framework that organizes the leadership of this top office was fixed with the Law of August 8, 1938, by means of which the Head of State was permitted to legislate, without needing to consult or hear the deliberations of the Council of Ministers, when he considered that there was a need for urgency. No later provisions, including the Organic Law of the State, would ever affect the set of powers that the will of the dictator himself set up during and immediately after the civil war. All the fundamental laws, from the Labor Charter of 1938 to the Organic Law of 1967, have proceeded from these powers, which Professor Fernandez Carvajal has called "constituent dictatorship."[10]

Post-Civil War Constitutional Evolution. Beginning in 1942, the institutionalization of governmental power was completed by means of dispositions which, although formally proceeding from the Cortes, the National Council, or the government, originated solely from the will of Franco. The law establishing the Spanish Parliament (Ley de Cortes) was promulgated in 1942. Parliament was defined as an advisory body that was to assist Franco in the exercise of his legislative powers. The Cortes did not approve laws. It prepared and elaborated them in accordance with the wishes of the Head of State.

Gibraltar: Frente a una Leyenda (Madrid: Ediciones y Publicaciones Españolas, 1947).

[10] Fernandez Carvajal, *La Constitucion Española*.

Franco retained the right to legislate without taking the Cortes into account, although he only used these prerogatives on certain occasions, most of which concerned constitutional matters.

In 1945, after having consolidated and institutionalized his power, the Head of State issued the Law of National Referendum, which placed explicit limitation on his own power and which afforded protection to Spaniards "against the deviation shown in recent political history, when, in matters of utmost importance or public interest, the will of the Nation can be supplanted by the subjective judgement of her rulers." The paradoxical, or cynical, nature of this law testifies to the confidence that Franco had in his control of the state apparatus in 1945.

Realities of Coalition. If we look at the real nature of Franco's leadership, we can affirm that its origin was military and that he consolidated his position as the leader among various leaders of the heterogeneous movements that supported the cause of the rebels in the civil war. In practice his leadership made use of coalition governments as an enduring instrument of rule. He created sufficient ambiguity so that no group of the victorious coalition could really say whether Franco was in favor of or hostile to a particular faction. The political panorama of supporters that surrounded him was composed of Falangists, "liberal monarchists," Carlists, corporatists, fascists of Renovacion Española, conservative Catholics of Opus Dei, and members of the Associacion Catolica Nacional de Propagandistas (a group of intellectuals and professionals committed to the infusion of religion in politics). When confronting each group, he always had an authoritative bargaining position, so he never succumbed to the temptation of founding his own party.

Franco's way of solving the conflicts between political factions was to use the principle of divide and rule. He never allowed himself to get carried away by the complaints or demands of the different political families and, as a last resort, simply delayed in order to let their demands cool down (the crises of 1941 and 1969, the notes and reports of Carrero from 1941 onward on the political situation, and the aftermath of the crisis derived from the assassination of Carrero Blanco are good examples of that).

Franco never tolerated any type of rival leadership, and when it arose he destroyed it. He selected ministers who never formed a homogeneous team, but who were isolated figures recruited for their loyalty to the Caudillo more than for their efficiency or competence. Franco did not create a group of personal advisers or a "political staff" to help him in formulating policies or to provide independent information. All that he had were his two households: the military and the civilian, whose employees functioned as gate keepers and managers of his daily schedule. They prepared reports on subjects of current interest and informed him of the political gossip in the different circles in which they moved. (An important source for any analysis of the palace world of the General is the memoirs of his cousin Teniente General Francisco Franco Salgado-Araujo, *Mis Conversaciones Privadas con Franco,* in which he relates his vision of the political life around Franco and his opinions on various leaders of the system. Franco's cousin spent his life near Franco in positions in the military household.)[11]

In the absence of a team of personal advisers, Franco had to depend on the advice of his ministers. The policy areas over which he exercised the most influence were the ones he considered strategic: the organization of the basic institutions of the regime, the control of the army, the public order, and foreign relations.

In the composition of his government he always tried to maintain a certain representation of the political families in specific ministerial departments. Thus, the army always controlled the military ministries. The Catholic groups controlled the Department of Education, which allowed the church to control private education. The Carlists occupied the Ministry of Justice. The Falangists were in the Ministry of Labor and Housing, and the economic ministries were controlled by the private sector, specifically by members or sympathizers of the Opus Dei.

This complex mechanism, through which the different interests were articulated, has to be understood within the context of the role of bureaucrats in the state apparatus. Thus, ministers tended to be recruited mainly from within the bureaucratic apparatus of the state. Franco divorced himself from the errors of his ministers, and he changed his ministers without ever incurring responsibility for their errors.[12]

Preparation for Succession. In 1947 the Cortes elaborated the Law of Succession of the Head of State, approved by the Spanish people in a national referendum on July 6 of that year. This law defined the

---

[11] F. Franco Salgado-Araujo, *Mis Conversaciones Privadas con Franco* (Barcelona: Planeta, 1976). It is difficult to know the part played by candor or animosity, caused by his political and economic disfavor, in the critical judgments contained in the important memoirs of Franco Salgado-Araujo.

[12] See K. Mudhurst, *Government In Spain: The Executive At Work* (London: Pergamon Press, 1973).

Spanish state as a monarchy, while the position of the Head of State continued to belong to the Caudillo. A Council of Regency was created for the purpose of filling in for the Caudillo in the event that he was no longer able to assume the position of Head of State. The law also created a Council of the Kingdom and specified how the succession was to take place and under what conditions the title of the Head of State would belong to the Regent or the King. The law required the approval of the Cortes, as well as a referendum for any modification of the provisions therein.

Ten years later (on July 26, 1957), the Law of the Legal System of the Administration of the State was passed. This law referred to the Head of State as one of the superior offices in the state administration, but it did not define his jurisdictions or prerogatives. It indicated that a special law must be passed to specify the precise functions of the holder of this office. The law did, however, make a distinction between the Head of State and the President of the Government, and it elaborates the jurisdictions of the latter. The law expressly recognized delegated legislation, which up to that time was an accepted constitutional custom. Finally, the law established that in the case of decree laws, in order to appreciate the urgency that prompted their adoption, the Head of State was required to hear the opinion of the Commission on Legislative Competence of the Cortes.

In 1958, the Head of State promulgated the Law of Principles of the National Movement, which constituted the doctrinal basis of the regime and the inspiring principle of the rest of the fundamental laws. These principles were conceived as the synthesis and quintessence of the Franco system. They had to be strictly obeyed by all the branches of the government, and they had to be explicitly mentioned in the oath required to assume public posts. Curiously, the referendum was not used to approve these principles, and it was established that they were "by their own nature permanent and immutable."

The process of the legal institutionalization of the regime culminated in the approval of the Organic Law of the State on January 10, 1967. This law was important in setting into motion the mechanisms for the succession, but it in no way changed the responsibilities of the top office.[13]

By way of illustration, it is sufficient to refer to what happened in the Council of Ministers on April 2, 1966, when the ministers broached the subject of the political future of the regime. Fraga is reputed to have observed to Franco that, "although he considered

---

[13] Sainz Rodríguez, *Testimonio*, pp. 338-39.

himself to be the last of the Ministers, he felt himself to have the right to request in the name of 30 million Spaniards that he [Franco] should define his position and clarify his vision of the future." There ensued moments of great tension. Franco replied: "Do you think that I don't realize, do you think I am a circus clown?" The debate on the future of the regime lasted an hour and a half. For most of the time Franco listened with a smile to the opinions of the ministers, who later attempted to decipher the significance of Franco's smile. Don Camilo, an intimate friend of Franco's family, and minister of the interior, said that it was his opinion that the smile meant only one thing: that Franco already had the law prepared.[14] Despite the importance of the Organic Law, Franco did not communicate his intentions to the ministers, who were left to puzzle the Caudillo's smile. Franco not only retained power with respect to constitutional matters, ordinary legislation, and the mode of the succession (which included the right to propose, to annul a proposition, or to reject a dynastic line of pretenders to the throne), but he accumulated the offices and powers of the Head of State and Head of the Government (in addition to being leader of the National Movement and Generalissimo of the Armed Forces). I shall refer later in some detail to the office of the President of the Government. For the moment, it is important to emphasize that despite the legal separation of the Presidency and the Head of State since 1939, a legality based on the Law of the Legal System of 1957 and the Organic Law of 1967, Franco did not appoint a President of the Government until 1973, and even then he did so with the stipulation that during his own life this would in no way affect his powers. Indeed, Franco continued to preside in the Council of Ministers, even as he lay dying at the end of 1975.

Having described the ideological and constitutional foundations of Franco's regime, we need to add that Franco's reign was also based to some extent on his charismatic qualities. The theory of *caudillaje*, the religious elements that surrounded his figure and his mission ("Caudillo of Spain by the Grace of God" says the coinage), the facility of mass mobilization in critical moments in the life of the regime, the perception that people had of him—all this suggests that there was an attachment to Franco, the person. There is no doubt that in the latter period of his rule, Franco's charismatic qualities subsided as technobureaucratic elements predominated in the structure of the political leadership.[15] Sainz Rodriguez has accurately described

---

[14] Lopez Rodo, *La Larga Marchahacia la Mouarguia* (Barcelona: Planeta, 1977), pp. 229-30.

[15] J. Conde Garcia, *Contribucion a la Teoria del Caudillaje* (Madrid: Vicese-

the essence of Franco's regime:

> Franco was dictator, but a dictator whose strength was no
> more than the army. . . . In Spain there has only been one
> personal dictatorship supported by the army and the accep-
> tance of the great social mass that was traumatized by the
> war. . . . Mussolini had the militia because he was not sup-
> ported by the army but by the Party. On the other hand,
> Franco was a soldier and the Party was only a loin cloth
> to conceal the military dictatorship. This led him to accept
> the construction of a fictional State, that was like a theatrical
> scene, lacking in reality. A Parliament that was not a Parlia-
> ment. Municipal Councils that were not Municipal Coun-
> cils. . . . The only thing that was authentic was his personal
> rule. To his military colleagues, he appeared as the Head of
> all this mechanical contrivance, and he never permitted that
> the appearances listed here should become political reality.
> For this reason, when Franco died, the scenery fell and the
> problem that arose was not how to reform a regime but how
> to bury it at the same time as its founder.[16]

The Government: President and Ministers

The Executive. The Franco regime was, as Carlos Rama has called it,
an institutionally hybrid regime. The political domination of General
Franco implied a mediation that altered the traditional bourgeois
domination. Franco was at first supported by a coalition of all the
traditional right-wing groups. He later widened his base of support
to include the middle classes. Consequently, Franco governed in a
pact with the economically dominant class and through terror, wide
police powers, the absence of individual freedom, corruption, non-
competitive elections, and a rubber-stamp parliament. The divisions
within the opposition to the regime undoubtedly contributed to the
stability of Franco's system. But the critical element in the Franco
regime was its capacity to coordinate the different divisions within
the executive in the absence of clearly demarcated jurisdiction. The
history of the Franco regime is, in large part, the history of the
regime's executive.

---

cretaria de Educacion Popular, 1942). Professor Conde, one of the most outstanding scholars, attempted a kind of legitimation of Franco's dictatorship. See
also F. Prieto, "La instrumentacion legal del liderazgo carismatico de Franco,"
Revista de Fomento Social (December 1971), pp. 401-407.

[16] Sainz Rodriguez, *Testimonio*, pp. 338-39. Franco never allowed himself to be
controlled by the army. He kept it out of the political arena. But he did make
symbolic use of the army as a way of warding off threats to the regime.

Having explained the main character of the regime, which clearly points to the predominance of the executive in general and of Franco in particular, we must avoid the temptation of concluding that Franco is responsible for all executive actions. This would be a highly simplistic view of the functioning of the executive of Franco's Spain.

The ministers in Franco's government were not without power and influence, even though they were always in a situation of dependence with respect to Franco, who conferred legitimacy upon them. But if they were in a wholly subordinate position (they could not even resign) with respect to Franco, they enjoyed considerable power within their own ministerial departments.

General Franco's cousin notes in his memoirs that ministers of the extreme right, of Accion Catolica, monarchists of Alfonso XIII, right- and left-wing Falangists "all ended by accepting the authority of the Caudillo who maintained them in power. Each one went his own way in his ministerial policy, but all were united by the desire to continue being ministers. . . . To be a minister of Franco is to be a little king who does what he wishes while His Excellency places no brake on his personal policy."[17] Salgado-Araujo criticizes Franco's frequent hunting parties (which also functioned as informal political arenas) because they did not leave Franco sufficient time to follow governmental affairs closely. The result of this negligence, according to Franco's cousin, was the transference of power to the ministers. "We Spaniards do not have a dictatorship of Franco, although it looks like that, but we do have a dictatorship of his ministers . . . some have been in their post for 14 years and do whatever they feel like because among other things, they know that they cannot be publicly criticized."[18]

It is interesting to note that Spanish texts tend not to distinguish between the government and the Council of Ministers, sometimes implying that they are one and the same, but sometimes also implying that the government is a political and policy-making organism whereas the Council of Ministers is essentially concerned with matters of administration. Until 1957 the legal provisions that could illuminate the respective jurisdictions of the government and the Council of Ministers were scant. A start at definition and clarification was made with the promulgation of the Law of the Legal System of the State Administration, which limits itself (as always during the Franco period, administrative reforms were a means of concealing and delaying authentic political reforms) to an administra-

[17] Salgado-Araujo, *Mis Conversaciones*, p. 68.
[18] Ibid., p. 130.

tive treatment of the government. By means of this law the ministerial departments were restructured into thirteen civil ministries, of which eleven were inherited by Franco (Foreign Affairs, Justice, Finance, Labor, Education, Interior, Public Works, Industry, Trade, Agriculture, and the Presidency) and two were new creations (the Ministry of Information and Tourism in 1951, which controlled the press and television network and which had censorship powers, and the Ministry of Housing, set up in 1957 to give a post to the dissident Falangist Arrese). In addition, there were three military ministries. The only change that occurred in this structure during the Franco period concerned the creation of the Commissariat of the Development Plan in 1962, which eleven years later attempted to function as Ministry of Planning, a ministry that was abolished three years later. The Law of the Legal System mentioned above created the Comisiones Delegadas del Gobierno (interministerial commissions) of which undoubtedly the most important one has been that of economic affairs.

The Organic Law of the State of 1967 completed the legal structure of the government. The main features of this law included (a) giving coherence to a variety of legal texts and clearing them of fascist and totalitarian elements, (b) separating the offices of Head of State and President of the Government and regulating their powers and functions, (c) including the army in the institutional apparatus of the regime by considering it as the guarantor of territorial integrity and national security and as the "defender of the institutional order," and (d) specifying by the constitutional device known as *recurso de contrafuero* the means by which to limit a possible conflict between a fundamental law and other laws.[19]

President of the Government. One of the most important offices within the overall executive structure was that of the President of the Government. The office had existed since 1938, but had remained vacant. In practice, the office had been combined with that of the Head of State until 1973, when it was given to Franco's alter ego, Carrero Blanco. A confidant of the Caudillo, Admiral Carrero Blanco (a key man for understanding the regime) was appointed under secretary to the President in 1940; after 1951 he gained ministerial status. He remained a member of the Cabinet until the end of his life. In 1967 he succeeded General Muñoz Grande as vice president of the government (a post created in 1962, which indicated that Franco

---

[19] On the government and the regulations of the Organic Law of the State see J. Tomas Villarroya, "El Gobierno" in *La España de los años 70.III*, pp. 1027-1982.

was beginning to think of the future and his possible death) and continued to occupy the post that he had occupied since 1940. In 1972 it was legally established that the vice president would automatically become President in the event of the sudden death of General Franco. In June 1973 Carrero Blanco was appointed President, thus definitively separating the office of Head of State and that of President of the Government.

In 1967, Carrero Blanco began to share functions that until that time Franco had reserved entirely for himself. Indeed, he became so important that, from the office of the President of the Government, and with the powerful intervention of Lopez Rodo (who was technical secretary general and then became commissar of the plan) he was able to introduce important administrative and constitutional reforms. Among these were the launching of a development plan and the provisions governing the succession of Franco, including notably the choice of the present monarch, Juan Carlos I. It is noteworthy that some high bureaucrats managed to ignore or eliminate demands for reforms by simply invoking Carrero Blanco's name even though they had never seen him nor discussed the matter in question with him. It was enough to say: "Don Luis Carrero does not want to know anything about this matter." A few months after he became President of the Government, an attack by ETA (the Basque terrorist movement) ended the life of Carrero Blanco, interrupting a political line that Franco had been preparing for over twenty years. Carrero Blanco had symbolized Franco's continuity or as Franco's supporters said: "after Franco, Franco" or "after Franco, Franco's institutions."

The assassination of Carrero Blanco gave rise to one of the most serious crises of the regime. In conformity with the Organic Law of the State (the first such application of the law) Arias Navarro was appointed President of the Government. Arias Navarro was a former prosecutor during the most repressive period of the regime, as well as a former mayor of Madrid, a director general of security, and minister of the interior. Much speculation surrounded his surprising appointment, particularly since he was responsible for the security services when President Carrero Blanco was assassinated. No doubt his closeness to the Prado and to the General's family and Franco's failing physical condition were part of the explanation.

Navarro's *aperturismo* consisted in little more than prolonging the life of Franco's political model. By the summer of 1975 his reforms were already languishing, while the regime advanced toward its end. The period after Arias Navarro opened the doors of power to an "apparatchiki" of the movement connected to the Opus Dei and broke a long tradition of political leadership.[20] It was the first time that someone "without the due qualifications" (that is to say, a career in the army or in one of the grand corps of the administration) acceded to the top office. Under Franco, the "apparatchiki" of the movement never climbed further than the middle-level positions.

Council of Ministers. The Council of Ministers (or Cabinet) was the most powerful organ in the executive of the regime. Its membership increased from eleven in 1938 to more than twenty in 1979. The changes that occurred during the Franco period can be summarized as follows: in 1951 Industry and Commerce were separated; in 1957 the president of the National Economic Council joined the Council of Ministers; in 1965 the commissar of the plan substituted as minister without portfolio for the president of the National Economic Council in the Cabinet, and in 1966 the commissar became a full member of the Cabinet.

The composition of the Cabinet changed gradually during the life of Franco's regime. From 1938 to the early 1950s Cabinets were composed essentially of politicians belonging to the Falange movement. From the mid-1950s on, as the importance of economic ministries increased, the technocratic element became much more important.

Another important change in the composition of the Cabinet concerned the forces that were represented in it. As we noted earlier, Franco's Cabinet tended to be a coalition of various ideological and economic forces. Starting with the Cabinet of Carrero Blanco (1969–1973) and of Arias Navarro (1974–1976), there was a tendency toward a greater homogeneity in the Council of Ministers. The aim was to form more homogeneous governments and more coherent policies.

Carrero Blanco's government of 1969 broke Franco's pattern of relying on a coalition of antiliberal traditionalists (such as Falangists, Catholic organizations, and the army). Carrero Blanco brought into his government thirteen newcomers who had not previously held ministerial posts. In fact, eleven of the nineteen ministers in the government were members of the Opus Dei. The pressures from the

---

20 On the Movement and Falange, see Juan J. Linz, "From Falange to Movimiento-Organizacion: The Spanish Single Party and the Franco Regime, 1936-1968" in Samuel P. Huntington and C. H. Moore, eds., *Authoritarian Politics in Modern Society* (New York: Basic Books, 1970). For the period of Arias Navarro, see R. Carr and J. P. Fusi, *España de la Dictadura a la Democracia* (Barcelona: Planeta, 1979); J. M. Areilza, *Diario de un Ministro de la Monarquia* (Barcelona: Planeta, 1977); and R. de la Cierva, *Cronicas de la Transicion. De la muerte de Carrero Blanco a la proclamacion del Rey* (Barcelona: Planeta, 1975).

economic crisis and the industrial working classes, as well as inter-ministerial squabbles, ended the life of the government and the policy of economic modernization without political change.

The 1973 Blanco government came to an end within six months of this inception, when the President was assassinated. The new government, headed by Arias Navarro, also sought homogeneity, though without the Opus Dei. The Navarro government was made up largely of technicians and of men closely linked to Navarro.[21] In both the Blanco and Navarro cases, a more homogeneous government was sought to inaugurate new policies. Both cases also indicated that the formation of a new government did not depend entirely on Franco. During the Carrero Blanco–Arias Navarro period, there were two types of Cabinet meetings: those presided over by Franco himself, which were really decisive Councils of Ministers, and those held without Franco, which were called "little councils" or *consejillos*.

There were several distinctive features of Franco's Cabinets. In general, they lacked unity and coherence, and the constant clash between ministers was reflected in some of the irrational decisions that were made. The bureaucratic struggles over control of specific areas of the administration and the lack of communication among the different ministerial departments resulted in incoherence in the policy-making process, despite the apparent centralization of the regime. The incoherence arose repeatedly in cases where technically complex projects involving several departments required cooperation. Departments generally refused to share information, with the result that the centralized regime was unable to influence favorably the communication process among bureaucratic agencies. This problem was compounded by the fact that ministers were sometimes spokesmen, more or less openly, of interest groups (such as the church, the army, the banking sector, or particular industries).

The Cabinet was powerful enough so that no important decision was ever made without its consent, but, within it, power centers could always be identified, either on an institutional basis or on a more personal level. Institutionally, the most important power center was the Ministry of Finance, which controlled the budget, budgetary allocations, and financial policies, the levers of fiscal and monetary policy. Moreover, this ministry had a veto over other departments. The military ministries and those of the interior and foreign affairs were always major forces within the Cabinet. The locus of power was sometimes located in one of the directors general, who was sometimes

---

[21] J. Amodia, *Franco's Political Legacy: From Fascism to Facade Democracy* (London: Allen Lane, 1977).

more important than a minister (this was the case of the director general of the budget and the director general of security at various periods in the regime).

In personal terms, the power of the ministers was often derived from their special relationships with Franco, their prestige within the regime, and their positions in the department. The best examples of this phenomenon are: Serrano Suner (a key figure in the first governments and Franco's brother-in-law), who was minister of the interior and of foreign affairs; Blas Perez, also minister of the interior for more than fifteen years (Suner and Blas Perez were the organizers of the political Social Brigade); Carrero Blanco; and Lopez Rodo. The relationship of Carrero Blanco and Lopez Rodo with the Department of the Presidency of the Government and the gradual entrance of members connected, directly or indirectly, with the Opus Dei, gave great importance to other economic ministries (Commerce and Industry above all). Despite the importance of these personal ties, we should bear in mind that, unlike leaders in other authoritarian systems, Franco never surrounded himself with ministers who were his friends. He avoided giving leadership positions to his companions from the civil war or to his own comrades. And he certainly never attempted—and this was probably one of the most serious historical errors—to use any of the human capital of the defeated side after the civil war, a factor that impeded the reconciliation of the country.

The weekly meetings of the Council of Ministers in the Palace of El Prado (residence of the General), frequently served to ratify Franco's policies. Normally discussions of important matters took place, but often matters of minute detail took most of the time. The occupant of a high post (a director general) in the Ministry of Labor told us in an interview that a meeting with his minister and Franco or a meeting of the Council of Ministers, would be the only occasions for the director to meet his minister. Franco wanted to be kept abreast of labor conflicts in various companies, and he would ask for the smallest details. Because the minister rarely had that kind of detailed information, he found himself obliged to have a meeting with the director general so as to procure all the details.

The ministers had absolute freedom to put forward routine questions or to raise technical matters in the Council of Ministers. If conflicts arose, the most powerful minister or the one who obtained most support usually decided the issue. If this solution was not possible, Franco imposed his will or, alternatively, he left the matter for further study. These conflicts normally arose in two circumstances: when an important political decision was about to be taken, or when there were departmental struggles. The conflicts would often result in a deadlock that Franco would eventually break. Moreover, the government was, in a sense, overloaded since, as is to be expected of a centralized and authoritarian executive, no matter was too small or unimportant not to warrant discussion by the highest executive organ. This could not bode well for efficiency. To solve some of these problems a number of instruments were used, most of which attempted to facilitate coordination among the departments. These instruments included the interministerial commissions, the Commissariat of the Development Plan, and the Commission of Undersecretaries (which remains fully active today and which prepares the agenda of the Council of Ministers and decides on minor matters, though the Council legitimates such measures).

The Ministers of Franco

On the basis of work carried out by Juan Linz, Amando de Miguel, and others, we can affirm that by comparison with previous periods the ministers of Franco display certain peculiarities.[22] In the period known as the Restoration (1874–1923), it was normal for ministers to have links with Parliament. They were orators and election makers. In addition, there was a considerable turnover, with conservative ministers lasting about a year on average and the liberal ones a year and a half. In the dictatorship of General Primo de Rivera (1923–1931) there was an abundance of technocrats and civil servants, but few professional politicians. With the Second Republic (1931–1936) there was a return to the type of minister common during the Restoration, and great importance was given to intellectual and professional groups, even those lacking political experience. During this five-year period (1931–1936), there were more ministers than in the thirty years of Franco's reign. Franco recruited a type of minister who was closer to those of the dictatorship of Primo de Rivera than to those of the Second Republic, and in fact ministers who had served under the Primo de Rivera dictatorship were reappointed under Franco. The ministers of the Second Republic represented the different Spanish regions; those of Franco were recruited in Old Castille, in the Basque

---

[22] Juan Linz, "Spanish Cabinet and Parliamentary Elites: From the Restauracion (1874) to Franco (1970)," mimeo; Amando de Miguel, *Sociologia del Franquismo* (Barcelona: Euros, 1975); P. H. Lewis, "The Spanish Ministerial Elite, 1938-1969," *Comparative Politics*, vol. 5, no. 1 (October 1972), pp. 83-106; and Equipo Mundo, *Los Noventa Ministros de Franco* (Barcelona: Dopesa, 1970), see the epilogue by Amando de Miguel; also M. Baena, "Los ministros burocratas," *ICE*, no. 522 (1977).

country, and in Navarra and, above all, in Madrid. It has been a constant feature in contemporary Spanish history that there has been a high proportion of lawyers and civil servants in ministerial posts.

The novel features of Franco's Cabinets were the accentuation of this trend and the greater place given to military men, financiers, and businessmen. An analysis of the composition of the Cabinets from 1938 to 1975 shows, to a certain extent, the changes in the composition of the social forces that controlled or supported the regime. From 1938 to 1957 military men predominated (military experts occupied positions of economic and political leadership). After 1957 only two military men occupied civil ministries, and the technocrats progressively displaced the Falangists and the Catholics. Since 1973 no military man has appeared in a civil department. (In the present Suarez government, for the first time since 1936, a civilian is minister of defense.) Of the 112 ministers between 1938 and 1974, 62 held office for less than five years, 35 held office for between five and ten years, and 17 ministers remained for more than ten years.

The ministers in civil departments used different channels for arriving at their positions, channels that reflect the heterogeneity of this group. The political career of the ministers did not require a specialized apprenticeship, but rather the occupation of a number of different posts. Of the eighty-five ministers in civil ministries, twenty-seven had previously been under secretaries, thirty-four were directors general, thirty-six had previously occupied high posts in autonomous branches of the central administration, twelve were ambassadors, and thirteen occupied high advisory posts. This is to say that those who took part in the government during the Franco era belonged to a political class to which they returned after their stint in the government. Ministers generally found that, as political parties or democratic life did not exist, the bureaucracy and the private sector were the only fields in which they could make themselves noticed. All ministers are ex-officio members of Parliament (procuradores de las Cortes), but practically half of Franco's ministers were procuradores after leaving the Cabinet. The great majority of these ministers-procuradores belonged to the group designated directly by the Head of State. Around 40 percent of the ministerial elite had connections with large public and private companies (there is a complex situation in which managers of both sectors are in a position of interchangeability). Almost 80 percent of Franco's ministers were recruited from the bureaucracy and of these, the great majority came from the corps of the super elite (the Spanish equivalent of the Grand Corps in France) with an absolute dominance of university professors and state lawyers.

TABLE 7–1

RECRUITMENT OF THE SPANISH MINISTERS FROM DIFFERENT PROFESSIONS
AND ADMINISTRATIVE CORPS, 1938–1975

Occupation/Corps	Number	Percentage
Military	34	30
Civil servants		
Univ. professors	12	11
Diplomats	6	5
Engineers	14	13
Judges & notaries	5	4
State lawyers & finance insp.		
(Finance Ministry Corps)	14	13
Jurist of the State Council	4	4
Total civil servants	55	50
Non-civil servants		
Lawyers	15	13
Economists	3	3
Total non-civil servants	18	16
Other and not available	5	4
Total	112	100

With the exception of the military, only 18 out of 112 of Franco's ministers were recruited outside of the state bureaucracy and they represented two different backgrounds: 11 were lawyers or economists linked with big business and 7 had studied law and were linked with the Falange and the party bureaucracy. (See table 7–1.)

The importance of the bureaucracy as a recruiting ground for those who occupied positions of political leadership in the Franco regime needs to be explored further because it suggests that the bureaucracy was not merely in the service of the regime, but actually was part of the decision-making apparatus.

The Bureaucracy and Ministerial Leadership

The ministerial departments, whose origin goes back to the Ancien Regime, have a dominant position within the administrative system. They are dissimilar in size and jurisdiction, and the absence of a unified civil service permitted each department to develop its own traditions and practices. Because the jurisdiction of each unit was affected by that of other units, jurisdictional battles are critical aspects of the administrative system. Finally, the corps system and the centralization of the state apparatus make the departmental organization of the Spanish system different from that of most other countries. Each department has a head—the minister—with one or two under secretaries (*subsecretarios*) who take care of administrative and personnel matters for the minister. Sometimes, and this is becoming more and more the case, they behave as vice ministers. Below the under secretaries is the director general, who is responsible for a division or sector within the ministry (each department having at least five or as many as fifteen directors). Within each directorate there are various under-directors general (*subdirector general*) who have as subordinates the chiefs of section (*jefes de sección*). Within the ministry there is also a general technical secretary (*secretario general técnico*) who is in charge of planning for departmental activities, for providing legal counsel, and for coordinating policies with other departments. The role of the technical secretary was very important in the 1960s, but is now declining in favor of the under secretaries.

The posts of director general, under secretary, and technical secretary in the ministries are the highest administrative posts in the central administration below the minister. The approximately 150 people who occupy these posts are, in effect, on the threshold of three sectors: the bureaucracy, the highest level of the political arena, and industry.

The activities of the directors general depend to a large extent on the functions that their ministry performs. Nonetheless, they share some important characteristics: all occupy the same position in the politico-administrative hierarchy, and all play an important role in the decision-making process, as well as enjoying an even greater autonomy in the implementation of decisions. Moreover, in the absence of representative institutions, of political parties, and of a real parliament, this group has been placed in the nerve center of the regime. In their strategic position, they can exert influence not only in long-term planning and projects but also in the day-to-day functioning of the political system. Finally, it should be noted that the homogeneity of this group derives largely from the recruitment of almost all its members from the bureaucracy, and particularly from the Grand Corps (*Cuerpos Especiales*). As such, the directors general are political appointees holding the highest positions in the administrative structure.

Under the Franco regime it was not possible to speak of a political career in the same way that one speaks of such a career in a democratic society. Nonetheless, we attempted to analyze the extent to which each occupational and social category contributed to the Spanish political elite. We were led to expect that in such a regime, membership in the Falange, the trade unions (*sindicatos oficiales*), the military, and the landowning class would be the most decisive categories for entry into the political elite. Our data, however, contradicted this hypothesis. We found that previous service in the central administration was crucial for entry into the political elite. Of the total number of directors, 41 percent had this common background in their careers, 21 percent had been provincial delegates of the central government, and around 20 percent had links with the economy through the banking system, industry, or enterprises of more than 1,000 employees. There was no communication between the local and the national elite, and there was no local channel to the national elite. (Obviously, this does not mean that localities enjoyed autonomy from the central government, since local officials were responsible to Madrid.)

It needs to be noted that this elite simultaneously needed several positions which reproduced at another level Franco's strategy of denying total commitment to any particular group. This means, in effect, that the bureaucratic elite did not, in a real sense, occupy full-time bureaucratic positions. Most of the members of this elite were employed in some other activity. The multiple holding of positions had one important functional advantage: it facilitated communication in the highly compartmentalized bureaucratic system.

The recruitment into the political elite, as well as the byproduct of communication within the bureaucracy, depended to a considerable extent on the existence of the Grand Corps within the politico-administrative system. A corps has been defined as units that "group civil servants who have a homogeneous professional specialization, who are recruited through a common procedure and who are trained to occupy, during the course of their career, a number of positions that are related to the preparation that was required of them for entry into the corps."[23] A corps remains united by the common interests—economic, professional, status—which its members share.[24] The members enter into the service of a particular corps, and not into the service of the administration as a whole. Consequently, their loyalty always remains first and foremost to their corps. Nor should we

---

[23] Oliva de Castro and A. Gutierrez Renon, "Los Cuerpos de Functionarios" in *Sociologia de la Administracion Publica Española* (Madrid: Centro de Estudios Sociales, 1968). A penetrating work is M. Beltran Villalba, *La Elite Burocratica Española* (Madrid: Ariel, 1977).

[24] For the similarities that the Spanish corps share with their French counterparts, see Ezra N. Suleiman, *Politics, Power and Bureaucracy in France* (Princeton: Princeton University Press, 1974), chap. 10, and his *Elites in French Society: The Politics of Survival* (Princeton: Princeton University Press, 1978).

underestimate the fact that the corps have remarkable powers of cooperation, as well as privileged access to top positions in the state apparatus and in the private sector. Furthermore, the members of the Grand Corps benefit financially from their positions because, in addition to the salaries of their members, they also charge for services rendered (a charge that is known as *tasas y exacciones para-fiscales*). As a consequence, the exact salaries of the members of these corps are unknown.[25]

What are the main elements of the Spanish Grand Corps? First, the corps are self-governing bodies and have total control over the recruitment of newcomers. Each corps has a leader whose task is to fight for the interests of the corps as a whole. Second, in the absence of competitive political structures, of free expression of political opinions, and of adequate channels of participation, these corps work as singular pressure groups from within the state, frequently by occupying political positions. Third, the political and administrative roles of the corps overlap and their participation in politics and in the policy-making processes exceed the limits of those distinctions made by Chapman while speaking about the civil servant: "Politics mean much more than the maneuvering of parties and their relations with particular clienteles. It is not possible forever to evade questions about the right kind of society, the purposes of the state, the basis and justification of government business. The determination of ends, the choice of means, the balance of social forces, are the stuff of politics. In these terms it is clear that some civil servants are engaged in politics. The word 'policy' is a recognition of this, it is a way of describing ends, choosing means and fixing priorities . . . 'policy' is then nothing more than the political activity of civil servants."[26]

Fourth, the principle of "leave of absence" (*détachement*) plays an important role. The members of the corps are detached from their "administrative" functions so as to be employed in political positions. Frequently, they remain permanently on leave "in the service of the state" (the corps acts as if it often lends personnel to the state), but stay linked with their corps so as to share in the additional incomes that the corps distributes periodically to its members. Being on leave is what gives the members of the corps their policy-making powers. For example, the corps of the state lawyers

---

25 A. Nieto, *La Retribucion de los Funcionarios en España. Historia y Actualidad* (Madrid: Revista de Occidente, 1967). With the hope of Rodo's reforms, the "tasas" were budgeted.

26 B. Chapman, *The Profession of Government* (London: Humanities, 1959), pp. 274-75.

has approximately 200 members, yet it has produced 15 ministers and 49 directors, as well as directors of public enterprises, banks, and holders of other local and national political offices. Over half of the members of this corps have been on leave permanently. As a member of this corps, who was also a director general, put it: "My political activity was closely associated with my professional formation and, putting aside previous activities, my vocation was decided the day I entered the Corps of the Abogados del Estado [state lawyers]. Entry into the corps presupposes, I apologize for the lack of modesty, a talent, a sense of responsibility, an objectivity and dedication—all these are very important aspects of a political career—and finally, it is also important that our political leaves of absence never raise questions in the minds of the people who make these decisions because returning to the corps is a guarantee."[27]

Fifth, the ubiquity of the corps within the state apparatus shows a kind of incongruity between the specialization of the members of each corps and the departments that they control. It also violates the organic links between a corps and a department by the practice that leads a corps to "colonize" other departments. Thus, the corps of state lawyers (which is organically linked to the Finance Ministry and specializes in financial matters) has occupied the following departments at the highest political levels: Interior, Foreign Affairs, Justice, Labor, Commerce, Education, Planning, Health, and others.

Sixth, there not only exists an interministerial mobility for members of the corps, but also a colonization of departments by the corps. Obviously, if a corps has all its members in its organic department, it does not have the potentiality to penetrate other sectors. If it is dispersed through all the departments, it does not have the possibility to control any one. The optimum is expressed by corps that have the control over their own departments *and* various others. Thus, the diplomatic corps has absolute control over Foreign Affairs, and also important sectors of the Information and Commerce Ministries; the state lawyers have a majority in their own department and also in the Interior and Labor Ministries. The corps of civil engineers has control over its department (Public Works) and over Housing; the corps of university professors substantially controls its own departments, and so on. The practice whereby certain positions are reserved for certain groups is now generally accepted.

Seventh, the polyvalency of the Grand Corps has two important consequences: the first is that ministerial decisions on the appoint-

---

[27] Declarations cited by de Miguel in *Sociologia del Franquismo*, p. 108.

ment of directors are influenced by the minister's risk of isolating himself if he recruits from only one corps; second, the extreme compartmentalization of the corps and the ministries can only be overcome by using the corps that has the greatest capacity for penetration. This means that the network of communication and information, as the base for policy-formation, comes to be determined by these corps. Hence, the trap: One needs to have a director who is a member of a polyvalent corps, but this means that there will be no way to overcome that rigid compartmentalization (*compartimientos estancos*) that Ortega y Gasset referred to in his *Inveterate Spain*.

Briefly, then, we can summarize our findings about the Spanish bureaucratic elite that has played so important a role in the Franco regime by noting the following: (a) about 57 percent of the directors general from 1938 to the present day came from these corps; (b) their tenure as directors has been longer than that of any other group; (c) the extent of their penetration of state activity has been, without a doubt, the biggest by any comparison; (d) through the thirty-six years of the Franco regime this has been the most permanent group; (e) the progressive demilitarization of the regime and the lack of strength of the fascists and ideologues of the early phase, allowed a hegemonic role to be played by the Grand Corps; and (f) the closed nature of this elite accounts in large part for its durability. The proportion of those who remained in the same position or moved to the position of under secretary or minister rose from 50 percent in 1938 to 82.7 percent in 1973.

We can generalize from the characteristics of the directors general as distinctive elements of the Spanish political pattern of leadership during Franco's period. We see the following: demilitarization under Franco implied a growing authoritarian bureaucratic system, in which a corporatist structure of control and interest representation, a general apathy toward politics, and a tendency toward political repression made possible a kind of arbitrary politics. This arbitrary politics did not require the mechanisms of phony elections, of an engineered democracy, or of the cooptation of the dissidents. In this vacuum, the elite, without national constituencies, became more and more isolated from the country and continued to practice self-recruitment in order to ensure its future. Politics in Franco's regime became largely bureaucratic politics. The absence of political parties and intermediate institutions meant that politics was largely played inside the bureaucracy.

Paradoxically, this closed bureaucracy was not a monolithic structure. It would be simplistic to conclude that the bureaucracy was a ruling class or that it expressed a deep unity. It did nothing of the kind because it had a stratification system and internal divisions, which implied the absence of common purposes and posed serious obstacles to a homogeneous policy-making process.

The Death of the Franco Regime

The Franco regime mixed nonconsensual bureaucratics and military power with a personal leadership that was at first charismatic and then bureaucratic. Despite the seeming pyramidal structure of the executive, Franco's concern with a limited number of policy areas (especially public order, foreign affairs, and constitutional issues) left considerable room for ministers and senior civil servants to play important political roles. The diffusion of executive responsibilities within the executive branch explains the complexities of the relationships among different parts of the executive branch in different phases of the regime. Each stratum within the executive branch could be particularly powerful within the framework established by their hierarchical superior. Thus, ministers could decide what they wished in areas that Franco conceded to them. In turn, directors general could enjoy considerable freedom of action in areas that their ministers chose not to be concerned with.

Franco's relationship with his ministers was never a particularly close one. He considered them concerned with sectional interests. The directors general related only to their ministers and never to Franco. In the early phase of the regime, the bureaucracy (including its upper reaches) was wholly subordinate to political power. In the aftermath of the civil war the elite corps contributed to the functioning of the state machinery, for which they were later rewarded. Toward the late 1950s, when the political class had renewed itself, a new situation came into being: The bureaucracy was now a partner in power and not merely an obedient organ of the regime. The basis for legitimation was no longer the civil war. The regime's concern with efficiency and with technological and economic change added further to the corps' importance. Nieto's argument that corps members were no more than politicians in disguise is basically correct.[28] They came to enjoy political power without having to be branded as politicians.

The Carrero Blanco assassination is certainly one of the events that signaled the end of Francoism. Blanco embodied the political

---

[28] A. Nieto, "De la Republica a la Democracia: La Administracion española del Franquismo," three articles published in *Civitas* (Oct.-Dec. 1976, Oct.-Dec. 1977, and July 1978).

continuity of the orthodox line, and the Organic Law had been elaborated with his own career in mind. The first Arias Navarro government (1974–1975) was an ambiguous and weak attempt at political reformism (which included pseudoparticipation in contrast to the irrevocable adhesion of the old days, as well as licensed political associations within the movement, and to some extent liberalization of the mass media). The challenges to the "reform from above" evidenced by social unrest and political terrorism pushed Arias Navarro to more intolerant Francoist policies. After Franco's death in November 1975, the political opposition became integrated, social conflict was exacerbated, and the economic situation became critical. Juan Carlos, as King of Spain, asked Arias Navarro to leave the government and Adolfo Suarez became President with the mandate to put into effect new democratic policies. The new government faced two models, both of which derived from the previous authoritarian rule: the rupture model (as in the Portuguese case) with a provisional government and political purges against the old political class, or the reformist model (the one that Arias Navarro attempted). Suarez arrived at a solution that rightists called *pacted reform* and leftists called *pacted rupture*.

In fact the instrument used was the Law for Political Reform, which called for free elections whose goal was to elect a legislative body in charge of writing a new constitution. While respecting the letter of Francoist legality, the elections represented an attempt to break the legal structure of the Franco regime. The political forces of Francoism were defeated in the elections. The UCD (Unión de Centro Democrático) as the governing party did not get a clear majority, and, for this reason, the leadership model that Suarez has had to follow has involved a complex network of agreements and consensual politics on both sides of the political spectrum. This kind of consensual politics (interpreted by some political scientists as the application of the consociational theory of democracy à la Lijphart) was used in the socioeconomic agreements with the opposition parties known as the Pactos de la Moncloa (after the name of the presidential palace), in the resolution of political issues in the constitution-making process (where agreements were reached outside the parliament and that body became more a kind of ratification chamber), in the statutes for Catalonia and the Basque country, and even in the nomination of members for the Constitutional Court.

Democratic consent, genuine representation, and popular sovereignty become the elements of the new legitimacy. The Constitution of 1978 has established the principles of Western democracies and has made detailed provisions for executive power (see titles II and IV). The King—who has been the motor for the political transition—has the power to "arbitrate," that is, to guarantee the working of the institutions, while the government directs domestic and foreign policy, manages civil and military administration, and ensures the defense of the state.

In this structure the President enjoys a very important position, shaping a structure that is clearly Presidentialist and where, in practical terms, the *Führerprinzip* is being applied. This strong Presidential structure can be founded, for example, in the confidence vote established in the constitution, whereby the President can obtain from the Congress of Deputies a vote of confidence without even making public the composition of the Cabinet.

Although Franco may have disappeared from the collective memory of the Spanish people, we do not as yet have sufficient perspective to decipher, even with the new constitution, the relationship between the leadership patterns of today and those of Franco's legacy. It does appear, however, that ministers today enjoy less leeway than in the old days. Suarez has placed himself above his ministers, and he tries to maintain a clear separation among, on the one side, his close political friends and staff with whom he reaches his political decisions, and, on the other side, the administrators or heads of departments. In some respects, therefore, the organization of the executive in the post-Franco era has tended to move toward a greater centralization, though it will be necessary to see how certain measures now being considered—such as the bill on the reorganization of the government, the administration, and the civil service—get implemented and how they will affect the decision-making process. Also, time will give a clearer picture of the relationship between the central government and the regional authorities.

8

Government against Sub-governments

A European Perspective on Washington

Richard Rose

"We must all hang together, or assuredly, we shall all hang separately."

Benjamin Franklin, at Philadelphia, 4 July 1776

Politics is about the representation of conflicting demands; government is about resolving these conflicts authoritatively and to a nation's benefit. In principle, the two activities should be complementary. In practice, politics and government can be in opposition, for what people want or what interest groups demand may not be what government can (or should) provide. A government must be responsive to popular demands to maintain political consent. Yet a government must also make decisions that are unpopular yet necessary to maintain its collective authority.

NOTE: This was written while the author was a visiting scholar at the American Enterprise Institute, Washington, D.C., for the first three months of 1980, a particularly stimulating time to be in a stimulating environment. Useful comments and criticisms on the ideas expressed herein were received from Bruce Adams, Dom Bonafede, Colin Campbell, I. M. Destler, Leon Epstein, Hugh Heclo, Tom Mann, B. Guy Peters, Michael Pitfield, Austin Ranney, James A. Reichler, Bert A. Rockman, Harold Seidman, Lester Seligman, James L. Sundquist, Peter Szanton, and Aaron Wildavsky. The author also benefited from discussing ideas at seminars of the Kennedy School for Government at Harvard; at a conference on the Institutionalized Presidency jointly organized by the National Academy of Public Administration and the White Burkett Miller Center at the University of Virginia; and at a joint seminar of the American Enterprise Institute and the Brookings Institution on Giving Direction to Government, organized with considerable efficiency and energy by Bradley H. Patterson, Jr. None of the above named is responsible for what the author has argued herein.

In view of the particular thrust of the chapter, it should be emphasized that the author writes from the perspective of a Truman Democrat, albeit a native Missourian who has "come a long way from St. Louis" since commencing the study of comparative politics by sailing to England in 1953, and has crossed the Atlantic many times since to study governments on opposite sides of the Atlantic.

The fundamental question facing governments on both sides of the Atlantic today is: How to combine the best of politics and government? Only if this is done can a government be open and responsive to voices demanding particular and sometimes conflicting policies, yet simultaneously have sufficient collective authority to make those big and often hard decisions that sacrifice particular concerns to a collective interest.

Nations differ substantially in how they meet the common challenge of giving direction to government. The foregoing chapters have provided ample evidence of differences among European governments, as well as major differences between the United States and European governments. The direction of government in Franco Spain and Italy differs notably from Britain and Norway. On the great circle tour of governments, Canada stands between the United States and Europe politically, combining American-style fragmentation by federalism of government functions and parties with a British form of Cabinet government.

Big differences can also be found in the way in which the same country governs itself at different times. The directing institutions of the Fifth Republic in France were a conscious reaction against the experience of the Fourth French Republic. The 1949 Constitution of the Federal Republic of Germany was even more a conscious reaction against the faith placed disastrously in leadership (the *Führerprinzip*) in Hitler's Third Reich.

Because the United States has the oldest continuous Constitution of any country examined in this book, the practical extent of change in governance is outstanding. The institutions of government found in Washington, D.C., today operate very differently from the political system that the Founding Fathers left as their heritage at Philadelphia. If scholars of American party politics can point to at least four different party systems, even more different constitutional "systems" have existed in America since 1789. The balance as well as the scope of government have changed greatly in two centuries. The character and problems of American government today more clearly resemble those of contemporary European countries than they do the United States of 200 or 100 years ago.

Within the past two decades we have altered substantially our appreciation of how and how well America is governed. Concern about "overloaded" government is common to all Western nations and the mixed economy welfare states of Western Europe have relatively greater fiscal burdens to carry than the United States.[1] America has also had unique problems. The Vietnam conflict and Watergate led to a dramatic fall in popular trust in public figures in America, extending well beyond popular disillusionment with Presidents Johnson and Nixon. Equally important, it led to changes in political parties, in Congress, and in the Presidency, each intended to strengthen popular demands against what was perceived as excessive presidential authority.

Changes in world politics have fundamentally altered America's role in world affairs. In July 1979, the President of the United States publicly proclaimed a "national malaise,"[2] while in many European countries, signs of material progress have been matched by a rebirth of political self-confidence. In economic as well as military terms, the United States can no longer consider itself the world's dominant nation. America's government must now compete with many nations that are neither remote nor are they necessarily allies. Involvement in world affairs, combined with relatively diminishing power, makes America increasingly vulnerable to events abroad. Cumulatively, these changes support the description of Washington today as the capital of *The New American Political System*.[3] The basic political question facing America today is not whether the world is changing, but *how* is it changing?

It is inverted snobbery to claim that the United States is worse governed than any other nation, just as it is chauvinistic to claim that the United States must be the best governed country in the world. The purpose of comparison here is positive, not invidious: to use examples from European experience as an empirical means of evaluating America's government today. The first object of this chapter is

---

[1] For a variety of European views of "overloaded" government, see Richard Rose, ed., *Challenge to Governance* (Beverly Hills: Sage Publications, 1980). On the causes and consequences of economic difficulties in major Western nations, see Richard Rose and B. Guy Peters, *Can Government Go Bankrupt?* (New York: Basic Books, 1978). For carefully argued discussions of America's distinctive difficulties, see, for example, James L. Sundquist, "The Crisis of Competence in Government," *Setting National Priorities: Agenda for the 1980s*, ed. Joseph A. Pechman (Washington, D.C.: The Brookings Institution, 1980), pp. 531-63; and Richard E. Neustadt, "Problems and Prospects for Presidential Leadership: Looking toward the 1980s," duplicated (Kennedy School of Government, Harvard University, 1979).

[2] Cf. President Carter's speech of July 15, 1979, in *Weekly Compilation of Presidential Documents*, vol. 15, no. 29 (Washington, D.C.: Government Printing Office, July 23, 1979), pp. 1235-1241; and two articles on "Crisis of Confidence" by Patrick H. Caddell and Warren E. Miller, *Public Opinion*, vol. 2, no. 5 (October/November 1979), pp. 2-16, 52-60.

[3] The title of a book edited by Anthony King (Washington, D.C.: American Enterprise Institute, 1978).

to compare how the United States and European governments give direction to government. The second object is to "size up" the many different policies of government in order to evaluate the relative advantages and disadvantages of contrasting approaches to making public policies. Attention is then turned to two major contemporary weaknesses in the direction of American government—the decline of party and the institutionalization of distrust. There is no intention to argue that the United States adopt European political institutions wholesale in some grand but misguided attempt to strengthen government by foreign imports. The evidence shows that there is no need to do so. Government can be improved if Americans are ready to move back (or forward) to practices that were normal in Washington until the upheaval of events in the 1970s that altered the unstable distribution of political power in Washington.

Since the questions raised in the following pages are political questions, the answers are rightfully matters of dispute. Analysis cannot by itself determine prescription. Those who wish a weak government will praise everything in the American Constitution (and any appropriate European example) that prevents the expansion of government's activities. Conversely, proponents of active government are likely to look favorably at European institutions that sustain big government. While analysis cannot substitute for political values, it can instruct political values and actions. A fuller understanding of how other countries are governed can also lead to a more sophisticated appreciation of the strengths of the American system, as well as a sharpened awareness of its shortcomings in the potentially more hostile world of today.

Different Ways of Directing Government

The role of a President differs radically according to the nature of the political system. A President's powers can approach those of an Imperial ruler only in an autocracy, that is, a system that so values the authority of government that it suppresses the representation of particular interests by competing political parties and pressure groups. By contrast, a President is almost a bystander in a system of government that so values the representation of particular demands that it provides hardly any institutions to make collective decisions. Where the institutions of government are so subdivided that few issues can be resolved in any one place, there is little central direction that a President can provide, and few central decisions can be made. Writings about the American Presidency are often flawed because authors concentrate upon the President as if he were endowed with the primary powers of government.

Contemporary European and American political systems have contrasting histories. European governments have evolved in political cultures that emphasize a unitary corporate will, whether it be known as the Crown in England, the State in France, or the Nation in Germany, Italy, or Norway. An *étatiste* tradition offers values justifying a government strong enough in its collective authority to make collective decisions. But this tradition has also justified the suppression of politics, that is, the legitimate articulation of popular demands. Of the six European countries examined here, only two—Norway and Britain—have enjoyed uninterrupted representative government since before World War II.

America began as a "governmentless" agglomeration of peoples. There was politics aplenty among the scattered colonies that nominally owed allegiance to one or another Crown and effectively gave allegiance to none. Politics as the articulation of demands against government was carried to the extreme in the American Revolution. But it left the ex-colonists with the need to establish some sort of government to provide collectively for their needs. The Articles of Confederation adopted in 1781 were based on the superiority of the thirteen separate states. The articles made no provision for an executive branch, or even a central authority. The system was found to be too weak, even by indigenous standards, and the Constitution went into force. But the tradition of putting politics before government remains strong today.

The evolution of government in Europe involved the fostering of politics, that is, allowing people to make political demands through competing parties and pressure groups. Making the authority of government responsive to popular demands began in the seventeenth century in England and a century later on the continent of Europe with the French Revolution. Resting government on popular consent as well as authority took centuries to secure. In Germany, Italy, and Spain contemporary institutions of representative government have only been developed since World War II.

By contrast, the great challenge in America has been to create effective government. The Civil War showed that by 1865 there was sufficient collective authority to enforce government's will against rebellious parties. The century since has been a history of attempts, such as the New Deal, to strengthen government's capacity to reconcile popular demands with collective policies facing the problems of an increasingly threatening world.

In comparative perspective, the American system stands out because it maximizes politics. The institutions of government incorporate the representation of popular demands into the very structure of governance. Politics starts at the grass roots. Electing councillors on a citywide basis—a logical corollary of the idea of a city as a community—may be challenged in the courts as suppressing the rights of ethnic (literally, "national") groups to representation. The referendum can give citizens the power to determine their own taxes or legislation. The institutions of federalism give individual citizens and groups a multiplicity of points of access to government. In Washington, too, the policy process is porous; interest groups unite with groups of congressmen, bureaucrats, and specialist advocates, as well as with state and local government officials, to establish networks to advance particular interests.

American politics has produced a system with many sub-governments.[4] For example, one study of local government in the greater New York area was called *1400 Governments*,[5] to emphasize the subdivision of legal authority in one limited metropolitan area. But 1,400, 14,000, or 140,000 sub-governments do not necessarily add up to one government. The Founding Fathers described the American system of governance as a system of checks and balances. The checks are easy to see: the opposition of Congress and the President; the independent powers of the courts; Washington's need to cooperate with states in the federal system; the prohibitions of government activity contained in the Bill of Rights. These checks subdivide political authority and sub-governments flourish.

The balances are more difficult to discern. Nowhere is there a single institution to declare the will of the government as a whole. If any institution can claim this status, it is the Presidency, for only the President is elected by the nation as a whole. But neither Congress nor history justify such a claim. The Madisonian model of government is a system of institutionalized checks: the balance is meant to result from these checks harmonizing in a more or less coherent whole.

Any critical review of modern European history is likely to draw at least one negative lesson: Beware the pretensions of governments

---

[4] The term "sub-governments" as a description for a well-established Washington phenomenon was given currency by Douglass Cater, *Power in Washington* (New York: Random House, 1964). For a contemporary modification and restatement, see Hugh Heclo, "Issue Networks and the Executive Establishment," in *New American Political System*, ed. King, pp. 87-124.

[5] Robert C. Wood with Vladimir V. Almendinger, *1400 Governments: the Political Economy of the New York Region* (Cambridge, Mass.: Harvard University Press, 1961).

claiming unlimited authority. This is true whether the government is dressed in the Imperial trappings of a divinely anointed autocrat or in the pseudodemocratic trappings of a mass mobilization totalitarian state. The hundreds of millions who have experienced the excesses of such governments are the first to praise the politics of popular representation and consent.

What, if any, is the major negative lesson to be drawn from the evolution of American government? To suggest that representative political institutions are too strong risks discrediting democracy by discrediting the people. The alternative is to suggest that *collective political authority is too weak*. This view has been enunciated by almost every modern study of the Presidency. For example, President Johnson's Task Force on Government Organization under Ben Heineman described the executive branch as an ill-designed feudal regime, "a collection of fragmented bureau fiefdoms unable to co-ordinate with themselves intelligently."[6] A 1975 Trilateral Commission report questioned whether American government today allows the President the necessary authority to act in the national defense.[7] From a very different political perspective, a socialist can argue that the multiplicity of particularistic institutions hobbles effective government action on behalf of the majority of Americans.[8]

The challenge to both American and European governments today is how to combine the politics of representation with the authority of government. In practice, all of these countries practice some form of "mixed" government. But the mixture is not the same on opposite sides of the Atlantic.

Fusing Government and Politics: The Cabinet System. The central mechanism in European governments is collective, not singular; it is the Cabinet. A Prime Minister is first among equals in the Cabinet. But it is the Cabinet, not the Prime Minister that is responsible collectively for the activities of government.[9] A European Cabinet,

---

[6] Quoted from the unpublished 1967 report of the Heineman Task Force on Government Organization in Richard Rose, *Managing Presidential Objectives* (New York: Free Press, 1976), p. 145.

[7] Conveniently available in Samuel P. Huntington, "The Democratic Distemper," *Public Interest*, no. 41 (Fall 1975), pp. 9-38.

[8] L. J. Sharpe, "American Democracy Reconsidered," *British Journal of Political Science*, vol. 3, nos. 1-2 (January, April 1973), pp. 1-28, 129-67.

[9] The reader should note that the discussion of the Cabinet system concentrates attention upon an ideal-type system in order to bring out clearly the fundamental difference between nearly every European nation and the government of the United States. The first seven chapters of this book provide ample evidence of particular national variations around this ideal type.

like its American counterpart, consists of the heads of the principal government departments: foreign affairs, finance, justice, defense, commerce, labor, and so forth. Because the range of activities of European mixed economy welfare states is usually larger and longer established than in the United States, it might be expected that departmentally based sub-governments would be a greater obstacle to collective authority than in the United States. But this is not the case, for Cabinet members act on very different terms than their Washington counterparts.[10]

A Cabinet does not govern by meeting together for endless discussion. Its authority is demonstrated by the behavior of politicians acting as individual ministers. Most hold their Cabinet position by virtue of directing a major ministry (that is, a department of government). If a Cabinet minister wants to do something, it is normally done through his ministry, for within his ministry an individual minister is politically supreme. The Cabinet is important because it gives the minister his authority to direct departmental affairs. A politician placed in charge of a ministry, major or minor, has considerable scope for making decisions within the ministry's defined area of responsibilities and for carrying out policies supported by the Cabinet collectively. Moreover, a minister has at hand a cadre of senior civil servants who are not only experienced in looking after the machinery of government, but also very experienced in dealing with pressure groups.

Politics, that is, the articulation of political demands, is first of all a matter of winning a minister's ear. Pressure groups wish to press where the power to take effective action is, and in Europe they normally head for the ministries. Political demands are not suppressed, but channeled to those with executive responsibility for action. When major issues affect several ministries, such as unemployment, the access points for political demands are greatly increased. By contrast with executive branch officials in Washington, a European minister deals with pressure groups without intimidation by a legislature with the powers of Congress; without supervision by courts with the power and activist inclinations of the United States Supreme Court; and usually without the constraints of federalism as well.

In a Cabinet system, pressure groups are neither ignored nor are their wishes necessarily frustrated. Ministers are politicians who wish

---

[10] That is, the separation of legislative and executive powers in Washington and the separate election of the President precludes the creation of a Cabinet that can effectively dominate both institutions. That is why the President's Cabinet has only a nominal existence. Federalism intensifies but does not cause the domination of sub-governments in America.

to be popular and, partisan values aside, they would rather say yes than no to a claimant group. Moreover, on both sides of the Atlantic, civil servants know that it is much easier to administer policies if, within limits, they are adapted to meet the particular concerns of affected groups. Cabinet government is consistent with pressure groups representing business and labor engaging in continuous consultations with a host of ministries. Social welfare ministries too attract a host of pressure groups. Although members of Parliament individually have much less influence than do congressmen, they too can be vocal advocates of particular policies. In short, Cabinet government incorporates many sub-governments.

But on any given issue, Cabinet government provides a strong political counterweight to the particularistic demands of pressure groups. A minister can terminate negotiations with a pressure group if the measures it advocates are inconsistent with the policy of the Cabinet. Whenever money is involved, a minister must defer to a Cabinet colleague (the budget minister) for spending authority. If a minister misinterprets the broad lines of Cabinet policy in dealing with a pressure group, the Cabinet may refuse to sanction the agreement. Individual Cabinet ministers thus have a positive incentive to take a broader view of policies than do pressure groups. The pattern of Cabinet policy establishes guidelines for what is and is not acceptable action by individual ministers. To be sure of retaining the backing of the Cabinet, a minister must stay within guidelines applying to government as a whole.

In Europe as in America, conflicting demands are put forward by different departments. In the modern mixed economy welfare state, particular ministries are likely to become spokesmen for groups that are their prime responsibility, for example, a labor ministry speaking for organized trade unions; an industry ministry speaking for business; agriculture for farmers; and so forth. In a European coalition government, particular ministries may be awarded to coalition partners because of the specific interests they represent, for example, a socialist party awarded the labor ministry and a religious or anticlerical party assigned the ministry of education. The ministries of government institutionalize political conflict in Europe as in Washington.

Where the Cabinet system differs from the American system is in having a single collective authority to reconcile disparate political demands. Cabinet deliberations bring politics into the center of government. Ministry is set against ministry, interest group against interest group, and the ambitions of individual politicians are also at war with each other. Political temperatures rise with the importance of the issue. The authority of Cabinet does not eliminate politics; instead, the *Cabinet permits the fusion of government and politics.*

A common bond of collective political interest is the force that gives a Cabinet the effective authority to make binding decisions reconciling diverse political demands. Party is the central force behind Cabinet government. Cabinet members represent the majority party or parties in Parliament. Because of a strong bond of party loyalty uniting politicians in the legislature and the executive, the Cabinet can be confident that Parliament will endorse its actions. Moreover, the doctrine of the collective responsibility of Cabinet requires that every politician in Cabinet accept a decision and not criticize it publicly. Any minister who does not wish to do so is expected to resign from Cabinet, thus jeopardizing his future political career.

Where there are departures from this "ideal type" model of Cabinet government, the results are a restriction of government's authority. Federalism imposes one restriction upon the authority of Cabinet. In federal systems, a Cabinet must take into account the powers of other tiers of government. This results in significant differences in government between the federal systems of Canada and Germany and such unitary states as Britain and France. Where divisions within the electorate deny one party a majority of seats in Parliament, a Cabinet is restricted by the bargains necessary to maintain support by a coalition of parties. Even where single-party majority government is the rule, there are often differences of opinion within a governing party. Cabinet government permits the representation of different factions in a Cabinet, and ministers with differing outlooks must moderate their differences to maintain the Cabinet's collective authority. Italy is an extreme example of this.

The distinctive feature of Cabinet government is that all of the participants in a debate are bound politically to collective decisions. The strongest phrase is not the expression of the volition of an individual politician, but rather a collective statement: The Cabinet has decided. A Cabinet decision can be voiced in the language of command, for all ministers and civil servants are bound to accept the collective decision or resign. A Cabinet decision will always be argued as well as arguable. In retrospect, it may even turn out not to have been the best decision. But the government of the day can and does produce policies that collectively commit the whole authority of government. *In the Cabinet system, there is a government as well as sub-governments.*

The Domination of Sub-governments: The American System. American government is organized, but not in a way that is easily amenable to description, let alone direction. There is no single locus of authority, contrary to the views of authors of classic treatises on sovereignty or modern-day television image makers. Nor is there a clear hierarchical relationship between the different parts of American government, as in a business school organization chart. Nor, for that matter, is there a stable pattern of power that can be illustrated in a textbook diagram. The fundamental fact of American government is that political power is divided among many dozens of sub-governments in Washington, whose tentacles extend throughout the federal system. The parts are greater than the whole.

Where sub-governments dominate, there can be no expression of the collective will of government. Major policies are likely to emerge gradually as the unintended byproduct of many separate decisions taken by interested parties comprising different sub-governments. Congress is the foundation for the politics of sub-governments. The specific institutions comprising sub-governments differ from issue to issue. For any given issue, they will normally include officials from bureaus within the executive branch; congressmen and staff from committees or sub-committees on Capitol Hill; pressure groups, including relevant representatives of state and local government and public employees; and more or less free-floating policy professionals—academics, consultants, journalists, and articulate spokesmen for single issues. Although sub-governments are not recognized in the Constitution, they constitute recognizable issue networks. Hugh Heclo argues that they are increasing in scale, controversy, and political significance, while simultaneously becoming more remote from direction by the one representative of collective authority in Washington, the President.[11]

Upon entering office, an American President faces a very different problem from a European counterpart. In the Cabinet system, a Prime Minister's problem is how to give direction to a government that is *already* there, that is, organized and capable of collective action. In America, by contrast, there is no collective authority ready at hand for the President's use. "The members of the Cabinet," in the words of former Vice President Charles G. Dawes, "are a President's natural enemies,"[12] because of their tendency to become a part of a sub-

---

[11] Heclo, "Issue Networks and the Executive Establishment."

[12] Quoted by Richard E. Neustadt, *Presidential Power: The Politics of Leadership from FDR to Carter*, 3d ed. (New York: John Wiley & Sons, 1980), p. 31. All subsequent citations to this volume are to the 1980 edition.

government network. Even if a President succeeds in tying particular Cabinet appointees close to him, they may lose effectiveness by losing their standing in a sub-government. The President's lonely eminence may make him a symbol of American government, but in a practical sense, he is far less a corporeal symbol of government than the Queen of England. The American political system is a *multi*-government system rather than a single collective institution. A President is required to create government, that is, to discover how to use powers and institutions at hand in ways that increase his collective authority, while falling short of that inherited by politicians in a Cabinet system.

The making of the budget is a classic illustration of the fundamental difference between policy making in a Cabinet system and in the United States. In Europe, the budget is decided by Cabinet ministers. The Cabinet is the arena in which spending ministers press sub-government claims against the government's minister of finance in months of bargaining between conflicting ministries. Up to this point, the process resembles what happens between the President's Office of Management and Budget and operating agencies of the executive branch. The difference is that once a European Cabinet resolves these disputes, legislative approval is almost certain, because of the Cabinet's collective authority. By contrast, the President's budget is no more than a set of recommendations to Congress. Within Congress, different committees then scrutinize particular recommendations according to criteria of different sub-governments. The budget of the United States is not what the President recommends, but what Congress enacts. And what Congress enacts is not so much what it collectively regards as best for the nation as it is the byproduct of many different decisions by sub-governments.[13]

The strongest phrase in Washington—the President wants this— is usually voiced as an aspiration. The people whom the President can immediately command in the White House do not have their hands on the operating agencies of government. Even those whom the President appoints to direct the major departments of government are only overseers of the bureaus that collectively constitute the principal operating agencies of the executive branch. The President can fire an appointee, but this is itself an admission of failure to gain satisfaction from the person appointed. It is not an augur that he can do any

---

[13] The changes induced by the Congressional Budget Office are interesting in American terms, but do not alter the fundamental trans-Atlantic differences. Cf. Aaron Wildavsky, *The Politics of the Budgetary Process*, 3d ed. (Boston: Little, Brown & Co., 1979); and Hugh Heclo and Aaron Wildavsky, *The Private Government of Public Money* (London: Macmillan, 1974).

better with a successor. Moreover, most of the money that the government spends is effectively uncontrollable, fixed by statutory obligations, such as pension payments or interest on the national debt. In domestic policy, the federal government gives almost as much money to state and local governments to administer as it manages itself.[14] In national security affairs, the President's position is relatively stronger as commander-in-chief, but it would be a bad thing if he spent all his time thinking of war.

By any measure, the responsibilities placed upon the President have grown greatly since World War II. But in no sense have the President's capabilities expanded in proportion. Modern technology has created communications systems by which the President, as commander-in-chief, can literally direct a military operation halfway around the globe, but it has not created the means to make an enemy surrender at the sound of the President's voice. The personalizing eye of the television camera brings news from around the world into the living room of nearly every voter, but this is a liability to a President during a controversial war or a scandal such as Watergate. Since the time of President Eisenhower, who presided over government as a noncontroversial head of state, each President has found himself a little less popular on average than his predecessor in opinion poll ratings.[15]

Almost every writer about the contemporary Presidency emphasizes the widening gap between what a President is required or expected to do (what Richard Neutstadt calls his "clerkship" functions) and the resources at hand. Sub-governments fill the gap, dictating what they think ought to be done from the perspective of their own particular interests. At the opening of the 1980 edition of his landmark study, Neustadt points out that Presidential *weakness* is the underlying theme of *Presidential Power*. At the conclusion, he asks: "Is the Presidency possible?"[16]

In the face of increasing difficulties in giving direction to government, Presidents have appointed a number of commissions to review the operations of the federal government in search of ways to make

---

[14] Cf. Frederick C. Mosher, "The Changing Responsibilities and Tactics of the Federal Government" (Conference on the Institutionalized Presidency, the White Burkett Miller Center, University of Virginia, Charlottesville, March 20-21, 1980).
[15] See Hugh Heclo, "Public Expectations and the Presidency," unpublished paper (Washington, D.C.: National Academy of Public Administration Project on the Presidency, 1980), p. 5.
[16] Neustadt, *Presidential Power*, pp. xi, 210 ff., and 241. For a related argument and prescription, see Aaron Wildavsky, "The Past and Future Presidency," *Public Interest*, no. 41 (Fall 1975), pp. 56-76.

it more "manageable." The commissions have sat for years and submitted lengthy reports. Some have emphasized the need for a President to be businesslike and encourage greater efficiency. Others have abandoned the rhetoric of the private sector and spoken of the need for leadership. Predictably, a third prescription is that a President should be both a leader and a manager.[17] None of these prescriptions has been effective. The fundamental point is that American government is not meant to be managed or led by one person. A President can no more manage the whole of government than he could manage a herd of wild horses. The President's task is to lasso what is needed for his purposes and not to attempt the impossible, riding herd over all the sub-governments of Washington.

The United States has a President, as a university has a President. But as Harold Seidman remarks, "Universities may have presidents, but presidents don't have universities."[18] A university has a single figure presiding over it, chairing meetings, and representing it to outside bodies. The structure of a university, however, is designed to prevent its nominal head from influencing what goes on inside it, that is, the work of faculty in specialized departments. Executive branch agencies are analogous to departments within a university in their variety and in their desire for autonomy. The President of the United States has far more political influence than a university president and has levers for acting internationally and sometimes nationally. But the eminence of a President is a lonely eminence. The President does not normally make decisions that determine the direction of government. Instead, he issues statements that are clear or vague according to circumstances; these are only one input to a complex process of bargaining within and among sub-governments.

The President has a hard time getting a handle on government because there is no handle there. There are a multiplicity of sub-governments making particular policies by a process of partisan mutual adjustment. There are few occasions when the President enjoys a monopoly of power in government. What is often described

---

[17] The typology is adapted from Michael McGeary, "Doctrines of Presidential Management," unpublished paper (Washington, D.C.: National Academy of Public Administration, 1979). For a more detailed discussion of attempts to make government more manageable, see Harvey C. Mansfield, "Reorganizing the Federal Executive Branch: the Limits of Institutionalization," *Law and Contemporary Problems*, vol. 25, no. 3 (Summer 1970), pp. 461-95; Richard Rose, *Managing Presidential Objectives*; and Peter Szanton, ed., "Papers on Government Reorganization," unpublished (Washington, D.C.: Administrative Conference of the United States, 1980).

[18] Harold Seidman, *Politics, Position and Power*, 3d ed. (New York: Oxford University Press, 1980), p. 135.

as Presidential influence may be better described as the planned (or fortuitous) conjunction of the interest of the President and the interests of particular groups within or outside government.

In the United States, there is no equivalent to the authority of a Cabinet in Europe. The Supreme Court is the one institution that, under certain limited circumstances, reconciles conflicting political demands and does so with final authority. The Supreme Court can do this because it is the custodian of the Constitution, and the Constitution is the ultimate authority in the Amercian political system. Supreme Court decisions are accepted by politicians and bureaucrats with an authority denied a Presidential request. But because its powers of decision are final, the Court is often cautious when it contemplates a case with major political implications. In the words of one legal scholar, the justices today "follow the normal Washington tactic of letting the issue stew for a while so that there is an opportunity for all to be heard and for the decision maker to absorb what is to be heard. They often make tentative or partial experiments in new areas before going the whole way. . . . When they miscalculate they sometimes retreat a bit."[19] Supreme Court action on race relations, when it ordered fundamental changes "with all deliberate speed," illustrates how the Court can, within fields amenable to judicial action, face up to sub-governments' conflicts and resolve them with binding decisions.

The authority of the Supreme Court is much less than that of a Cabinet, however, because a Cabinet can and must be concerned with the manifold of public policies. By contrast, a court can only be concerned with justiciable issues, which are often procedural rather than substantive. But in most fields of public policy the Supreme Court simply sets very broad constitutional parameters for policy makers. It cannot and does not give positive direction about the major substantive problems facing the country such as the economy, national security, or energy.

Lopsided Government. The essential similarity between American and European governments today is their openness to politics. On both sides of the Atlantic, institutions of contemporary government give great scope for individuals and organized interests to press their particular demands on government. In the United States, the federal system and the powers of Congress institutionalize this openness to an extreme degree. In European countries, even in a state without

---

[19] Martin Shapiro, "The Supreme Court: From Warren to Burger," in *New American Political System*, ed. King, p. 27.

elections such as Franco Spain, interest groups press their demands upon ministries.

Nonetheless, there remains an ocean of difference between the collective authority of a Cabinet and the American political system. The primary contrast is a matter of balance—or the absence of balance. The Cabinet provides collective authority sufficiently strong to reconcile differences among sub-governments. The force of a Cabinet is not that of a dictator; instead, it is the force of government based upon elected politicians with common loyalties and a common need to secure reelection. Conflicting interests can and do state their case in Cabinet. But after that is done, there is a government there, that is, a Cabinet with the political and institutional strength to reconcile differences.

The American system, by contrast, is best described as lopsided, because the power of sub-governments is so great in relation to collective authority. The Supreme Court can make decisions binding upon other branches of government, but its authority is strong only when other branches act unconstitutionally. It is far too simple to dismiss the lopsided strength of sub-governments in the United States as a consequence of the Constitution, and therefore unalterable.

The Constitution fixes major institutions of government, but it does not determine their relationships or the bulk of their activities. The most important changes in modern American politics have occurred independently of constitutional amendments, which since 1920 have been trivial in political significance. Neither the New Deal nor the global political commitments undertaken by the United States after World War II required constitutional amendments. The role of Congress, of political parties, and of the bureaucracy alters without constitutional amendment. At any given time, there is an "unwritten constitution" influencing power in Washington. Like any unwritten document, it is amenable to change.

If the American system is changing, the question follows: How *should* it be changing? For more than a decade, the power of sub-governments has been growing. Without the means of making collective decisions effective, there is no way in which any elected official can reconcile the conflicting views of many competing sub-governments. But trends are not immutable, least of all in institutions as open and responsive as those constituting the unwritten constitution of the United States. The pages that follow consider ways in which the American system could alter in the future. None of the changes considered depends upon constitutional amendment, and none depends upon a few simple devices of institutional engineering. The structure of a nation's politics is not solely a matter of institutions. It is also determined by how well politicians adapt institutions at hand to the problems that confront the country.

Sizing Up Public Policies

Problems of public policy come in many different sizes. A decision about whether to put a stoplight at an intersection or build a community swimming pool is a decision of government, just as is a decision about national wage and price controls or building a neutron bomb. When the impact of public policies differ greatly in size, there is good reason to want different decisions taken by institutions of very different scale. Questions of local traffic or recreation can be decided by a local council or a local referendum, whereas questions of national impact require effective decisions by a national government. Every political system requires the capacity of miniaturization, that is, the ability to make small-scale decisions. Equally, it requires the capacity to mobilize collective authority to make big decisions for the nation as a whole.[20]

A wise nation adapts its political structure to the size of the problem at hand. We do not need to submit all our problems to the collective authority of national government, but neither can we do without the benefits of collective authority. What we need to do is identify under what circumstances different types of government deal best with different types of problems—and then consider whether the American political system is properly sized for major challenges that confront it today.

The Strengths and Limits of Sub-governments. The American system of politics is especially good at dealing with a large number of small-scale decisions. Contrary to the arithmetic logic of democracy as majority rule, the American system can respond quickly and easily to the particular concerns of smaller groups because of the existence of so many sub-governments. The federal system divides substantial governmental powers among thousands of territorial sub-governments,

---

[20] For favorable discussions of disaggregating decisions, see especially C. E. Lindblom, *The Intelligence of Democracy* (New York: Free Press, 1965) and Mancur Olson, Jr., *The Logic of Collective Action* (Cambridge, Mass.: Harvard University Press, 1965). For this writer's views, see Richard Rose, "Coping with Urban Change," in *The Management of Urban Change in Britain and Germany*, ed. R. Rose (Beverly Hills: Sage Publications, 1974), pp. 5-25, and R. Rose, *What is Governing? Purpose and Policy in Washington* (Englewood Cliffs, N.J.: Prentice-Hall, Inc., 1978), p. 125 ff.

with populations of anything from a few hundred to California, with a population larger than all five nations of Scandinavia. The openness of the political system to popular participation is taken advantage of by organized groups as well as individuals. In Washington, the philosophy of giving everybody "a piece of the action" reaches its ultimate expression in the contemporary Congress, where 535 congressmen each try to represent their small fraction of the American people and service the demands of individual interests and voters within their own district.[21]

The strength of sub-governments in America is rooted in the political philosophy of pluralism, a celebration of the variety of American life and a desire to provide institutions that respond to some needs of every group of citizens.[22] Fourth-class cities are created to deal with fourth-class problems, and counties whose boundaries were determined by travel time in a horse and buggy continue to play a significant part in the sub-government of America. To decry the institutional atomization of contemporary American politics is to miss an important point. An atomized political system should be good at making small-scale political decisions. Equally, to decry "majorities of the moment" is to overlook the fact that shifting coalitions enable individuals to satisfy different political demands by combining in different ways.[23] To decry the strength of market forces in American society is to ignore the extent to which mutual adjustment in the marketplace can meet some demands far better than centralized decision making, a proposition that is as true in politics as it is in economics.[24]

The conventional way to resolve the inevitable conflicts between sub-governments is to rely upon political brokers. Brokers are not sources of authority. However, they play a critical role in negotiating agreements between and within the many sub-governments. The primary function of a broker is to secure a majority for some policy, whatever its content. If a leader is defined as a politician who influ-

---

[21] See, for example, Morris P. Fiorina, *Congress: Keystone of the Washington Establishment* (New Haven: Yale University Press, 1977), and Richard Fenno, *Home Style: House Members in Their Districts* (Boston: Little, Brown & Co., 1978).

[22] See, for example, E. Pendleton Herring, Jr., *The Politics of American Democracy* (New York: Rinehart & Co., 1940). Contrast T. J. Lowi, *The End of Liberalism* (New York: W. W. Norton & Co., 1969).

[23] The complaints are voiced by Anthony King in his conclusion to *New American Political System*, pp. 389, 391.

[24] Cf. Lindblom, *Intelligence of Democracy*; Alec Nove, *The Soviet Economic System* (London: Allen and Unwin, 1977), and C. E. Lindblom, *Politics and Markets* (New York: Basic Books, 1977).

ences the views of others, then a broker can be defined as a politician who accepts the views of others for the sake of creating a majority. If there is not a sufficiently broad consensus to create such a majority, then inaction is the expected outcome. Sub-government politics often lead to nondecision making, when the number of more or less autonomous groups involved is large, and some refuse to reconcile their conflict in a brokered consensus.

The advantage of exercising authority on a smaller scale than the national level is shown by the fact that in the past two decades most European governments have faced political demands to disaggregate authority and to provide increased opportunities for popular participation and regional decision making. The growth of the welfare state has also led European governments to adopt a variety of devices to reduce the role of ministries in making or delivering such basic welfare services as health, housing, and social work. Where responsibility for policies remains concentrated in national ministries, there is a growing attention to pressure groups clustering around them. Simultaneously, demands to decentralize or devolve authority to regions or "nations" demanding greater autonomy have been voiced, and voiced vigorously, in Britain, Canada, France, Italy, and Spain.[25]

Big issues require decision making by government collectively, for they raise questions that commit the country as a whole. International affairs is the most obvious example, for half a nation cannot be at war with a foreign power while the other half remains at peace. An all-or-nothing choice, binding on everyone, must be made. Major issues of macroeconomic policy also require collective decisions of government. For example, a government must make central decisions about monetary policy, for if half of its citizens normally deal in foreign currencies, then it no longer has effective authority in the national economy. Energy policy is a third contemporary example of the need for central decisions. While individuals may decide what kind of home heating or what type of transportation to consume, only a government can determine collectively what quantity, price, and mixture of imported and domestic energy resources will be available to individual consumers.

The issues of greatest concern to government are aptly described as collective, for they have a pervasive effect upon society as a whole. As such, they are appropriate for determination by a government elected to look after the major concerns of society as a whole. When

---

[25] See, for example, James Cornford, ed., *The Failure of the State* (London: Croom-Helm, 1975).

issues arise that affect all citizens collectively, such as matters of war and peace, then some part of the nation must decide for the whole. When inflation arises, collective action offers means of counteracting inflation that cannot be taken by individuals. When oil is in short supply, an individual may wish to buy a lot of gasoline cheaply, below world prices. But if the collective effect of millions of people doing so is to jeopardize a nation's economic or military security, then decisions are properly made by government. A popularly elected government has a better claim than any sub-government or private organization to determine national policy.

Major collective issues are literally vital because they concern the defining attributes of the modern state. Modern government commenced with the creation of authorities strong enough to provide national security, impose domestic order, and sustain an economy in the face of tariffs by principalities, baronies, and lesser jurisdictions in Europe and in dispersed colonies in America. The growth of government, particularly in the twentieth century, has added many more responsibilities. Today, social welfare policies make first claim upon the government's material resources, but the defining responsibilities of modern government necessarily remain its first priority.[26] Any modern state must deal effectively with these problems or cease to be a sovereign state.

Big, pervasive problems have major consequences spilling over into many areas. For example, energy problems have implications for the economy and for national security; national security problems have major economic implications; and economic problems have a major impact upon money available for social services as well as upon a country's status in the world. If decisions were only made by sub-governments, then every sub-government would become the object (or victim) of decisions elsewhere in government about which it was not consulted.

Collective problems require a collective response. The politics of sub-governments is inadequate to resolve conflicts about issues of pervasive importance to society. Sub-governments come into conflict with each other, and decision making is made more difficult, as perhaps it should be when large stakes are involved. Conflicts can only be resolved by something larger and stronger than particularistic political networks, namely by the collective authority of government.

---

[26] See Richard Rose, "On the Priorities of Government: A Developmental Analysis of Public Policies," *European Journal of Political Research*, vol. 4, no. 3 (1976), pp. 247-89.

Although important collective issues might be expected to unite politicians in the name of a putative national interest, their immediate impact is to generate politics as usual. In default of an authoritative definition of the "national" interest, different sub-governments are each free to advocate views that are not so much selfish as they are narrow and particular. Each department has a different perspective on multifaceted national problems. For example, a Defense Department may see an international issue as a military problem, whereas the State Department may see it as a diplomatic problem.[27]

In their initial response to complex collective issues, governments in Europe and America tend to act similarly, for the advocacy of competing views is built into the policy process. It is welcomed philosophically, for Europeans and Americans both tend to believe in the free competition of ideas in the marketplace. It is institutionalized politically, by rights of free speech and the stimulus to debate given by party competition. And it is present organizationally by the conflicting interests of different government departments or ministries.

Collective problems normally involve a number of different sub-governments. Everybody wants to get into the act when an issue is "hot" politically and affects their interests. For example, in addition to energy agencies, environmentalists, national security agencies, and treasury officials will have views about the use of natural resources. A collective problem is disaggregated into its component parts for consideration separately by different departments, each from its own point of view. The resulting recommendations will not meet the requirements of a collective policy. Instead, they will be a laundry list of particular concerns, requiring reconciliation by the authority of government. Such conflicts cannot easily be resolved by asking brokers to intervene. Attempts to arrive at a consensus are likely to lead to inaction, when major sub-governments disagree about what is the nation's interest.

By definition, collective problems cannot be resolved by the conventional method of providing something for everybody. For example, farmers and motorists cannot be given cheap energy, while advocates of energy conservation are given higher prices. When collective issues have "zero sum" properties (that is, what one group wins the other must lose), then there must be sufficient collective authority in government to enforce decisions upon losers as well as winners.

Giving Government the Priority. The political problem forced forward by collective issues is: How to get a collective decision? When interests

[27] See Graham Allison, *Essence of Decision* (Boston: Little, Brown & Co., 1971).

conflict and departments recommend mutually exclusive alternatives, a conscious choice is needed. The risks and costs of making a decision cannot be avoided; that is in the nature of politics. What is variable is whether a policy is merely the byproduct of separate sub-governments pursuing particularist interests, or is a conscious and singular decision about what is good for the country collectively.

The Cabinet system differs greatly from the American system when confronted with the need to make a collective choice. A Cabinet can invoke the power of government against politics *because there is a government there*. A Cabinet can produce a "shut up" decision, that is, a decision that must be accepted by all the affected ministries. The decision may be complex and contain a number of compromises. But it is nonetheless a political decision, making choices and stating them in a way that is binding upon sub-governments.[28] Each member of the Cabinet must either go along with the decision or resign from office. That is the price that individual politicians pay for being part of a Cabinet government.

By contrast, the United States lacks a single institution that can effectively assert the collective authority of government on major issues of the day. In the Madisonian system of dispersing power, there is no assurance that any decision will be made. Whereas a lawyer would think it odd if, after a lengthy judicial hearing, the Supreme Court refused to issue any decision or its decision was ignored by other courts, we do not think it odd when there is no decision in Washington about a major collective issue.

The benefits of sub-government policy making are real and continuing, but they are also limited. At a time when the collective problems facing the United States are both immediate and of great importance, it is particularly costly to make decisions in bits and pieces that do *not* add up to a collective policy. Moreover, it is increasingly difficult to find the extra resources needed to invest (or waste) in making big decisions in small ways. The price can be just as high for the United States as the price the Soviets pay for having an over-centralized economy.

Because the agenda of political issues facing the United States in the 1980s is dominated by collective problems, there is now a need to strengthen the collective authority of government as well as maintain the established authority of sub-governments. The American problem

---

[28] In many circumstances, especially economic policy, a decision may involve "trade-offs" or compromises. The point here is that there is a big difference between compromises consciously made by a collective authority and compromises that are simply the byproduct or result of conflicts between sub-governments.

is not that the sub-governments are too strong. The opposite is the case: *The countervailing collective force of government is too weak.*

The President is the official most concerned with problems of the nation collectively, because he is elected by the nation as a whole. The authority of the President to order the dropping of an H bomb is often cited as proof of the awesome power that one politician can have over mankind's collective fate. Yet this prompts the question: What does the President do when he is not dropping H bombs? The answer was given by President Truman many years ago: "I sit here all day trying to persuade people to do the things they ought to have sense enough to do without my persuading them."[29] The President is not so much the chief decision maker in American politics, as he is the chief persuader. The institutions to which he applies his powers of persuasion are the sub-governments of the United States. He proposes, but they dispose of most public policies, whether large or small.

The conventional way to recommend strengthening government is to suggest strengthening the Presidency. The "backlash" against the White House of the early 1970s appears to have subsided, and calls for a "strong" President once again resound. The prescriptions lead in a variety of directions.

The simplest advice concerns the personal character and behavior of the President. Be wise. Be firm. Be popular. Be good. But such injunctions, however well intentioned, risk failing through naiveté. Stated negatively, they are unexceptionable. Who would want a stupid, weak, unpopular, and evil President? If followed literally, however, they can lead to defects arising from an excess of these virtues. A President may be handicapped if intelligence leads to indecision, if firmness leads to stubbornness, if a concern with popularity leads to enslavement to opinion polls, or if goodness is pursued to the point of self-righteousness.

More meaningful are injunctions about the political behavior that an individual President should pursue. Particularly relevant here is the approach of Richard Neustadt, whose theme is the politics of personal power: "What a President can do to make his own will felt within his own Administration; what he can do, as one man among many, to carry his own choices through that maze of personalities and institutions called the government of the United States."[30] While Neustadt emphatically declares his allegiance to the cause of promoting

---

[29] Quoted from Neustadt, *Presidential Power*, p. 9.
[30] Neustadt, *Presidential Power*, p. v.

Presidential power, the words in which he does so pay tribute to the power of the sub-governments of the United States.

As government has grown bigger (a process often assumed to make it less manageable or even unmanageable), Presidents have turned to the nostrums of management in search of authority: reorganize; plan; coordinate. These prescriptions are typically voiced by persons who wish the President (or, at least, staff in the Executive Office of the President) to assert collective authority against a multitude of sub-governments. Logically, the call for coordination is appealing because it appears to address the problem of reconciling conflicting views of sub-governments. But as long as sub-governments are strong, coordination is bound to be weak. Coordination can work well only after the power of sub-governments is overcome or where there is little or no conflict about "apolitical" issues. European experience shows that planning, too, is more attractive in theory than in practice. Even if (a heroic assumption) useful planning documents could be produced in Washington, they would be of limited value without a collective authority that could act authoritatively upon a plan. The reorganization efforts of Presidents Nixon and Carter have shown how little scope there is for major institutional change; the people who have organized the many sub-governments wish to keep things as they are.[31]

An easy prescription to accept is that the President should receive the views of a multiplicity of advocates.[32] By actively soliciting views from different sources, a President can check one source of information against another and prescriptions for one policy against another, incidentally making a virtue of a major feature of sub-governments. This goal is easy to achieve, for the major problems that the President considers are by their nature multidimensional. At a minimum, the White House should have staff sufficiently detached from departmental loyalties and sufficiently committed to the idea of "due process" in policy making so that the President does in fact receive the views of all relevant sub-governments before he makes a decision. But the more the President is given the differing views of multiple advocates, the harder his job is likely to be. As President Warren Harding once moaned: "I listen to one side and they seem right and then I talk to

---

[31] For an up-to-date review, see the collection of papers produced by Peter Szanton, ed., "Papers on Government Reorganization," especially Allen Schick, "Alternatives to Reorganization"; and Seidman, *Politics, Position, and Power*, chap. 5.

[32] See Alexander L. George, "The Case for Multiple Advocacy in Making Foreign Policy," *American Political Science Review*, vol. 66, no. 3 (September 1972), pp. 751-951, including comments by I. M. Destler.

the other side, and they seem just as right, and there I am where I started. . . . God, what a job!"[33]

The President's job is not just to listen to the views of sub-governments but also to resolve disputes between them. No procedures or institutions will be of value to a President in the absence of the collective authority needed to make decisions binding upon sub-governments, as can be done by a Cabinet. Reviewing the major collective problems facing the United States today emphasizes how difficult it is for the President (or any other part of American government) to do that because the American system values sub-governments more than government.

In international affairs, the United States government has a well-established set of institutions for making policy under Presidential authority.[34] The National Security Council gives institutional expression within the White House to a large complex of agencies and interests. But the circumstances in which the President's authority is sufficient to make foreign policy are very restricted. That authority is at its most potent in short-lived international crises, such as the 1962 Cuban missile crisis. But the object of international affairs is to avoid crises, not to seek international confrontations as compensation for a lack of power domestically.

The President's representatives can discuss mutual action with foreign governments, but they usually cannot commit the United States to endorse an agreement. The concurrence of Congress is almost invariably needed, whether in the form of legislation, appropriations, or tacit agreement not to use its considerable powers of oversight to obstruct or alter the implementation of a given policy. Of course, European officials often have to refer back to their national government for instructions about negotiations and the full force of Cabinet disagreement may be felt on an important matter, for example, the terms of an International Monetary Fund loan. But once a Cabinet has made up its mind, then a European government can quickly commit the country in international affairs. By contrast, in the United States most noncrisis decisions approved by the President do not commit the government until they have also been reviewed and acted upon by one or more sub-governments.[35]

---

[33] Quoted by Theodore C. Sorensen, *Decision-Making in the White House* (New York: Columbia University Press, 1963), p. 42.

[34] See, for example, I. M. Destler, *Presidents, Bureaucrats and Foreign Policy* (Princeton: Princeton University Press, 1972); and Graham Allison and Peter Szanton, *Remaking Foreign Policy: the Organizational Connection* (New York: Basic Books, 1976).

[35] On the significant claims of Congress for involvement in foreign policy making

Presidential endorsement of a foreign policy initiative is not tantamount to the commitment of the United States government. For example, there can be no dispute about the national and international importance of SALT II (Strategic Arms Limitation Treaty). The inability of President Carter to obtain any binding decision about America's acceptance or rejection of the treaty months after its negotiation highlights the relative weakness of American government. The President initially found it easier to agree with America's major international adversary than with his own party in Congress. To argue that Congress was wiser than the President on this issue is to defend the American system in American terms. It is hardly an inducement to foreign nations to enter into commitments with a President, if Congress concludes that the President is not even worthy of trust within Washington!

The management of the economy today presents no easy answers —but there are nonetheless important decisions to be made. Moreover, decisions concerning the money supply, the level of public expenditure, America's relationship with its foreign trading partners, and national wage and price controls are collective issues. But the institutions for making economic policy in the United States are much more fragmented than in any Cabinet system. The very substantial revenue raising and spending powers of state and local governments compete with federal decision, and the greater scope of private-sector economic activity further reduces the scope for federal decision. Within the federal government, the President consults with at least three different major economic policy advisers—the Treasury, the Council of Economic Advisors and the Office of Management and Budget—as well as such agencies as Commerce, Labor, Agriculture, and Housing and Urban Development. The Federal Reserve Board stands at a greater distance from the executive branch than do most European central banks. The increasing severity and importance of America's economic problems have led Presidents to seek new means of managing the flow of economic recommendations coming to their attention, with mixed success.[36]

---

today, see, for example, Thomas M. Franck and Edward Weisband, *Foreign Policy by Congress* (New York: Oxford University Press, 1979), and such journalistic comments as Martin Tolchin, "Congress Broadens Its Influence on Foreign Policy," *New York Times*, December 24, 1979.

[36] Cf. Roger Porter, "Presidential Decisionmaking: the Economic Policy Board" (Ph.D. diss., Harvard University, 1978, and forthcoming as a Cambridge University Press book); and Sidney L. Jones, *The Development of Economic Policy: Financial Institution Reform* (Ann Arbor: Graduate School of Business Administration, University of Michigan, 1980).

To complicate matters further, there is an increasing need for American economic policy to balance domestic with international concerns, for the American economy is now greatly influenced by what happens elsewhere in the world. The growing interdependence of international and domestic issues implies a need for collective authority to reconcile conflicts across an even wider range of concerns than heretofore. But a careful review by I. M. Destler of the direction of America's foreign economic policy concludes with a message that is "predominantly negative." The President is advised to treat international economic policies through domestic economic policy-making institutions, but these institutions are relatively weaker than the President's agencies for national security. Furthermore, the influence of congressionally based sub-governments is greater in economic policy than in international affairs.[37]

The specialization of economic policy institutions is not unique to the United States. When European governments nationalize major industries, they create very complex institutions; the case of Italy is an extreme example. The differentiation of economic institutions is part and parcel of the complexities of a mixed economy. What distinguishes governments on opposite sides of the Atlantic is the relative capacity to resolve differences. A European nation can refer economic issues to a Cabinet in which the Treasury will control far more of public-sector spending (and far more of the economy as well) than the President does, as well as having more collective authority in Cabinet.

The 1973 OPEC oil embargo has fundamentally altered the character of the energy issue. Prior to that date, there was no consensus that the United States needed to have a national energy policy. There were a plurality of energy policies, mostly made by a process of mutual adjustments in the marketplace. Individual consumers determined their use of energy by individual decisions. Producers and suppliers of energy used the profit motive to guide their actions. Political decisions affecting energy use were made at local and state as well as federal levels. The whole apparatus of sub-government politics persists to the present.

Political events of the 1970s, however, have made energy questions an issue of collective choice. Crucial questions today concern the total amount of energy that America should seek from domestic and foreign suppliers in a given year; how much in foreign exchange it can pay for energy supplies; and how the economy can adapt to

---

[37] See I. M. Destler, *Making Foreign Economic Policy* (Washington, D.C.: The Brookings Institution, 1980), chap. 13.

abrupt changes in oil prices. Questions of collective supply and demand have supplanted issues of individual supply and demand. The questions concern government because of the scale of costs involved and because of the interdependence of energy, economic, and foreign policies.

Energy policy is intrinsically complex and uncertain; there is no easy or assured course of action that the United States or any European government can follow. European governments are advantaged in responding to these complexities because of their greater collective authority in government. But in the United States, the President's ability to take any action on major energy issues is hamstrung by sub-government politics.

In the face of such major collective challenges, it is little wonder that James Reston described Washington as "a troubled city" as it entered the 1980s. Reston diagnosed the cause as "structural defects in our government that must be repaired if we are to deal with our present and coming problems."[38]

In international affairs, in the economy, and in energy, there is great scope for debate about the substance of collective decision. No institutional mechanism can guarantee that big decisions will always be made wisely or that their consequences will be widely acceptable. European governments differ in their ability to stimulate economic growth or control inflation, notwithstanding similarities in their institutions for economic policy making. Moreover, a Cabinet government usually consults pressure groups about major decisions. The important point here is that a Cabinet can make a binding decision. By contrast, in the United States, the need to secure the concurrence of many different sub-governments tends to deflect attention from the substantive merits or demerits of decisions and to concentrate attention upon tactics. In the Washington obstacle race, the crucial question is not only "how good is this policy?" but also "what sort of chance does it, or something that still looks like it after a host of amendments, have of enactment?"

The logic of the foregoing analysis points clearly to the need to strengthen government against already strong sub-governments. The next two sections elaborate on ways in which this strategy can be pursued. Unlike most prescriptive works, no claim is made that the President is (or can be) greatly strengthened. Being President is a one man job and the holder of that office is going to remain only one man—and something less than a superman. Instead, attention is given to ways in which the *collective* element of government can be strength-

[38] James Reston, "Where Are We Going?" *New York Times*, December 23, 1979.

311

ened by altering existing relationships between the President and other major political figures and by altering relations between the President and major policy makers nominally under his authority.

These changes may appear to hamper the President by making him more subject to collective authority, but the opposite is the case. By comparison with European political leaders, an American President is weak because of the absence of collective authority. To strengthen collective authority would impose new restrictions upon the President, but unlike most post-Watergate changes, those considered here are intended to strengthen collective authority.

Better a government strong enough even to constrain the President than the present experience of both a weak President and a weak government. In Europe, taming the collective authority of government was once the first problem of the makers of constitutions. In America today, the issue of first importance is how to increase collective authority. The problems facing America in the 1980s provide justification enough for doing so. To make collective policies effectively, "We may need to give as much attention to reinventing the state and its institutions as to reinventing the car."[39]

Disciplining Leaders

Ambition is the common element that unites politicians of diverse views on both sides of the Atlantic. To become a Prime Minister or a President, an individual must have a strong desire for office and a willingness to do whatever the system requires to reach the top. Europe and America differ, however, in what they demand of an ambitious politician. In Europe, the emphasis usually is upon skills relevant to running a government; in America, the first emphasis today is upon running a skillful election campaign.

The Cabinet system disciplines political leaders; their authority is not derived from followers attracted by their personality but from an organized party. The party is the organization that selects one of its members to be its leader. The party can continue without any particular personality as its leader, but a politician, whatever his personal attributes, cannot expect to give direction to government without the confidence of a political party.[40]

---

[39] Bert A. Rockman, "Constants, Cycles, Trends and Persona in Presidential Governance: Carter's Troubles Reviewed" (Paper delivered to the annual meeting of the American Political Science Association, Washington, D.C., 1979), p. 48.

[40] Since the direct election of the President, the party politics of the Fifth French Republic constitute an exception in Europe in some respects resembling the American system of "partyless" candidates running personal campaigns, such as the use of the "run off" ballot in France.

The Cabinet system is based upon party discipline, for the Cabinet must be able to rely upon a majority in the Parliament to sustain its existence. No government can last without a party or coalition to deliver these votes. The weaker the party discipline (or the greater the divisions within a party) the more frequent are changes at the top, as the frequent reshuffling of coalition governments in Italy illustrates. Political parties do not need a distinctive left- or right-wing ideology to be a force giving direction to government. The parliamentary cohesion produced by party loyalty is enough; by sustaining a Cabinet in office, the party maintains the collective authority of government against sub-governments.

Team Captain or Self-Employed? In Europe, the party makes the Prime Minister. A European politician must serve a long apprenticeship in the party before being elected its leader. The route to the top is lengthy, commencing when an individual joins the party in a relatively humble status and at an early age. In Norway, the typical Labour Prime Minister spends a lifetime in the labour movement. In Britain, the average postwar Prime Minister has spent more than a quarter-century as a member of Parliament before entering Downing Street and joined the party as a youth, some forty years before reaching the top of politics. Decades spent working within the party give an individual politician a clear idea of what his colleagues think, how they act, and what they will expect and accept from their leader. Socialization is a process of disciplining individuals to act in accord with collective norms. Socialization into the party is a precondition of election to its leadership.

By contrast, American Presidents are self-selected and self-employed. Presidential candidates may spend years in building a political following, but it is first and foremost a *personal* following. In the case of the Kennedy brothers and Nelson Rockefeller, family ties and family wealth sustained a substantial staff and also created a national network of personally loyal supporters. Dwight D. Eisenhower, America's only two-term President since World War II, illustrates the weakness of American party loyalties. It was not known whether Eisenhower was a Republican or Democrat until shortly before he began to run for the Republican party's nomination for the Presidency.

To become a party standard-bearer, an American politician must first of all *divide* his party by contesting primaries against fellow partisans. Each contestant must build an organization outside the party, relying upon professional campaign consultants and individuals attracted by his personal appeal or issue stands. A Presidential convention is no longer the grand conclave of the state and local leaders of the party, but a candidate-centered electoral college whose members are recruited on grounds of candidate orientation, sex, race, age, or other criteria. In Austin Ranney's succinct phrase, it is best today to think of "parties as prizes, not judges." [41]

The winner of a Presidential election is in an even stronger position to maintain a personal party of followers. A President is likely to distrust the party's own National Committee staff, having an organization of personal loyalists whom he can discipline, but to whom he owes no obligations. An incumbent President must have a good personal political machine because of the threat of a major primary fight for renomination, as occurred in 1968, 1976, and 1980. He can use his media prominence to gain publicity and use White House staff for campaign as well as Presidential purposes. Congressmen cannot criticize a President for creating his own party, since individual congressmen are today increasingly inclined to create a personal following, independent of the party on whose ticket they run.

European countries trust the party caucuses to select their leaders, and thus to determine who can become Prime Minister. The method can hardly be described as undemocratic when it is used by parties of all ideologies, ranging from left to right (and also by conventions nominating every American President up to the 1970s). While the methods of caucus choice differ within Europe from party to party and country to country, there is a common negative factor: open competition for popular favor through primary elections is rejected.

To become party leader, a European politician must cultivate the good opinion of persons most involved in the party. The electoral college is small, but it is also unusually sophisticated for the people casting the votes have known all the candidates for years, or even a political lifetime. They will know their personal and political shortcomings, as well as their strengths and have seen how the candidates perform in adversity as well as in office. Thus, an aspiring party leader needs to show by actions as well as words that he has what it takes to give direction to government.

The European system of selecting leaders by party caucus strengthens party unity, and this in turn strengthens the collective authority of government against sub-governments. A party leader or Prime Minister is a team captain leading the team where it is willing

---

[41] Austin Ranney, "The Political Parties: Reform and Decline," in *New American Political System*, ed. King, p. 236.

to follow. A party leader knows what the party expects because he has spent years working in it, often in subordinate positions that chasten the ego. Insofar as European parties have some more or less distinctive principles, a party also offers guidance on policy. To retain office, a European party leader must maintain the continuing confidence of his political colleagues, some of whom will be looking for occasions to undermine that confidence to their personal benefit. The position of a European party leader is that of a politician subject to party discipline as well as using party discipline to sustain collective direction of government.

Both European and American parties face the common problem of winnowing a few national leaders from an electorate of tens of millions. The European reliance upon the caucus vests the power of choice in a jury of party peers. By contrast, the American primary system gives the mass electorate the power to name Presidential candidates. However, millions of primary voters cannot make the same kind of informed judgment about politicians as can party professionals. The scale of contemporary primary campaigning makes it impossible for candidates to be seen in the flesh by most voters, and the style of campaigning creates a greater concern with a candidate's image than with the substance of government policies.

In the United States today the mass media are the brokers or gatekeepers, mediating relations between candidates and voters. The evaluation of candidates by television and the press has replaced the endorsements formerly given by old-style party machines. An individual voter must rely upon the media to tell him what the candidates are like, in the absence of guidance offered by parties in face-to-face ward or township meetings. Candidates resent the potential influence of broadcasting mediators and seek to project their image to voters themselves with all the paraphernalia of modern telecommunications: television commercials, press advertisements, direct mailings, and canvassing by phone banks.

An American President is not a team player; he is more like a golfer who has just won the National Open by playing against and defeating everyone around him. Contemporary campaign conditions lead Presidential candidates to stress vacuous symbols that could be used interchangeably by candidates of either party, such as "strength" or "goodness" and to make the personality of the candidate the issue. In the words of Richard Nixon's chief media adviser in 1972: "We thought that the issue was clearly defined, that there were two choices —the President (and I meant that distinction—not Richard Nixon, but the President) and the challenger, the candidate George McGovern.

We wanted to keep the issue clearly defined that way."[42] A similar viewpoint was put forward by a senior aide to Jimmy Carter in 1976: "Issues are not our problem now—we've got to have good advance, good and precise targeting, good media, better polling, and a hell of a lot more on turn-out. We've got one major goal between now and November: to sell Jimmy and Mondale as leaders whom voters will trust. *They* are *the* issue."[43]

Rootless candidates risk becoming rootless in government. Insofar as a politician concentrates his attention upon the relatively contentless concerns of campaigning, distancing himself from any organization besides his own personal following, he loses a stable commitment of party to invoke against the sub-governments of Washington. Stephen Wayne succinctly draws the moral: "The personalization of the presidential electoral process has serious implications for governing. To put it simply, it makes it more difficult."[44]

European experience shows that it is not important whether a party elects its leader by a national conference of delegates or by a parliamentary caucus. Nor is it particularly important whether the leader is a strong personality (as is often the case in Britain or Germany), a servant of the party (as in Norway), or the leader of a temporarily dominant faction (as in Italy). The important point is that *there is a party there*, that is, an institution to recruit and socialize would-be national leaders, so that a leader can be selected who is well enough known to be trusted by the party and who can govern with collective support.

What is here called the European method of selecting party leaders was until very recently the American method as well. Until the 1960s, the standing of the President and of would-be challengers for that office was largely determined by the judgment of party professionals, congressmen, executive branch officials, and journalists. Since that time, presidential selection has become "in substance, if not in form, something closely approaching a non-party system."[45] It is a system in which critical judgments about the credibility and viability

---

[42] Quoted in Stephen J. Wayne, *The Road to the White House* (New York: St. Martin's Press, 1980), p. 173.

[43] Quoted in Jeff Fishel, "From Campaign Promise to Presidential Performance: The Carter Administration in Contemporary Historical Perspective" (unpublished paper prepared for a colloquium of the Woodrow Wilson International Center, Washington, D.C., June 20, 1979), p. 40.

[44] Wayne, *Road to the White House*, p. 246. See also Nelson Polsby, "Presidential Cabinet Making: Lessons for the Political System," *Political Science Quarterly*, vol. 93, no. 1 (Spring 1978), pp. 15-25.

[45] Ranney, "Political Parties," p. 245.

of candidates are made by professional media people who, whatever their skills in communication, remain amateurs in government.

Because these changes in American politics are both recent and volatile, it should be practicable to strengthen political parties, making them once again something more than mere flags of convenience. The opportunities to strengthen the parties are multiple and recurring— decisions about primary election laws, campaign finance, Presidential convention delegations, national party organizations, and procedures in Congress. To argue that parties cannot be raised from their present weak state or even that they are doomed to disappear is the counsel of despair. It would encourage a President to become a loner in a system of sub-governments in which few things can be accomplished by a politician on his own.

Experienced Governors or Skilled Campaigners? In any democratic system the ideal is identical: to give power to politicians who are successful both in winning office and in giving direction to government. The founders of party government in America believed that "running for office and governing the nation were (and ought consciously to be) indissolubly linked."[46] With the advent of mass suffrage in Europe, conservative as well as social democratic politicians came to realize that only a party with mass appeal could elect caucus nominees to office. But there is no logical necessity for all politicians to be equally skilled at campaigning or governing.

European party leaders vary widely in their native intelligence, political backgrounds, and programmatic goals. But the great majority have shared the common experience of an apprenticeship in governing. In the course of a long political career, an aspiring leader is likely to serve first as an assistant or deputy to a minister before becoming entrusted with directing a second-rank Cabinet department. Then, on the basis of demonstrated skills in office, the politician can be named to direct a major ministry—the treasury, foreign affairs, or an important welfare agency. In the course of a decade or more in office, a politician will become familiar with the routine of departmental briefings, Cabinet meetings, and Cabinet battles. It is by conducting himself well in these principal activities of government that an ambitious politician gains the stature needed to win election to its leadership.

---

[46] James W. Ceaser, *Presidential Selection: Theory and Development* (Princeton: Princeton University Press, 1979). Cf. the less optimistic view of James Bryce, "Why Great Men are Not Chosen Presidents," in *The American Commonwealth*, 3d ed. (London: Macmillan, 1893), pp. 78-85.

Skill at campaigning is desirable but not essential to become a senior Cabinet minister. The proportional representation system of election used widely in Europe concentrates powers of parliamentary nomination in the hands of the party organization. A talented politician can find a safe parliamentary seat by work within the party. Once elected to Parliament, MPs usually find their seat is safe electorally, because of the strength of voters' party loyalties. Even where voters can cast a ballot for an individual candidate and not just for a predetermined party list, MPs find that the party label, not their personality, is the cause of their continuing reelection.

To become Prime Minister a politician does not need to win a national election. The post can be gained at short notice during the life of a Parliament, if the incumbent Prime Minister retires. In Britain, Winston Churchill, Anthony Eden, Harold Macmillan, Sir Alec Douglas-Home, and James Callaghan all entered 10 Downing Street after their party was already in power, and the last two never led their party to an election victory. A continental variant in reaching the top is to benefit from the reshuffle of a coalition government. When no party has a parliamentary majority, then the choice of a coalition Prime Minister depends upon negotiations between parties and not upon popular election. In Italy, the negotiations involve factions within the ruling Christian Democratic party as well as interparty bargaining.

Of course, every party must have a leader to head it during a general election campaign. In the selection of European party leaders, attention is increasingly being given to a potential leader's image, as well as to substantive evidence of capability in government. In many parties, a leader must be better than passable in his personal image to secure election. But the need to be better than passable in government is equally important, thus producing *doubly* qualified leaders. The short duration of a European election campaign, relative to American practice, greatly reduces the amount of attention that a party leader must give to electioneering.

Typically, an American Presidential candidate solicits popular support as an act of faith. His previous record is unlikely to cast much light on how the candidate would act if confronted with the mammoth challenge of the White House. Unlike a Prime Minister, a President almost invariably has no previous experience of directing a major federal agency. No postwar American President has previously headed an agency in the executive branch, thus learning about the direction of government at first hand.

So many accidents have marked the succession of postwar American Presidents that generalization from the record should be undertaken with caution. Nonetheless, one clear pattern is present. Five of the seven postwar Presidents have served in Congress and four have also served as vice president. Since only one of the four vice presidents subsequently entered the White House by popular election (and even then Richard Nixon did so only after being defeated in an attempt to move directly to the Oval Office from his subordinate post), it is reasonable to regard congressional experience as the most characteristic experience, and this has been true throughout American history.[47]

Congress provides all of its members with rich exposure to the sub-governments of the United States. The particular exposure given depends upon home-district interests and committee assignments. Given the greater powers of Congress, particularly in the oversight of executive agencies, a congressman may learn more about how agencies work than his counterpart in a Parliament in Europe. On the other hand, a congressman does not have to accept party discipline and is free to ignore the problems facing the President and can take popular positions on issues without any idea of what it means to be responsible for the policies at stake.[48] The great difference between congressmen and members of Parliament is that the latter do not jump from being a spectator to being the chief director of government.

The vice presidency is not so much a training ground for the Presidency as it is an antechamber in which an ambitious politician sits uncomfortably, wondering whether "lightning" will strike the President. The post gives its incumbent a broad overview of a number of problems of government, but the vice president is in no sense a deputy President. White House officials far below the vice president in formal status see much more of the President and his work. Nor does the President wish to give the vice president "on the job" training as his successor. Instead, he is likely to be jealous of very favorable attention that the vice president receives. The post is "too close for comfort," and the vice president is the one politician in the executive branch whom the President cannot dismiss at will. The President tends to use the vice president for select and limited purposes, to do things that the President would rather not do. Allison and Szanton conclude: "The consistent experience of all post-war Vice Presidents

---

[47] Calculated from data presented in Thomas E. Cronin, *The State of the Presidency*, 2d ed. (Boston: Little, Brown & Co., 1980), p. 382.

[48] See, for example, David R. Mayhew, *Congress: The Electoral Connection* (New Haven: Yale University Press, 1974).

begins with high expectations based on Presidential promises of a major role rapidly followed by deep disappointment about being kept in the closet."[49]

Historically, the governor's office was once a recruiting ground for the White House. More than half of all Presidents from Thomas Jefferson to Franklin D. Roosevelt had previously served in the executive mansion of a state. In the days when the federal government had little to do and its problems were domestic problems, the transition from State House to White House involved limited changes. Today, however, the transition is more complicated in two respects. The first is the difference in the types of issues on which Presidents and governors concentrate. A President is primarily concerned with collective problems—national security, foreign affairs, and the management of the economy and energy. By contrast, governors are concerned with such state and local issues as education and roads, services important to individual citizens but remote from the collective issues confronting the White House. Moreover, the growth in the complexity of Washington government and politics makes it much harder for a governor who has not had previous experience as a congressman or executive branch official to learn the ways of a town which is infinitely more complex in its politics than any state capital.

The postwar President with the greatest prior experience in executive branch politics was Dwight D. Eisenhower. As a career soldier, Eisenhower had ample opportunities to watch the bureaucracy at work and to develop skills for dealing with the huge defense establishment. It was Eisenhower's skill in working with the military bureaucracy and in interdepartmental and interallied relations, not battlefield performance, that brought him to the top of the defense establishment, thus giving him the visibility that led to the White House.

The American system of selecting a President is now biased against people who know how the executive branch works. It is hardly an accident that those who serve a President in a major department—State, Defense, or Treasury—do not subsequently become President themselves. A President will normally wish to keep the limelight to himself and take credit for major successes. Moreover, because the holders of major offices are closely identified with the President in public, they suffer in popular eyes from being tied to a President whose popularity is likely to wane after years in office.

---

[49] Allison and Szanton, *Remaking Foreign Policy*, p. 83.

The extreme contrast between the prior government experience of a Prime Minister and the campaign demands upon a President raises the question: Is the government of the United States easier to understand than that of a European nation? Observers on both sides of the Atlantic would certainly say the opposite. Yet the President and most of those around him start their governing career in Washington with far less experience than their European counterparts of how government agencies work.

For a European political leader, the transition from dealing with particular issues of departmental politics to broad issues of government is gradual. The job of a Prime Minister is not to make, let alone manage, specific policies of government but to be concerned with meta-policy, that is, relationships between the particular policies of different ministries or sub-governments. Having had experience as a minister of how departmental policies are reconciled by the collective authority of the Cabinet makes it easier for a party leader to reconcile policies that collectively concern government.

By contrast, an American President enters office abruptly, with no prior experience of how the concerns of different sub-governments can or should be balanced against each other in the face of major collective concerns of government. A President with a congressional orientation may think the job of the White House is simply a problem in building coalitions of interests to enact legislation. But in fact it is very different. The President's primary responsibility today is to mobilize political forces to countervail against coalitions mobilized by sub-governments. Only if a President can do this is it possible to develop major policies in which the collective concerns of government take precedence against the particularistic claims of sub-governments.

Popular election confers legitimacy upon a President, but it does not confer wisdom about the ways of government. Of course, any politician skilled enough as a campaigner to be elected President can pick up some of the skills of governance on the job. But there is a risk in making this assumption, and the time spent in on-the-job learning may be costly for the President, for the country, or both. Moreover, the "hazards" of transition[50] have increased as political atomization tends to increase the number and potency of sub-governments, thus making it more difficult for an inexperienced and newly installed President to assert the collective authority of government.

---

[50] See Neustadt, *Presidential Power*, chap. 11.

The logic of the foregoing analysis points to a simple, almost self-evident proposition: *government is best strengthened by those who understand how it works.* Equally, the more ignorant a President is of the government over which he presides, the harder it will be for him to direct it. The efforts of President Nixon and his staff to alter fundamentally what they perceived as a hostile executive branch bear witness to the difficulties of effective change without knowledge. An insider's account of these uninformed attempts to redirect government is aptly entitled *The Plot That Failed.*[51] The slight record of achievement of President Carter's much trumpeted reorganization program is also evidence of the difficulties that an outsider faces in trying to redirect American government. The fact that many people knowledgeable in Washington's ways do not want to alter their actions makes it even more important that those who desire change be the equal of their opponents in understanding government.

Insofar as prior experience in the federal government is an asset, then the American electorate has a remedy ready at hand. Although anyone may run for the Presidency, voters should regard with skepticism any candidate who lacks significant previous experience in Washington. All other things being equal (a necessary and sometimes crucial qualifying phrase), those influencing the choice of Presidential candidates—whether party stalwarts, media commentators, or voters in primaries—should look to talent already in Washington. Washington is a critical political audience, aware of both individual shortcomings and strengths. Moreover, there is an ample supply of candidates successful in Washington for each party to choose from. If this is not done, then the American people risk electing a President who learns about giving direction to government by making his first mistakes at the top.

Introverted or Extroverted Leaders. Introverted political leaders give first priority to what is going on within government. Extroverted political leaders give first priority to what is going on in the country. In principle, a President or Prime Minister should be knowledgeable both about the actions of government and about the mood of the country. But there is not world and time enough to attend to everything of political importance. The choice a politician makes reveals as much about a political system as it does about his own personality.

---

[51] See Richard E. Nathan, *The Plot That Failed: Nixon and the Administrative Presidency* (New York: John Wiley & Sons, 1975). Cf. Frederic V. Malek, *Washington's Hidden Tragedy: the Failure to Make Government Work* (New York, Free Press, 1978).

The character of government in Europe makes politicians introverted. They are concerned first and foremost with the operations of government, and those who judge them are an elite of colleagues, opponents, and political commentators. In Cabinet, politicians judge each other by how well they handle their departmental affairs and how readily they secure Cabinet endorsement for their proposals. A Prime Minister is judged by how well he manages the Cabinet and by the overall direction he gives the work of government. Parliament judges ministers by their performance in debate against political opponents, a far more demanding test than that of public opinion polls. The party organization judges ministers less in terms of their personal popularity and more in terms of their performance on issues of significance in the party.

Of course, European politicians are also judged by the mass media and, once every four years or so, by the electorate. But these judgments are not a pervasive and persisting influence upon government. An election tends to be an interruption (or sometimes a termination) in the career of a government, not the chief or only event to concentrate upon. European election campaigns are much shorter than in the United States and the preparations for a campaign are far less demanding. If an election need not occur at a fixed date, it can be brief and called at short notice.

In contemporary Washington, the President is pressed to be extroverted, to look outward to the national electorate. There is an established and well argued case for saying that the President should regard popular communication—the so-called preaching and teaching functions of the Presidency—as primary responsibilities. The White House affords a "bully pulpit," as Theodore Roosevelt once said, to explain the country's problems to the people and to inspire the nation in the face of difficulties.[52]

The President is constantly pressed to turn his back on Washington in order to renew his popularity with those who elected him, even though an American President's fixed term of office gives him greater job security than most European Prime Ministers. What makes the American President unique is the need to run a permanent national popularity campaign as a condition of influencing the government. It is necessary for the President to appear popular in the nation in order to affect government, for a President's influence in Washington depends upon how others perceive the President's popular standing at the moment.

---

[52] On the "preaching and teaching" functions of the Presidency, see Clinton Rossiter, *The American Presidency* (New York: Harcourt, Brace & World, 1960).

As long as the nomination of Presidential candidates (or the renomination of the President) was in the hands of political professionals, a President was judged primarily by what he did rather than by what he said. Periodic consultation with the electorate was considered necessary but not sufficient to give direction to government. The electorate was not expected to make any but the most general judgment about the collective performance of the competing parties for, as V. O. Key, Jr., emphasized, "The voice of the people consists mainly of the words 'yes' or 'no,' and at times one cannot be certain which word is being uttered."[53] Judgments on specific actions were made by political professionals in Washington and reinforced by the very self-interested judgments of local machine politicians. If the President met the standards of the professionals, he rose in their esteem; if not, then the President's status fell, and with it his influence. The picture of judgment by partisan colleagues that Richard Neustadt paints of Washington in the 1940s and 1950s is similar to that existing in Europe today.[54]

Today, Presidents tend to distance themselves from Washington, preferring the continuing judgment of public opinion polls to that of Washington professionals. The Nixon White House was pervaded with a spirit of continuous electioneering. Many of the campaign staff, brought in unprecedented numbers to the White House, had no background in the federal government and had little or no substantive knowledge of policies. Henry Kissinger's memoirs are replete with anecdotes about offensive behavior by brash advance men from the White House who sought to give orders to officials of sovereign states in order to extract better coverage on prime-time American television.[55] Following victory in the November 1972 election, President Nixon abandoned a plan to conduct an elaborate talent search for new appointees to his administration in order to make appointments that would strengthen his appeal to major voting groups.[56] It is not accidental that a majority of Presidential aides convicted as Watergate conspirators were brought to the White House because of their campaign expertise rather than their knowledge of government.

---

[53] *Politics, Parties and Pressure Groups*, 5th ed. (New York: Thomas Y. Crowell, 1964), p. 544.

[54] Cf. the description of the British Prime Minister in chapter 1, with Neustadt's argument, especially well set out in "The Constraining of the Presidency: the Presidency after Watergate," *British Journal of Political Science*, vol. 4, no. 4 (October 1974), pp. 383-97, and presented diagramatically in Cronin, *State of the Presidency*, p. 130.

[55] Henry Kissinger, *The White House Years* (Boston: Little, Brown & Co., 1979).

[56] See Malek, *Washington's Hidden Tragedy*, pp. 78ff., 259-64.

President Carter won the 1976 Presidential nomination under a new primary system that greatly encourages candidates to concentrate campaign efforts upon voters at the grass roots, rather than upon professional politicians and opinion leaders. Upon entering the White House he was cautioned by his pollster, the youthful Pat Caddell, "Too many good people have been defeated because they sought to substitute substance for style."[57] President Carter has been particularly in need of political "plums" to sustain a personal following, for he had no particular party following even after winning his nomination. In making initial appointments to office, President Carter appears to have gone well beyond his predecessors in his desire to "reach out" to appoint people previously unidentified with government or for representativeness of race, sex, or ethnic origin. His July 1979 request to all senior appointees to submit their resignations in order to have a "born again" administration was a further sign that executive agency heads are seen more as *symbols* to the mass electorate than as effective executive agency heads.[58]

Moreover, the Carter Presidency has opened up the White House to special interest groups important in the President's campaign strategy by creating a quantity of special assistants to provide liaison with Hispanic Americans, blacks, the aged, women, Jews, Italians, and other ethnic groups. Earlier Presidents have, of course, made a point of keeping on good terms with leaders of major groups in American society. But they did not think it necessary (or desirable) to appoint to their staff individuals whose chief function was to press the cause of particular interest groups within the White House Office.

In a revealing statement made in Detroit on July 16, 1979, after a "crisis of confidence" retreat into the mountains of Maryland, President Carter appeared to draw a stark contrast between his responsibilities in government and his responsibilities to the nation's electorate. He confessed:

---

[57] As quoted by James T. Wotton, "Pre-Inaugural Memo Urged Carter to Emphasize Style over Substance," *New York Times*, May 4, 1977.

[58] For a detailed review of the appointments process in the 1976-1977 transition, see Bruce Adams and Kathryn Kavanagh-Baran, *Promise and Performance: Carter Builds a New Administration* (Lexington, Mass.: Lexington Books, 1979). On the Johnson years, compare Matthew B. Coffey, "A Death in the White House: the Short Life of the New Patronage," *Public Administrative Review*, vol. 34, no. 5 (September/October 1974), pp. 440-44. For an interpretation of the significance, see, for example, the ongoing work by Nelson Polsby, "The American Party System and the Conduct of the Presidency" (Paper delivered to a conference of the White Burkett Miller Center, University of Virginia, Charlottesville, November 1979).

> Many of the people have said, "Mr. President, you're not out among the people enough, you don't listen to us enough. You've been so bogged down managing the government that you haven't been leading our nation." Well, I listened to that and I've learned my lesson. So, for the rest of the time I'm in office, I'm going to spend more time among you.[59]

In other words, the President promised to give priority to the pastoral and inspirational task of spending time among people as against spending time in giving direction to government. No European Prime Minister would make that choice. They see their job as that of governing, not quasi-spiritual counseling.

An extrovert President risks confusing appearance with reality. Even with the most elaborate of mass media or metaphysical efforts, a President cannot make his presence felt nearly so much outside Washington as inside the capital. There he occupies a unique office. Outside, he is but one more source of inspiration or guidance, and a partisan source at that. To attempt to be the leader of "all the people" *except* the two million staff of the federal government is a curious way to assert political leadership. To try to claim the popularity usually accorded only a monarchical Head of State is to misunderstand the reason why Europe's surviving monarchs have remained popular. Monarchs have maintained popular esteem only by acting apolitically and avoiding controversy.[60]

There is nothing wrong with a President seeking publicity from the Oval Office as long as this can be done at little or no cost to his powers of governance. But a President urged to "look" Presidential by signing legislation in the White House Rose Garden may become more concerned with appearances than with influencing what he signs. Nor is there anything wrong in asking of a proposed measure: How will this play in Peoria? Yet if the President is to have influence on government, he must also subject each of his actions to another test: *How is this playing in Washington?* Otherwise, in the words of Bert Rockman, a President risks becoming "a public relations junky."[61]

The growth of modern publicity techniques and the international decline of deference to leaders has affected Prime Ministers as well as Presidents. But the need for Prime Ministers to look to public opinion

---

[59] *Weekly Compilation of Presidential Documents* (July 23, 1979), p. 1257. In his speeches at this time, President Carter also indicated a desire to flee from the Washington news media as well, stating a preference for media people "uncontaminated" by contact with the judgmental standards of Washington.

[60] Cf. Richard Rose and Dennis Kavanagh, "The Monarchy in Contemporary Political Culture," *Comparative Politics*, vol. 8, no. 3 (April 1976), pp. 548-76.

[61] Rockman, "Constants, Cycles," p. 46.

is occasional and intermittent. Their first priority remains exercising authority within government. Even when a Prime Minister such as Harold Wilson gives first priority to public relations, he does so as an agent for his party, and not simply as a self-employed promoter. If a Cabinet makes a mess of things, then all the clever speeches and quiet chats with media people will be of little avail to a Prime Minister who rises and falls with the performance of his party in government.

To communicate effectively requires deeds as well as words. The substance of government has more effect upon the lives of ordinary people than does the style of national leaders, and television offers more appealing entertainment than do late-middle-age politicians. In the short run, a President may find that he does well in the polls because even though "his policies may be wrong, his politics have been brilliant."[62] But in the long run, it is what government does that has an enduring impact upon society.

If a President reduces, or even flees from his responsibilities in government, there is no doubt that America can still be governed. But in default of collective political authority, it will be government only by sub-governments.

You've Got To Trust Somebody

Since time immemorial, kings, priests, and warrior chiefs have faced the challenge of how to extend their power beyond face-to-face discussions or hand-to-hand combat. The authors of the American Constitution. thought they had resolved the difficulty by creating a Presidency that Thomas Jefferson praised for providing "unity of action and direction" in all the branches of government.[63] The Constitution vested executive authority in the President. It did so clearly and succinctly. It gives no indication, however, of how one person should conduct the affairs of the United States government, and many occupants to the office have puzzled about what to do. By contrast, European countries vest executive authority in a Cabinet collectively responsible to Parliament.

The idea of one person constituting, let alone directing the whole of the executive branch of American government is not difficult: it is

---

[62] James Reston, "Carter's Successful Failures," *New York Times*, February 6, 1980.

[63] Quoted approvingly by Louis A. Brownlow, "The Executive Office of the President: a General View," *Public Administration Review*, vol. 1, no. 2 (Winter 1941), p. 103.

merely impossible. The executive branch is not a unitary organization, capable of direction from a single place. It is a vast congeries of disparate institutions. No one could be in charge of all the departments, agencies, bureaus, and commissions listed in the 717 pages of the *United States Government Manual, 1979–1980*. Even more than the checks of the Constitution, the constraints of the clock are the ultimate limit upon the personal power of a President. The finiteness of time limits what any President can do in the course of a day, a week, or a year.

The record of any leader's time in office is, for the most part, a record of what others do in his name. By himself, a President or a Prime Minister can do very little. European governments recognize this. A Prime Minister is referred to as a nondepartmental minister, that is, a politician who does *not* have any particular executive responsibilities. These are in the hands of particular departmental ministers. Detachment from day-to-day executive responsibilities gives a Prime Minister time to think about broad questions of governmental direction. It also makes the Prime Minister institutionally neutral in the inevitable conflicts between ministers representing different sub-governments. A President is nominally the chief executive officer for the whole federal government. In fact, a President must make use of others to extend his influence upon government. The more use a President can make of others, the better he can give direction to government.

Political relationships are based upon trust or distrust. Any national leader—whether President, Prime Minister, or Emperor—must make some assumptions about how those around him will behave. This is necessary to make life predictable. A political leader must decide whether to trust others to cooperate with him, either because their self-interest coincides with his self-interest or because of shared loyalties. The more people a political leader can trust, the better he can multiply his influence upon the government. To build a critical mass capable of making a major impact upon the direction of government, a politician must extend trust beyond the limits of face-to-face contacts and call upon the loyalties of hundreds of people whose positive cooperation is necessary in the direction of government.

Government without trust is a jungle in which unmitigated self-interest rules. A politician who does not trust anyone else risks becoming alienated from those who should be his political colleagues and allies. Isolation from others is a sign of political weakness. In its extreme form, distrust can produce paranoia, in which a politician alternates between delusions of persecution and delusions of grandeur. Anyone who doubts that distrust can be carried to extreme lengths in politics should read President Nixon's conversations on the Watergate tapes and study the attempts of the Nixon White House to take over the executive branch.[64]

Personal loyalty is a political leader's typical criterion for deciding whom to trust. One approach to human nature, an approach canvassed by political theorists since the time of Machiavelli, stresses the importance of self-interest as the best guarantor of loyalty.[65] A political leader may expect people to be loyal to him only when it is in their self-interest to do so. A President is often advised to be distrustful, for not even those he appoints may remain loyal to him. Instead, they may cultivate favor with others who influence their political fortunes or claim Presidential authority unduly and go into business for themselves.

Impersonal loyalty offers another basis for sharing authority. Impersonal loyalty exists when individuals show loyalty to something more than self-interest: to the ethic of a profession, be it the military, civil service, or the law; to the ideology or associations of a political party; or to the formal and informal responsibilities of an office. Impersonal loyalty makes collective action much easier because it encourages cooperation in the direction of government. Elected politicians may then trust civil servants to do what is expected of them. Impersonal loyalty also makes for a greater degree of cooperation, or at least civility, between politicians representing different views within government.

Ultimately, the question facing any President or Prime Minister is not whether to delegate responsibilities, but how? The pile of papers in the In basket would bury a national leader in a week, if he did not learn to trust others to deal with many major issues. The greater the number of memorandums, the greater the confusion of conflicting views that must be confronted and the more intense the claims made by interested parties and sub-governments. On both sides of the Atlantic, the question is the same: *Whom should you trust?* The answers, however, are different on opposite sides of the Atlantic.

---

[64] Nathan, *The Plot That Failed*, passim; and *The White House Transcripts* (New York: Bantam Books, reprint of Watergate tapes, edited by the *New York Times*, 1974).

[65] For an interesting attempt to compare Machiavelli's approach to the role of the Florentine prince with Richard Neustadt's approach to the Presidency, see William T. Bluhm, *Theories of the Political System* (Englewood Cliffs, N.J.: Prentice-Hall, 1965), chap. 7.

Collegial Trust. Cabinet government fosters trust. It does this by requiring that self-interested politicians give loyalty to something larger than their own careers. First of all, Cabinet members must be loyal to the party that creates and sustains the Cabinet. It is the party, not the individual who is in power. A minister (including a Prime Minister) who loses the confidence of the governing party loses his office as well. Second, Cabinet members are expected to be loyal to the Cabinet collectively. Ministers are expected to accept decisions that go against their wishes when the Cabinet reconciles conflicting claims of sub-governments. Even self-interest will lead a politician to show impersonal loyalty as a necessary condition of personal advancement in a career in Cabinet government.

Cabinet government accepts the division of political labor. A Cabinet institutionalizes the articulation of conflicting political demands by different ministries, and the ambitions of individual ministers amplify the voices of sub-governments. But a Cabinet also maintains the collective authority of government. As part of the process of making policy, individual ministers are expected to show loyalty to whatever decision is collectively endorsed in the name of the whole.

Cabinet government is collegial. A college is a group of people bound together in a common fate, like a group of monks in a monastery or the faculty of a liberal arts college. The members of a college are not expected to have identical interests. They may be divided by subject matter in a teaching institution, by territory in an ecclesiastical body, or by departments in government. Nor are they all necessarily equal in status or authority; for example, the Roman College of Cardinals elects a Pope in whom supreme authority is then vested. The important point about a collegial body is that it creates a strong sense of solidarity between members who share a common political fate.

Collegial government does not deny self-interest, but disciplines it. A Prime Minister expects his colleagues to disagree with each other and perhaps to covet his job. The party's next leader and quite possibly the country's next Prime Minister, will sit in Cabinet as a colleague. Just as an American President brings politicians of diverse outlooks into his Cabinet, so too a European Prime Minister regards the making of a Cabinet as an exercise in building a political coalition, in which the different parts balance each other to mutual advantage.

In effect, a Cabinet is a team, rather than a collection of politicians brought together for an all-star game. Each minister wishes to think of himself as already or potentially the team's most valuable player. But a collective interest in the team's victory makes each individual prepared to cooperate with teammates; politics and government are combined in ways that are good for the country and good for the governing party's own electoral prospects.

A Prime Minister can act either as a playing captain or as a coach. A playing captain is in the thick of political action and is expected to justify his position by superior individual performance. But even a playing captain knows that he cannot score all a team's goals. The team as a whole must score more goals than any one member can do. Moreover, every player knows that the total number of goals that a team will score depends upon cooperation between players, including the readiness of one to pass the ball to a teammate who has a better chance of scoring. A Prime Minister may often act like a coach on the sidelines, a vantage point that saves him from getting his shins kicked. It also avoids potentially awkward comparisons between the performance of individual departmental ministers and the Prime Minister. A coach cannot call all the plays or score all the goals, but he is held responsible for the collective performance of the team. Whether a Prime Minister acts as a playing captain or coach, he accepts the discipline of loyalty to a collective political fate.

The sources of collegial loyalty are multiple and vary somewhat from country to country. In Britain, years of living with colleagues in party and Parliament give each Cabinet member a good idea of the ways in which colleagues can be trusted. In Germany, a tradition of legalistic thinking makes formal departmental powers and institutions of greater importance in regulating relationships between colleagues. In Norway, a lifetime of continuing involvement in the Labour movement makes colleagues into friends or at least, old and familiar antagonists. In Canada, the Cabinet has shown an increasing readiness to trust small committees of ministers to make many decisions in the name of the Cabinet as a whole. In Italy, the very weakness of trust and loyalty makes even more important the retention of that minimum collective loyalty that is a precondition of any Christian Democratic politician enjoying the benefits of Cabinet office. The history of Franco Spain shows what can happen when there is not a political structure based upon loyalty and trust: sub-governments became strong as personalistic loyalties to Franco weakened through time. In the Fifth French Republic, the directly elected President has used a Prime Minister and Cabinet to ensure legislative support, while he also worked closely with a coterie of very senior civil servants.

The relationship between Cabinet colleagues is only half the story of political administration in a European government. Equally important is the relationship between ministers and the permanent civil service. The most immediate sign of their importance is the numerical superiority of the higher civil service. A party that has gained millions of votes at a general election may place only a few dozen people in major positions of authority within government: senior civil servants very greatly outnumber the ministers held account-able by the electorate. Experience is a second cause of the importance of civil servants; collectively, they are the institutional memory in government. Civil servants attain high-ranking positions by demon-strating skills in managing the machinery of government. Because they serve many governments, officials acquire a fund of knowledge far beyond that of a politician, whose tenure of office is normally short-lived. In a very real sense, senior civil servants are the main-stay of government. At the highest levels, senior civil servants are very different from rule-bound clerks. They are very political animals, albeit of a different species than ministers.

Impersonal loyalty is the central value of a civil servant. Civil servants see themselves as loyal not only to the party in power, but also to the institutions of government that continue whatever party the electorate returns to office. The loyalty is to the concept of "the state," "the Crown," or "the Constitution." It is thus public and political, but is also far broader than that of a party politician; it requires a civil servant to distance himself from identification with individual politicians. The ethic is most familiar in the military.

Just as ministers may pride themselves on party loyalty, so civil servants pride themselves on their political pliability, that is, a readiness to serve ministers of different parties. Even if personally disagreeing with a particular policy, a civil servant should, as the saying in London's Whitehall puts it, "carry out ordained error with loyalty and even enthusiasm." Paradoxically, many continental civil servants would claim that the fact that national laws allow them to stand for elective office while a civil servant is proof of their profes-sional capacity to distinguish between different political roles, some-times showing impersonal loyalty to government and, at other times, acting as a party loyalist.[66]

The doctrine of impersonal loyalty is sustained in European governments by the civil service. As a distinct and honored status group within society, it recruits from the ablest university graduates and offers a permanent career. In the first few years of office a civil

---

[66] For surveys comparing the relations of European politicians and civil servants, see, for example, Mattei Dogan, *The Mandarins of Western Europe* (New York: Halsted Press, 1975).

servant learns the ethic of impersonal loyalty and to suppress individual opinions in favor of views consistent with the impersonal values of the service. Because the higher civil service to a large extent regulates its own promotions, younger civil servants seek to demonstrate skill in serving impersonal ideals as a means of promotion to the higher ranks of their chosen career.

Ministers usually develop a trusting relationship with civil servants, because their roles are complementary. Ministers are or ought to be skilled at voicing political demands and bargaining in Cabinet on behalf of their ministry. While a minister is concerned with the "external" relations of a ministry, senior civil servants can manage the direction of its continuing activities. At the highest levels, civil servants should also be expert in advising their minister about the conflicts that can arise between what a politician may desire and that which is administratively "do-able." By trusting civil service advisers, ministers expect to gain ideas and policies designed to anticipate major political criticisms and capable of implementation with a minimum of administrative difficulty. When a minister is under attack, he can turn to civil servants for ammunition to use in self-defense. In return, a civil servant trusts that the minister will take responsibility for everything the ministry does—including civil servants' mistakes. Civil servants do not mind letting their political superior take the credit—as long as he will also take the blame. What they value is security and anonymous influence.

Because civil servants have a long career in government, they are a force for continuity from election to election. This may lead some ministers newly returned to office to look at their advice with skepticism. A good civil servant will react by welcoming the stimulus of a new set of political masters. If a minister refuses to trust his civil servants, he is in difficulty. He will not know what to make of the mountains of information and advice sent to him. Nor will he have an alternative source of advice or a network of sub rosa contacts within the ministry. To implement policies without involving ministry staff is virtually impossible. Hence, a minister distrustful of his impersonal advisers can rarely give effective direction to government. Trust is a necessary condition of effective political action by a minister.

The reciprocal trust of ministers and civil servants tends to strengthen the collective voice of government against sub-governments. Just as ministers have a collective loyalty to their party and Cabinet, so civil servants have a collective loyalty to enduring institutions of government. Moreover, this loyalty is reinforced by their own career ladder. The result is that politicians in a Cabinet can normally assume when making decisions that the alternatives from which they choose have been formulated by civil servants with an eye to ready implementation and that an experienced and skilled career service is ready to carry out the choice that the Cabinet collectively makes.

Institutionalized Distrust. The President's position is unique, but he pays a price in distrust for his lonely eminence. In the absence of the solidarity of Cabinet government, a President's appointees are likely to identify with the agency in which they serve. In the absence of strong party loyalties, congressmen may identify with particular constituency or subcommittee interests. Given the strength of American sub-governments, a civil servant may put loyalty to his sub-government ahead of loyalty to government in the abstract. The President may conclude that he cannot trust anyone else in "his" administration to see problems from the perspective of the Oval Office.[67]

In such circumstances, the President tends to see loyalty as a chimera at worst and a one-way street at best. He would like those he appoints to be loyal to him, whether they serve in the White House or elsewhere in government. But even a cursory reading of the literature about the Presidency will remind him that even close Presidential aides, not to mention remote departmental officials, have a tendency to identify the President's interests with their own personal interests, and he cannot hope to have enough influence to prevent this happening frequently. In fear of being captured by subordinates invoking his authority for their goals, a President may refuse to trust those he appoints. Whereas a Prime Minister has no choice but to defend decisions made by other ministers, since he too is bound by collective responsibility, a President may limit the backing he gives to projects of others for fear of becoming a captive of a particular sub-government or adviser.

However great a President's distrust of others in government, he nonetheless must have *some* trust in others as a necessary condition of extending his influence in government. A President looks first to White House staff for loyalty. The people appointed to posts there ought to be loyal to the President, for their jobs depend on the President retaining office and on the staffers retaining the personal confidence of the President. White House staff are typically assigned

---

[67] This prescription is part of the conventional wisdom of Presidential advice today and has been particularly stressed by Richard Neustadt. For an insider's account of how even honest staff may become deluded by their position, see George Reedy, *The Twilight of the Presidency* (New York: Mentor Books, 1970).

functional rather than program responsibilities; they look after press relations, or congressional relations, or are involved on an ad hoc basis with issues of Presidential interest.

A President has no difficulty in finding staff personally loyal to him. In running for office, a President accumulates a substantial personal retinue and the most senior of his campaign aides tend to move into positions in the White House. An unintended consequence of recruiting campaign staff for White House posts is that it enhances the pressures there to run a continuing campaign rather than a government. Campaign staff typically have little or no previous experience in the intricacies of executive branch operations. The skills required to be an advance man, to write campaign speeches, or to organize state primary races are very different from those required to put together a budget or review complex disputes about energy policy. While a President can continue to trust campaign staff to look after the electorate, he is ill advised to rely upon them to look after many problems of government.

The biggest questions of loyalty and trust concern the hundreds of people whom the President appoints to take leading positions in federal agencies. In contrast with Europe, a President is not restricted to appointing congressmen to office as a Prime Minister may be restricted to appointing MPs as ministers. Potentially, the hundreds of Presidential appointees can greatly multiply the influence of the President. As Hugh Heclo asserts: "In affecting the everyday work of government, these hundreds of personal selections add up to a cumulative act of choice that may be at least as important as the electorate's single act of choice for President every four years."[68]

In making appointments a President employs a multiplicity of criteria: personal friendship, loyalty, and campaign contributions; representation of voting blocs and interest groups; previous evidence of management abilities or intellectual achievement outside Washington; or previous success in an administrative position within government. Often, the criteria are seen to be in conflict, as in the simple judgment of one Presidential personnel adviser that the task was to achieve "the marriage of two opposing objectives: quality appointments and political reward."[69] But there is no necessary conflict between these objectives: talented people can also be enthusiastic supporters of a President. The real difficulty in making appointments

---

[68] Hugh Heclo, *A Government of Strangers* (Washington, D.C.: The Brookings Institution, 1977), p. 88, and see pp. 38 and 85 for Heclo's estimate of the numbers involved.

[69] Quoted in Adams and Kavanagh-Baran, *Promise and Performance*, p. 24.

is that a President is unlikely to know (or to care) much about the second, third, and fourth echelon posts or the people who receive White House commissions to fill them.

A President wants immediate support from executive branch officials—as and when his business and theirs intersect. The Cabinet does not secure the closure of conflict, as in a European system of government. Presidential appointees in the agencies have divided loyalties. Although the President gives them their commission, the pressures that go with the job tend to give precedence to the political demands of sub-governments. These pressures come from Congress through its oversight of the agency; from the bureaucrats within the agency; from pressure groups that are clients of the agency; and from a host of other influences that loom far larger to a Presidential appointee than to the President himself.[70]

The irony (or tragedy) is that while a President may sacrifice competence to secure loyalty, he may not gain loyalty in return. After working in the White House for President Lyndon Johnson, Joseph Califano described the relationship between the President and Presidential appointees thus:

> From his window in the Oval Office, the President looks out on a jumble of irrationally organized departments and agencies. Politics teaches him about the inherently divided loyalties of Cabinet and agency heads who must testify before Congressional oversight and appropriations committees and live with cross-pressures from their peers, their constituencies and the bureaucracies they administer.[71]

Two years later Califano had the opportunity to view the Presidency from a different perspective, when appointed Secretary of Health, Education, and Welfare in 1977. He promptly acted in accord with his new position. After prolonged friction with the White House, the President decided he was not securing enough of Califano's divided loyalties and fired him in 1979.

Even though both Republican and Democratic Presidents endorse the idea of "Cabinet" government, it has failed in practice in Washington. By Thomas Cronin's reckoning, less than one-quarter of the officials in a President's Cabinet are likely to be both loyal and expert. Those who are both disloyal and amateurish can easily be fired. Those who are loyal but inexpert cannot easily be dismissed. And those

---

[70] See Bradley H. Patterson, Jr., *The President's Cabinet* (Washington, D.C.: American Society for Public Administration, 1976), chaps. 2 and 3.

[71] Quoted by Bradley H. Patterson, Jr., in "White House Staff: the Bashful Bureaucracy" (Unpublished paper, Washington, D.C., c.1977), p. 4.

who are disloyal but capable politicians must be handled with care; if fired, this is best done at a moment of their temporary vulnerability. No wonder a White House aide lamented, "Everybody believes in democracy until he gets to the White House and then you begin to believe in dictatorship."[72]

The President's distrust of his own appointees is compounded by an increasing tendency to distrust the highest-ranking civil servants. The distrust was initially fostered by the Eisenhower administration's suspicion that career officials administering many agencies spawned by New Deal and Fair Deal legislation were of "a distinctly Democratic cast." In the words of one of them, "The line between the career service and the political appointees was a blurred one and relationships were close and trusting, based on the assumption—and for the most part, the fact—of a shared political philosophy."[73] The Eisenhower administration sought to induce change in the career grades by forcing out individuals closely identified with some New Deal programs and bringing in new appointees sympathetic to the Republican outlook. This could be done in two ways: giving civil service status to partisan recruits and increasing the number of Presidential appointees at the top of agencies.

With changes of party in 1960, 1968, and 1976, the number of political appointees has grown, and the layers of Presidential appointees at the top of agencies has more than doubled in two decades. A post held by a Presidential appointee is assumed to be a post "captured" from the bureaucrats and "won" for the President's will. Successive Presidents have increasingly devalued the expert knowledge of their own career budget staff in the Executive Office of the President, even though there is no one but the President to whom this staff could be loyal.[74] An extreme example is in the change in the direction of the Office of Management and Budget (formerly the Bureau of the Budget), a crucial agency in the Executive Office of

---

[72] Quoted from a Kennedy aide by Cronin, *State of the Presidency*, p. 223; estimates of loyalty and competence of Cabinet ministers also from Cronin, p. 261.

[73] James L. Sundquist, "Jimmy Carter as Public Administrator: an Appraisal at Mid-Term," *Public Administration Review*, vol. 39, no. 1 (January/February 1979), p. 7; see also, Joel D. Aberbach and Bert A. Rockman, "Clashing Beliefs within the Executive Branch," *American Political Science Review*, vol. 70, no. 2 (June 1976), pp. 457-68; and Richard L. Cole and David A. Caputo, "Presidential Control of the Senior Civil Service: Assessing the Strategies of the Nixon Years," *American Political Science Review*, vol. 73, no. 2 (June 1979), pp. 399-413.

[74] Cf. Hugh Heclo, "OMB and the Presidency—the Problem of 'Neutral Competence'," *Public Interest*, no. 38 (Winter 1975), pp. 80-98. See also Louis Fisher, *Presidential Spending Power* (Princeton: Princeton University Press, 1975), chap. 2.

the President. By 1980, the top ten staff were political appointees. Of the ten top OMB officials that President Carter initially appointed, nine were without any previous experience in the executive branch that they were meant to monitor on his behalf.

The 1976 election of a President without any previous Washington experience can be dismissed as the freak outcome of public reaction to a "mess" in Washington. But the readiness of the Carter administration to appoint inexperienced people to key positions (albeit modified by its readiness to appoint some old hands, too) is indicative of a longer-term trend.

The first consequence is the reduction in the collective memory of public officials. Newly appointed directors of agencies do not wish to ask about the past, for the past is a record of agency defeats as well as victories. Because they are determined to ignore the lessons from the past, each fresh flight of appointees runs the risk of rediscovering rather than learning from past mistakes.

A second consequence is the progressive "amateurization" of the central direction of government. Most Presidential appointees now have limited previous knowledge or no knowledge of Washington. It takes a year or two for a Presidential appointee to come to grips with the complexity of the institutions and programs under him. Yet most appointees only stay in a particular office for one or two years. By contrast, the European system of appointing ministers from within Parliament (or even, from the civil service) puts a premium upon prior knowledge of how government works. This greatly reduces the time needed to learn the specific operations of a department and most ministers are likely to remain in a given office longer than two years.

Estrangement is a third consequence of increasing the number of Presidential appointees at the top of an agency. Most agencies are staffed at the top by individuals appointed for a wide variety of political considerations, and who have not met before. There is no Presidential team. Instead, there is "a government of strangers," most of whom leave town or take another job before they become friends or working partners.[75] There is also estrangement between career civil servants and Presidential appointees. The former believe their chances for promotion are blocked unless they too become partisans. Some do, but others quit for better-paying jobs elsewhere in Washington; retreat into defensive positions that give them considerable autonomy; or collaborate with congressional subcommittees

---

[75] See Heclo, *A Government of Strangers*.

to direct particular programs as they, rather than the White House, think best.

Demoralization as well as distrust flourishes in such an environment. In the words of one former assistant secretary of the Treasury:

> The operating agencies and departments feel that White House aides unwisely isolate the President and influence his decisions without considering the technical advice that others have provided. White House assistants retort that Cabinet officials are immersed in operating details and become captives of institutional goals rather than concentrating on the needs of the President. Political appointees are placed in a no win situation: the career employees responsible for their programs resent pressures they believe are politically motivated and White House officers argue that the appointed officials should be better team players.[76]

Directing Government as a Cooperative Task. The President's title of chief executive is a misnomer; he can more accurately be described as a nonexecutive chief.[77] To visualize the President as in command of a hierarchical organization is misleading in the extreme. Insofar as a President is viewed as the man on top, this only emphasizes his remoteness from what is going on in the ranks of government. The powers of American government are divided among many institutions and individuals. The political questions of greatest importance to the President concern his nonhierarchical relationships with the rest of American government.

Governing is a cooperative task. Politicians in a Cabinet system recognize and welcome this. Each minister is given a measure of trust by his colleagues and allowed to proceed with matters of immediate concern within his department. In turn, each minister trusts his colleagues to meet common political responsibilities. When disputes arise between colleagues, each is expected to fight his case staunchly. But once the Cabinet resolves the dispute, they are expected to cooperate with each other. In the background, senior civil servants strengthen cooperation because their impersonal loyalty to the Cabinet reduces the animus that conflicts of personal loyalties can generate.

---

[76] Jones, *Development of Economic Policy*, p. 284. The complaint is not unique to Jones's experience in the Nixon and Ford administrations. Cf. Robert Wood, "When Government Works," *Public Interest*, no. 18 (Winter 1970), p. 95.

[77] See Richard Rose, "The President: Chief but not an Executive," *Presidential Studies Quarterly*, vol. 7, no. 1 (Winter 1977). On the significance of "chieftainship" as a form of leadership, see Brian Farrell, *Chairman or Chief? The Role of the Taoiseach in Irish Government* (Dublin: Gill and Macmillan, 1971).

Prime Ministers accept without hesitation the self-restraints of cooperative government. It is part of the job description. A Prime Minister is not expected to become closely involved in formulating or carrying out policies for which particular ministers have operational responsibility. A Prime Minister expects to be consulted about the formulation of major policies, and expects Cabinet colleagues to cooperate when changes are suggested in departmental policies for the sake of broader considerations of government. Moreover, in hidden and not so hidden ways, the Prime Minister's hand can influence these policies. But he usually has neither the staff nor the inclination to distrust colleagues or to try to shadow, second-guess, or overrule their actions. By giving trust a Prime Minister secures sufficient detachment so that, when troubles arise, he is not primarily responsible; that dubious privilege is given to a Cabinet colleague.

Governing is a cooperative task in Washington as well. The reality of the Presidency is that in almost every field a President depends upon cooperation with others. Insofar as a Presidential proposal requires legislation or appropriations, Congress must cooperate if the President's wishes are to be made into government policy. Insofar as a government policy requires administrative action, public officials—often in state and local as well as the federal government—must cooperate if it is to be implemented. Insofar as implementation requires a positive response from citizens, the intended beneficiaries must also cooperate, whether business firms or unions encouraged to fight inflation, or people in poverty encouraged to better themselves. The President has far greater scope for independent action in international affairs, but American foreign policy depends upon the willing or unwilling cooperation of other nations to produce desired effects.

When enunciating policy proposals, a President gives guidance, not orders. The President is expected to indicate, from his unique perspective, what he thinks ought to be done in the name of the government of the United States. But he is also expected to take the views of other significant actors in the policy process into account. For this reason, a President may delay giving any indication of what he thinks the government should do until reasonably confident that Congress, executive branch agencies, and others in sub-government networks will cooperate with him. A President may also give guidance in very general, even intentionally vague, terms in order to avoid conflict, leaving others to give specific meaning to government policy.[78] A President may even employ "hidden hand" leadership as

---

[78] See the extended discussion in Rose, *Managing Presidential Objectives*, pp. 155ff.

Eisenhower has been shown to have done, using others to promote controversial policies in order to remain out of the firing line himself.[79]

The President is exceptionally well placed for giving guidance on broad questions of public policy. Because his office is at the intersection of many conflicting sub-government demands, the President is well aware of how different domestic, economic, and international issues relate to each other. Because he ordinarily has no commitment to any departmental perspective, a President can view relationships among policies with a detachment denied departmental officials. Because the President has a unique political status, he can also command great publicity for any proposals he puts forward.

Important as the President is, he can only come to terms with the responsibilities of his office by trusting others. The government of the United States is not a single man, but a cooperative network of individuals and institutions. The 1960s and 1970s saw Presidents who rejected this belief, pursuing "efforts to govern without the government—a circumvention of the cabinet departments and the Congress that has deepened the isolation of the President, demoralized able bureaucracies and embittered executive-congressional relations." In the judgment of national security analysts Graham Allison and Peter Szanton, the consequence of this for major collective policies "is not simply inefficient, it is dangerous."[80]

To increase trust within the federal government requires reducing existing friction induced by distrust. Positive action requires the identification of people whom the President will trust to get on with their jobs as best they can. By doing this, the President can gain greater detachment from government and the practical political advantages that come from "not going to firefight every problem that comes along." It is often forgotten that strategies of inaction are important means of realizing the President's second priority: "keeping out of trouble."[81]

An immediate step that any President can take to reduce second-guessing of responsible agencies is to reduce the size of the White House staff. Because a President regards White House staff as personally loyal, his initial instinct is to trust them more than any other officials in government. But doing this has major disadvantages.

---

[79] See Fred I. Greenstein, "Eisenhower as an Activist President: a Look at New Evidence," *Political Science Quarterly*, vol. 94, no. 4 (Winter 1979-1980), pp. 584ff. Cf. Allen Yarrell, "Eisenhower and McCarthy: an Appraisal of Presidential Strategy," *Presidential Studies Quarterly*, vol. 10, no. 1 (Winter 1980), pp. 90-98.

[80] Allison and Szanton, *Remaking Foreign Policy*, pp. x-xi.

[81] See Rose, "President: Chief but not an Executive," pp. 11ff.

341

There is a constitutional obstacle: a President cannot formally delegate his powers to staff subordinates. The Constitution does not make provision for multiple Presidents, nor does it authorize a building to make demands on executive agencies.[82] (Compare, for instance, the staffer's use of the phrase: "The White House wants . . .") Nor can White House staff normally claim to have knowledge of federal programs matching that of operating agencies. In such circumstances, a staff may simply broker deals with no knowledge of the content of policies or design policies with insufficient understanding.

Political prudence offers the most compelling argument against a large White House staff. The swelling of the Presidency increases the number of individuals purporting to speak in the name of the President, while reducing the proportion who can be in frequent enough contact to know which issues the President wishes to pursue or avoid. A President then finds that staffers give directions contrary to his wishes or involve the White House in needless controversy. Agencies find, in the words of a former Bureau of the Budget official, "There are too many people trying to bite you with the President's teeth."[83]

A second step that a President could take to strengthen government would be to make *fewer* Presidential appointments. This would reduce a burden that is now well beyond the powers of an incoming President. As John F. Kennedy said, when faced with the task of naming Cabinet and sub-Cabinet officers: "I don't know any people (for Cabinet jobs). I only know voters! How am I going to fill these 1,200 jobs?"[84] With fewer jobs to fill, the President could give more attention to selecting small and complementary teams of people to give direction to major agencies or programs. It would also reduce the errors that campaign staff make in arranging the appointment of people they do not know to jobs that they are unfamiliar with.[85] Cutting down the layers of untried Presidential appointees would reduce the amount of inexperience and unfamiliarity at the top of government. To overload agencies with novices is to weaken rather than strengthen the direction of government.

---

82 See the rules of President Ford's adviser, Donald Rumsfeld, quoted in Cronin, *The State of the Presidency*, p. 247.

83 Roger Jones, quoted by Joel Havemann, "OMB's Legislative Role is Growing More Powerful and More Political," *National Journal*, vol. 5, no. 43 (October 27, 1973), p. 1592.

84 Quoted in Arthur M. Schlesinger, Jr., *A Thousand Days* (Boston: Houghton Mifflin Co., 1966), p. 127.

85 For an extreme example, see the account of the Carter administration's first-term efforts, in Adams and Kavanagh-Baran, *Promise and Performance*.

One positive measure that a President could take would be to give more appointments to people already experienced in the ways of government. Fortunately, the sources of experienced appointees are multiple. For more than a generation there has been a pool of "In-and-Outers," that is, individuals who are ready to accept short-term appointments in government, while at other times holding jobs outside government, and often outside Washington as well. In-and-Outers can be found in both Democratic and Republican ranks, and the frequent rotation of the parties in office increases the number of available personnel, that is, appointees turned out of office by the electorate.

In-and-Outers can also be complemented by the appointment of Super Grade civil servants (GS levels 16 to 18) to noncareer as well as career posts. Because they have served up to twenty years or more in government, there are few tricks of the political trade that Super Grades do not know. A President could show more trust in the impersonal loyalty of Super Grades, returning them to positions of authority and responsibility commensurate with those held prior to adding more layers of Presidential appointees in the past two decades. Alternatively, a President might offer more Presidential appointments in the noncareer service to Super Grades. A person accepting such a post becomes doubly qualified, having already demonstrated impersonal loyalty before accepting a public loyalty to the President of the day. Ironically, a President might find that placing greater reliance upon Super Grades would also ease his problems with Congress, for the views of American upper-level civil servants correlate very highly with those of congressmen.[86]

A President might also consider the advantages of appointing a few Cabinet secretaries with a "passion for visibility." Such secretaries could be used as buffers by the President to deflect political controversy from the White House. President Eisenhower was well aware of the advantages of trusting subordinates to make decisions. In phrases that almost exactly reverse President Truman's motto ("The buck stops here"), Ike believed that aides should be "free to solve their own problems wherever possible and not to get in the habit of passing the buck up."[87] Allowing select Cabinet secretaries to play a more public role in directing government would only recog-

---

[86] See Bert A. Rockman, "The Roles of Bureaucrats and Politicians: Styles and Prescriptions," typescript (University of Pittsburgh, 1979), figure 2.

[87] See Greenstein, "Eisenhower as an Activist President," p. 581. The memorandum quoted was written in wartime, but Eisenhower was consistent in trusting delegation thereafter as well.

nize what is an accomplished fact. There is no need to imitate European-style Cabinet meetings when this has failed before. A newly elected President might instead encourage a few sophisticated secretaries to try out ideas—always with the warning that he retained the right to repudiate them or ask for their resignation, if they went beyond acceptable limits.

Today, a President must accept the need for partnership in policy making. If major collective policies are to be made, they cannot be made by the President alone. The Vietnam war showed that there are even limits to the President's role as commander-in-chief.

The most important partner for the President is outside the executive branch—Congress. Congress has always shown a major interest in initiating policies. The motto of congressmen is: "If you want to get along, you have got to go along." This motto applies to a President as well as to a freshman member of the House of Representatives. Only by voluntary cooperation between major parts can the American system produce collective authority sufficient to counteract sub-governments. To see the improvement of the nation's policy making simply in terms of strengthening the President is to mistake cause and effect. A President can be strengthened by measures that strengthen other institutions as well. To think otherwise is to mistake the part—the important but hardly exclusive prerogatives of the President—for the whole. In the face of major collective challenges and entrenched sub-governments, what is needed in America is not simply a stronger President. *What America needs most of all is a stronger government.*

Cooperation and Competition

By comparison with the United States, European nations are better organized to make collective decisions, because there *is* a government there. The collegial system of government permits complex decisions to be sorted into constituent political parts, yet it also provides the authority needed for collective choice. Interestingly, European governments most nearly resemble Washington when they meet in the institutions of the European Community. The explanation is simple: the nine member nations of the European Community meet as sovereign states—even more sovereign than the committees of Congress or well-entrenched Washington bureau chiefs.[88]

[88] See Helen Wallace, William Wallace, and Carole Webb, *Policy-Making in the European Communities* (New York: John Wiley & Sons, 1977).

The United States is at a competitive disadvantage in its relations with European countries because the strength of American sub-governments makes it difficult for a President to commit the nation's resources to the achievement of any policy. In addition to the difficulties presented by other nations, a President simultaneously faces the problem of dealing with Washington's sub-governments. When the United States had world political hegemony, it could be argued that it was an advantage for the nation not to be able to commit itself readily in foreign affairs. The threat of congressional intervention could be a strategic bargaining counter for extracting concessions from other nations—and the fact of congressional recalcitrance could lead to further concessions before approval of a treaty. But when America does not exercise world political hegemony, its inability to make policy commitments quickly and confidently makes the United States more vulnerable. European leaders are well aware of this. In the opinion of a veteran Washington columnist, James Reston, "It's hard to remember a time since the last World War when the ambassadors of the major nations in Washington were more anxious about the American economy or the handling of its foreign policy."[89]

The tempting thing for an American to do when confronted with evidence of national weakness and the possible advantages of other systems of government is to dismiss the whole question as "interesting but academic." America is as it is for reasons rooted in its national history, and European governments owe their present forms to past (and not always happy) political histories.

But no nation, not even one of the dimensions of the United States, can today act like an island unto itself. Whereas European countries have been doomed to live with the fact of interdependence for centuries, the shift from continental isolation to world involvement has occurred in America in a little more than a generation. Dollar devaluation in 1971 can be taken as the symbolic turning point, when decisions made by the large number of foreigners who held American dollars began to exert abrupt and unwanted influence upon Washington's direction of America's domestic economy. Decades of world dominance is not the best preparation for America facing interdependence in the 1980s. As the former British Prime Minister James Callaghan commented sympathetically after a visit to Washington early in 1980, "Americans don't know how to live with problems

---

[89] "This Funny Capital," *New York Times*, March 19, 1980.

because they are always assuming that they can lick them."[90] I..
frustration, Americans may wish to retreat to isolationism, but this
is hardly practicable in an era of nuclear missiles and global economic
interdependence. An aggressive response to frustration is also of no
avail. It is one thing to express a desire to "nuke" enemies. But it
is impossible to use force against allies and friends.

As the leader of a major political alliance, the United States today
is continuously involved in cooperative actions with many nations
affecting diplomatic and military affairs, the economy, and energy
resources. While each country involved shares some common interests,
each also has national interests to protect. In consequence, these
relationships are also competitive. *Today, the United States finds
itself competing against as well as cooperating with other major
Western nations.*

In matters of military security, Western nations want to cooperate for mutual defense against potential aggressors. But the
same allies also compete in trying to find ways to minimize their
share of the collective defense burden. European politicians are no
more anxious than American politicians to spend more on defense
if this also requires a cut in spending on major social programs or a
significant increase in taxation to meet increased bills for defense.

In the international economy, the United States cooperates with
many nations by being an active trading partner. Insofar as the United
States exports goods in large quantities to other countries, its economy
becomes interdependent with that of its major trading partners. When
the United States imports large quantities of goods from other countries, the skeins of interdependence tighten. The President's special
representative for trade negotiations can define the major goals of
United States trade policy, but he can achieve these goals only in
cooperation with nearly one hundred other nations in complex multilateral trade negotiations.

In energy, Western nations have a common interest in not having
abrupt changes in world oil prices that disturb standards of living
and national security. But they are very differently endowed with
energy resources. Of the eight nations studied in this volume, four
have substantial oil resources of their own and four are almost
entirely dependent upon imported oil. Differences in national resources lead nations to adopt competitive policies when each perceives

---

[90] Henry Brandon, "Carter learns the power game," *Sunday Times* (London),
January 13, 1980. For a fuller discussion of the varieties of North Atlantic
relationships, see, for example, Christopher W. Makins, "The Atlantic Alliance,"
in *Setting National Priorities: Agenda for the 1980s*, ed. Pechman, pp. 459-96.

346

its national interest to be more immediate and compelling than a general Western interest vis-à-vis the Middle East.

The major collective problems facing America today involve international as well as national interdependence among security, economic, and energy policies. Making policy now requires more than the creation of sufficient authority in government to resolve disputes between sub-governments within the United States. It also requires the marshalling of well-defined collective policies to assert vis-à-vis other nations. Insofar as national security matters are defined as the overriding policy concern in Washington, the President is likely to spend more time thinking about enemies than allies, a pattern of behavior that intensifies stress in Washington, as well as risking friction with friends elsewhere.

For nearly two decades after World War II, European countries were relatively weak vis-à-vis the United States. Decisions made in Washington could be "coordinated" with other nations after the event. But Washington today cannot devote all its attention to resolving domestic political disputes and worrying about unfriendly nations. To take the support of allies for granted is risky when international relations are increasingly competitive as well as interdependent.

To suggest that the President pay more attention to the opinions of friendly governments is not to suggest that the United States should refrain from thinking in terms of its own self-interest. Instead, it is to argue that the self-interest of the United States now requires it to pay more attention to what other nations do. This is because the policies of other European nations (and Japan should here be counted as a "European country) now have a clear and significant impact upon the success or failure of American politics.

In the 1980s America's *interdependence is likely to increase, in spite of the growth of neo-isolationist sentiments.* After all, wishing that international problems would disappear cannot reduce interdependencies based upon established economic, political, and security policies. The obstacles that sub-governments create in making collective policies in Washington affect America's capacity for international policy making. If nothing is done to alter this state of affairs, then the President may find that the government of the United States is a liability rather than an asset in efforts to advance America's national interests in an increasingly interdependent world.